HINDUSTANI
AS IT OUGHT TO BE SPOKEN

HINDUSTANI
AS IT OUGHT TO BE SPOKEN

Romanised

J. TWEEDIE

THIRD EDITION

GYAN

Published by

GYAN

Gyan Publishing House
5, Ansari Road
Daryaganj, New Delhi-110002
Phone: 011-47034999, 9811692060
E-mail: books@gyanbooks.com

Distribution Network
gyanbooks.com
India, USA, Canada, UK, Australia, France

ISBN : 978-81-212-4427-5 (PB)
First Published, Calcutta, 1900

2nd Impression 2020

Printed at: Gyan Press, Delhi.

Hindustani
Author: J. Tweedie

HINDUSTANI

AS IT OUGHT TO BE SPOKEN.

BY

J. TWEEDIE,

Bengal Civil Service.

"It is really surprising, when you come to think of it, how ungrammatically people do talk."

Third Edition.

Calcutta

THACKER, SPINK & CO.

LONDON: W. THACKER & CO., 2, CREED LANE, LUDGATE HILL.

1900.

PREFACE TO THE SECOND EDITION.

THE Author must express his regret at this little work having been out of print for a time. His excuse is the unexpected rapidity with which the First Edition was absorbed by the public. It is, however, satisfactory to know that the book is fulfilling the purpose for which it was written; and has already become, in a great measure, *the book*, which even those who must eventually know the vernacular character, read, in order to gain a rapid knowledge of the construction of the language, and a large stock of guaranteed words and phrases. Nothing is then left but to study the Vernacular Alphabet.

The present volume is larger than its predecessor. This is because many complaints reached the Author that there was too little in the book. The cry was for more. This is a good sign. But, on the other hand, there were complaints of inability to remember words only 'once given' in the course of the "Lessons." The collecting of all words given in the body of the book into the Glossaries at the end, is one cause of the increased size.

Another is that the number of Exercises has, on demand, been largely added to, implying the introduction of many additional words.

It has been considered proper to retain in the body of the book the lists of words there given, though now also to be found in the Glossaries. They are selected words which, in the opinion of the Author, one *must* know; and whether one learns them or not as they stand above the Exercises—one certainly would never learn them, if they stood only in a "Dictionary."

Perhaps the humble "Index" deserves mention. Thus by turning to the proper Sub-Head under the General Head "VOCABULARIES," you will find where all the words relating to any one subject, (as 'Animals,' 'Birds,' 'Vermin,' and so on,) are to be found collected in the body of the book.

Another feature which certainly deserves notice here is that in both Glossaries, nouns which are masculine but have feminine terminations are marked (m.), while feminine nouns not ending in the recognised feminine terminations (see page 8,) are marked (f.). At page 105 you will find a useful (but of course incomplete) list of such feminine nouns. False genders grate horribly on the ear; '*Mon soeur est très-beau.*'

But the chief new feature of this Edition is "The Reader," which contains a collection of modern extracts of fable, story, dialogue and oratory. These should be enough to satisfy all those who have ventured to 'ask for more.'

As the First Edition was complete in its exposition of the grammatical structure of the language, much could not be added on this subject. Some sections however have been now more fully treated than before; as for example, the Pronoun 'apna,' on page 30.

Thus has the Author endeavoured to give some return to the public for its kind reception of the First Edition, by making the Second Edition more copious, more complete and more convenient than the First.

The Author also hopes to be able to give the student —very soon—a translation of all the Exercises, and of 'The Reader.' This will both shorten labour, and render a correct acquisition of the language more certain and easy.

It remains for the Author to acknowledge the services rendered by Moulvi Záhir-ud-dín of Patna in perusing the Hindústáni additions, as they passed through the press.

Paṭna, February 1893.

PREFACE TO THE FIRST EDITION.

THIS little book has been written at the request of ladies, so that no apology for its appearance is called for. Their complaint was that no book exists from which they can gain a complete and correct knowledge of the Hindústáni language suited to their daily requirements; and so they have to struggle with books which give them both too much and too little. Therefore they requested that a small book should be written by aid of which the true grammatical structure of the language might be learned, and a stock of words acquired *which are actually in daily use.* It is hoped, that those who have learned the lessons of this book *vivâ voce* with the Author will remember him kindly when they see these lessons in print.

The scope of the book is not ambitious. Thus, there are no dissertations on the origin of the language, or on the derivation of words, or on philological analogies. Very little will be found of ornate Persian or Arabic phraseology. Even some of the refinements of the alphabet—for instance, the distinction between '*alif*' and '*ain*'—'*te*' and '*toė*,' have not been insisted on.

The aim has been to make the book a thoroughly practical one, suited to all and every, whose mid-life has to be spent in India. The lessons remain in the form of familiar oral teaching, dry rules being, as far as possible, avoided. It is hoped that the book will thus be interesting to read, as well as easy to learn. A special feature will be found in the lists of English and other foreign words which have become naturalised, at least among those natives who come much in contact with Europeans.

It is believed that the Alphabetical Vocabularies—in combination with a grammar—supply what does not at present exist in any form. Each of these contains about two thousand five hundred words and phrases, for the most part additional to the copious lists of words and phrases given during the course of the Lessons. All these have been selected and tested with the greatest care; so that the reader may feel quite sure that he is getting in all cases the *words actually used* by natives of ordinary education when speaking of the common affairs of daily life. The spelling is everywhere uniform; and may be said to be the Government system of transliteration. Thus is the student of Hindústáni (as is believed for the first time) provided with an adequate and readily accessible stock of really colloquial, every-day words; alphabetically arranged in Roman type, both Hindústáni-English and English-Hindústáni, on a uniform system of spelling approved by Oriental Scholars and by Government, combined with a short and easy grammar.

It cannot be denied that by far the greater number of Englishmen and Englishwomen in India speak a very peculiar language under the name of 'Hindústáni'—and this, both as regards grammar and pronunciation. The excuse is sometimes made, that they hear natives speak as they speak. There is some truth in this; but it is forgotten that the natives referred to learned the language which they so speak from their masters and mistresses, and that if credit is due to anyone, it is due to the natives who have had the wit to understand, and the skill to acquire the dialect which they hear addressed to them.

That dialect is occasionally spoken of in the following pages as 'Anglo-Hindústáni.' It is the Author's hope that by means of this little book, it will—in some degree at least—be replaced by Hindústáni as it ought to be spoken.

The contents of the book may be mastered in one month's study, even by those who are 'not good at languages.' It is recommended that at the first-reading little or no attempt should be made to translate English into Hindústáni. This should be made at the second perusal. At the first perusal, the twelve lessons should be completely mastered, the Hindústáni exercises carefully analysed, pronunciation practised aloud, and as large a stock of words learned as the reader can possibly retain.

It only remains for the Author to express his obligations to Sayad Wájid Hossen, K. B., and to Baboo Sheo Darshan, learned scholars of Bihár, for their kind labours in revising, and, in some respects amending, the letterpress of these lessons,—labours which render it probable that the book contains nothing which will mislead the student.

Paṭna, December 1889.

PUBLISHERS' PREFACE TO THIRD EDITION.

OWING to the lamented death of the Author, Mr. Tweedie, before the present edition was completed, the Publishers have had to seek other aid in passing it through the press. The work was entrusted to a distinguished linguist, and the very careful manner in which he has performed his task leads the Publishers to hope that the present edition will receive the same cordial support that was accorded to its predecessors. The features of the book remain in all respects the same, and no trouble has been spared to make the work as complete and accurate as possible.

CALCUTTA, 1900.

PARADIGM of the Verb 'Hona,' *to be*, or *become.*

According to the forms most commonly used; but see Page 14, Sect. 9.

To be read before the PARADIGM on page 16.

The second of two bracketted lines gives the Feminine forms.

See Page 10, Sect. 6.

Various Parts.

Stem, Ho. Infinitive, Ho-na. Pres. Part., Ho-ta. Past Part., Hú,a. (fem. hú,i; [1] hú,íṇ.[2])

Tenses.

Singular.			Plural.		

Subjunctive and Imperative, *I may be; Be thou, &c.*

Ho-úṇ,	Ho-we,	Ho-we.	Ho-weṇ,	Ho,	Ho-weṇ.

Future, *I shall* or *will be, &c.*

Húṇ-ga,	Ho-ga,	Ho-ga.	Hoṇ-ge,	Ho-ge,	Hoṇ-ge.
Húṇ-gi,	Ho-gi,	Ho-gi.	- - - same as the Masc. - - -		

Present, *I am, &c.*

Húṇ,	Hai,	Hai.	Haiṇ,	Ho,	Haiṇ.

Past, *I was, &c.*

Tha,	Tha,	Tha.	The,	The,	The.
Thi,	Thi,	Thi.	Thíṇ,	Thíṇ,	Thíṇ.

The Compound Tenses are the same in formation as those shown on page 16, viz.:— Ho-ta húṇ, &c., *I am being.* Ho-ta tha, &c., *I was being.* Hú,a húṇ. &c., *I have been.* Hú,a tha, &c., *I had been.* Hú,a húṇga, &c., *I shall have been.*

Special Parts.

Ho-ke, *or* ho-kar, *having been.*

Ho-te-hi, *immediately on being.*

Húјiye, *be pleased to be.*

---

[1] Singular. [2] Plural.

CONTRACTIONS

USED IN THE BODY OF THE BOOK.

THE ordinary grammatical ones, as 'Sing.' for 'Singular'; 'Plur.' for 'Plural,' and so on, speak for themselves. 'Anglo-Hind.' stands for 'Anglo-Hindústáni.' (See Preface to the First Edition.) (E.) means that the word beside which it is placed is an English* one in common use by natives. 'Ex:—' stands for 'Example.' (H.) means that the word may only be used of Hindus. (M.) means that the word may be used of Muḥammadans. (L.B.) means that the word is current only or chiefly in Lower Bengal.

---

* Some words, e.g. 'frikasi,' 'áspik,' &c., are so obviously English, (or anyhow not Hindústáni,) that they have been printed without the (E.).

CORRIGENDA.

THE following corrections should be made, as far as possible, before beginning the perusal of the book :—

Wherever 'Huzúr' occurs, *read* 'Ḥuzúr.' See page 28, also page 51, Exercise No. 16, &c

Wherever 'tarah' occurs, *read* 'taraḥ.'

Page 16, after the line beginning 'Girta húṇ,' *insert* :—

Imperfect, *I was falling, &c.*

Gir-ta tha, tha, tha. | Gir-te the, the, the.

" 43, *place* an asterisk before 'sáth.'

" 47, Note 1, For 'It is also' *read* 'Another particle,' '*ṭho,*' is... Next line but one, for 'to' *read* 'ṭho.'

" " (last two notes,) for 'v' and 'vi.' *read* 'iv' and 'v.'

" 103, (first line,) for 'Ordinal,' *read* 'Cardinal.'

" 121, (second line,) for 'ghisarta, ghisarta,' *read* 'ghisaṭta, ghisaṭta.'

" 149, (line 17,) for 'ghisarna,' *read* 'ghisaṭna.'

TABLE OF CONTENTS.

HINDUSTANI

AS IT OUGHT TO BE SPOKEN.

FIRST LESSON.

THE ALPHABET AND PRONUNCIATION.

The Consonants.

1. These, in Hindústáni, correspond closely with the English Consonants; but in Hindústáni there are some additional sounds. There is no x; its place is supplied by "ks." There is also no "c" whether soft or hard; "q" does not occur in the Hindústáni in this book.

2. The unmarked "t" and "d" must be pronounced with the tip of the tongue touching the teeth. When these letters have a dot under them, pronounce with the tongue against the bars of the roof of the mouth; so with "r" and "ṛ."

3. Pronounce "ch" as in "church,"..."sh" as in "short,"..."g" as in "get,"..."ng" as in "king,"... "j" as in "jet,"..."y" as in "yet,"..."w" as in "wet," though sometimes the sound of "v" in "vet," is given to this letter. You should be careful also to pronounce even a single "s," with a full hissing sound, not confounding it with "z." In Hindústáni, we have both an "f," and "ph;" "f," as in English; "ph" as directed in the next section; "h" is as much a consonant as any other; it is to be lightly sounded like an ordinary English "h." When it is the last letter of a word, *and is preceded by another consonant*, the "h" is to be sounded like "ha," cut short as you pronounce it; "ḥ," (with dot) is a rough aspirate, such as is commonly heard in the border-country at home; "k" (without a dot) is sounded from the root of the tongue; "ḳ" (with a dot) is sounded low in the throat.

4. Many words and syllables begin with a consonant followed by "h." This "h" must not be ignored, as it nearly always is by Europeans. By ignoring it, you may call in a "loafer" when you merely want your "horse;" or a native woman instead of your brother. The effect of this "h," is to give sounds not familiar in English. You may acquire them by separating the consonant and the "h" with a very faint echo of any short vowel sound; and practising the gradual withdrawal of that sound, till you can pronounce the consonant and the "h" as one sound. *Any plan is preferable to leaving out the* "h." As laid down in the last preceding section, "ch" is sounded as in "*church;*" and "sh," as in "*short;*" "th" and "ph" also "kh" when not underlined, fall under this section. 'Ch' and 'sh' are *single letters* in Hindústáni.

5. Kh (underlined) is used to express a hard guttural sound. No English word begins with it. The Scotch word "loch" ends with it. The "ch" in the German word "ach!" comes still nearer it.

6. Gh represents a sound hardly attainable by adult Western throats. The most you will be able to do, is to treat it as a plain "gh," under Section 4 above; or you may try and catch its true sound by getting a more or less educated Muhammadan to give you the word for a "domestic fowl."

7. Ṇ (with dot) gives a strong nasal twang *to the whole syllable* in which it occurs.

The Vowels.

1. The *short* ones :—
   - a pronounced as the "u" in "*fun.*"
   - i pronounced as the "i" in "*fin.*"
   - u pronounced as the "u" in "*full.*"

2. The *long* ones :—
   - e always long (and to be pronounced at the end of a word, as well as elsewhere): like the "e" in the German word *mehr;* or the *Scotch* pronunciation of words like "*there,*" "*fare,*" "*dare.*"
   - o always long, pronounced as "o" in *pole;* but more protracted in sound.
   - á pronounced as the "a" in *far.*
   - í pronounced as the "i" in *machine.*
   - ú pronounced as the "u" in the German "du," or "oo" in "*fool;*" but more protracted in sound than the latter.

Throughout this book when "a," "i," and "u," are *short*, they are not marked; nor are they marked *when final letters*, for then they are nearly always long; when not final letters *and long*, they are marked ', "e" and "o," being always long, are never marked. The instances in which words *end* in a short vowel are shown by an "h" following the vowel.

Diphthongs.

8. Take it that there are no diphthongs: when one vowel follows another *and the two are not separated by the mark* "," pronounce the second rapidly after the first as in Italian. When that mark occurs, the two vowels belong to different syllables.

VOCABULARY No. I.

ádmi, *a human being.*[1]
mard, *a man.*
aurat, *a woman.*
ma, *a mother.*
báp, *a father.*
má-báp, *parents; a benefactor.*
beṭa, *a son.*
beṭi, *a daughter.*
k̲hasam, *a husband.*
joru; zaujah, *a wife.*
laṛke-bále, *children.*
bahin, *a sister.*
bhá,i, *a brother.*
bá,i, *a native woman; a dancing girl.*
bíbi, *a native lady.*
ghoṛa, *a horse.*
gora, *a European.*[2]
k̲hidmatgár, *a table-servant.*[3]
murg̲hi, *a hen.*
g̲husl, *a bath.*
khána, *dinner.*
k̲hánah, *a room (much used in composition.)*

---

[1] But translate it, ordinarily, by '*man*,' or '*woman*,' according to the context. [2] Really means '*fair-complexioned*,' often means a European soldier; is not applied to Europeans of rank. [3] So among Europeans; among natives, the word is applied to any domestic servant.

SECOND LESSON.

NOUNS: their CASES, NUMBERS, AND GENDERS.

Cases.

1. "Cases," are marked by certain small words, which follow the original word. The original word, however, *sometimes* undergoes a slight modification before the word indicating the "case" is written. For this modification, see next section; but note here, in anticipation, that there are two accusative cases, the "*simple accusative*," which is always the same as the nominative; and an accusative formed with the particle "ko."

2. The words used to indicate case-relationship are these:—

ka, ke, ki, *of;*	se, *by; with* (of the instrument); also *from;* also "*since*" (of time); *ago.*
ko, *to; at.*	
par, *on; at;*	meṇ, *in; into.*
ne, *by* (of agency)	tak; talak, *up to; as far as.*

3. The selection to be made from ka, ke, ki is a difficulty which should be mastered once for all, as there are many analogies to it in the language. Note, therefore, the following explanations:—

i. The *thing owned* regulates the selection.
ii. If *that thing* be feminine, always use 'ki.'
iii. If *that thing* be singular, masculine and nominative, or *simple* accusative, always use 'ka.'
iv. If *that thing* be (a) singular, masculine and any case *except* the nominative or simple accusative: or: (*b*) plural, masculine, and any case: then always use 'ke.'

4. The English style *with "apostrophe* s," will always give the correct Hindústáni order of the words. An inversion is required in our form with "of."

Modifications in forming Cases and Numbers.

5. Proper names and words expressing family relationships do not change in the Singular; Ex. Khuda, *God:* Chacha, *a paternal uncle:* Bába, *a father:* also, in Bengal, *a child.*

6. Note again that the nominative and the *simple* accusative - both singular and plural—are always the same.

7. As regards the other cases SINGULAR:—

i. Most masculine nouns ending in "a," also many ending in "ah," change these into "e."
ii. No change is made in any other word, masculine or feminine.

8. As regards the NOMINATIVE (and simple acc.) PLURAL:—

i. Most masculine nouns ending in "a", and many ending in "ah" change these into "e."
ii. No other masculine noun changes at all.
iii. Feminine nouns ending in "i," add "áṇ."
iv. Feminine nouns ending in any *letter* other than "i," add "eṇ."

9. The OBLIQUE cases of the PLURAL (including the acc. in "ko") are formed by adding "oṇ," to the Nom. Sing. of nouns not ending in "a," or "ah"; or by substituting "oṇ" for "a" or "ah" in nouns which do end in these vowels.

Note.—Plurals are sometimes further formed by adding the word "log" *people*, (oblique cases, logoṇ) to the Nom. Plural, particularly to express the idea of a 'class.' Confer the use of 'Leute' in German. Ex laṛke-log, *the children*. This idiom is used only of human beings.

The Accusative in "ko."

10. This, in form, is the same as the dative. Its effect is often said to be to particularize a special thing. But this is not always so. The selection as between the two accusatives is a nicety of the language, for which no rule can be given. Avoid using the form with "ko" so as to cause confusion in the sense as to which word is dative and which accusative.

The Vocative.

11. The Vocative Singular is the same as the Nominative, except that "a" or "ah" becomes "e." The Vocative Plural ends in "o."

Gender.

12. Names of males are masculine. Names of females are feminine.

Things called '*neuter*' in English, are either masculine or feminine in Hindústáni. *They should be taken to be masculine, unless known to be feminine.*

13. No detailed rules for gender can be given; but *most* nouns which end in 'i,' 't,' 'ṭ' and 'sh' are feminine. Even to this rule, such common words as "*páni*," water; "*ghi*," a sort of butter; "*moti*," a pearl; "*dahi*," curd, are exceptions; these being masculine. See Appendix, No. 3.

Paradigm of Nouns.

i. *Masc nouns ending in "a," and some in "ah":—*

Cases.	Sing.	Plur.
Nom. and simple acc.	laṛka (*boy*)	laṛke.
Oblique cases,	laṛke	laṛkoṇ.

So; bandah, *slave*, bande; bande, bandoṇ, &c.

ii. *Any other Masc. noun:—*

Cases.	Sing.	Plur.
Nom. and simple acc.	mard (*man*)	mard.
Oblique cases,	mard	mardoṇ.

So; ádmi, *man;* moti, *a pearl;* guru, *a spiritual teacher*, &c. But '*ádmi*' has also a Nom. Plural, *ádmí,áṇ*.

iii. *Fem. nouns ending in "i":—*

Cases.	Sing.	Plur.
Nom. and simple acc.	bíbi (*lady*)	bíbí,áṇ.
Oblique cases,	bíbi	bíbí,oṇ.

So; any other feminine noun ending in "i."

iv. *Fem. nouns ending in any other letter:—*

Cases.	Sing.	Plur.
Nom. and simple acc.	rát (*night*)	ráteṇ.
Oblique cases,	rát	rátoṇ.

So; any other feminine noun not ending in "i."

VOCABULARY No. II.

Note.—There are no "ARTICLES" in Hindústáni; they are either omitted in translation, or "*a*" or "*an*" is translated by "*ek*" = one; and "*the*" by the demonstrative pronoun, which you have not yet learned. N.B. *Verbs* are placed at the *end* of a clause or sentence. See page 61.

larka, *a boy.*
larki, *a girl.*
roti, *bread.*
páni, *water.*
dúdh, *milk.*
taiyár, *ready.*
házir, *present.*
do, *give.*
lá,o, *bring.*
já,o, *go.*
á,o, *come.*
lejá,o, *take away.*
suno, *listen to me.*
bolo, *speak; say.*
hai, *is.*
hain, *are.*
aur, *and.*
bhi, *also.*
magar, *but.*
kitáb, *a book* (fem.)
kalam, *a pen.*
bulá,o, *call; summon.*
chup raho, *hold your tongue.*
rahne do, *let alone; leave.*
sabr karo, *have patience; wait a little.*
hat-já,o, *get out of the way.*

EXERCISE No. 1. TRANSLATE.

Mard ki ma házir hai. Aurat ka beta aur mard ki bahin házir hain. Larke ki roti taiyár hai. Ek ádmi bulá,o. Ek ádmi ko bulá,o. Suno! bá,i ke bete ko bulá,o. Suno! bá,i ki beti ko lejá,o. Bá,i ka bhá,i házir hai. Gore ka ghora taiyár hai. Ghusl ka páni taiyár hai. Sabr karo! Chup raho. Hat-já,o. Rahne do.

Account to yourself *in writing* for all the ka, ke, ki's, and for the changes of a into e, in the foregoing sentences.

THIRD LESSON.

AGREEMENT.

1. "Ka, ke, ki" agree *with the thing owned*, according to the rules above given.

2. Adjectives ending in a consonant, or any vowel except 'a,' agree without change.

3. Adjectives used in making compound-verbs (see *post*, page 21) do not change.

4. Adjectives in "a," become "i" in the feminine, and then never change further, whether singular or plural.

5. *If the noun be masculine*, "a" of the adjective remains unchanged in the nominative and simple accusative singular. It changes into "e" in all other cases of the singular, and in every case of the plural.

6. Such parts of verbs as end in "a" also "agree," under the same rule as applies to adjectives ending in "a," and one rule more: for the feminine *plural* of verbs in "agreement" is in "íṇ." But note, that if there be more than one word thus changeable, *only the last* takes the "ṇ": the other stop at the "i." The agreement is, ordinarily, [1] with the nominative.

---

[1] See *post*, Fourth Lesson, page 19, section 25.

Example of a Verb agreeing in Gender with its Nominative.

With Singular Nominative Masculine.
tha, tha, tha, *was.*
hota tha, hota tha, hota tha, *was becoming.*

With Plural Nominative Masculine.
the, the, the, *were.*
hote the, hote the, hote the, *were becoming.*

With Singular Nominative Feminine.
thi, thi, thi, *was.*
hoti thi, hoti thi, hoti thi, *was becoming.*

With Plural Nominative Feminine.
thíṇ, thíṇ, thíṇ, *were.*
hoti thíṇ, hoti thíṇ, hoti thíṇ, *were becoming.*

VOCABULARY No. III.

dhán, *rice in the field, or in the husk.*
cháwal, *uncooked rice.*
bhát, *cooked rice.*
dál, *a kind of pea.*
dál-bhát, *a native phrase for native food generally.*
makkhan, *butter.*
dahi, *curd.*
ghi, *native butter much used for cooking purposes.*
chá,e, *tea.*
káfi, (E.); ḳahwah, *coffee.*
chíni, *sugar.*
achchha, *good.*
k͟haráb ; bura, *bad.*
lamba, *tall ; long.*
úncha ; baland, *high.*
kotáh, *short.*
baṛa, *great.*
chhoṭa, *small.*
bahut, *much.*
thoṛa, *a little.*
bas, *enough ; that's enough.*
chhoṭi ḥáziri, *early tea.*
baṛi ḥáziri, *breakfast.*
nahíṇ, *not.*
nahíṇ, to, *if not, then.*

Note.—When two things are intimately connected, *and* is omitted, as *dál-bhát, roṭi-makkhan* (*bread and butter*), &c.

EXERCISE No. 2.

Chá,e taiyár hoti hai. Thoṛa dál-bhát do. Ghi achchha nahíṇ hai. Sabr karo! makkhan nahíṇ hai. Dahi le-já,o, dúdh lá,o. Khidmatgár ḥázir nahíṇ hai. Á,o, káfi taiyár hai. Ádmi lamba hai, magar aurat kotáh hai. Aurat ka bhá,i bura hai. Mard ki beṭi achchhi hai. Bas! já,o.

EXERCISE No. 3.

Call the good boy. Call good boys. Take away the little girl. Take away little girls. Take away the bread and butter of the little girls.[1] The little girls are present. The men are ready. The horses are ready. The women are good. The boy is tall. The girls are tall. Call the table-servant. Call the table-servants. The early tea is very good. Give (me) (some) dál-bhát. Give dál-bhát to the women. Bring the cooked rice. Bring the uncooked-rice. Give (me) a little cooked-rice. The man was bad. The woman was good. Early tea was getting (=*becoming*) ready. Have patience, the rice is getting ready. A good book. Breakfast is ready. All right! (=*very good*).

---

[1] Genitives and datives come, in order, before accusative. See *post*, page 61.

FOURTH LESSON.

THE VERB.

1. There is only one conjugation, and very few irregularities.

2. *Simple* tenses are those in which no "auxiliary verb," (as "am," "have," "shall," "will,") is used to form them.

3. *Compound* tenses are those which are made of (generally) the present or the past participle of the chief verb, *and an "auxiliary."*

4. The future tense, the present subjunctive, and the imperative, (with 'let') though *compound* in English, are *simple* in Hindústáni.

5. Nearly all languages use the verbs "*to be*" and "*to have*," as their chief auxiliary verb. Ex. "I *am* speaking," "I *have* spoken." In Hindústáni, there is no verb "to have."[1] The verb "*to be*" is therefore used *as the only* "*auxiliary*," and must be generally translated by our verb "*have*" in all compound tenses of the past participle. This is a little difficult at first, as the tenses look like tenses with the sense of a *passive* voice, but it will soon become familiar to you. Compare the German "*Ich bin gewesen*" and the

---

[1] See *post*, page 75.

Italian, *Io sono stato,* literally, I *am* been, but, in English, French and Spanish "I *have* been."

6. Subject to what has just been said as to translating the Hindústáni auxiliary by "*be*" or "*have*," as the English idiom may require, compound tenses are got *by a literal translation of the English.* Remember, however, that the auxiliary verb comes last in Hindústáni—"I speaking *am*" : "They spoken *had.*" See, also, clause 4 above.

7. Every verb consists of an invariable "stem;" and a variable termination. Starting with the "Infinitive," which always ends in "na," it is to be noted that that part of the word which precedes "na," be it only a single letter, is the "stem" to which the terminations are added.

8. The terminations are these:—(only *masculine* forms are given, but see Third Lesson, section 6, page 10).

–úṇ –e –e –eṇ –o –eṇ, Imperative and Subjunctive.
–úṇga –ega –ega –eṇge –oge –eṇge, Future.
–ta, Present Participle.
–a, Past Participle.
–ke, kar, *or* karke, . Perfect Participle.
–te hi, A special form, meaning '*immediately on,*' or, '*immediately after.*'
–iye, A respectful or polite form of the 2nd person of the imperative; meaning, '*please to,*' &c.

Note.—The Imperative, the Subjunctive and the last three never change; 'a' agrees under the rules already given.

9. The Future, the Subjunctive, and the Imperative of "hona," *to be*, are *usually* written in a contracted form. The Future is as follows: the Subjunctive and the Imperative being reached by dropping "ga" and "ge."

Sing., húṇga, hoga, hoga. *Plur.*, hoṇge, hoge, hoṇge.

10. Sometimes these words are met with in the regular form, ho,úṇga, ho,ega, &c.; sometimes a euphonic "w" is inserted, and then the words would be "howúṇga, &c.": but the contracted forms are, perhaps, the most common.

So also the "e" of the stem of "dena" *to give*, is generally omitted; also, the "e" of the stem of "lena," *to take:* so we get "dúṇga" or "de,úṇga," &c. "*I shall give:*" and "do," or "de,o" Imperative, "*give:*" so, lúṇga, or le,úṇga; lo, or le,o, *I shall take; take.*

11. Only the following parts of "*hona*," therefore, can be considered as materially "irregular":—

Past Part., hú,a, *been.*

Pres. Tense,—hai, hai; haiṇ, ho, haiṇ, *am, &c.*

Past Tense,—tha, tha, tha; the, the, the, *was, &c.*

[Always bear in mind Section 6 of the Third Lesson.]

12. The compound tenses of "hona" *are made with hona as the auxiliary*, the same as any other verb. Ex.:—Maiṇ hú,a húṇ; ham hú,e the. *I have been; we had been.*

13. All "Infinitives" are Verbal Nouns. Present Participles are never verbal nouns.

14. When, by inflection, two "a"s meet, they are separated by a "y," as ána *to come;* stem á; past participle á,a; but written "áya."

15. When by inflection, an "a" and an "e" meet, they are *usually* separated by a "w." Thus from "ána," we may write "á,ega," or "áwega."

16. The plain stem is sometimes used as a 2nd person of the Imperative; but it is insulting to the person to whom it is addressed. Ex:—ja, *go.*

17. On the next page is given a Paradigm of a Hindústáni Verb.

PARADIGM OF A HINDÚSTÁNI VERB.

Active Voice: Gir-na, *to fall*, Stem, gir.

Various Parts.

Infin.	Gir-na, *to fall.*
Pres. Part.	Gir-ta, *falling.*
Perf. Part.	Gir-ke, *or* Gir-kar, *having fallen.*
Past. Part.	Gir-a, *fallen.*

Tenses.

Singular.			Plural.		
Subj. and Imperative. *I may fall. Fall thou, &c.*					
Gir–úṇ,	–e,	–e.	Gir–eṇ,	–o,	–eṇ.
Future. *I will fall, &c.*					
Gir–úṇga,	–ega,	–ega.	Gir–eṇge,	-oge,	–eṇge.
Present. *I am falling, &c.*					
Gir–ta húṇ,	hai,	hai.	Gir–te haiṇ,	ho,	haiṇ.
Past. *I fell.*					
Gir–a,	–a,	–a.	Gir–e,	–e,	–e.
Perfect. *I have fallen, &c.*					
Gir–a húṇ,	hai,	hai.	Gir–e haiṇ,	ho,	haiṇ.
Pluperfect. *I had fallen, &c.*					
Gir–a tha,	tha,	tha.	Gir–e the,	the,	the.
Fut. Perfect. *I shall have fallen, &c.*					
Gir–a húṇga,	hoga,	hoga.	Gir–e hoṇge,	hoge,	hoṇge.

Special Parts.

Gir–te-hi, *immediately on falling.*

Gir–iye, *be good enough to fall; fall.*

So with nearly all other stems in the language.

16. *The present participle*, used without the auxiliary, forms the tense which is usually called "The Conditional." It expresses a condition *with reference to past time.* The next clause, which gives the *consequence*, is also thrown into the same tense. Ex. :—If the man had come, (then) I would have given him one rúpi : (= Agar ádmi áta, to, maiṇ us-ko ek rúpíya deta).

ii. The same tense also expresses *continuity of action in past time* or *what usually happened* ; as, "whenever the king visited the town, he gave gratuities to the poor ;" here also both clauses are put into this tense : Jab rája shahar ko áte, tab g͟haríb logoṇ ko bak͟hshish dete.

[The verb is here made *plural*, out of respect to the rája.]

17. *The past participle*, used without the auxiliary, forms a tense which expresses an absolute, completed action in past time. Ex. :—"He *wrote* a letter yesterday." It also expresses a hypothetical *future* event. The ordinary future, or subjunctive, expresses the same sense ; so you may use any of the forms noted. When this participle is used *as an adjective*, it is followed by "hú,a," both words agreeing with the noun : as, písa hú,a cháwal, *ground rice ;* mári hú,i laṛki, *a beaten* (female) *child.*

18. *The future perfect tense*, (see Paradigm) is much used to express what you think *must have occurred*, though you don't actually *know* that it has occurred. Hence the common phrase, "hú,a hoga," literally "*it will have been ;*" but meaning "no doubt it *has* so happened, though I don't *know* it," and so, in similar senses. Ex. :—"pahuncha hoga," "no doubt he has arrived," "diya hoga," "it will have been given," *i.e.*, no doubt, it has been given.

19. "*Shall have*" is often equivalent to "*must*"— being used either where we give a peremptory order, or

recognise what is inevitable. The phrase is translated by the Verbal Noun (infinitive) followed by "*hoga.*" Ex. :—

Eng. We shall have to go in the carriage to-day (áj).

Note. Maiṇ, *I.* Ham, *we.* Ham-ko, *to us.*

Hind. To-day, to us in the carriage going will-be. A'j ham-ko gáṛi meṇ jána hoga.

Eng. The table-servant must bring dinner.

Hind. To the table-servant, bringing dinner is obligatory. K͟hidmatgár-ko khána lána hoga.

20. "*Must*" when used politely, and not peremptorily, is rendered by the word "*cháhiye,*" which is (in effect) an irregular 3rd personal verb—meaning "*it is necessary,*" "*proper,*" "*desirable*" or the like. It is also used (without any polite sense) of what applies to one's self. Ex. :— A'dmi-ko jána cháhiye, (*to the man going is-proper*) *the man must go.* Ham-ko roṭi cháhiye, (*to me bread is-necessary*) *I must have some bread.*

21. "*Ought,*" which is a sort of modified "must," may be translated by the same word "cháhiye;" or by appropriate adjectival phrases, *e.g.*, "it is necessary" (zarúr); "proper," (munásib) that I, you, the man, should do such and such. The easiest construction is the same as that given above, 'ham-ko jána cháhiye.'

22. "*May*" and "*can,*" denoting *permission* and *ability* are translated by the verb "sakna," to be able. This is properly added to the "stem" of the principal verb: but is often used (incorrectly) even by natives with the genitive of the infinitive. Ex. :—

He can speak [bolna] = wuh bol-sakta hai.

The children may remain = bába-log rahne sakte haiṇ.

23. To "*have done,*" or "*finished*" with a thing is translated by "chukna" added to the "stem" of the principal

verb. Ex. :—He has done speaking = wuh bol-chuka hai. Sometimes it is found added to *the past participle.*

Hence, the common "ho-chuka" meaning "*it's finished*," "*it's done*," "*it's all over.*" "Ho-gaya," irregular past from the compound verb "ho-jána," *to become*, is often used as equivalent to "ho-chuka." You may use either word; and *when used alone*, *i.e.*, not as part of a sentence, you need not alter the word in any way. But you would say, "*chhoṭí ḥáziri ho-chuki hai*, if you wished to make a sentence of it.

24. The language abounds in verbs intensified in meaning by one verb being added to the "stem" of another, the latter only being conjugated. They should be used rather than simple verbs. Here are some examples :—

ḍálna, *to throw*,	*plus*	dena, *to give*,	gives,	ḍál-dena, *to throw down.*
dena, *to give*,	„	dena, *to give*,	„	de-dena, *to give up.*
dekhna, *to see*,	„	lena, *to take*,	„	dekh-lena, *to take a look at a thing.*
kahna, *to tell*,	„	dena, *to give*,	„	kah-dena, *to inform.*
khána, *to eat*,	„	lena, *to take*,	„	khá-lena, *to eat up.*
khána, *to eat*,	„	jána, *to go*,	„	khá-jána *to eat up.*
lena, *to take*,	„	ána, *to come*,	„	le-ána *or* lána, *to bring.*
lena, *to take*,	„	jána, *to go*,	„	le-jána, *to take away.*
márna, *to strike*,	„	ḍálna, *to throw*,	„	már-ḍálna, *to kill.*
rakhna, *to place*	„	dena, *to give*,	„	rakh-dena, *to put a thing down.*
pína, *to drink*,	„	lena, *to take*,	„	pí-lena, *to drink up.*
pína, *to drink*,	„	jána, *to go*,	„	pí-jána, *to drink up.*

and very many more.

25. The (so-called) Nominatives in the tenses of the

past participle of transitive verbs are peculiar: but this is what you have to do:—

i. Change the nominative into the case with "ne."

ii. Take the accusative, and consider it to be a nominative.

iii. Make *it*, so looked upon as a nominative, *and the verb* "agree," according to Section 6 of the Third Lesson.

Ex.:—*The man struck a boy*, mard-ne ek laṛka mára.[1]

The man struck a girl, mard-ne ek laṛki mári.

The man has struck two boys, mard-ne do laṛke máre haiṇ.

The man had struck two girls, mard-ne do laṛki,áṇ mári thíṇ.

The explanation of this strange construction which is usually given is that it is equivalent to "*by a man, a boy was struck*." But the explanation is faulty; for that English phrase is in *the passive voice*, while the Hindústáni is *in the active voice*. You must just accept the construction as it stands.

26. Whenever it is possible to use *the accusative with* "*ko*," you partly avoid the difficulty; for *then* the verb is always in the third person singular, masculine.

Ex.:—Mard-ne laṛke ko mára, *the man struck the boy.*

Mard-ne laṛki ko mára, *the man struck the girl.*

Aurat-ne laṛki ko mára hai, *the woman has struck the girl.*

Auratoṇ-ne laṛki,oṇ ko mára tha, *the women had struck the girls.*

Also note that verbs such as those given on page 19, of

---

[1] "Márna" may also mean *to kill.*

which the last part is got from "ána," or "jána" (*e.g.* lána, to bring) (though transitive) follow the ordinary rule, and not the rule given at Section 25.

27. By adding "karna," or "dena" to certain adjectives and nouns, you can reach a large number of corresponding verbs, Ex. :—

taiyár, *ready*,	taiyár karna, *to prepare ; make ready.*
sáf, *clean*,	sáf karna, *to clean.*
kála, *black*,	kála karna, *to blacken.*
ḥázir, *present*,	ḥázir karna, *to bring one in ; introduce.*
supurd, *trust*,	supurd karna, *to entrust.*
báwar, *belief*,	báwar karna, *to believe.*

and many more.

28. Other forms of derivative verbs are such as the following :—

bolna, *to speak*,	bulána, *to call.*
márna, *to strike*,	marna, *to die.*
khána, *to eat*,	khilána, *to give to eat ; to feed.*[1]
pína, *to drink*,	piláná, *to give to drink ; to water.*[1]
dena, *to give*,	dilwána, *to cause to be given.*
dekhna, *to see*,	dikhlána, *to show.*

and many more.

29. There are some irregular forms of the "respectful imperative," Viz. :—i. Díjiye, from dena, *be pleased to give.* ii. Kíjiye, from karna, *be good enough to do* or *make.* iii. Líjiye, from lena, *be pleased to take.* iv. Píjiye, from pína, *drink ;* v. Húјiye, from hona, *be* or *become.*

30. One other useful idiom should be learned, *viz.*, the use of the pres. part. to express that you do one thing while

[1] Governs the accusative

also doing another thing. Ex. :—Wuh mard bolta chalá-játa hai, *that man goes along, talking.*

Note.—This idiom is often strengthened by doubling the participle. With a fem. nom. it will be (*e.g.*) *bolti*, and in the plur. masc *bolte*, according to the ordinary rules of agreement.

The Irregular Past Participles.

31. There are six irregular past participles (including "hú,a" from "hona" already given). They are as follows :—

	Sing.		Plur.	
	Masc.	Fem.	Masc.	Fem.
From jána, *to go*	gaya,	ga,i.	ga,e	ga,íṇ.
„ karna, *to do*	kiya,	ki.	kí,e	kíṇ.
„ dena, *to give*	diya,	di.	dí,e	díṇ.
„ lena, *to take*	liya,	li.	lí,e	líṇ.
„ hona, *to be*	hú,a,	hú,i.	hú,e	hú,íṇ.
„ marna, *to die*	mú,a	mú,i	mú,e	mú,íṇ.

Note.—"In Bengal, *gaya* is frequently corrupted into *gíya*" in ordinary talk. *Marna* has also a *regular* past participle, *mara.*

The Passive Voice.

32. Never use the passive voice, if you can express your meaning in the active voice.

In making the passive voice, use "jána," *to go*, where English uses the verb "to be." Confer Italian, which makes much use of '*venire*,' in forming the passive; also the German, *verloren gegangen.* Ex. :—

The man is struck = The man is going struck. Mard mára játa hai. ... *The woman was struck = The woman was going struck.* Aurat mári játi thi. ... *The horse will be beaten = The horse will go beaten.* Ghoṛa mára já,ega.

VOCABULARY No. IV.

ABOUT THE HOUSE.

House, ghar; (not 'gar') makán; koṭhi.
The verandah, barámdah.[1]
Office, áfis (E.) daftar; kachahri.
Room, kamra.
The stairs, síṛhi.
The floor, zamín.
The roof, chhappar; chhat.
The Walls, díwár.
The door, darwázah.
The window, khiṛki.
The glass-door, shíshe ka darwázah.
The venetians, jhilmili.
The dining-room, kháne ka kamra.
The drawing-room, hál-kamra.
The private-room, k͟hás-kamra.
The bed-room, sone ka kamra.
The bath-room, g͟husl-k͟hánah
The furniture, sámán; chíz sab.
The pictures, taswíreṇ (fem.)
The carpet, dari.
The mat, chaṭá'i.
The curtains, pardah.
A table, mez (fem.)
A chair, kursi; chauki.
An easy-chair, árám-kursi.
A bracket, bráket. (E.)
The books, kitábeṇ (fem.)
The ornaments, árá,ish.
The vases, gul-dán.
The store-room. godám (corrupted from "godown").
The stables, astabal.
The cook-house, báwarchi-k͟hánah.
The hen-house, murg͟hi-k͟hánah.
The cow-shed, gáo-sálah.
The flower-garden, phúl-bág͟h (*or* bág͟hcha).
The vegetable-garden, sabzi-bág͟h (*or* bág͟hcha)
The orchard, bág͟h.
Land in which a house stands, 'compound.'[2]

---

[1] Derived from the Persian, "*bar-ámadan*," to come out.

[2] Pronounce as in English; the derivation of this word is not known to the author. The word is used only by English people.

VOCABULARY No. V.

Useful Verbs.

To open, khulna (*intr.*).

To open, kholna ; khol-dena (*trans.*).

To close, band-karna.

To read, paṛhna.

To push, ṭhelna.

To pull, khíchna, (L.B.) tánna.

To sleep, nínd-lena.

To lie down, sona, *often used to mean* 'to sleep.'

To get up, uṭhna.

To raise, uṭhána.

To take a walk, sair karna ; hawa khána.

To ride, sawár hona.

To go in a carriage, gáṛi meṇ swár honá.

To run, dauṛna.

To wash, dhona.

To write, likhna.

To do accounts, hisáb likhna.

To sew, sína; silá,i karna.

To learn, síkhna.

To teach, sikhána, *or* sikhlána.

To dance, náchna.

To sing, gána.

To put on clothes, kapṛe pahinna ; oṛhna.

To take off clothes, kapṛe utárna.

To drive, háṇkna.

To get out of the way, haṭ-jána.

To laugh, haṇsna.

To weep, rona.

To take the air, hawa khána.

To go away; *go*, chalájána.

To put into motion, or *cause to go faster*, chalána.

To run off, bhág-jána.

The master of the house, ghar ka sáḥib.

The lady of the house, ghar ki mem-sáhibah.

The young lady of the house, ghar ki mís-sáḥibah.

The young gentleman of the house, chhoṭa sáhib.

Note.—The first three phrases are required by the exigencies of Europeans; but are not *good* Hindústáni. The *proper* feminine of "*sáḥib*" is "*sáḥibah;*" but '*sáḥib*' is often used as if of both genders. Never allow "*mís-bába*" for a *grown-up* young lady. *Mem-sáḥibah* is used to mean a married lady, plur. *mem-log*, the ladies. '*Chhoṭa sáḥib*,' used in an official sense, means 'the Assistant Magistrate,' junior partner, or the like.

VOCABULARY No. VI.

khula, *open.*
band, *shut.*
baland, *high.*
nícha, *low.*
achchha, *good.*
kharáb ; bura, *bad.*
nahíṇ, *not,* often contracted, *na'.*
nahíṇ to, *otherwise ; if not, then.*
ḥákim, *ruler ; judge.*
tajwíz, *investigation ; justice* (fem.)
naukar, *a servant.*
naukar-log, *the servants.*
laṛke-log, } *the children.*
bába-log, }
bál-bachche, }
khabar, *news.*
khabar ka kághaz ; akhbár, *the newspaper.*
bakhshish, *a gratuity ; a "tip."*
khurák, *food,* (fem.)
zor se, *forcibly ; "hard."*
agar, *if.*[1]
kih, *that* (of narration).
ek sáth ; báham, *together.*
juda ; alag, *separate.*
aksar, *frequently.*
jab, } [2] *when.*
tab, } *then.*
khusúsan, *especially.*
poshák, *dress ; fine clothing.* (fem.)
sharm, *shame* (fem.)
janam, *birth.*
nikáḥ ; shádi, *marriage.*
zindagi, *life.*
maut, *death* (fem.)
ḥuzúr, *Your Honor.*
band-o-bast, *arrangements* (of any kind).
koshish, *endeavour ; struggle ; attempt.*
apna-e-i, *own,* reflexive ; all persons, both numbers.

EXERCISE No. 4.

Ghar ki mís-sáhibah ghar meṇ nahíṇ hai. Jhilmili khuli hai. Darwáze ko band karo. Pankha táno. Pankha zor se khícho. Naukar log házir nahíṇ haiṇ. Bába-

[1] Always followed by "to" at the beginning of the second clause: Ex.: —If he comes, (then, "to") I shall leave.

[2] "*Jab*" of the first clause is followed by *tab* in the second : Ex.:— When he came, (then, "tab") I left. See Appendix No. II, page 104.

log gáṛi meṇ hawa kháte haiṇ. Darwázah band hai.[1] Agar ádmi ka bhá,i áwe, to bolo, kih darwázah band hai. Agar ádmi áta, to band-o-bast achchha hota. Mard-ne laṛki bulá,i hai. Mard-ne laṛki ko buláya hai. Mard-ne apni joru ko poshák di hai. Hákim-ne achchhi tajwíz ki hai. Naukaroṇ-ko bulá,o. Mís-sáḥibah ghar ka ḥisáb taiyár karti hai. Roṭi do, dúdh díjiye, páni líjiye. Laṛke log-ko le-já,o. Khána taiyár.[2] Hál-kamre meṇ játa húṇ. Chup raho, so,enge. Huẓúr má-báp.

EXERCISE NO. 5.

N.B.—Datives come before accusatives.[3] Wuh = he, she, it, that.

Put the book on the floor. Shut the glass-door. Open the venetians. Please to bring bread, water, milk. Take away the children into the dining-room. Push hard, the door will open. Open the door. Please give bread to the European. Water the horse. If the man had called out, the children would have come into the house. Immediately after speaking, he called the servants. The Sáḥib[4]

---

[1] This phrase is used in India as equal to "*not at home*" (as well as in its plain material sense).

[2] "Hai," is often left to be "understood," but it is better to express it.

[3] For full instructions as to arrangement of words, the reader may refer to page 61.

[4] Custom warrants the use of this word by itself, or after a personal name, with reference to any European of fair social position Its correct use is (not after a personal name but) after a designation, or name of office, *whether European or native:* as Judge-sáḥib, *the Judge;* Díwán-sáḥib, *the diwán;* Munshi sáḥib *the* (*Muhammedan*) *writer,*' &c. The phrase "call my Baboo," meaning "call writer, &c.," should be cut out of our Anglo-Hindústáni.

has given a gratuity to the table-servant. He is striking the boy. She will strike the boy. The man has struck a boy. The man has struck a girl. The man has given food to the woman. The woman has made many attempts. I'm going. He has gone. Keep quiet! the 'sáḥib' is lying down; the 'mem-sáḥibah' is sleeping: the 'mís-sáḥibah' is learning Hindústáni. Wait a little! I am reading the newspaper. The children will go into the garden. The children may (can) go into the drawing-room.

FIFTH LESSON.

The Pronouns.

These seem at first intricate; but if you will notice the analogies which run through them, they will become easy.

2. To begin with a simple point. There is the pronoun of respectful address to be used to equals and superiors, "áp." The word is unchangeable; but takes the case-signs after it. With the case-signs of the genitive, it of course means "your."—It is joined to the third person plural for politeness sake.

3. If you are addressing a person of not less rank than "rája," you may use the noun "ḥuzúr" (with the third person plural). Ex. :—" Huzúr ka mizáj kaisa hai ?" *Your Honour's health, how is it?* Huzúr nahíṇ jánte haiṇ (kih &c.) *Does your Honour not know* (that &c.). The *ordinary* address to inferiors is made by the second person plural. The second person singular is used only in abusive or contemptuous address, and therefore ought to be always avoided.

4. The PERSONAL PRONOUNS are as follows :—

The First Person.

	Sing.	Plur.
Nom.	maiṇ, *I.*	...ham, *we.*
Gen.	mera.[1]	...hamára.[1]

Form to which to add all particles, except 'ne':—

	mujh.	...ham.

The Second Person.

Nom.	tu, *thou.*	...tum.
Gen.	tera.[1]	...tumhára.[1]

Form to which to add all particles, except 'ne':—

	tujh.	...tum.

Notes :—

i. "ne" is always added *to the Nominative* forms.

ii. You will never be wrong if you use only these forms; but there are also these other forms :—

Dat. and Acc. *Sing.* "mujhe," "tujhe." } no particles.
Dat. and Acc. *Plur.* "hameṇ," "tumheṇ." }

Oblique plur. forms, "hamoṇ," "tumhoṇ" These take the particles, *including* "*ne.*"

iii. Never use the Sing. of the 2nd personal pronoun. Always use the plural throughout. (See para. 3, above.)

iv. You will never be wrong in using also only the plur. of "maiṇ;" but when speaking to an equal or superior, it is better to use the singular.

v. Even natives of rank, when speaking of themselves, generally use a noun of humility, with the 3rd person singular. Persons of inferior rank to you, *ought* always so to speak to you of themselves. Such words are :—"Ghulám," *your servant*; "Bandah," *your servant*; "Fidwi," *your faithful one*; Tábidár," *your subordinate.*

---

[1] These follow the rules for "ka, ke, ki," but, *being already genitive*, they do not take these particles after them.

The Third Personal Pronouns.

Nom. and simple accusative,	yih, *he, she, it.*	ye, *they.*
Oblique forms *for all particles*,	is, *him, her, it.*	in, *them.*
Nom. and simple accusative.	wuh, *he, she, it.*	we, *they.*
Oblique forms, as above.	us, *him, her, it.*	un, *them.*

'Yih' is *he, she, it* of a person or thing *near* you; 'wuh,' of a person or thing more or less *distant.*

THE DEMONSTRATIVE PRONOUNS.

5. Yih and wuh are also THE DEMONSTRATIVE PRONOUNS; *this, that; these, those.*

Notes:—

i. You will never be wrong if you use only these forms; but there are also these other forms:—

Dat. and Acc. *Sing.*, "ise," "use." } no particles.
Dat. and Acc. *Plur.*, "inheṇ," "unheṇ." }

Oblique plur. forms. "inhoṇ," "unhoṇ." These take the particles, *including "ne."*

ii. When "yih" and "wuh" are *personal* pronouns, the case-particles are added to the oblique forms direct; when they are *demonstrative* pronouns, these particles are added to the noun only. Ex.:—is-ko do, *give (it) to him*; is ádmi ko do, *give it (to) this man.*

iii. It is polite to use the plural for the singular of these *personal* pronouns. Ex:— un-ko do, *give* (it) *to him.*

THE POSSESSIVE PRONOUNS.

6. These are the Genitive cases of the three *personal* pronouns, used as adjectives in agreement with the thing owned. Ex.:—Mera ghoṛa, *my horse*; mere ghoṛe, *my horses*; tumhári khúshi, *your pleasure*; is-ka ghar, *his* (or, *her*) *house*; is-ka rang, *its color*; un-ki bahin, *his sister.*

THE REFLEXIVE PRONOUN 'APNA.'

7. This word is a stumbling-block to Europeans.

8. It is a plain Adjective agreeing with a person or thing owned, according to the rules of ka, ke, ki; but when it means "*self*," it is necessarily used without a noun. It never takes any of the terminations of the oblique cases in the plural. We have, therefore, only the three words 'apna,' 'apne' and 'apni.'

9. It means *my own*, *thy own*, *his own*, *her own*, *its own*; *our own*, *your own* and *their own*, whenever these words 'refer back' to a preceding Nominative, relating to the same person or thing.

10. It also means "*self*," "*selves*," as these words are added to *my*, *thy*, *his*, *her*, *its*; *our*, *your*, *them*, when they 'refer back' to a Nominative of the same subject. Ex.:— I want that horse for *myself*.

11. When "*myself*," etc., follow a personal pronoun merely as *strengthening adjuncts*, they cannot be translated by 'apna.' You must use the indeclinable word '*khud*.'

Notes:—

i. Not to use 'apna' where it is the proper word, or to use where it is not the proper word, is sure to give a meaning which you do not wish to express.

ii. Observe that the Nominative is nearly always left to be 'understood' in the second person of the Imperative Mood; and that pronouns, as Nominatives, are also very generally omitted. These facts make no difference in the necessity for 'apna.'

iii. 'Own' is generally omitted in English, but if the context requires it, the omission does not remove the necessity for 'apna.' Thus, the sentence '*he wants his horse*' will be translated according as '*his*' means *his own* horse, or the horse *of another man*. In the former case, the translation will be, *wuh apna ghoṛa cháhta hai*; in the latter, *wuh is-ka* (or, *us-ka*) *ghoṛa cháhta hai*. Everything turns on the second pronoun relating back (or not) *to the same person or thing as the Nominative.* When it does so relate back, use 'apna'; when it does not so relate back, use an ordinary possessive pronoun.

EXERCISE No. 6.

Yih ghoṛa mera hai. Yih mera ghoṛa hai. Maiṇ apna ghoṛa pasand karta húṇ. Maiṇ us-ka ghoṛa pasand karta húṇ. Hamára ghoṛa lá,o. Mera ghoṛa mere wáste lá,o. Main, apna ghoṛa, apne wáste, cháhta húṇ. Main, apna ghoṛa, us-ke wáste, cháhta húṇ. Wuh ádmi apne bhá,i ke wáste ám le-áta hai. Wuh ádmi us-ke bhá,i ke wáste ám le-áta hai. Apna kám chhoṛ-do; mera kám karo. Apne bá,eṇ já,o. Apna khána khá,o. Us ka khána khá,o. Us-ne apna khána kháya hai. Us-ne us-ka khána kháya hai. Teri bát se teri badzáti maalúm hoti hai. Maíṇ-ne, apne wáste, bahut koshish ki[1] hai. Wuh aurat, apne wáste, bakhshish mángti hai. Maiṇ khud já,úṇga.

EXERCISE No. 7.

Pull your own rope; leave his alone. He calls his (own) servant. He calls his (another person's) servant. Turn to your right-hand. He, by his labour, has become rich. He, by his (another person's) assistance, has got promotion. He will eat his (own) dinner. He will take his (another man's) place. He fetched a chair for his (own) mother. He has brought ten (das) Rupees for his (another person's) servant. I wish this for myself. This is my hat He has brought my pony. I myself will do it. The rája himself said.

[1] 'Ki' is either from 'ka, ke, ki' or is the fem. past part. of 'karna.' Here, it is the latter.

THE INTERROGATIVE PRONOUNS.

12. These are "kaun?" *who? which? what?* and "kya?"[1] *what?*

13. "Kaun" is used, properly, of persons only; but is often used for animals or things. It may either stand alone, or be followed by a noun.

14. "Kya"[1] is used of animals or things. It may either stand alone, or be followed by a noun.

15. Declensions.

	Sing.	Plur.
Nom. and Simple Acc.	kaun?	kaun?
Form for the oblique cases	kis?	kin?
Nom. and Simple Acc.	kya?	kya?
Form for the oblique cases	káhe?	káhe?

THE RELATIVE PRONOUN.

16. This is "jo," *who, which.*

A little attention is here needed. In Hindústáni the "relative" pronoun is put *before* the noun to which it relates; and so we form the first clause; then we pick up the thing by a *personal* pronoun in the second clause.

Ex.:—Eng. Call-in the man, who is at the door.
Hind. What-man is at the door, *him* call-in.
" Jo ádmi darwáze par hai, us-ko-bulá,o.

17. The easiest declension of this word is as follows:
Nominative and Simple Accusative, singular and plural *jo.*
Form to which case-signs of the *singular* are added ...*jis.*
Form to which case-signs of the *plural* are added ...*jin.*

The "correlative" or word with which the second clause begins is, ordinarily, the demonstrative "wuh," see

[1] Hence the common phrase "kya hai?" "*what is it?*" *what do you want, &c.*

the example above:—"jo ádmi darwáze par hai—*us-ko-bulá,o.*"

For *things*, 'so' (indeclinable,) is often used.

Note.—You will sometimes find the Relative Pronoun used in Hindústáni *following* its antecedent as in English. Especially when *a clause* stands as antecedent.

VOCABULARY No. VII.

Giving some English (and other) words, which (generally in a more or less corrupted form) have become common in English houses: and which may be freely used. They are both singular and plural.

[The word "ḳamís," (fem.) a shirt, or chemise, is of Arabic origin.]

brúsh, *a brush.*
baks *or* bakkas,[1] *a box.*
botal, *a bottle* (fem.)
bíṛ-sharáb,[2] *beer* (fem.)
brándi-sharáb,[2] *brandy* (fem.)
wiski-sharáb,[2] *whiskey* (fem.)
tost, *toast.*
búṭ, *a boot; boot.*[3]
pín, *a pin.*
dráz, *a chest of drawers.*
patlún, *pantaloon; trousers.*
sílpaṭ; slipaṭ, *slippers.*
minaṭ, *a minute.*
butám, *a button.*
súl-dráz, *body-drawers.*
kálar, *a collar.*
shál, *a shawl.*
dares, *a lady's dress.*
farák, *a frock; dress.*
piṭi-koṭ, *a petticoat.*
kanṭar, *a decanter.*
lamp,[3] *a lamp.*
almári; almaira, *a wardrobe.*
glás, *a glass.*
tambleṭ,[3] *a tumbler.*
wain-glás, *a wine-glass.*
peg, *a mixture of spirits and soda-water; a 'peg.'*

---

[1] Hence "bakkas-wála" a "box-wála," a pedlar.

[2] Also with "sheri" (sherry), "poṭ" (port), "simkin (champagne), &c.

[3] Preserve your pronunciation of the Hindústáni short '*a*'.

VOCABULARY No. VIII.

House Servants.

sirdár *or* sardár-berer *or simply* 'berar,' *the head house-servant not connected with the table or food.*

khánsámán, *the butler.*

báwarchi, *the cook.*

grass-cut, (E.) *he who cuts fodder for the horse.*

sá,is, *the groom.*

máli, *the gardener.*

darbán, *the gate-porter.*

chaprási, *the messenger.* (Literally wearer of a "chaprás" or badge.)

áyah, *the female attendant on a lady or children.*

pankha-wála, *the punkha-puller.*

kochbán; (half E.) gáribán, *the coachman.*

chaukídár, *the watchman; a police officer of inferior grade.*

mashálchi, *the scullion.*

bheri-wála, *the shepherd.*

mihtar, *the sweeper.*

mihtráni, *the female sweeper.*

khidmatgár, *the table-servant.*

darzi, *the tailor.*

bihishti, *the waterman.*

dhobi, *the washerman.*

dhobin, *the washerwoman.*

dá,i, *the wet-nurse.*

kiráni, *the Hindu writer.*

munshi, *the Muhammadan writer;* also, *a teacher of languages.*

"met" (E. mate) is used to express "under"-servant, as met-máli, met-berer, met-báwarchi, &c.

VOCABULARY No. IX.

áj, *to-day.*

kal, *to-morrow* or *yesterday* (according to context).

pahunchna; á-jána, *to arrive.*

chalá-jána, *to depart.*

safar, *a journey.*

bímár, *sick.*

bímári, *sickness.*

hán, *yes.*

na, *no.*

kab? *when?*

kyún, *why?*

EXERCISE NO. 8.

Fidwi áj safar se pahuṇcha hai. Áp ka mizáj achha hai? Áp kab chale-já,eṇge? Ghulám kal já,ega. Kal maiṇ bímár tha. Kal mera bhá,í bímár hú,a; áj achchha hai. Uski beṭi ḥázir hai. Kab ḥázir hú,i? Us ádmi-ko roṭi aur bír-sharáb do. Maiṇ-ne ek laṛkí bulá,i hai. Ḥázir hai? Háṇ, ḥázir hai. Ham ko ek sáf kálar do. Is laṛki ka báp mar-gaya hai. Us laṛke ki ma mar-ga,i hai. Wuh ádmi kharáb hai. Nahíṇ! Wuh kharáb nahíṇ hai Yih kharáb hai. Kyúṇ játe ho?

EXERCISE NO. 9.

When did you arrive [are you arrived] from your journey? I arrived yesterday. I shall leave to-morrow. My sister became sick yesterday: to-day her health is good (or, she's all right to-day). That man's son is here (ḥázir, *present*). I called him. The house-lamps (= lamps of the house) are not clean. Khidmatgár[1]! bring (me) a peg. Yes, sir! (sáḥib).

EXERCISE NO. 10.

Pyár karna, *to make dear, fondle, pet, love.*

Jo ádmi darwáze par hai—usko bulá,o. Jis ádmi ka ghoṛa ḥázir hai—us ka báp bulá,o. Jo laṛke kharáb haiṇ—unko saza do. Jo laṛki,áṇ achchhi haiṇ,—unko pyár karo. Jo páni glás meṇ hai—wuh ham-ko do. Nahíṇ sáhib! wuh páni sáf nahíṇ hai; sáf páni ghulám le,áta hai. Kaun buláta hai? Kaun ádmi buláta hai? Kya hai? Jo gora darwáze par hai,—usko páni do. Jo laṛki áj pahuṇchi hai —wuh bímár hai.

---

[1] Never call this servant your "kitt."

EXERCISE No. II.

Pet that good girl who is in the drawing-room. Call the man whose father arrived yesterday. (*Hind.* Of what man the father arrived yesterday—him call.) Bring me the collars which are in the drawers. The washerman has not brought the shirts which I gave (him) yesterday, (=what shirts I (maiṇ—ne) gave yesterday—these the washerman has not brought). Who is there[1]? What boy is there? What children are there? Which is a good house? (=which house is good?) The European's house is a good one (*say*, *only*, 'is good').

---

[1]Házir.

SIXTH LESSON.

Various Words allied to Pronouns.

1. "Ko,i" and "kuchh" should first be noted. They may stand alone, or be followed by a noun. They are not interrogative; though the sentence in which they stand may be interrogative.

2. "Ko,i" is used of persons, and of things specifically indicated. It may be translated, *some, any*—"ko,i" followed by "*nahíṇ*" gives us "*no*" or "*nobody.*" Ex. :—ko,i nahíṇ hai, *nobody is there*. Ko,i ádmi nahíṇ hai, *There is no man present.* Sab ko,i, *everyone*. Sab ko,i chale-ga,e haiṇ, *every one has gone away*.

3. "Kuchh" is used of *matter* or *mental feelings*, and has generally an *abstract* sense. It is unchangeable and is also translated *some, any*. With "nahíṇ" added, we get "*no,*" "*none,*" and "*nothing.*"

4. Declension of Ko,i.

	Sing.	Plur.
Nom. and Simple Acc.	ko,i.	ko,i.
Form for the oblique cases	kisi.	kin.

Examples :—Ko,i hai, *some one is there*. Ko,i hai[1]? *is any one there?* Ko,i ádmi hai, *some man is there*. Ko,i ádmi hai? *is any man*

[1] Kaun hai? Means *who is there?*—you knowing or believing that *some one* is there.

there? Ko,i kursi lá,o, *bring some chair or other.* Kuchh roṭi hai, *there is some bread;* kuchh roṭi hai? *is there any bread?* Kuchh nahíṇ hai, *there is none.* [Kya hai? What's the matter?] Kuchh nahíṇ, *nothing.* Kuchh parwáh nahíṇ hai,' *there is no matter; pray don't trouble yourself.*

5. With "jo," and 'ko,i and 'kuchh,' compound pronouns are made as in English—viz :—

jo ko,i, *whoever* ... ... jo kuchh, *whatever.*

Note.—Both 'jo,' and 'ko,i' change in the oblique cases according to the declensions of these words already given. Of course, in 'jo kuchh,' only the "jo" can change.

6. The words given below are plain adjectives. They follow the rules of ka, ke, ki.

dúsra, *another,* whether meaning *a different* thing of the same kind, or *an additional* thing of the same kind. In the latter sense "aur ek" (meaning *one more*) may be used and ambiguity avoided.

aisa, *like this,* waisa, *like that.*

kaisa? *like what? what like? what sort of a? how?*

kitna? *how much? how many?*

itna, *this much.*

jaisa, taisa, *as, so.*

jitna, titna, (*or* itna) *as much as; or as many as—so much, so many.*

Notes:—

i. Aisa...waisa and the two pairs last given are used correlatively. As :—Jaisa málik, taisa naukar, *as is the master, so is the servant.* Jitna dúdh hai, titna (*or* itna) do, *give me as much milk as there is.* See Appendix No. 2, page 104.

ii. Here notice the useful phrase 'Jaisa cháhiye,' *as you please;* 'taisa kíjiye' (*so do*) being 'understood.'

7. The following words do not change :—

ek, *one,* or '*a*' or '*an,*' also, "*about,*" or "*or so,*" in such phrases as '*about* ten rupees;' 'there were a dozen men *or so.*'

har, *each*; har-ek, *each one*.
bahut, *much, many*.
chand; baaze, *several*.
aur do, aur tín, aur chár, &c.
donoṇ, *both*.
aur, *more*.
aur ek, *one more; another*.
two more, three more, four more, &c.

sab, *all; the whole*, may be used without change, and either with or without a noun. Ex.:—Ham sab log, *all we people*. When used without a noun you may say "sab" or "sabhoṇ," in the oblique cases.

8. DISTRIBUTION is marked by doubling the numeral: or by the use of "har-ek," *each*. Ex.:—

Ek ek ádmi ko, ek rúpíyah do, or,
Har ek ádmi ko ek rúpíyah do. } *give each man a rúpi.*

VOCABULARY No. X.

FURNITURE AND SOME THINGS ABOUT A HOUSE.

chaṭá,i, *matting for floors*.
shatranji; ghálícha; dari, *a carpet*.
mez, *a table* (*fem.*)
'kháne ki mez,' *the dinner-table*; 'likhne ki mez,' *a writing-table*; 'kitáb ki mez,' *a table with books on it*; 'tásh ki mez,' *a card-table*, and so on.
chháta, *an umbrella; parasol*.
kursi, (*also*, chauki), *a chair*.
sáil-bod, (E.) *a sideboard*.
ti-pá,i, *a tea-poy; any small table*.
pardah, *a curtain; hangings in a doorway, &c.*
taswír, *picture* (*fem.*)
chíz, *a thing* (*of any sort*), (*fem.*)
árá,ish, *the ornamentation*.
kitáb; bahi, *a book* (*fem.*)
ḳalam, *a pen*.
pensil, *a pencil* (E.)
kághaz, *paper*; lál-kághaz, *red paper*; *i.e.*, *blotting-paper*.
siyáhi; roshná,i, *ink; blacking*.
batti, *a wick*.

mom-batti, *a wax-candle.*
tel-batti, *an oil-light; a night-light.*
bája, *any musical instrument;* par excellence, as regards European houses, *a piano.*
pá,o-dán; moṛha; ishṭúl, *a footstool.*
palang, *a bed.*
kauch, (E.) *a couch.*
pankha, *a pankha; a fan.*
kunji; chábi, *a key.*
pauti, *a work-basket.*

Dán, a termination which means a vessel for holding anything, as: "gul-dán," *a flower-vase;* chá,e-dán, *a tea-caddy;* ág-dán, *a fire-holder* (for *e.g.*, lighting cigars), &c., &c.

VOCABULARY No. XI.

jalna, *to burn (intr.)*
jalána; jalá-dena, *to burn or kindle (trans.)*
bujhna; bujh-jána, *to go out (as a light.)*
bujhána; bujhá-dena, *to extinguish.*
átash-khánah; *the fire-place; grate.*
ág, *fire (fem.)*
hezam; lakṛi, *fire-wood.*
ko,ila, *charcoal.*
patthar ka ko,ila, *stone-coal, i.e., coals.*
asbáb, *goods and effects.*
kahna,[1] *to say a thing.*
ya, *or.*
ya, ya, *either...or.*
jaldi; shitábi, *haste; speed.*
jald, *quickly.*
darakht, peṛ; gáchh, *a tree.*
par, *a feather.*
loha, *iron* or *steel.*
lohu, *blood.*

Exercise No. 12.

Sirdár! átash-kháne meṇ ág do. Lakṛi dúṇ, ya patthar ka ko,ila? Patthar, ka ko,ila. Kaun mez taiyár karúṇ?

---

[1] Governs the Acc. so has Nom. with "*ne.*" "*To,*" after this verb, is translated by "*se*"—Us-ne mujh-se kaha.

ásh ki mez. Sardár se kaho kih sab hamára asbáb jald bakkas meṇ rakh-de. Tel-batti nahíṇ jalti hai, mom-batti jald lá,o. Par ka ḳalam (*quill*) lá,o, yih lohe ka ḳalam achchha nahíṇ hai. Sab ghar, chaṭá,i, shatranji, mez, taswír, aur dusre dusre[1] asbáb sáf karo. Tum kaise ádmi ho? Jaise sáhib, taise naukar.

Exercise No. 13.

What sort of a fellow is that? Bring me all the milk in the house (= *as much milk as is in the house, so much bring to me.*) How many things are (there)[2] in the wardrobe? There are[2] many men present (= *many men are present.*) Light the fire. There is no fire-wood. Bring some from the cook-house. Please give me (*i.e.*, *to me*) some blotting-paper. This night-light has gone out: bring another. Put (it) on the chair, and go away.

---

[1] Doubling an adjective idiomatically enhances its force.

[2] See page 75, section 12.

SEVENTH LESSON.

Prepositions.

1. These generally *follow* their noun or pronoun.

2. Most of them follow the genitive with *ke*; a few follow the genitive with *ki*.

3. Of course, when a word *is itself a genitive*, the preposition follows it directly, without *ke* or *ki*. Ex.:—Mere wáste, *for me; for my sake;* tumháre liye, *for your sake, for you.* Kis wáste, *on what account? why?*

VOCABULARY No. XII.

1. Prepositions which follow the genitive with *ke*, or a genitive word in *e*. Those with an asterisk may also be used as adverbs.

* áge, *in front.*
* andar; bhítar, *inside.*
* úpar, *up; above.*
baad, *after (time).*
bá,is, *by reason of*
* báhar, *outside.*
badle, *instead of.*
* bích, *among; between.*
pár, *over; across.*
pás, *near; beside.*
mutábiķ; mu,áfiķ, *like; in conformity with; according to.*
ba-műjib, *according to; agreeably to.*
* nazdík, *near.*
* píchhe, *behind.*
sáth, *along with.*

* sámne, *in front of.*
sabab, *by reason of.*
siwa ; siwá,e, *except.*
ewaz, *as a substitute for.*
* ḳaríb, *near.*
* gird, *around.*
liye, *for the sake of ; for.*
máre, *by reason of ; on account of.*

* níche, *under.*
wáste, *for the sake of.*
* darmiyán, *in the midst ; by the way (i.e., road) between ; among.*
yaháṇ, *beside ; in presence of.* (the French "*chez;*" German "*bei.*")

2. Of these which follow *ki*, or genitive word in *i*, you need only learn these :—

bábat, *concerning.*
jihat, *on account of.*
k̲h̲átir, *for the love of*; *for the sake of.*
taraḥ, *like :* is taraḥ, *in this manner :* us taraḥ, *in that manner.* *
taraf, *towards :* is taraf, *this way*, (*i.e.*, direction); us taraf, *that way*,* (*i.e.*, direction).
márfat, *by the hands of ; through* a person.
nisbat, *concerning ; relative to ;* ba-nisbat is ki, *in comparison with this.*

* *Note.*—In such quasi-adverbial phrases as these, made with "*is*" and "*us*," *demonstratives*, the "*ke*" or "*ki*" is omitted before the preposition. Other examples are "*is liye*," on this account ; "*us liye*," on that account.

EXERCISE NO. 14.

Ghar ke áge baṛa darak̲h̲t hai. Ḍar ke máre báhar nahíṇ ga,e the. Mere nazdík ek rúpíya bhi nahíṇ hai. Tumháre liye sab ko,i koshish karega. Is taraf mat á,o ; us taraf já,o. Ba-nisbat is ki, wuh achchha hai. Yih kám kis taraḥ karúṇga? Jaisa cháhiye. Mere yaháṇ bahut ghoṛe haiṇ.

EXERCISE NO. 15.

The European soldiers have gone across the river. Under the lamp (is) darkness.[1] By the way, I saw two tigers. He was going towards the city. In this manner he became rich. For my sake he underwent much labour. Compared with this, dying is better. Among friends, quarrelling is bad. There are many good pictures in the Judge's house.[2] He has done the work, agreeably-to my orders.

---

[1] Andhera. The sentence is an Eastern proverb. [2] Use 'yahán.'

EIGHTH LESSON.

Conjunctions and Allied Words.

VOCABULARY No. XIII.

These present no difficulties. Those which suggest a "subjunctive" sense (as, '*if*,' '*though*,') are often, but not always, followed by the Subjunctive Mood. The principal conjunctions are as follows:—

agar ; jo, *if.*
agarchih, *although.*
aur, *and ; also.*
balkih, *rather ; on the contrary.*
chúṇkih, *in as much as ; as ; since ; because.*
kih, *that* (of narration).
Sometimes it has the sense of '*or*,' as 'kih na,' *or not.*
khwáh...khwáh, *either...or.*
kyúṇkih, *because.*
go-kih, *given that ; although.*
magar ; lekin ; par, *but.*
nahíṇ, to, *if not ; otherwise.*
bhi ; ham, *also.*
harchand, *although.*
pas, *therefore ; so.*
to, *then.* (See *Notes*, p. 47.)
tau bhi, *even then ; still.*
warna, *and if not ; or else.*
hanoz, *yet ; still ; up to this time.*
ya, *or.*
ya...ya, *either...or.*
na...na ; na yih...nah wuh, *neither...nor.*

See also Appendix No. II, page 104.

'Both...and' ;—'Both' is not translated ; 'and' is usually translated by 'o,' sometimes emphasised by adding 'bhi' after the second word. Ex.:—'Ádmi wahán̤ the,' o laṛke bhi the, *Both men and boys were there.*

Notes.—'To' is used in the second clause to introduce the consequence, result, &c., of the first clause. Ex.:—Agar tum yih kám nahín̤ karoge, *to* main̤ g͟hussah hún̤ga, *If you don't do this work, I shall be angry.*

i. *As a particle* 'to' has several idiomatic uses. Thus, it is used to emphasise an Imperative. Ex.:—dekho to, *look now!* suno to, *just you listen!* It is also used after a numeral, instead of a repetition of the thing spoken of. Ex.:—Ap-ko kitne rúpíye darkár hain̤? Das to káfi hon̤ge, *How many rupees does Your Honor require? Ten will be enough.*

ii. 'Kih' is much more frequently introduced in narration than is 'that' in English. It is generally pronounced as if spelt with a short "e," like our "e" in *kennel.*

iii. There is a peculiar idiom in the use of 'jab tak' (or, talak) and 'tab-tak' (or, talak)—words which, taken together, give us one sense of the English 'while,' and 'till'. The idiom is that you must *always insert a negative* before the verb of the first clause. *We* fix our minds on (for example) the moment of our *return; the natives*, on the duration of the absence. Ex.:—jab-tak main̤ nahín̤ phir-á,ún̤, tab-tak baiṭhiye, *so long as I do* NOT *return, so long take-a-seat,* i.e., *till I return, take a seat.* Jab-tak ghoṛa taiyár nahín̤ hoga, tab-tak ek kitáb paṛhiye, *as long as the horse is* NOT *ready—so long read a book*, or, *read a book, while the horse is getting ready.*

v. When two *unrelated* events are spoken of, as happening at the same time, use 'jis-wak̤t' and 'us-wak̤t.' Ex.:—Jis-wak̤t main̤ chiṭṭhi likhta tha, us-wak̤t wuh ak͟hbár dekhta tha, *while I was writing a letter, he was taking a look at the newspaper.*

vi. 'Chún̤kih' of the first clause is followed by 'is wáste' in the second clause.

VOCABULARY No. XIV.

Useful Verbs (*continued*) and Notes on Some.

bajna, *to sound* (*intr.*)

bajána, *to sound; to play* (*trans.*)

báz-rakhna, *to keep back; withhold; conceal.*

bánṭna, *to divide.*

bánṭ-lena, *to divide and appropriate.*

bándhna, *to bind; tie.*

baiṭhna, *to sit; sit down.*

biṭhána, *to seat.*

bajá-lána, *to carry out; perform.*

bachna; bach-jána, *to escape.*

bachána, *to rescue; save.*

baṛhna, *to grow; increase.*

baṛhána, *to cause to grow,* or *increase; advance* (*trans.*)

barasna, *to rain.*

bújhna, *to understand.*

bujhána, *to explain.*

bhágna; bhág-jána, *to flee; escape; bolt.*

bhejna; bhej-dena, *to send.*

bhúlna, *to forget; to make a mistake* (bhúl).

bhúl-jána, *to forget; to be forgotten.*

cháhna, *to wish; desire.*

chaṛhna, *to ascend.*

chaṛhána, *to cause to ascend; raise.*

chilláná, *to scream.*

ḍúbna, *to sink; be drowned.*

ḍubána, *to cause to sink; immerse; lower.*

dauṛna, *to run.*

ḍálna; ḍál-dena, *to throw; throw down.*

daryáft karna, *to find out about a thing.*

ḍhúnḍhna, *to search for.*

farámosh-karna, *to forget.*

gána, *to sing.*

guzarna; guzar-jána, *to pass over* (e.g., *a river.*)

girna; gir-jána, *to fall.*

girána; girá-dena, *to cause to fall; to throw down.*

gumán-karna, *to fancy; opine.*

ghabrána, *to be confused; perplexed; put out;* (also *trans.*)

ghulna, (*intr.*) *to melt.*

ghulána, (*trans.*) *to melt.*

háṇkna, *to drive.*

jágna, *to be awake.*
jagána, *to waken (trans.)*
jánna, *to know.*
jína, *to live.*
jítna, *to win.*
jhagaṛna, *to quarrel.*

ḳabúl karna, *to agree to ; consent ; admit a charge, &c.*
kám-ána, *to be serviceable.*
kiráya-lena, *to borrow ; hire.*
kasna, *to pull ; make tight.*
khujlána, *to scratch ; tickle.*
khodna, *to dig.*
khulna, *to be open ;* after rain &c. ; *to clear.*
kholna, *to open ; unfasten.*
khelna, *to play ; sport.*
khojna, *to search for.*

ladna, *to be laden.*
ládna, *to load.*
lapeṭna, *to wrap up (as with paper.)*
laṭkána ; laṭká-dena, *to suspend ; hang-up.*
lajána, *to be ashamed.*
laṛna, *to quarrel.*
lagna, *to touch ; be in contact with ; reach ;* also *begin.*
lagána, *to apply one thing to another ; to cause to touch ; to lay on (and, so, to moor a boat, &c., &c.)*

leṭna, *to lie down ; rest.*

mángna, *to ask ; demand ; want.*

[púchhna, is to *ask a question.*]

mangwána, *to send for.*
mánna, *to obey,* also, *to believe ; acquiesce-in.*
malna, *to rub ; chafe.*

nikalna ; nikal-jána, *to go out ; sally forth.*
nikálna, nikál-dena, *to extract ; take out ; turn out ; show-the-door-to.*

pána, *to get ; obtain.*
paṛhna, *to read.*
paṛhána, *to instruct.*
pakaṛna, *to catch hold of.*
pakna, *to grow ripe.*
pakána, *to cause to ripen ; to cook.*
pukárna, *to call out.*
púchhna, *to ask a question.*
ponchh-dena, *to wipe ; dust.*
pháṛna, *to tear (trans.)*
phaṭ-jána, *to split ; burst, (intr.)*
pahchánna, *to recognise one ; know one again.*
phir-ána, *to come back.*
phir-jána, *to go back.*

pahuṇchna, *to arrive.*

pahuṇchána, *to escort; conduct; cause to arrive.*

paiṭhna, *to enter.*

rahna, *to stay; remain; dwell.*

samajhna, *to comprehend.*

samjhána, *to explain.*

sochna, *to meditate on.*

tákna, *to turn; look this way; guard; watch.*

talab-karna, *to seek for; send for.*

taráshna; káṭna, *to cut.*

ṭhaharna, *to wait; stay where you are.*

toṛna, *to tear; break; destroy.*

utarna, *to descend.*

utárna, *to cause to descend.*

uṭhna, *to rise; stand up.*

uṭhána, *to raise.*

uṭh-jána, *to get up and go; to depart.*

uṛna, *to fly.*

uṛána, *to dissipate; to fly*, e.g., a kite (guḍḍi.)

wáḳif-hona, *to be*, or *become aware of anything.*

yád-rakhna, *to remember.*

zikr-karna, *to mention.*

Notes:—

i. The verb '*milna*' occurs most frequently as a 3rd personal verb only. What is our Nominative becomes a Dative, and our Accusative becomes the Nominative. *Confer* the Latin, '*Liber est mihi,*' I have a book.

With this construction always preserved, '*milna*' means every phase of a thing *coming-to*, *reaching*, *meeting* a person or thing. Its precise English must vary with the context, and includes *have*, *find*, *get*, *procure*, *meet*, *come-across* or whatever else suits.

'*Mila*' (3rd pers. past tense,) is a handy word—used alone—to mean '*I've found it*;' '*I've got it.*' Or you may say—more fully—'*ham-ko mila hai.*' 'Ham mile,' 'wuh milega,' and so on, *are not Hindústáni.*

EXAMPLES:—Jangal meṇ ham-ko do sher mile the, *In the jangal I met two tigers.* Mujh-ko bakhshish milegí, *I shall get a reward.*

Us-ko ḥukm-námah mila hai, *he has got a written-order.* Darmiyán ráh ke, ek naddi mili thi, *In the middle* (or, *by the way,*) *they came-on a* river ; ('*unhoṇ-ko*' being 'understood.')

ii. From 'pakna,' comes the Anglo-Hindi. 'pucca.'

iii. 'Lagna,' when it means *to begin.* is preceded by the inflected form of the Infinitive : Ex :—Wuh bolne laga, *he began to say.*

iv. 'Ḍarna,' *to fear,* requires '*se*' of the thing feared. Ex— maiṇ tum-se ḍarta húṇ, *I am frightened for you.*

v. 'Kahna,' *to say, tell,* also takes '*se*' where we use *to.* Ex. :— Us-ne ham-se kaha, kih, &c , *he told* (*to*) *us, that, &c.* So with 'púchhna' :—us-se púchhiye, *ask of him, ask him.*

vi. To express *purpose, intention* or *object,* the inflected form of the Infinitive followed by '*ko*' or '*ke wáste,*' is used Ex :—Wuh kháne ko játa hai, *he is going to dine.* Khelne ke wáste báhar játa húṇ, *I am going out to play.* Or you may say—'ke matlab se'=*with the intention of.* Ex :—Us shakhs-ne, mujh-ko nuḳsán pahuṇcháne ke matlab se, yih bát kahi hai, *that fellow has told this story in order to cause injury to arrive to me,* i.e., to injure me.

Exercise No. 16.

In donoṇ meṇ se, áp kaun pasand karte haiṇ? Meri rá,i meṇ, *yih* achchha hai. Huzúr líjiye ; fidwi ke pás dúsra hai. Bahut achchha! Ghulám áj shám ko ḥuzúr ke pás bhej-dega ; nahíṇ to kuchh kám ka nahíṇ hoga. Achchha ! bhej-díjiye.

Khet meṇ dhán hai ; báwarchi-kháne meṇ cháwal hai ; mez par bhát hai. Agarchíh maiṇ us-ko phir dekhúṇ, tau-bhi nahíṇ pahchán-sakúṇga. Maiṇ us bát ko yád nahíṇ rakhta húṇ. Baaze ádmi kahte haiṇ, kih shahr meṇ bahut chor-log rahte haiṇ. Maiṇ Hindústáni zabán meṇ hoshyár hoti húṇ.

VOCABULARY No. XV.

ḳaisar-i-hind,[1] *the Empress of India.*
bádsháh, *or* pádsháh, *a king.* (M.)
malikah, *a queen.* (M.)
mahárája;[2] rája[2] *a king.* (H.)
maḥárání;[2] rání[2] *a queen.* (H.)
sháh-zádah, *a prince.* (M.)
kúṇwar; jub-ráj, *a prince.* (H.)
díwán, *a minister of state.*
arkán-i-daulat,[3] *the nobility.*
k͟hás-o-ám,[4] *the people generally.*
k͟hud, (indec.) *self.*
baṛa Láṭ[5] Sáḥib, *the Governor-General.*
láṭ Sáḥib, *the Lieutenant-Governor.*
zamín, *land.*
zamíndár, *a land-holder.*
mulk, *a country.*
milki, *landed property.*
khet *a field.*
kheti, *cultivation.*
raíyat;[6] káshtkár; kisán, *a cultivator.* [(*fem.*)
fasl, *the crops; the harvest*
rabi, *the spring crop.*
k͟haríf, *the autumn crop.*
ápas meṇ, *among themselves.*
bát, (*fem.*) *word; affairs; business; news.*

Notes:—[1] This "*i*" is Persian for "*of*"...[2] These words are best left untranslated.... [3] Literally, "*the Pillars of the State,*"... [4] Literally, *The Exclusive and the Common.* "o" is Persian for "*and.*" [5] i.e. "*Lord.*" [6] The Anglo-Hind, '*ryot*' The *plural* is ri,áya, *tenants; subjects.*

When speaking of persons of distinction, you put the Verb in the Plural, even though the Nom. be singular.

Exercise No. 17.

Ḳaisar-i-Hind ke beṭe is mulk meṇ á,e the. Baṛe Láḍ Sáḥib ke sáth rahe the. Ḳaisar-i-Hind k͟hud nahíṇ á-saki thíṇ. Sab Bádsháh, Mahárája, Rája, K͟hás-o-ám, Ḳaisar-i-Hind ke beṭe-ko dekhne ke wáste, Kalkatta[1] ga,e

[1] Calcutta.

the. Sháhzáde-ne bhi logoṇ-ko dekhne ke wáste, sab mulk meṇ safar kiya tha. Is-se sab ko,i niháyat khush hu,e.

Agar yih bát áp-ko pasand nahíṇ hai, to, maiṇ chalá-já,úṇga. Yih ádmi daulatmand nahíṇ hai, balkih gharíb hai. Chúṇkih tum-ne yih kám nahíṇ kiya hai, is wáste tum-ko saza milegi. Jab barsát achchhi hai, tab ri,áya khush haiṇ. Jab maiṇ taiyár húṇga, tab áp ke sáth báhar já,úṇga. Mujh-ko khush karne ke matlab se, bakhshish di hai.

Exercise No. 18.

Given that Your Honor is unwell, still there is no fear of death. Although Your Honor has given the order, still I will not do this work. Just you listen! I shall go to Calcutta, and you shall stay here till I come back. Don't come till I shout. While I say a word to this man, you take-a-look-at to-day's paper.

The land-holders of this country are rich, and often quarrel among themselves. Their tenants get excellent crops when the rains are good. This year,[1] the rains have not been sufficient; therefore (*pas*) the crops are bad.

I am frightened for tigers. I saw two in the forest. They, becoming frightened at me, ran-off, making a loud cry. In the way, we also reached a river; we crossed-over in a boat.

---

[1] The Persian 'im sál' is in common use. It is an *accusative* of time, and must not be used as if it were a Nominative.

NINTH LESSON.

Adverbs, and Allied Words and Phrases.

VOCABULARY No. XVI.

These do not change. You may make up adverbs, by putting 'se' after any noun which will make sense. Ex. :—'Zor-se (Anglo-Hind. 'jorsy,') *with force; forcibly.* 'K͟habardári se' *with care; carefully.* Learn also :—

ab, *now; at present.*
áhistah, *slowly.*
albattah, *certainly; 'no doubt.'*
aslan-mutlaḳan, *by no means; most certainly not.*
bá,eṇ, *to the left hand.*
be-shak, *without doubt.*
bihtar. *better.*
bil-fel, *immediately; at once.*
bil-kul, *entirely.*
dáhine, *to the right hand.*
ek dam, *this instant.*
hameshah, *always.*
ho sakta hai, *it may be; perhaps*
ittifáḳan, *it so happened that; by chance.*
is waḳt, *at this time; now.*
jald, *quickly; soon.*
jhaṭ-paṭ, *very quickly; now; at once.*
kabhi-kabhi, *sometimes.*
mat, *the negative always used with the Imperative Mood.*
masalan, *for example.*
niháyat, *exceedingly.*
raftah-raftah, *gradually.*
sháyad, *perhaps.*
thoṛa thoṛa, *by little and little.*
turat, *at once; now.*
us waḳt, *at that time; then.*
zarúr, *of necessity.*
ziyádah, *more,* often with the sense of, '*too much.*'

EXERCISE No. 19.

Maiṇ niháyat khush húṇ; mere báp-ne ham-ko bahut rúpae di,e haiṇ; maiṇ bil-fel ghoṛe mol-lúṇga. Kapṛe almári meṇ jald laṭká-do. Zarúr jána hoga. Ittifáḳan, murgh-ko ek moti mila tha; kaha, kih "yih chíz kis kám kí hai? maiṇ bhúkh se be-táb húṇ; moti, jauhari, oṇ ki chíz, hai; mere wáste ek dánah ja,i bihtar hoga;" bolte-hi, bhúkh se mar-gaya.

EXERCISE No. 20.

I met a friend on the road. On his journey he came upon a river. A cock came upon a pearl. It came to pass that[1] the king's daughter found a child on the bank of the river. He began to say (that) 'I met two tigers on the road;' but his friend said (that) 'there are no tigers in this place,' so he shut-up.[2]

---

[1] Ittifáḳan. [2] Chup-rahna.

TENTH LESSON.

INTERJECTIONS.

Those in common use are as follows :—

are, (*if a female is addressed*, 'ari,') *hey you !*
kya bát, *what a statement ! stuff ! nonsense !*
wáh-wáh ; shábásh, *bravo ! well done !*
achchha ; k̲h̲úb ; k̲h̲air ;[1] *good ! well !*
bahut achchha,[2] *very good ! all right !*
wá,e-wá,e, *woe is me ! oh dear, oh dear !*
bápre-bápre, *expresses astonishment at some disagreeable news, or the like.*
báp-báp, *help ! mercy !*
duhá,i, *or* duhá,i-duhá,i, *justice !*
duhá,i Mahárání ki, *grant justice, oh Great Queen !*
afsos, *or* afsos hai, *what a pity ! how sad !*

---

[1] We, in telling a story, often *begin* a sentence with the exclamation 'well !' Natives, in like circumstances, often *end* a sentence in the same way. Their word is 'k̲h̲air.'

[2] 'Bahut achchha' or 'bahut k̲h̲úb' is also a common answer given by a servant on receiving orders. Or he may answer, 'jo ḥukm,' *whatever your orders* (be)—' I shall attend to them' being understood. Or he may say, simply, 'Háṇ, k̲h̲udáwand,' or, Ji ! háṇ, *Yes, Your Honor !*

chhi-chhi,[1] *ugly! nasty!*
dúr; dúr-dúr; dúr ho! *be off! get out!*

VOCABULARY No. XVII.

Useful Adjectives—*(continued.)*

achha; k͟húb, *good.*
k͟haráb; bura, *bad.*

úṇcha; baland, *high.*
nícha, *low.*

baṛa; bazurg, *great.*
chhoṭa, *small.*

bahut, *much.*
thoṛa; zarrah, *little.*

moṭa, *thick; coarse; stout.*
patla, *thin; weak in texture, or in body.*
bárík; mihíṇ, *fine in texture.*
dubla, *thin; scraggy.*
mazbút; *strong; firm.*
kam-zor, *weak, (deficient in strength.)*
nátáḳat, *infirm; shaky.*
zoráwar, *strong in body; oppressive.*

kaṛwa, *strong, (as liquor,* or *tea.)*

lamba, *long.*
kotáh, *short.*

chauṛa, *broad.*
kam-arz, *narrow.*

gol, *round.*
chau-kona, *square.*

kharkhara, *rough.*
chikna, *smooth.*

garm, *warm; hot.*
ṭhanḍh; ṭhanḍha, *cold.*

sáf, *clean.*
maila, *dirty.*

sak͟ht, *hard,* also, *difficult.*
narm; mulá,im, *soft.*

ásán; salís, *easy.*
mushkil, *difficult.*

---

[1] This word must never be used as an adjective describing any of Her Majesty's subjects; or their dialect; as in these lines from the "*Lays of Ind*"—

> "What though upon her lips there hung
> The accents of the *chhi-chhi* tongue."

bhári, *heavy.*
halka, *light.*

tázah, *fresh.*
saṛa ; purána, *decayed.*

naya ; nau, *new.*
purána, *old.*

gaihra, *deep.*
uthla, *shallow.*

tez ; tezrau, *fast.*
tez nahíṇ, *slow.*

nazdík, *near.*
dúr, *distant.*

pyára, *dear* (of affection.)
mahṇga, *dear* (of price.)
sasta ; manda, *cheap.*

tang ; *narrow ; too tight.*
tez, *sharp* (as a knife.)
kund, *blunt.*

káfi, *sufficient ; enough.*
kam, *deficient ; 'short.'*

daulatmand, *rich.*
g͟haríb ; kangál ; muflis, *poor.*

mag͟hrúr, *proud.*
g͟haríb ; miskín, *humble ; poor in spirit.*

andha, *blind.*
bahra, *deaf.*

gúṇga, *dumb.*
langṛa, *lame.*
langa, *naked.*

maalúm, *known.*
ná-maalúm, *unknown.*
k͟hush, *pleased ; happy.*
ná-k͟hush, *displeased ; unhappy.*

pasand, *agreeable ; approved.*
ná-pasand, *disagreeable ; disapproved.*

chálák ; tez-zihn ; aḳlmand ; } *clever ; sharp-witted.*

dána, *wise.*
be-wuḳúf, *foolish.*
kund-zihn, *dull of intellect.*
diwánah, *mad.*
hoshyár, *skilful ; up in your work.*
be-hosh, *senseless ; stupid ; 'no good ;'* also, *'in a swoon.'*
umdah, *great ; noble.*
páji, *mean ; base ; contemptible.*
álim, *learned.*
jáhil, *ignorant.*
sáf, *clear.*
andhera, *dark.*

súkha, *dry.*
bhíṇga ; tar, *wet.*
sach ; sachcha; rást, *true ; just.*
jhúṭha, *untrue.*
ná-rást, *unjust ; wrong.*
durust, *right ; proper.*
ná-durust, *not right ; improper.*
sufed, *white.*

kála, *black.*
barun (E.), *brown.*
sabz, *green.*
níla, *blue.*
lál, red.
zard, *yellow.*
uttar ; shamál, *the North.*
dakhan ; janúb, *the South.*
púrab ; mashriḳ, *the East.*
pachchham ; maghrib, *the West.*

Notes :—

'Kam' is much used as a prefix, signifying deficiency. 'Maalúm,' 'Ná-maalúm,' are much used colloquially, by themselves alone, to mean '*I know it,*' '*I don't know it.*' 'Muflis' is said also to mean '*a bachelor,*' but there is probably some error in this use of the word.

The words 'uttar,' 'dakhan,' 'púrab,' and 'pachchham,' are those most commonly used. From 'dakhan' comes the Anglo-Hind, 'Deccan.'

All natives know the points of the compass ; and all directions should be given by them. Thus you may tell your servant if you want him to bring you an article, (and know yourself where it lies,) that it is, *e.g.*, on the North-West corner of your table. He is then sure to find it, if there.

EXERCISE No. 21.

Are ! kidhar játe ho ? 'Áp kyúṇ púchhte haiṇ ? Kya bát ! tum jawáb nahíṇ de,oge ? Háṇ khudáwand ! fidwi jawáb dega ; fidwi bázár játa hai. Bahut achchha ! ḳusúr nahíṇ hai, chalo. Duhá,i Mahárání ki ! chor logoṇ-ne mere sab mál lúṭ-liye haiṇ ; ḥukm díjiye kih polís (E.) ke sipáhi,án fouran taḥḳíḳát kareṇ. Wá,e ! wá,e. Afsos hai! cháron taraf[1]

[1] 'Cháron taraf'—(chár, *four*) idiomatic ; *on all sides ;* "chár" is made plural ; 'taraf' is unchanged ; no preposition is required.

uttar, dakhan, púrab, pachchham, talásh kareṇge, kaho! kya kya mál gum ho-gaya hai?

Yih ádmi aḳlmand hai; wuh, be-wuḳúf hai. Yih aurat bahut dubli hai; lekin uska khasam bahut moṭa hai. Yih kapṛa patla aur kam-arz hai, mujh ko kapṛa mazbút aur chauṛa darkár hai; tumháre pás aisa kapṛa hai? Kála kapṛa mazbút hai. Be-wuḳúf! maiṇ sufed kapṛa mángta húṇ, tum kála kapṛa báhar karte ho—já,o! Berar! Háṇ khudáwand! barun ghoṛa bimár hai. Bápre! bápre! kaisa hú,a? Maiṇ kya jánta! Jald dauṛo—bázár-se julláb ki dawa maṇgá,-do. Tábidár chaprási bhej-dega. Nahíṇ! tum sust ádmi! is darmiyán meṇ, ghoṛa mar-já,ega; khud dauṛo; dúr!

Exercise No. 22.

Hey you! what are you up to? (=*doing.*) Nothing. Then, what is all this noise? We are only chatting among ourselves. Don't chatter in the verandah; by reason of the noise, I cannot work. Who are these men? They are cultivators. What do they want? They say that owing-to (se) the oppression of their (own) landlord, their crops have been attached; they desire justice. But is their story true; God knows! as a rule, there is some truth and some falsehood on both sides. Certainly these poor people won't tell lies. Your Honour has been six months in the country and knows everything; but (your) slave's opinion is that whoever believes only half[1] will do good justice.[1]

---

[1] From 'nisf,' *half*, is derived 'insáf,' *justice*; also 'Munsif,' *a dispenser of justice*, a '*Moonsiff*' (Anglo-Hind).

ELEVENTH LESSON.

ARRANGEMENT OF WORDS IN A SENTENCE.

The arrangement of words in a sentence is left a good deal to taste, subject to one fixed rule that your Verb must come at the end of the clause or sentence; and if there be an *auxiliary*, it is the last word. You cannot divide the parts of a verb; making such a sentence as 'He had, after some delay, made a full confession.' All the component parts of a compound tense come together.

2. Taking the ordinary words and clauses which occur in a sentence, the following order will be found idiomatic:—Nominative, preceded by the qualifying word, or words, if any; Object, purpose, intention, or the like; ..Dative.... Adverbial, or participle clause;...Accusative; ... Verb. Ex.:—Us kharáb ádmi-ne—nuksán pahuncháne ke matlab se—mujh-ko—niháyat baland awáz se—gáli di thi, *That bad man, with the object of causing (me) loss, to me, in a very loud voice, gave abuse.* If you wish to state the *place*, you might say, *e.g.* 'bázár men' before 'gáli.' The *time* would probably stand first of all: as, áj, din-ko, tín pahar ke wakt, (us kharáb ádmi, &c.,) *to-day, by day, at the time of three-watches*, i.e., *at three o'clock this afternoon, &c.*

3. INTERROGATION is expressed in several ways—

1st.—By the mere inflection of the voice; the words

remaining in the same order as in an affirmative sentence. Ex. :—Tum nahíṇ jánte, kih, &c. *Don't you know that &c.?*

2nd.—By the use of a plain interrogative word. Ex. :—kyúṇ deri karte ho? *Why are you delaying? why are you so slow?*

3rd.—By first naming a thing, and then asking about it; as often occurs in French. Ex. :—Áp ka mizáj—kaisa hai? *Your Honor's health—how is it?*

[Hai ádmi ḥázir? and the like, are not Hindústáni.]

Some Interrogative Words.

Kab, *when?* Kaháṇ, *where?* Kidhar, *whither?* Kyúṇ, *why?* Kaun, *who?* Kya, *which? what?* Kab-tak, *how long?* Ka,eber; ka,e dafah, *how often?* Kis-wáste, *on what account; why?* Kyúṇ-kar; kis-tarah; kaisa, *in what manner; how?* Kitna, *or* ketna, *Plur:* kitne, *or* ketne, *how many? how much?*

VOCABULARY No. XVIII.

The Body and some of its Parts.

badan; jism, *the body.*	áṇkh; chashm, *the eye.*
sir, *the head.*	nák, *the nose.*
bál, *the hair.*	rukh; gál, *the cheek.*
zulf, *curly hair.*	múṇh, *the mouth.*
múchh, *mustachios.*	tálu, *the palate.*
dáṛhi, *the beard.*	dáṇt *or* dant, *a tooth.*
ru; chihrah; múṇh,[1] *the face.*	jíbh; zabán,[2] *the tongue.*
pesháni, *the forehead.*	jabṛa, *the jaw.*
abru, *the eyebrow.*	lab, *a lip.*

[1] Pronounce, nasally, 'moo.' [2] Zabán means also '*a language.*'

ṭhuḍḍi ; zanakh, *the chin.*
kán, *an ear.*

gardan, *the neck.*
gala *or* gula, *the throat.*
bázu, *an arm.*
háth ; dast,[1] *a hand.*
hatheli, *the palm.*
ungli, *a finger.*
nákhun, *a nail.*

káṇdha, *the shoulder.*
chháti, *the breast.*
sínah, *the bosom.*
godi, *the lap.*
pánjar, *the side.*
píṭh, *the back.*
chútaṛ, *the buttocks.*

ṭáng, *the leg.*
jángh, *the thigh.*
pinḍli, *the calf.*

pá,oṇ, *the foot.*
talwa, *the sole of the foot.*
eṛi, *the heel.*
pá,oṇ ki ungli, *a toe.*

haḍḍi ; háṛ, *a bone.*
paṇjari, *a rib.*
khún ; lohu, *blood.*
pit, *bile.*
pasínah, *perspiration.*
dam[2] ; sáṇs, *the breath.*

rag ; nas, *a vein.*
maghz ; dimágh, *the brain.*
dil, *the heart.*
peṭ ; shikam, *the belly.*
midah, *the stomach.*

phepṛe, *the lungs.*
tilli, *the spleen.*
gúda, *the marrow.*

chamṛa, *the skin.*[3]

---

[1] Hence, dast-ánah, (*not* das-tánah,) *a glove.*
[2] Not to be confounded with 'dum,' *the tail of an animal.*
[3] Means also '*leather.*'

TWELFTH LESSON.

NUMERATION.

The first things to learn here are the following fractions:—

pá,o, *a quarter.*	deṛh, *one and a half.*
ádha, *a half.*	aṛhá,i, *two and a half.*

also these:—

sáṛhe, *one half* MORE *than the unit named.*

sawa, *one quarter* MORE *than the unit named.*

paune, *one quarter* LESS *than the unit named.*

2. Then learn these words:—

ganḍa, *a bundle of* 4.	hazár, a *thousand.*
kori, *or* kurí, *a score.*	lákh, *a hundred thousand.*
sau, *a hundred.*	kaṛoṛ, *ten millions.*

3. There are separate words from 'one' to 'one hundred,' but it will be sufficient for you to learn the words only from 'one' to 'twenty.' They are as follows:—

1, ek.	8, áṭh	15, pandrah.
2, do.	9, nau.	16, solah.
3, tín.	10, das.	17, satrah.
4, chár.	11, igyárah,	18, aṭhárah.
5, pánch.	12, bárah.	19, unís.
6, chhah.	13, terah.	20, bís.
7, sát.	14, chaudah.	

———

4. The other numbers up to 100 will be found in Appendix No. I, page 103. With the materials now given you, you can express any number, in a perfectly idiomatic way: by using karoṛs, lákhs, thousands, hundreds, *scores*, and units. Ex.:—557 = five hundred, two scores, and[1] seventeen, pánch sau, do kúri, satrah. 9,991 = nau hazár, nau sau, char kúri, unís.

5 The ORDINAL numbers are as follows:—Paihle, *first*; dúsra, *or*, doyum, *second*; tísra, *third*; chautha, *fourth*. These, when ending in 'a,' follow the rules of ka, ke, ki. After 'chautha, *fourth*,' the ordinals are got by adding 'wáṇ' to the cardinals. 'The sixth' is, for euphony's sake, 'chhaṭwáṇ.'

6. 'Once,' 'twice,' 'thrice,' &c., are expressed by 'ek dafah,' 'do dafah,' 'tín dafah,' and so on.

7. 'A,' in such phrases as 'a yard,' 'a foot' is expressed by the word 'fi.' or by 'ek ek' Ex.:—fi—*or* ek ek—gaz kitne rúpae hoṇge? *how many rupees a yard.*

8. As there are sixteen annas in a Rúpi, 16 is much used to give the idea of a 'whole,' 'a unit,' or 'full quantity,' of anything; "*eight annas*" meaning a half; '*four annas*,' a quarter; *two annas*, an eighth, and so on. Confer the words 'quadroon,' 'octoroon.'

---

[1] 'AND' is never expressed with numerals.

THIRTEENTH LESSON.

Time.

The English Months are sure to be known by all your servants, and are also known to natives generally. But you must catch the pronunciation in use in your locality.

The following is pretty near the ordinary pronunciation:—

Janṛi.	Julai.
Fabṛi.	Agast.[1]
Marich.	Saptambar.
Apríl.	Oktobar.
Mai.	Navambar.
Jún.	Dichambar.

2\. The Days of the Week are not known by their English names.

The names most commonly used are these—

Itwár; rabibár, *Sunday.*
Sombár; pír ka roz, *Monday.*
Mangal, *Tuesday.*
Budh, *Wednesday.*
Brihaspat; biphe, *Thursday.*
Shukrbár; jumah, *Friday.*
Sanichar; sanibár, *Saturday.*

[1] Accent on the last syllable.

3. The HOURS are now-a-days always counted by the English watch when possible. But the native division assigns so much time to the day-light, and so much to the night. The reckoning is by the "pahar," (pronounced in Lower Bengal, 'prohor,') which consists of three English hours; four "pahars" being counted to the day, and four to the night. Then the word 'ghanṭa'—which means *a bell*, or *gong*—is used to mean 'an hour,' as in many parts of India a gong is struck after each hour. Again, there is a word 'ghaṛi,' which is said to be equal to about *one-third of an English hour;* but is often used very vaguely; as indeed all words of time are, when not referred to a watch or clock. 'Ghaṛi' is also used for the English '*clock*,' or '*watch*' itself.

4. 'The clock' is known to all servants as well as to superior natives. The verb 'bajna' (*intr.*) *to sound;* or the verb 'bolna' (*intr.*) *to say*, is used with reference to a clock or watch. If you will study the following clauses you will be master of 'the clock' in Hindústáni:—

kya baja hai, *what has sounded? what o'clock is it?*
do baje haiṇ, *two have sounded; two o'clock.*
aṛhá,i baje haiṇ, *a half more than two has sounded.*
sawa do baje haiṇ, *a quarter more than two has sounded.*
paune do baje haiṇ, *a quarter less than two has sounded.*
do baj-ke, bís mínaṭ, *two having sounded, twenty minutes* (more have passed), *twenty minutes past 2.*
bís mínaṭ ke baad, do bajega, *after twenty minutes, two will strike; twenty minutes to 2.* Or this may be expressed thus:—bís mínat kam, do baje, (*by*) *20 minutes less, two o'clock.*

deṛh baje, *half past one.* . . . aṛhá,i baje, *half past two.*
ka,e baje? *at what o'clock?* tín baje, *at three o'clock.*

5. Time in a vague sense is expressed by an accusative without government, as in English. Ex:—guzashte sál, *last year*; pari roz, *on the following day*.

6. When precision is aimed at, 'at,' or 'by,' (of time) is translated 'ko,' or 'ke wakt' Ex:—Áj, shám-ko, *to-day, at evening; this evening*. Rát ke wakt, *by night, at night*.

7. 'Ago,' 'since,' 'for,' are translated by 'se,' or by 'hú,a' in agreement. When 'since' can be resolved into *that I have not*, you must use a negative. Ex.:—Tín baras hú,e, maiṇ Kalkatte meṇ raha tha, *three years ago, I was living in Calcutta*. Kal se, maiṇ is-ko khojta húṇ, *I am searching for it since yesterday*. Chár mahínoṇ-se, wuh bímár hai, *he is (has been) sick for four months*. Páṇch barsoṇ se, maiṇ-ne apna watan nahíṇ dekha hai, *since five years, I have not seen my native country*, or, in good English, *it is five years since I have seen my native country*.

8. In naming a date (táríkh, fem.) you use 'ko.' Ex.:—Navambar mahíne ki pánch táríkh ko, Kalkatte já,úṇga, *I shall go to Calcutta on date 5. of the month November*.

9. 'Meṇ' is also often used for 'in,' or 'during,' expressed or understood.

10. In using the numbers, '*and*' is always left untranslated. Ex.:—*five hundred* AND *forty-three*, páṇch sau, do kúri tín.

VOCABULARY No. XIX.

Words and Phrases relating to Time, Money, Weight, and Measurement.

Time.

táríkh (fem.), *a date.*

baras; sál, *a year;* in dating, san.

mahínah, *a month.*

haftah, *a week.*

roz; din, *a day.*

chaudah roz, *fortnight.*

ghanta; ghari, *an hour.*

minat (E.), *a minute.*

lahzah, *a second,* (*lit. twinkling of an eye*).

áj; im roz, *to-day.*

kal, *to-morrow,* or *yesterday* (according to context)

parson, *the day after to-morrow,* or *the day before yesterday* (according to context.)

tarson, *the fourth day* (forwards or backwards.)

pari roz, *the day after* (*any event*); *next day.*

guzastah; jo bít-gaya, *the past.*

guzastah baras (*or* sál), *last year.*) (Nom.)

guzashte baras (*or* sál), *last year.* (Acc.)

yih baras (*or* sál), *this year.* (Nom.)

is baras; is baras men; im sál, *this year; during this year,* (Acc.) 'im' is Persian; but 'im sál' is in common use.

á,indah, *the future.*

á,indah, baras, (*or* sál,) *next year.* (Nom.)

á,inde baras; á,inde baras men (or with 'sál'), *next year.* (Acc.)

ab; hál; is wakt, *the present.*

ek din nághah karkē; ek din chhor-kar, *every alternate day*

din ke wakt, *by day.*

rát ke wakt, *by night.*

ala-s-sabáh, *at early dawn.*

tarka; fajr; bhor; subh, *early morning.*

do pahar din, *noon.*

do pahar rát; ádhi rát, *mid-night.*

shám, *the evening.*

shám-ko, *in the evening.*

Money.

mablag͟h, *a lump sum.*

rúpíya, *a rupee.* Plur. rúpíye; rúpae; rúpi; rúpae is also used to mean '*money.*'

ánah, *an* '*anna,*' $\frac{1}{16}$ of a rúpi.

pá,i, *a* '*pie,*' $\frac{1}{12}$ of an 'ánah.'

rúpi, *a rúpi-piece.*

aṭh-anni, *an 8-ánah-piece*

chau-anni *a 4-ánah-piece.*

do-anni, *a 2-ánah piece.*

paisa, *a 3 pa,i-piece* (4 make an 'ánah'), often means '*money.*'

Weights.

man, *a* '*man;*' Anglo-Hind. 'maund,' equal to about 80 lbs.

ser, *a* '*seer,*' equal to about 2 lbs.

ádhá-seṛ; ek paun (E.), *half a* '*ser,*' or *one pound.*

chhiṭáṇk, *a* '*chittack,*' $\frac{1}{16}$ of a 'ser.'

tola, *a* '*tolah;*' *the weight of a rúpi;* by which letters, gems, gold, silver, &c., are weighed.

Measurement.

ek kos, *a* '*coss;*' about two miles.

ádhá-kos, *half a* '*kos;*' *a mile.*

bhíga, *a land measure;* varies in different parts of India.

kaṭṭha, *a* '*cottah,*' $\frac{1}{20}$ of a 'bígha.' (square measurement).

rassi, *a measure of length about* 60 *yds.*

gaz, *a yard.*

háth, *a cubit.*

fúṭ (E.), *a foot.*

musht; muṭṭhi, *a fist, i.e., a* '*hand,*' (as in measuring horses.)

inchi (E.), *an inch.*

Exercise No. 23.

Jo haftah bít gaya hai, us meṇ maiṇ-ne do ghoṛe mol-liye haiṇ, Guzashte sál, ri,áya bahut g͟haríb the; im sál, un-ki fasl achchhi hai, is liye k͟hush haiṇ. Angrezi[1] baras—Janṛi ki paihli táṛík͟h ko—shuru hota hai. Meri ghaṛi bigar ga,i hai. Us-ki ghaṛi tez chalti hai, aur mere bhá,i ki ghaṛi sust chalti hai. Kuchh kám ki[2] nahíṇ haiṇ. Maiṇ-ne paune

[1] English.

[2] Agreeing with 'ghari.'

chár gaz mol-liye. Unhoṇ-ne aṛhá,i man ko,ila kharíd kiya. Ham-ko paune páṇch baje jagá,o. Ka,e baje báhar já,eṇge? Áj, shám-ko, báhar já,úṇga; ka,e baje maiṇ ab nahiṇ jánta húṇ. Sab chíz ṭhík hai? Háṇ khudáwand! Tel-batti ghusl-kháne meṇ rakh-do.

Exercise No. 24.

Her ear is small. Her breast is white. Her cheek is red. Her heart is light. His jaw is large. There are gloves on her hand. There was much perspiration. His shoulder is strong. Give me one quarter. He has bought fifteen horses. How much has he given for them? Rs. 9,786. Five hundred and forty-two men were present. Give me 2¾. He is first, and she is second. I spoke to him three times. This year is hot. This year, the rains are good. To-day at one pahar, I shall go to Calcutta. At what o'clock did he go out? At a quarter to three.

FOURTEENTH LESSON.

MISCELLANEOUS.

The PRONUNCIATION given in this book is the purest known; but you must not expect that here, any more than in England, pronunciation is everywhere the same; or even the same in one locality, as uttered by educated and by uneducated people. Thus you will often hear 'z' and "j" confounded with each other; and will even learn to know "nazdík," under the metamorphosis of 'nagích.'

2. You must also remember that there is such a thing as ACCENT in addition to 'quantity.' Thus a long 'a' at the end of a word will be sounded less strongly than the same elsewhere.

3. Besides quantity and accent, there is also the CADENCE of a sentence. This, and the appropriate action of hands, face and body, can be acquired only by imitation.

4. THE GREAT FAULT OF EUROPEANS—next to leaving out the non-initial 'h'—is "clipping" their words as they speak, ignoring double consonants, and forgetting that Hindústáni, when well spoken, is a language of vowels and double consonants, and must be vocalized like Italian. It is miserable to hear such sounds as *hamreh garry low*,[1] *pinnykypanny do*, *eggy barrow*,[2] *sarry das bajy*, and so on.

---

[1] Pronounce as in '*how*.'

[2] No doubt, for 'áge baṛhá,o.'

4. In concluding the instructions of this little book, a few matters which have not found place in the earlier lessons will be gathered up here.

5. IDIOMS of a peculiar kind are not very numerous in the language. You have already learned (page 47) that you require 'not' in such phrases as '*wait here till I come back;*' and (page 68) '*it is three years since I saw you.*' Note also that words of time, measurement, quantity and so forth often stand in the accusative without any government. "Of" is not translated in such phrases as 'a cup *of* tea,' 'a yard *of* cloth,' 'a piece *of* bread.' The words stand in 'apposition'—ek piyálah chá,e—ek gaz kapṛa—ek ṭukṛa roṭi. In such phrases, again, as 'he fell from the wall,' the natives say, he fell from *on* the wall (díwár par se); also our phrase 'out of' is taken in the reversed light, and becomes 'from in.' Ex.:—lomṛi bil meṇ se nikli, *the fox came out of* (from inside) *its hole.* There is also a favourite idiom by which the pluperfect tense (with *had*) is used where we use a plain past. See Example, Exercise 17, page 52; and (as in many other languages), the Future Tense is often used, where, strictly speaking, the Subjunctive Mood is the correct thing. The omission of pronouns, where no ambiguity will be caused, has already been pointed out. Doubling words in order to strengthen the force is common in Hindústáni, and not unknown in English: 'My love is like the red red rose.' Ex.:—wuh achchha achchha ádmi hai, *he is a very good man.*

6. You will sometimes find PLURALS IN 'AN.' This is from the Persian; and occurs chiefly in words ending in—dár. It does not change in the oblique cases. Ex.:—Zamindár-án, tábidár-án, chaukídár-án, &c.

7. WÁLA-WÁLI (masc. and fem,; declined like nouns in

'a' and 'i') are very useful terminations. They are joined usually to the Nom. Sing. of a common noun, or to the inflected form of the Verbal Noun. They indicate a person connected with the thing the noun expresses, or one who does the action expressed by the verb. Ex. :—pankhá wála, *a pankha-puller;* roṭi-wála, *a baker*; machhli-wála, *the fish-monger;* likne-wáli, *the* (female) *writer*, and so on, *ad-infinitum.* They are also added to Adverbs.

8. The DEGREES OF COMPARISON are made thus :—For the comparative degree you compare the thing you are speaking of with *one thing* of the same kind. For the 'superlative degree,' you compare it *with all conceivable things* of the same kind. Your adjective has no change indicative of 'degree;' but coutinues to 'agree,' as usual. Ex. :—

Yih ghoṛa . . . us ghoṛe se . . . achchha hai.
This horse . . compared with that horse . . is the good one.
Yih ghoṛa . . . sab ghoṛoṇ se . . . achchha hai.
This horse . . compared with all horses . . is the good one.

9. Occasionally you may find the Persian terminations of the comparative and the superlative degrees, *viz.*, 'TAR' and 'TARÍN,' used with adjectives derived from the Persian language. But this is not common. The only familiar word is 'bihtar,' *better;* the 'positive degree' of which in Persian is 'bih,' *good.* Superlative, 'bihtarín.'

10. In NARRATION, you must use the same pronouns and verbs as the original speaker used : Ex. :—

Eng. :—He said he would go to Calcutta to-morrow.
Hind. :—He said, (that) 'I will go to Calcutta tomorrow.'

11. So, in sending a VERBAL MESSAGE (which you

should never do if you can help it) give your messenger the very words he is to use. Ex. :—

Eng. :—Go and tell him, I can't come.

Hind. :—Go and tell him, (that) 'The Judge sáḥib (or as the case may be) can't come.'

12. 'IT IS;' 'THERE IS;' 'THERE ARE.' These idioms do not occur in Hindústáni. The plain noun and verb only are used. Ex. :—kaun hai,? rája sáḥib haiṇ, *who is it? It is the rája sáḥib.* Khabardár ! ág hai, *take care! there's fire.*

13. TO HAVE. There is no verb for this. You must use the verb 'to be;' on the *liber est mihi* principle. Ex. :—Ham-ko kuchh ummed nahíṇ hai, *I have no hope.* Us ke pás bahut kitábeṇ haiṇ, *he has many books.* Us-ke do ghoṛe haíṇ, (*his are two horses*) *he has two horses.* When 'have' has the sense of 'get,' 'obtain,' &c. 'milna' may be used. Ex. :—Us-ko ek ḥukm-námah mila hai, *he has, holds, has got, a pass.*

14. "THANK YOU." To a servant this phrase is properly expressed by "bahut achchha;" "achchha:" or even "bas." The last word means '*enough;*' '*that'll do.*' To equals and superiors the word "shukr-guzár" (literally 'thanks-passing') should be used—by itself—on all fitting occasions.

Note.—Exaggerated civility to an inferior is regarded by him as sarcasm. As you may never use any word of abuse, a little exaggerated politeness may be used instead.

15. TO SALUTE "Salám karna;" "salám bolna;" "salám dena" "Salám karna" is to perform an act of salutation. "Salám bolna" and "salám dena" are about equal to each other in meaning. You will have to use

them chiefly in two instances: *first*, as a polite mode of sending for a person: Ex.:—"kiráni bábu ko salám do" (or bolo), *i.e.*, "*give* (or *say*) *my* '*salám*' *to the* (Hindu) *clerk*" —the rest is eliptic; but the clerk will understand that he is to come to you: so, *secondly*, when a caller sends in his card, you say "salám do;" or "salám bolo" to the servant. He carries your salám to the caller, who comes upstairs and pays his visit, on receiving your "salám" but not before. A '*visiting-card*' is ṭikaṭ (E.)

16. The PARTICIPLE "IN KE" OR "KAR," (sometimes "*karke*" or "*karkar*," all being derived from *karna*, sometimes only the plain stem), is much used in Hindústáni, to lead up to the principal verb—and avoid the repetition of "*and*" Ex.:—Yih bát bolkar chalá-gaya. *Having said this much* (lit. this *word*), *he went away*: or, *He said this much and left.*

17. This little book contains none of the high-flown, and somewhat exaggerated style of phraseology which abounds in Oriental languages; nor any of the phrases adopted from Arabic. These belong to an advanced course. You should, however, provide yourself with two phrases of a superior kind, to be used to native gentlemen of rank. They are words meaning shortly, "*to arrive*," and "*to depart;*" and are "tashríf-lána," *to arrive*, "tashríf lejána," *to depart.* Tashríf means "*the honour of your presence:*" the first phrase (to arrive) therefore means "*to bring the honour of your presence*"—and the second (to depart)—*to take that honour from us.* "Huzúr," is the correct word whereby to address natives of high rank. The verb will of course be in the third person plural; and so you will say:

Huzúr kab tashríf lá,e haiṇ? = *When did you arrive?*
Huzúr kab tashríf le-já,eṇge? = *When do you go away?*

18. Then, the polite form by which to ask for a person's health is, 'mizáj sharíf.' To which the answer may be 'huzúr ki mihrbani se,' *by Your Honour's kindness*, or 'ḥuzúr ki inayat se,' *by Your Honour's favour*, or 'ḥuzúr ki du,a se,' *by Your Honour's blessing*, or 'shukr Khuda ka hai,' *thank God*,—'I am well' being understood.

19. Connected with this matter, I mention, in conclusion, that in the middle of many names of Arabic origin, you will find the syllable "*ul*" or "*ud*," occasionally "*us*." They all mean, "*of the*" and the whole name has generally a grand significance. Thus Shams-ud-dín means "The Sun of the Faith;" Siráj-ud-daulah[1], "The Lamp of the Commonwealth," and so on.

VOCABULARY No. XX.

Khuda, *God.*
firishtah, *an angel.*
auliya, *the saints.*
iblís ; shaitán, *the Devil.*
bihisht,[2] *heaven.*
aráf *or* iráf, *purgatory.*
jahannam, *hell.*
rúh, *the soul.*
dín ; mazhab, *religion.*
duniya, (fem.) *the world ; universe.*
neki ; bhalá,i, *righteousness.*
gunáh ; páp, *sin.*
Khairát, *alms ; charity to the poor.*
rozah, *a fast.*
rozah rakhna, *to fast.*
namáz (fem.), *prayer.*
namáz paṛhna, *to say prayers.*
gharíb-log, *the poor*
girja, *a church.*
masjid, *a mosque.*
maṭh, *a temple.* (H.)
padṛi sáḥib, *an English minister;* also, *a Catholic priest.*

---

[1] The "Sir Roger Douler" of the British soldier of the last century.

[2] Hence is derived the name of that one of your servants whom you will probably call—this little book not withstanding—your "Beasty." (Bihishti.)

láṭ Pádṛi Sáhib, *the Bishop.*
imám, *a Muḥammadan minister.*[1]
mahant; guru, *a Hindu priest.*
bíbal (E.), *the Bible.*
ḳurán, *the religious book of the Muḥammadans.*
bhagwat, *ditto of the Hindus.*

---

bíj, *seed.*
chára, *a seedling.*
bigaṛ-jána, *to go wrong; get out of order* (as health, a watch, &c.); *to miscarry,* (as plans.)
kisán, *a cultivator.*
bona, *to sow.*
ropna, *to plant.*
nirauni, *weeding*; nirauni karna, *to weed.*
gídaṛ; siyál, *a jackal.*
zarrah, *a little somewhat.*
kheti-karna, *to cultivate.*

Note.—'Láṭ' is corrupted English for 'Lord.'

Exercise No. 25.

Bhala ádmi g͟haríb logoṇ ko k͟hairát dega. K͟hairát dena, namáz paṛhna, rozah rakhna, ye tín chizeṇ k͟huda ko pasand haiṇ. Is-girje ke pádṛi-sáḥib ka nám kya hai? Ham nahíṇ jánte. Rúḥ ka árám bihisht meṇ hai; k͟haráb ádmi,oṇ ki saza jahannam meṇ hogi. Ko,i mazhab nahíṇ hai, kih us meṇ bhale ádmi aur bure ádmi nahíṇ haiṇ Ek baras meṇ bárah mahíne haiṇ. Har ek baras meṇ tín sau tín kúri pánch din haiṇ. Kisán log paihle bíj bote haiṇ; is ke baad, chára khet meṇ ropte haiṇ. Agar páni kam ho, to, fasl k͟haráb hoti hai; g͟haríb logoṇ ko kabhi-kabhi sirf chár áne ya do áne ki fasl milti hai. Tab zamíṇdárán bhi bure ḥál meṇ haiṇ. Unhoṇ-ko k͟hazánah nahíṇ milta hai; sarkári mál-guzári náhíṇ de-sakte haiṇ; pas, un-ki zamíṇdári,áṇ nílám meṇ bar-bád haiṇ.

---

[1] Muḥammadans have no "priests."

EXERCISE No. 26.

This year the ryots will get a sixteen annas crop. Every one will be pleased; tenants, landlords, and Government. Satan is the enemy of man; God is his friend. From religion, is the peace of the soul. The Bishop will be here the day after to-morrow. The church is open every alternate Sunday.

Is my watch correct? No. It is fast. How many rúpis are in the house? Three hundred and ninety-three. In the evening, jackals come into the garden. I have not been here since the day before yesterday. On what date did he go away? On 7th July last.

FIFTEENTH LESSON.

The difference between words given in the body of this book and words in the Glossary at the end, is that the former are words which you *must know*, and must learn up as soon as possible; while among the latter, are many words which you may or may not require to use, and for which you must search if wanted.

2. The following lists—among which Exercises are placed by way of rests—complete the words which you *must* know. Some of the words already given are allowed to appear again here.

VOCABULARY No. XXI.

The Seasons and Weather.

mausam, *or* músim, *a season; weather.*

garmi ka mausam, *the hot weather; summer.*[1]

jáṛe ka mausam (*or* músim), *the cold weather; winter.*[1]

barsát ka mausam, *the rainy weather.*[1]

---

[1] The durations of these three seasons may be roughly given thus: 'The cold weather,' 15th October to 15th March. 'The hot weather,' 15th March to 15th June. 'The rains,' 15th June to 15th October. The cold weather is longer in North-Weastern India. There is plenty of hot weather everywhere during 'the rains.'

áṇdhi ; túfán, *a storm.*
khula din, *a fine day ; fair-weather.*
dhúp ; tapish ; garmi, *heat.*
jáṛa ; sardi, *cold.*
barf, *snow ; ice.*
yakh, *ice.*
barsát ; bárish ; páni, *rain.*
patthar, *hail.*
sáf ; khula, *clear.*
andhera, *dark.*
abr ; badli, *a cloud.*
hawa ; batás, (L. B.) *wind.*
kohásah, *fog.*
garaj, *thunder.*
bijli, *lightning.*
garajna, *to thunder.*
bijli chamakna, *to lighten.*
barasna ; páni hona, *to rain.*

Note. –'Adjectives' may be made by using a noun and ka, ki, ke. Ex. :—
Áj páni ka din hai, *this is a rainy day.*

VOCABULARY No. XXII.

Nature, the Landscape, Towns, &c.

ásmán, *the sky.*
súraj ; áftáb, *the sun.*
chánd, *the moon.*
tára ; sitárah, *a star.*
dunya, *the world.*
miṭṭi ; khák, *earth.*
páni ; áb ; jal, *water.*
hawa, *air.*
áb-o-hawa, *climate.*
samúndar ; kála páni, *the open sea.*
darya ; naddi, *a river.*
kinárah, *the shore ; bank.*
nála, *a ditch ; 'nullah,'* (Anglo-Hind.)
nahr, *a canal.*
tál, *a lake.*
táláb ; taláo, *a reservoir ; a 'tank.'*
áhar ; khazánah, *a reservoir made by damming up natural supplies.*
kú,a ; indára, *a well.*
pahár : koh, *a mountain.*
tará,i ; dáman-i-koh, *the land at the base of mountains.*
maidán ; ramnah, *a plain ; meadow.*
darakht ; gáchh ; peṛ, *a tree.*
ábádi, *cultivated land.*

parṭi, *waste-land; uncultivated land.*
jangal, *forest; high-grass,* or *forest trees on land; a weedy place; 'jungle.'*
jháṛ; jháṛi, *underwood; scrub.*
kíchaṛ, *mud.*
bálu; ret, *sand.*
patthar, *a stone.*
patta, *a leaf.*
ḍál; shák͟h, *a branch.*
jaṛ, *a root; roots.*
ghás, *grass.*
phal; mewa, *fruit.*
phúl, *flowers.*
shahr; nagar, *a city; a town.*
gáṇw; basti; grám (L. B.) *a village.*
ghar; makán; koṭhi, *a house.*
hopṛi, *a cottage.*
ráh; (*fem.*) rásta, *a road.*
saṛak, *the highway.* (*fem.*)
gali, *a lane; a 'gully,'* (Anglo Hind.)
chauk, *a square* (often used as the market-place.)
bázár, *a collection of shops, or stalls; a market; the 'bazaar.'*
háṭ; mela, *a fair.*
dúkán, *a shop.*
hoṭel, (E.) *a hotel.*
isṭeshan, (E.) *the railway-station.*
jel-k͟hánah, (jel, E.) *the jail.*
ḳilah; gaṛh, *a fort.*
pul, *a bridge.*
rel-rásta, ('rel,' E.) *the railway.*
rel-gáṛi, *a railway carriage; a train.*

Exercise No. 27.

Barsát ke mausim meṇ, jangal aur jháṛ bahut úṇche hote haiṇ; darya sab baṛe haiṇ; gáchh, maidán, ghás, sab chizeṇ sabz rang ki hoti haiṇ. Garm dinoṇ meṇ, darkár hai kih ko,i ádmi dhúp meṇ nahíṇ jáwe; magar aksar hota hai kih garmi ke mausim meṇ, sab ko,i tandurust rahta hai; jáṛe ke mausim meṇ, áb-o-hawa niháyat pasand hai; lekin sardi ke bá,is, zukám aur chand ḳism ki bimárí ádmi,oṇ-ko taklíf deti haiṇ.

Exercise No. 28.

A storm is coming from the West. I see lightning there. Listen! there's thunder. I can't hear it. There are many shops in the city; but the streets are narrow. There are fogs in the cold weather. The train will arrive at noon. There are no shops in this square. It is near the bazar, therefore there are no shops. The water of the reservoir is better than the water of the canal. There is a large tank on the 'maidán.'[1] A fair will take place (say, '*there will be a fair*') on the 10th of next January. Have you been at (say, '*ever gone to*') the Sonpúr fair (*mela*)?

VOCABULARY No. XXIII.

Common Animals.

jánwar; haiwán, *any animal.*
háthi; fíl *or* píl, *an elephant.*
sher-babar; singh, *a lion.*
sher; bágh, *a tiger.*
chíta, *a leopard.*
bhál; bhálu, *a bear.*
jangli sú,ar, *a boar.*
bheṛiya, *a wolf.*
gídaṛ; siyál, *a jackal.*
lomṛi, *a fox.*
haran *or* hiran, *a stag; a deer.*
gilehri, *a squirrel.*
k͟har-gosh, *a rabbit; hare.*
úṇt; shutur, *a camel.*
ghoṛa, *a horse.*
mádiyáṇ, *a mare.*
gadha,[2] gadhi, *an ass.*
ṭaṭṭu, *a pony; a 'tatt'* (Anglo-Hind).
kutta, kutti, *a dog.*
billi, *a cat.*
sáṇḍ,[3] *a bull.*
bail, *an ox.*
bhaiṇs; bhaiṇsa, *a buffalo.*
gá,o *or* gá,e, *a cow.*
bachra, *a calf.*

---

[1] Used as an English word; especially in Calcutta.

[2] Also used figuratively.

[3] The pronunciation of this word does not admit of being reproduced by letters, you must *hear* it pronounced before attempting it.

bheṛi, *a sheep.*
bakri ; chhágul, *a goat.*
sú,ar,[1] *a pig.*
bandar, *a monkey.*

Vermin and Insects.

sáṇp, *a snake.*
bichchhu, *a scorpion.*
gojar, a *centipede.*
indúr, *a rat.*
chúha, *a mouse.*
chha-chhúṇdar, *a musk-rat.*
cham-gídaṛ, *a bat.*
ṭikṭikki, *a lizard.*
til-chaṭṭa, *a cockroach.*
chúṇti, *an ant.*
dímak, *a white ant.*
machchhar, *a musquito.*
makkhi ; magas, *a fly.*
pissu, *a flea.*
khaṭ-mal, *a bug.*
ganḍi, *a 'gundy.'*

Birds.

chiṛiya, *a bird of any kind.*
murgh-ábi, *water fowl.*
gidh, *a vulture.*
chíl, *a kite.*
chakwa, chakwi, *the Brahminy goose.*
mor, *a peacock.*
sáras ; bogla, *a crane.*
kauwa, *a crow.*
ullu,[2] *an owl.*
háṇs, *a swan.*
ráj-háṇs, *a goose.*
bat ; battakh, *a duck.*
murgh, murghi, *cock, hen.*
píru, *a turkey.*
pekan, *a capon* (English word with '*c*' and '*p*' misplaced).
kabútar, *a pigeon.*
cháha ; isnaip (E.) *snipe.*
baṭer, *quail.*
ṭil, (E.) *teal.*
tota, túti, *a parrot.*
maina, *a 'maina.'*
bulbul, *a bulbul* (often confounded with a nightingale).
sháma, *a nightingale.*

Exercise No. 29.

Jangal meṇ bahut jánwar rahte haiṇ. Sher-babar jangal ke bádsháh haiṇ, Hindústán meṇ sher-babar kam haiṇ.

---

[1] [2]Also used figuratively.

Sher bahut haiṇ: aksar admi,oṇ-ko pakaṛ-kar kháte haiṇ. Sab ko,i un-se ḍarte haiṇ. Barsát ke mausim meṇ sáṇp kabhi-kabhi ghar meṇ áte haiṇ: bahut k͟habardár hona cháhiye. Díwár meṇ se bichchhu nikal-áte haiṇ. Hindústán ki chiṛiyáṇ nahíṇ gáti haiṇ. Mor ki áwáz bahut ná-pasand hai. Sáḥib log bahut murg͟hi,áṇ kháte haiṇ; is mulk meṇ sasti haiṇ.

EXERCISE No. 30.

When the grass is long, (then) there are many snakes. At the base of the mountains, the hunter gets many tigers and elephants. The bear lives in the hills. Pig-sticking is the best sport in the country. A fast horse is necessary for pig-sticking. Ponies are serviceable for children. In this country, the three seasons are—the cold weather, the hot weather, and the rains.

VOCABULARY No. XXIV.

THE BÁZÁR.

bázár, *the market.*
bázár karna, *to market.*
mol-lena; k͟haríd-karna, *to buy.*
bechna, *to sell.*
bikna, *to be sold.*
ḳímat; dám, *price.*
nirk͟h (Anglo-Hind nirrik); bhá,o, *rate.*
k͟haríd-farok͟ht, *buying and selling; trafficking.*
sauda; mál; chíz, *merchandize; goods.*
nafa, *profit.*
nuḳsán; ghaṭi, *loss.*
púṇji, *capital.*
súd, *interest.*
dúkán, *a shop.*
dúkándár, *a shopkeeper.*
sarráf, (Anglo-Hind. 'shroff'), *a banker.*
mahájan, (*lit.* the great man), *a money lender; merchant.*
saudágar, *a merchant; trader.*
saudágari; tijárat, *trade.*
dastúri, *discount; allowance given by the seller to your servant.*

ráj, *the mason.*
lohár, *the smith.*
nál-band, *the farrier.*
baṛha,i, *the carpenter.*
bálbar ; hajjám, *the barber.*
sonár, *the gold,* or *silver-smith.*
júti-wála, *the shoe-maker.*
mochi, *the cobbler, worker in leather.*
tarázu, *a weighing-machine.*
baṭ khara, *a weight for ditto.*
taul ; wazn, *the weight of a thing.*
taul karna, *to weigh.*
kapṛa, *cloth.*
thán, *a piece ; a web.*
namúnah, *a pattern ; sample.*
resham, *silk.*
mal-mal, *muslin.*
katán-kapṛa, *linen, calico.*
rú,i, *cotton.*
ún ; pashm, *wool.*
bánát, *broad-cloth.*
flálen, (E.) *flannel.*
márkín, (*i.e*, 'American') *calico.*
lambá,i, *length.*
chouṛá,i, *breadth.*
motá,i, *thickness.*

VOCABULARY No. XXV.

The Dinner Table.

kháne ki mez, *the dining-table.*
mez ki chádar, *the table-cloth,* also *table-cover.*
bartan, *a plate ; dish.*
kháne ke bartan, *the dinner things.* [*service.*
mewe ke bartan, *the dessert-*
dúṇga, *the dish in which a side-dish or vegetables are served ; a side-dish,* which servants are fond of calling also 'sai-dís.' (E.)
dís, (E.) *the pièce de résistance*
sekan *or* síkan (*i.e.*, 'second' E.), *the second course.*
chhuri, *a knife.*
káṇṭa, *a fork.*
chhuri-káṇṭa, *the knives and forks.*
chammach ; chamchah, *a spoon.*
ḍhakna ; sarposh, *a cover ; lid.*
háth-boli, (half E.) *a finger-glass.*
háth ka tauliyah, *a napkin.*

glás, (E.) *a glass; the glass-service.*

piyálah, *a cup.*

pirich, *a saucer.*

peṇch-kash, *a cork-screw.*

kág, (for E. 'cork') *a cork.*

k͟hilál, *a tooth-pick.*

pík-dán ; ugál-dán, *a spittoon.*

VOCABULARY No. XXVI.

THE KITCHEN.

báwarchi-k͟hánah, *the kitchen.*

degchi, *a copper cooking vessel.*

ḳalá,i, *the tinning of the same.* (has to be done once a month.)

háṇḍi, *an earthen pot.*

ghaṛa, *a water-pot.*

rasú,i, *cooking.*

rasú,i ke bartan, *the cooking pots.*

háṇḍi-bartan, *vessels generally.*

ketli, (E.) *the kettle.*

fará,i pán, (E.) *the frying-pan.*

sík͟h, *a spit.*

tanúr, *an oven.*

chúlha, *a stove; fire-place for cooking.*

ko,ila, *charcoal; coals.*

hezam ; lakṛi, *wood; fuel.*

doli, *a hanging meat-safe.*

tháli, *a brass plate.*

loṭa, *a native brass-vessel for liquids.*

tháli-loṭa, *native brass-vessels generally.*

VOCABULARY No. XXVII.

THE BED ROOM.

(See also pages 34 and 94.)

sone ka kamara, *the bed-room.*

siṇgár-mez, *a dressing-table.*

á,ínah, *a looking-glass* (accent on first syllable.)

háth-boli, (E.) *a washing-basin.*

áftábah, *a water-jug; a ewer.*

sábun, *soap.*

brúsh, (E.) *a brush.*
kanghi, *a comb.*
sábun-dán, *a soap-dish.*
manjan, *tooth powder* or *paste.*
khush-bu, *scent.*
bál ka tel, *hair-oil.*
palang ; chárpá,i ; kháṭ, *a bed.*
musahri, *musquito-curtains.*
chádar, *the sheets.*
kammal ; kamli, *the blankets.*
razá,i, *the quilt.*
takiyah ; bálish, *a pillow.*
ghiláf, *a covering slip, e.g.,* case for a pillow.
toshak, *the mattress.*
ṭab, (E.) *a tub.*
tauliyah, *a towel.*
isfanj, *a sponge.*
ṭokri, *a basket.*
jháṛan, *a duster.*
jháṛu, *a broom.*

VOCABULARY No. XXVIII.

GAMES.

anṭa ; geṇd ; goli, *a ball.*
khelne ki lakṛi ; thápi, *a bat ; a cue or the like.*
anṭá-ghar, *the billiard room ; the club.*
khel-gáh, *the play ground.*
geṇd-gáh, *the racquet court.*
satar, *a line.*
rassi, *a rope ; string.*
jál, *a net.*
khamba, *a post.*
khúnṭa ; mekh, *a peg.*
shatranj, *chess.*
tásh, *cards.*
páse, *dice.*
takhtah-nard, *backgammon.*
ṭenis, *lawn-tennis.*
polo, *polo.*

Note.—And so of other games. The English word must be used because the natives not having *the thing*, cannot have a name for it.

EXERCISE No. 31.

Áyah ! sab chíz taiyár hai ? Háṇ mem sáḥibah ? sab durust hai. Tum kaisi ádmi ho ! kuchh sábun nahíṇ hai, aur tum sab durust' bolti ho. Mera ḳusúr ! mu,áf kíjiye ! Ṭab meṇ páni hai? Nahíṇ mem-sáḥibah! biḥishti áj bímár hái. To ham kya kareṇge? Ek ḳuli ko chár paise díjiye, to wuh páni le-áwega. Achchha! achchha! ḳuli ko bulá,o—aur sábun, tauliyah bhítar rakh-do. Darzi bhi nahíṇ áya hai! sab ko,i áj bímár haiṇ! Mem sáḥibah! sach bát yih hai, kih áj baṛa tamáshah hai; is liye sab log bímári ka bahánah karte haiṇ; bandi ḥázir hai.

Exercise No. 32.

Bring clean sheets for[1] the bed. All the sheets are at[2] the washerman's? Since when are they at the washerman's? Since yesterday. Put all the books on the table, and clean the book-shelves. See! how dirty (they) are: clean (them) with warm water (and) soap; (and) then rub (them) with polish. Sometimes snakes come into the house; so[3] one must always be careful. Scorpions also and cock-roaches come out of the walls, and fleas and bugs and mosquitoes are everywhere.

Exercise No. 33.

Do pahar ke waḳt tumhára báp ghar meṇ se nikal-áya. Aṇdhere ke waḳt phir-gaya. Áj kaun tárík͟h hái? Áj júlá,i mahíne ki áṭh tárik͟h hai. Hamára badan kamzor hai; mede meṇ dard hai. Jíbh dekhlá,o. Zard rang ki[4] hai; dawa zarúr nahíṇ hai: subḥ ko, shám ko, ghoṛe par hawa khána cháhiye. Nahíṇ! chand roz hú,e, kih maiṇ apne ghoṛe par se gir-paṛa; bihtar hai, kih áp dawa deṇ. Achchha! maiṇ dúṇga.

Exercise No. 34.

One day, at evening, a fox, having come out of the jungle, saw grapes in a garden. He said (that) "see there:

[1] Ke waste. [2] Ke pás. [3] Pas.
[4] Feminine, because 'jíbh,' which is feminine, is understood.

"certainly these grapes are large and sweet, I shall seize "some." But the grapes were on the roof of a house. The fox began to jump; but was not able to get up,[1] and could not lay-hold-of[2] even one grape.[3] Becoming vexed, he said (that) "no-doubt you are very sour," and went away.

VOCABULARY No. XXIX.

The Stable and Harness-Room.

istabal, *the stable.*
thán, *a stall.*
sáz, *the harness.*
rás, *the reins.*
jot, *the traces.*
bág : lagám, *a bridle.*
dahánah, *a bit.*
nuktah, *the head-stall.*
zanjír, *a chain.*
dumchi, *the crupper* (strap).
zín, *a saddle.*
zer-band, a *martingale.*
ḥalḳah, *a collar.*
peṭi ; tang, *a girth.*
brúsh, (E) *a brush.*
k͟hark͟harah, *a curry-comb.*
rikáb, *a stirrup.*
rikáb-díwál, *stirrup-leathers.*
káṇṭa, *a spur.*
chábuk, *a whip.*
chauri, *a fly-flicker.*
gáṛi, *the carriage.*
ṭhíká-gáṛi, *a carriage for hire; a 'fly'; a cab.*
ṭam-ṭam, (E.) *a dog-cart.*[4]
fiṭan-gáṛi, (half E.) *a phaeton.*
band-gáṛi, *a brougham.*
baṛúsh-gáṛi, *a barouche.*
ghoṛa, *a horse.*
mádiyán, *a mare.*
ṭaṭṭu, *a pony.*
joṛi, '*the pair*' (of horses).
joṛi-gáṛi, *the carriage and pair ready for use.*
kampás, (E) *the shafts; a one-horsed carriage.*
nál, *a horse-shoe.*
nál-bandi, *shoeing a horse.*

---

[1] Charhna. [2] Pakarna. [3] Ek angúr bhi.
[4] Supposed to be the English 'tandem.'

khol-bandi, *taking off the shoes, paring the hoofs* (som) *and putting the old shoes on again.*
thaili, *a bag.*
bálṭi, *a pail.*
rassi; bágḍor, *a rope.*
sáz ka ghoṛa, *a harness-stand.*
mom-raughan, *grease; oil; harness-paste; polish.*
bárnish, (E.) *varnish.*
rang, *paint.*
dánah, *grain; corn.*
chaná, *gram.*
ja,i, *oats.*
jau, *barley.*
bhúsi, *bran.*
sattu, *a kind of flour, given in water to horses when tired, &c.*
ghás, *grass.*
dub-ghás, *a kind of grass which is best for horses.*
namak, *salt.*
bichhauna, *bedding.*
bicháli *straw.*

VOCABULARY No. XXX.

ARTICLES OF FOOD.

shorbah, (*vulg.* súrwah) *soup.*
machhli, *fish.*
sáman-machhli, *salmon.*
chingṛi, *shrimps.*
gosht,[1] *meat of all kinds.*
kaṭlis, (E.) *cutlets.*
mínch, *mince.*
isṭew, (pronounce as in English, with short 'i' before,) *stew.*
airan-i-stew, *Irish-stew.*
frikasi, *fricassee.*
áspik, *aspec.*
murghi, *a fowl; fowls.*

---

[1] In English houses, the servants distinguish 'bíf-gosht,' 'maṭan-gosht,' &c. The parts of an animal, as used at table, are also generally called by the English names; as, 'hed,' 'sholdar,' 'leg,' 'fore-kártar;' 'sedli' (*saddle,*) 'cháp,' (*chop,*) 'istek' (*steak*), &c. Many English people drop the 't' of gosht,' and so reach a word which means 'an ear.' But the servants come to know what is meant.

murghi-rost, (half E.) *roast-fowl.*
murghi-boil, (half E.) *boiled-fowl.*
murghi-katlis, *chicken-cutlets.*
kári, *curry.*
bhát, *cooked rice.*
kári-bhát, *curry and rice.*
pulá,o, *fowl cooked with rice and condiments.*
sassich, (E.) *sausage.*
pátis, (E.) *potted meat.*
anda, *an egg.*
ham, (E.) (pronounce as English, 'hem') *ham.*
bekam, *bacon.*
anda-bekam, *ham and egg.*
koftah, *rissole.*
púding, (E.) *pudding.*
panír, *cheese.*
roti, *bread.*
rol, (E.) *dinner rolls.*
tost, (E.) *toast.*
makkhan, *butter.*
chapáti, *a scone.*
kulchah; 'kek,' (E.) *cake.*
biskit, (E.) *biscuit.*
murabba; jám,(E.) *jam; jelly.*
jeli,(E.) *jelly*, as taken with mutton, &c., or as '*a jelly.*'
barf, (*vulg.* 'baraf') *ice; an ice.*

VOCABULARY No. XXXI.

CONDIMENTS.

masálah, *spices, generally.*
namak, *salt.*
rá,i, *mustard.*
mircha (*vulg.* 'mirich') *pepper.*
gol-mirch, *black pepper.*
lál-mircha, *cayenne-pepper.*
sirkah, *vinegar.*
sás, (E.) *sauce.*
wiláyati[1] tel, *olive oil.*
adrak, *green ginger*, used also to mean *preserved ginger.*
sonth, *dry ginger.*
haldi, *turmeric.*
lahsan, *garlic.*
párslí, *parsley.*
pudínah, *mint.*

---

[1] 'Wiláyati' means *foreign*; especially, *European*, or *English.* It is the 'belátee,' or 'bilatty' of Anglo-Hindústáni.

chilli,[1] *chillies.*
chaṭni, *chutnee.*
miṭhá,i, *sweets,* also, '*the dessert.*'
chíni ; shakar, *sugar.*
miṣri, *crystallised sugar.*
tambáku, *tobacco.*
churuṭ, (E.) *a cigar.*
sigareṭ, (E.) *a cigarette.*

VOCABULARY No. XXXII.

VEGETABLES.

tarkári ; sabzi, *vegetables, generally.*
álu, *potatoes.*
maṭar, *peas.*
boṛa, *a bean.*
múli, *radish.*
kobi, *cabbage.*
phúl kobi, *cauliflower.*
ság, *spinach ;* '*ság.*'
shalgham, *turnips.*
gájar ; gajrah, *carrots.*
piyáz, *onions.*
tamátu, *tomatoes.*
haṭichok, (E.) *artichokes.*
salád, (E.) *lettuce ; salad.*
silaṛi, (E.) *celery.*

Note—Many other vegetables are also used, and called by their native names, some having no English equivalent. Among these are, 'kaddoo,' palwal,' 'bhinḍi,' 'brinjál' *or* 'baigan,' 'kachhu' (*Jerusalem artichoke*), &c., &c. Your '*máli*' will point them out to you.

VOCABULARY No. XXXIII.

FRUIT.

mewah, *fruit generally.*
ám, *a mango.*
amrúd, *guava.*
anár, *a pomegranate.*
angúr, *a grape ; grapes.*
anjír, *a fig.*
bádám, *almonds.*
bel, *the* '*bel,*' *fruit.*

---

[1] Not a Hindústáni word.

kaṭhal, *the jack fruit.*
kela, *plantains.*
khajúr, *dates.*
k̲harbúzah, *melon.*
kishmish, *raisins.*
imli, *tamarind.*
jauz, *a nut*; *nuts.*
lemu, *or* laimún, *a lemon.*
líchi, *the leechee.*
nárangi, *an orange.*
náryal, *the cocoa-nut.*
pistah, *pistachio nuts.*
seb, *an apple.*
shaft-álu, *a peach.*
sharífah, *a custard-apple.*
strábari, (E.) *strawberries.*
ṭipári, *cape gooseberries.*
k̲húbáni, *apricots.*

Note.—In 'angúr' the 'ng' has not a nasal sound. Pronounce as if the syllables were separate, 'an-gúr.' You will not find on European tables in India many more fruits than those given above. You may add '*pamalo*' also anannás, *pine-apple.*

Wine and Drinks.

See page 34. Wines on English tables are called by their English names, (generally more or less altered,) followed by the word 'sharáb,' *wine.* 'Claret' is generally called 'lál sharáb.' Sometimes 'kalárat' (without 'sharáb' added.)

VOCABULARY No. XXXIV.

barf-páni, *iced-water.*
wiláyati-páni, *soda-water.*
míṭha páni (*sweet water*), *lemonade.*
títa páni, *bitter, i.e., tonic water.*
chá,e, *tea.*
ḳáfi; (E.); ḳahwah, *coffee.*
koko, (E.) *coco.*
dúdh, *milk.*
malá,i, *cream.*

Exercise No. 35.

Ek ádmi ke ghar meṇ, ek sau rúpíye, chori se, gum-hoga,e the. Us-ne ḳázi ko k̲habar di. Kázi-ne sab naukaroṇ ko talab karke, ek ek ádmi-ko ek lakṛi, náp meṇ barábar, di; aur kaha kih, "jo ádmi chor hai, us ki lakṛi ek uṇgli baṛh-já,egi." Tab sabhoṇ-ko rukhsat di. Rát ke waḳt, chor-ne, apni lakṛi se, ek uṇgli káṭ ḍáli; is taur se, ḳázi-ne chor pahchána, us-se rúpíye liye, aur saza di.

EXERCISE No. 36.

One man asked another, 'you, on the sea have often made journeys: say, what[1] wonderful-things[2] have you seen? He gave answer: 'Than all,[3] this is wonderful,[4] that I, at the shore, arrived in safety.

VOCABULARY No. XXXV.

(See also pages 34 and 87.)

THE TOILET AND ITS ACCESSORIES.

kapṛa; kapṛe, *clothes generally.*
kháne ka kapṛa, *dress clothes.*
ṭopi, *a hat.*
chhoṭi topi, *a cap.*
solah[5] ṭopi, *a pith hat.*
pagṛi, *a cloth head-dress; a turban;* also *linen, or silk, bound round a* 'topi.'
kálar, (E.) *a collar.*
gala-band, *or* gulu-band, *a neck-tie; neck-scarf.*
kamar-band, *a waist-band; belt.*
belaṭ (E.) *a belt.*
moze, *boots;* but used in English houses to mean *socks; stockings.*
buṭ (E.) *boots.*
júti, *or* júta, *a shoe.*
silpaṭ *or* slipaṭ (E.); páposh, *a slipper.*
dastánah, *gloves.*
rúmál, *a pocket-handkerchief.*
resham ka rúmál, *a silk ditto.*

---

[1] 'Kya kya;" doubling the pronoun gives the idea of number.
[2] Wonderful things; wonders, 'ajá,ib.'
[3] See page 74, section 8.
[4] 'ajúbah.'
[5] *Not* derived from sol, solis, the sun.

labádah, *a cloak.*
kurti, *a coat.*
báráni-kurti,[1] *a great coat.*
barsáti-kapṛa, *waterproofs.*
fráḳ, (E.); dares, (E.) *a lady's dress.*
frák-koṭ, (E.) *a frock-coat.*
dáman, *the skirt.*
ástín, *a sleeve.*
waskaṭ, (E.) *a waistcoat.*
patlún, (E.) *trowsers.*
brichis, (E.) *breeches.*
gális, *braces.*
piṭi-koṭ, (E.) *a petticoat.*
ḳamís, *a shirt; chemise.*
sul-daráz, *drawers.*
bani,en, *an under-flannel shirt.*
rát ka kapṛa, *night dress; night things.* [*'pyjamahs.'*
pá-e-jámah, *night drawers;*
rát ki kurti, *a short night-coat.*
rát ki ḳamís, *a night-shirt.*
baṛoch, (E.) *a brooch.*
aṇgúṭhi, *a ring.*
sone ki aṇgúṭhi, *a gold ring.*[2]
istad, (E.)[3] *a stud; studs.*
pín, (E.) *a pin.*
brúsh, (E.) *a brush.*
bál ka brúsh, *a hair-brush.*
kapṛe ka brúsh, *a clothes-brush.*
dáṇt ka brúsh, *a tooth-brush.*
kanghi, *a comb.*
ḳaiṇchi, *scissors.*
ḳalam-tarásh, *a penknife.*
sút, *thread; string.*
fítah, *tape; shoe-lace; boot-lace.*
sú,i, *a needle.*
sú,i-tága, *a needle-and-thread.*
sábun, *soap.*
sábun-dán, *the soap-dish.*
isfanj, *a sponge.*
manjan, *dentifrice.*
bál ka tel, *hair-oil*
k͟hush-bu, *scent.*

---

[1] Gentlemen generally call this their 'brandy-kurti.' On the contrary, it is derived from the Persian 'báráu,' which means *rain.*

[2] And so of other metal or gem rings; use 'ki' before 'aṇgúṭhi.' The principal gems are:—Almás; híra, *diamond.* Zamurrad; panna, *emerald.* Yáḳút, *ruby.* Fírozah, *or* pírozah, *turquoise.* Lahsuniya, *cat's-eye.* Dúdhiya-patther, *opal* (from dúdh, *milk*). Moti, *a pearl.*

[3] Uneducated natives require a preliminary '*i,*' to help them to pronounce a word beginning with an 's,' followed by another consonant. Another common word is, 'isṭríṭ,' *street:* and there are many others.

THE ARMY.

English titles of rank, of course somewhat altered, are used, followed by the word 'sáḥib.' The principal are:—jarnail sáhib (*the General*), karnail sáḥib, mejar sáḥib, kaptán sáḥib, sárjan sáhib (*the sergeant*). Native officers are called the súbadár sáhib, hawaldár sáhib, jamadár sáḥib, &c., though it is to be feared that 'sáḥib' is not always used to native officers.

VOCABULARY No. XXXVI.

fauj; lashkar, *the army.*
palṭan, *a regiment.*
gore ki palṭan, *a European regiment.*
sawár, *a horse-soldier.*
sipáhi, *a foot-soldier; a 'sepoy.'*
bája, *the band.*
jhanḍa; nishán, *a flag; the standard.*
ḍera, *a tent.*
ḍera karna, *to encamp.*
kúch karna, *to march.*
chháuni; lá,ins (E.), *the barracks; the lines.*
jang; laṛá,i, *war.*
roz-i-maidán, *the day of the plain, i.e. of battle.*
saff-i-jang, *battle order.*
laṛá,i; ḥamla; muḳábalah, *battle; attack; onset.*
sámán-i-jang, *equipments of war.*
zarb, *a stand of arms.*
top, *a cannon.*
bandúḳ, *a gun; musket.*
talwár; shamsher, *a sword.*
ballam; barchhi, *a spear.*
taghmah; urdi,[1] *a uniform.*
goli, *a ball; bullet.*
top ki goli, *a cannon-ball.*
ṭonṭa; kártús (cartouche), *a cartridge.*
bárút, *powder.*
chharrá, *shot.*
mártaul, *a hammer.*
kudál; kudáli, *a spade; pickaxe.*
ṭánga, *an axe.*
rasad, *forage; provinder.*

---

[1] Not Hindústáni; but in common use.

Exercise No. 37.

Naḳl hai kih barsát ke mausim meṇ, ek úṇṭ aur ek gadha sáth sáth safar-ko ga,e the. Darmiyán ráh ke, unhoṇ-ko ek naddi mili. Pahle úṇṭ páni meṇ paiṭha; gadha kináre par píchhe raha. Uṇṭ-ne kaha, 'Are! dost! kyúṇ nahíṇ áte ho? páni thoṛa hai.' Us-ne jawáb diya, 'albattah páni sirf tumháre peṭ tak hai, lekin mere kán tak hoga, main ḍúb-já,úṇga, áge já,iye, mujh-ko mu,áf kíjiye.'

Exercise No. 38.

A miser said to a rich man, 'Oh! friend! I am going 'on (*ko*) a journey; give me your ring; seeing (it) on my 'finger, I shall keep remembrance[1] of (*se*) you.' The rich man said, 'When you see your finger bare, you can remember[1] me.' He did not give the ring.

VOCABULARY No. XXXVII.

The Telegraph and Post Office.

tár (*wire*), *the telegraph.*
tár-ghar, *the telegraph-office.*
tár ki khabar, *or* chiṭṭhi, *a telegram.*
fáram (E.), *a telegraph* (or any other) '*form.*'
ḍák; ṭappál,[2] *the post.*
ḍák-munshi, *the postmaster.*
ḍák-wála, *the postman.*
ḍák piyádah,[3] *the postal-runner.*
ḍák-ghar, *the post-office.*
chiṭṭhi-ḍák, *the letter-post.*
bahangi-ḍák, *the parcel post;* (Anglo-Hind. 'bánghi dawk.')
maḥsúl, *postage.*
ḍák-ṭikaṭ, *a postage-stamp.*
chiṭṭhi ḍák meṇ dena, *or,* ḍálna, *or,* rakhna, *to post a letter.*

---

[1] Yad-rakhna. [2] Not used in Lower Bengal.

[3] There is a word pí,an,' generally spelt 'peon,' in very common use for a 'messenger' of any kind. The natives think the word is English; Englishmen think that it is Hindústáni.

VOCABULARY No. XXXVIII.

MISCELLANEOUS.

árám, *comfort.*
jawáb, *an answer.*
jawáb dena, *to answer; dismiss.*
chiṭṭhi; k͟hatt, *a letter; a note,*. (Anglo-Hind. a 'chit.')
nám, *a name.*
sust, *lazy; out of sorts.*
bu, *a smell.*
k͟hush-bu, *a nice smell; scent.*
bad-bu, *a nasty smell.*
tab, *or* tap; buk͟hár, *fever.*
muhri, *a drain.*
lákh; láh, *sealing-wax.*
le,i, *paste.*
náshtah[1]; háziri, *breakfast.*
ṭifin, *lunch.*
rokna; thámna, *to stop* (*trans.*)
khaṛa-rahna, *to stop* (*intr.*)
chalna; chalána; áge baṛhána, *to go on.*
shikár, *hunting; sport; game.*
shikár-karna, *to hunt; shoot, &c.*
shikári, *a hunter.*
kám, *any business, or work; use.*
yih kis kám ka hai, *of what use is this?*
parwáh, *importance; 'matter.'*
kuchh parwáh nahíṇ, *it's no matter; 'don't trouble about it.'* (The 'kuch-parwanny' of Anglo-Hind.)
parwánah, *a written order of command.*
kya kya, *what* (*various*) *things; what sorts of...?*
nazdíki, *neighbourhood.*
mihrbáni kar-ke (*lit. doing the kindness*), *'have the kindness,' 'goodness,' &c.*
mu,áf kíjiye, *means either* (*seriously*), *'pardon me,'* or (*courteously*), *'pray! excuse me.' 'I beg your pardon.'*
K͟hán: Bahádur: K͟hán Bahádur, *native titles, best left untranslated.*
wag͟hairah, *et cetera.*
faḳat, *finis.*

---

[1] Not used in Lower Bengal.

Exercise No. 39.

Apni ma ke wáste árám-kursi barámde meṇ rakh-do. Rát aṇdheri hai, lamp báhar lejána hoga. Achchha! lejá,o. Yih chiṭhi jarnail sáḥib ke pás le-já-kar, jawáb lá,o. Hamára sá,ís bahut hoshyár hai: Áj shám ko, hamára ghoṛa bhága-játa tha; usne, ek baghal se dauṛkar, lagám-ko pakaṛ-kar, ghoṛe-ko roka: is-tarah ham bach-gaye.

Bálu par ek bhál chalta hai; ḥuzúr ke iḳbál se, bandah már-ḍálega: ṭoṇṭa-díjiye.

Laṛá,i ke waḳt, ri,áya khush nahíṇ haiṇ. Lashkar sab ádmi,oṇ, sab chízoṇ ka málik hota hai; bahut zulm karta hai: khet ki fasl lúṭ le-játa hai; aur ádmi o aurat-ko, bojhe uṭháne ke wáste, zor se, chhín-leta hai; wá,e! wá,e!

Yih chiṭṭhi ḍák meṇ rakh-do. Sáḥib! ṭikaṭ nahíṇ hai. Durust! ham bhúl ga,e; ṭikaṭ lagá-do, aur jald dauṛo! paune páṇch baje ḍák band hogi; aur suno! hamáre wáste, chár ṭikaṭ, chár chár áne ki, mol-lo. Faḳat.

Exercise No. 40.

We shall go (out) shooting to-day. What sort of game[1] are there hereabouts?[2] Tiger, leopard, and wild-pig. Any water-fowl? Yes! duck; and there 's also snipe. We shall have to ride two kos. No matter! it is the cold season. Yes! but the sun is hot at noon. We have solah-topís! That's true. Wait a little! my gun is not clean.

When shall we be back? At seven in the evening. But what will the ladies do? They can play lawn-tennis with each other.[3] That won't suit[4] my wife,—we must be back by 3. All right! we 'll come back together.

Khuda salámat rakhe. Ámín.

May God preserve you! Amen!

---

[1] Shikár. [2] In this neighbourhood. [3] Among themselves.
[4] Be agreeable

APPENDICES.

I.

Numerals from 21 to 100.

II.

Relative and Co-relative Words.

III.

A List of Feminine Words in various final letters.

Appendix No. 1.

Showing the Ordinal Numerals from 21 to 100.

(See page 64.)

From 21 to 30.

ikkís...bá'ís...te,ís...chaubís...pachís...chhabbís...satá,ís ... aṭhá,ís...un,tís...tís.

From 31 to 40.

iktís... battís... tetís...chautís... paiṇtís...chhattís...saiṇtís... aṛtís...untális...chális.

From 41 to 50.

iktális... be,ális... tetális...chau,ális... paiṇtális...chhí,ális... saiṇtális...aṛhtális...unchás...pachás.

From 51 to 60.

ikáwan...báwan . tirpan... chauwan... pachpan... chhappan santáwan...anṭháwan...unsaṭh...sáṭh.

From 61 to 70.

iksaṭh... básaṭh...tirsaṭh .. chausaṭh ...paiṇsaṭh...chhí,ásaṭh saṛsaṭh...aṛsaṭh...unhattar...sattar.

From 71 to 80.

ikhattar ... bahattar.. tihattar ... chauhattar ... pachhattar... chhihattar...sathattar...aṭhatter ..unási...assi.

From 81 to 90.

ikási ... be,ási ... tirási ... chaurási ... pachási ... chhí,ási ... satási...aṭhási...nau,ási...nauwe.

From 91 to 100.

ikánawe ... bánawe...tiránawe...chauránawe...pachánawe... chhí,ánawe...santánawe...anṭhánawe...ninánawe ...sau, *or* sai.

APPENDIX No. II.

Showing a list of Relative and Co-relative words, the latter to be used in Hindústáni, even though not required in English.

agar; jo, *if.*	to, *then.*
agarchi, *although.*	tau-bhi, *even then; still.*
jab, *when.*	tab; to, *then.*
jab-tak (*or*, talak), *till when.*	tab-tak (*or*, talak), *till then.*
jahán, *where; wherever.*	tahán, *there.*
jahán-tak, *however for; up to where.*	tahán-tak, *so far; up to there.*
jaisa, *as.*	taisa; waisa, *so.*
jaun, *whoever; whatever.*	taun; wuh, *he; she; that.*
jidhar, *whithersoever.*	tidhar, *thither.*
jis-ḳadar, *in whatever degree.*	us-ḳadar, *in that degree.*
jis-waḳt, *at what time; when.*	us waḳt, *at that time; then.*
jitna, *or*, jetna, *as much as; as many as*	itna, *or* utna, *so much; so many.*
jo, *if.*	to, *then.*
jo; jo-ko,i, *who; whoever.*	wuh, *he; she; that*; we, *they; these.*
jo-kuchh, *whatever.*	so, *that.*

EXAMPLE.

"Jidhar áp já,engi, tidhar bandi bhi já,egi; jahán áp rahengi, tahán bandi bhi rahegi. Jo log áp ke hain, we bandi ke honge; jo Khuda áp ka ho, wuh mera bhi hoga."

APPENDIX No. III.

Giving a few common words, in various final letters, which are FEMININE in gender.

ág, *fire.*
akl, *sense; intelligence.*
áṇkh, *an eye.*
ástín, *a sleeve.*
áwáz, *the voice; a cry.*
bandúk, *a musket; a gun.*
bát, *word; news; affair.*
bhúkh, *hunger.*
bu, *smell.*
chádar, *a sheet.*
chál, *one's conduct, habits, &c.*
chaukaṭh, *the frame of a door.*
chhappar, *a roof; a thatch.*
chilam, *the part of a native pipe* (hukkah) *in which the fire and the tobacco are placed.*
dastár, *head-dress.*
dawa, *medicine.*
ḍhál, *a shield; target.*
díwár, *a wall.*
dohar, *a double-woven cotton-cloth.*
du,a, *benediction.*
dunya, *the world; universe.*
dum, *a tail.*
ḍar, *fear.*
guft-o-gu, *conversation.*
hawa, *air.*
ḥaya, *modesty; shame.*
iba, *a cloak.*
íṇṭ, *a brick.*
jíbh, *the tongue.*
kitáb, *a book.*
kiwáṛ, *a door; gate; entrance.*
kamís, *a shirt; chemise.*
khabar, *news; tidings.*
khák, *earth.*
khuráḱ, *food; victuals.*
mez, *a table.*
misl, *a file of papers.*
nakl, *a story; a copy of a writing, &c.*
namáz, *prayer; prayers.*
nok, *a point* (e.g. of a stick).
palak, *an eye-lid.*
palṭan, *a regiment.*
píṭh, *the back.*
piyás, *thirst.*
poshák, *dress.*
ráh, *a road.*

saṛak, *the high way.*
saza, *punishment.*
sharáb, *wine.*
sharm, *modesty ; shame.*
shakl, *shape ; form.*

taaríf, *praising ; praise.*
taawíz, *recourse to God ; an amulet.*
tahrír, *a written statement.*
tahsíl, *collection of dues.*
táḳ, *a niche.*
taḳrír, *recital ; narration.*
taḳsím, *division into shares.*
taḳsír, *fault ; crime.*

táláb, *a reservoir ; a tank.*
talwár, *a sword.*
taswír, *a picture.*
tajwíz, *investigation ; trial.*
tír, *an arrow.*
toshak, *a mattress ; bedding.*
túfán, *a storm ; 'typhoon.'*

ummed, *hope.*
umr, *age,* i.e., *period of life.*

zabán, *the tongue ; a language.*
zamín, *land ; the ground.*
zanjír, *a chain.*

zulf, *curly hair.*

A HINDÚSTÁNI READER.

CONTENTS.

NOTE.

The following Extracts have been taken from several modern sources, so as to give the student good samples of Hindústáni as written and spoken at the present day. The modern style of composition is less ornate than the older style, at least, when the súbject in hand is of a non-poetic kind. English words for which there are no vernacular equivalents are freely used; and the Relative Pronoun is not unfrequently found following its antecedent as in English, *e.g.*, 'ádmi jo,' instead of 'jo ádmi ..wuh.'.

As regards further exercise in writing Hindústáni, the student cannot do better than translate these stories into English, and after some time, retranslate them into Hindústáni.

It only remains for the author to acknowledge the kindness of those gentlemen who have allowed him to make Extracts from their several Works.

A HINDÚSTÁNI READER.

1. Gadha aur Sher.

Kisi gadhe-ko, barsát ke mausim meṇ, charne ke waste, bágh ki tar o tázah ghás mili; aur píne-ko,[1] chashme ka sáf aur ṭhanḍa aur míṭha páni muyassar áya. Gadha, khá-pí-kar,[2]-khúb moṭa hú,a. Usi nawáḥ meṇ, ek sher bhi rahta-tha. Ek din, gadha sher ke sáth khush-taba,i karne laga. Sher-ne, ná-khush ho-kar, dáṇt dikhá,e. Gadhe-ne, usko haṇsi samajh-kar[3], aur ziyádah[4] chheṛ-chháṛ shuruki.[5] Sher-ne kaha :—'agar yih gustákhi, jo[6] tu karta hai, aḳl ke sáth hoti,[7]

---

[1] 'Píne-ko,' *for drinking.*

[2] 'Khá-píkar,' *i.e.*, 'khá-kar, pí-kar,' *having eaten and drunken.*

[3] '*Understanding laughter*,' i.e., *taking it for laughter.*

[4] 'Aur ziyádah,' transl., *still further.*

[5] Remember that 'ki' may be the fem.: sing. past tense, or past part. of 'karna,' as well as the fem. of 'ka,' 'ke,' 'ki.'

[6] Relative here follows antecedent, as in English; contrary to the ordinary rule.

[7] 'Agar.—aḳl-ke sath hoti,' transl., *if...were along-with*, i.e., accompanied with, *sense*, or, *understanding.*

to maiṇ tujh-ko zarúr saza deta; magar, mujh-ko, teri be-wuḳúfi par, raḥm áta hai.'[1]

Ḥásil:—Baṛe log, aḥmaḳoṇ ki bátoṇ par, khiyál nahíṇ karte.[2]

2. Murgh aur Moti.

Ek murgh, bhúkh-se be-táb ho-kar, dáne ki just-o-ju meṇ kúṛe ke ambár ko[3] kured-raha tha. Bahut der ke bád, nágáh, ek besh-ḳímat moti nikla. Moti-ko dekh-kar, murgh-ne, baṛi ḥasrat ke sáth, kaha:—'Afsos! itni jánkani ke bád, mujh-ko mila bhi to[4] moti—jis-se na mere dil-ko tashaffi ho sakti hai, o na meri bhúkh-ko taskín. Yih moti agar kisi jauhari ya daulatmand-ko milta, to, is ki ḳadar karta, aur is-ko azíz-rakhta; lekin, mere liye, aise zor ki bhúkh meṇ,[5] jo,ár ya chane ka ek dánah, is-se,[6] kahíṇ bihtar tha.'

Ḥásil:—Numá,ish aur árá,ish ki chízeṇ, zindagáni ki asli zarúratoṇ meṇ, kám nahíṇ átíṇ.[7]

---

[1] 'Mujh-ko...rahm áta,' *to me comes compassion*, i.e., *I have compassion on thy*, &c.

[2] 'Khiyál karna' is a verb which has to be translated according to the context. The idea is the *action of the mind in connection with any subject*. Here you may transl. '*does not attach importance to.*' In other connections, it may mean '*to remember;*' or,—with 'nahíṇ,' '*to forget;*' and so on. "Khiyál" is one's '*knowledge,*' '*idea,*' '*notion,*' on any subject.

[3] '*At,*' or, '*in.*'

[4] Indicates *a unit*; also *here* contempt. 'Mujh-ko mili bhi to moti,' '*to me has-come-to hand this thing* called *a pear*;' or '*this wretched pearl.*'

[5] Aise zor ki bhúkh meṇ, '*in hunger of such force.*'

[6] '*Than this*' (pearl).

[7] 'Átíṇ' (for áti haiṇ') 3rd pers. plur. pres. indic. *feminine* of 'ána:' transl. '*Things of appearance and ornament—in life's real necessities—are of no use.*' The agreement is 'chízeṇ átíṇ (haiṇ). See page 10, section 6.

3. PILLE AUR GADHA.

Ek kisán ke ghar-meṇ ek gadha tha, aur ek kutiya bhi páli hú,i thi. Kutiya-ne bachche diye. Jab bachche baṛe hú,e, to k͟húb k͟húb kheláṛ,i,áṇ karte, aur uchhalte, kúdte; o kisán in bachhoṇ ki piyári piyári ḥarkateṇ dekhkar, bahut k͟hush hota,[1] aur un-ko, apne háth-se roṭi khiláta,[1] aur chumkárta.[1] Gadhe-ne dil meṇ socha, kih 'iṇ pilloṇ ki nisbat,[2] maiṇ bahut kám karta húṇ; magar hamára málik in-par ziyádah mihrbáni karta hai; lá,o ![3] maiṇ bhi pilloṇ ki taraḥ[4] kúdá-karúṇ, tá-kih málik mujhe bhi azíz-rakhe.'

Yih soch-kar, gadha,ek din, be-taraḥ dolatti,áṇ jháṛne laga. Kisán-ne pahle, to, gumán kiya, kih 'sháyad makkhiyáṇ ya machchhar is-ko satáte haiṇ;' magar ák͟hir-ko maalúm,hú,a, kih sirf sharárat-se kúdta hai. Tab, to, kisán-ne gadhe ki píṭh meṇ páṇch, chár ḍaṇḍe aise zor-se lagá,e, kih úchhal kúd sab bhúl-gaya.

HÁSIL :—Be-samajhe-bújhe[5] kisi ki rís karna zarúr k͟harábi láta hai.

4. SING YA ṬÁNGEN.

Ek bárah-singe-ne chashmah-e-áb meṇ apna aks dekha; to, apne síṇgoṇ ki shán-o-k͟húbsúrati dekhkar, bahut k͟hush hú,a; lekin jab us-ki nazar, patli patli[6] ṭáṇgoṇ par, paṛi, to kahne laga :—'kih k͟huda-ne mujh-ko we bad-shakl, ṭángeṇ

---

[1] '*Would become, &c.*' See page 17, section 16, ii.

[2] 'As *compared with these pups.*'

[3] As interj. '*Take it so.*' '*So be it.*'

[4] Acc. of manner. '*After the manner of puppies,*' or, '*as the puppies do.*'

[5] Be-samajhe-bújhe, '*without considering* (*and*) *understanding*; '*heedlessly*;' '*without thought.*'

[6] Doubling the adj. gives greater force.

kyúṇ bakhshi haiṇ, jo[1] mere síṇgoṇ ki khúbsúrati-ko bhi aib lagáti haiṇ.' Yih dil meṇ soch-kar raha tha; kih[2] itne meṇ, ko,i shikári á-pahuṇcha. Bárah-singa aisa tez bhága, kih shikári-ko us-ki háth-áne ki ummed na rahi; lekin, thoṛi dúr já-kar, jangal ki jháṛi meṇ, síng aṭak-ga,e, aur pakṛa gaya. Tab kahne laga, 'Há,e! meri bad-akli! síṇgoṇ se maiṇ khush tha: we meri halákat ka sabab hú,e haiṇ; aur ṭáṇgoṇ-ko maiṇ bura-jánta tha, unhoṇ-ne[3] mujhe, maut-se bacháne meṇ kuchh kami nahíṇ ki.'[4]

HÁSIL:—Jo chíz wakt par[4] kám-áne-wáli ho, is-ko azíz-rakhna cháhiye, go-kih khush-numa na ho.[5]

5. BUḌḌHA NAUKAR.

Ek shakhs ke pás baṛa zabardast shikári kutta tha. Har roz apne áka ke waste shikár láta; aur málik bhi us kutte-ko bahut azíz-rakhta tha. Ákhir-ko, wuh kutta buḍḍha hú,a; dauṛne ki tákat báki na rahi; ba-sar, zauf ke sabab-se,[6] dúr ki chíz nahíṇ dekh-saka tha. Gharaz, shikár-karne-se, sab tarah maazúl ho-gaya. Aisi ḥálat meṇ, málik-ne bhi nazar-i-iltifát kam kar-di. Rátib maukúf hú,a. Ákhir-ko, ghar se báhar nikál-diya. Jab kutta rukhsat hone[7] laga, to, ro-kar, málik-se[8] arz ki, kih, 'maiṇ-ne,[9] jawáni, áp-par nisár ki; barasoṇ

---

[1] Refers to 'ṭáṇgeṇ;' transl.—*which*, or, *for they*.

[2] *So that.*

[3] *They*, i.e., the legs.

[4] *Opportunely.*

[5] A relative clause 'jo...is-ko' transl., *what thing—opportunely—a service-bringing one may be*—THAT *to esteem—is proper, although*, &c

[6] 'Ba-sar, zauf ke sabab se,' *at last* (be-sar), *by reason of debility*.

[7] 'Rukhsat-hona,' *to take leave; depart*.

[8] Observe, the prep. same as with púchhná. See page 51, v.

[9] Acc. of time; no prep.

se[1] shikár ki just-o-ju meṇ dauṛa, aur bahut zak͟hm khá,e; lekin, kya! is k͟hud-g͟haraz dunya ka yihi dastúr hai, kih, ab maiṇ láchár húṇ,[2] to, mere rahne tak[3] ka, ko,i rawádár nahiṇ hai;[4] aur meri pichhli k͟hidmateṇ sab akárat haiṇ.'

ḤÁSIL:—Buḍḍhe naukar,[5] jin-se[6] kám nahíṇ ho-sakta, un-ke píchhle ḥuḳúḳ-ko bhúl-jána[7] baṛi ná-iḥsán-mandi hai.

6. KAUWA, AK͟HROṬ AUR GILEHRI.

Ek kauwa ak͟hroṭ-ko choṇch-se toṛ-raha tha; magar ak͟hroṭ par kuchh asar nahíṇ hota tha. Gilehri-ne dekha, aur kauwe-se kaha:—'Kyúṇ itni zaḥmat uṭháta[8] hai'? Kauwe-ne kaha:—'maiṇ-ne suna hai, kih ak͟hroṭ bahut maze ki chíz hai; aur jab K͟huda-ne, is sak͟hti ke sáth, is-ko band-kiya hai, zarúr is ke andar,[9] kuchh baṛi niimat hogi; so, maiṇ—jis-taraḥ ban-paṛega[10]—is-ko toṛ-kar rahúṇga.'

Gilehri-ne kaha:—'Maiṇ ek ásán tadbír batá,úṇ; ak͟hroṭ-ko, baṛi dúr, hawa meṇ úpar le-jákar, patthar ki samne-wali chaṭán par[11]—chhoṛ-de; girne ke sadme se, k͟hud pásh-pásh ho-já,ega.'

---

[1] *Since*, transl., '*for years back.*'

[2] '*Now (that) I am helpless,*' or, '*useless.*'

[3] '*Up to the point of my remaining.*'

[4] Transl.: *there is no consenter of* (Eng. *to*) *even my remaining.*

[5] There is no verb to this Plur. Nom. It is left standing, and referred back-to by 'un-ke'; as we might say. 'This man, why, he's a fool.'

[6] Oblique form of plur. of 'jo.'

[7] Verbal Noun.

[8] 'Uṭhána' and 'khána' are often used regarding mental feelings or sufferings.

[9] '*It must be that inside it.*'

[10] '*In whatever way it may be practicable.*'

[11] '*On an opposite slab of stone.*'

Kauwe-ne aisa hi kiya; lekin, níche utar-kar, kya dekhta hai? Kih wáḳe meṇ aḵẖroṭ to pásh-pásh ho-gaya, magar magẖz[1] gilehri le-kar chal-di; sirf chhilke chhoṛ-ga,i.

ḤÁSIL:—Ḵẖud-gẖaraz ádmi, jo[2] saláh deta hai, us meṇ[3] kuchh-na-kuchh apna fá,idah zarúr soch-leta hai.[4]

7. SHER, JANGAL KA BÁDSHÁH.

Sher aur ríchh aur chíta aur bheṛiya, chároṇ[5], shikár ki just-o-ju meṇ the; sab-ne saláḥ kí[6]:—'á,o, darya-kináre meṇ shikár kareṇ; jo shikár[7] milega, chároṇ barábar ḥisse báṇṭ-leṇge.'—Ittifáḳan, níl-gá,o-ko mára; aur, ba-mújib aḥd o paimáṇ ke, barábar chár hisse kiye! ḳaríb tha, kih har ek apna apna[8] ḥissah le;[9] itne meṇ, sher, lapak-kar, bola:—'Ṣuno, bhá'i! yih ek hissah, to, ba-mújib ḳaul-o-ḳarár-ke, mera hai; aur dusre ḥisse ka maiṇ is wáste dáwídár húṇ, kih maiṇ jangal ka bádsháh húṇ, kahíṇ shikár ho, mujh-ko chahárum, ba-taur ḵẖiráj ke, milta hai; aur tísra ḥissah maiṇ is wajah-se lúṇga, kih us meṇ dil aur jigar hai, jis-ko[10] tum

---

[1] Acc. governed by 'le-kar.'

[2] Instance of the Relative Pronoun used as in English.

[3] Namely, in his advice.

[4] 'Ádmi' is Nom. to 'soch-leta-hai' (*takes thought for: considers*). 'Fá,idah,' is the Acc. after this verb: or it may be looked on as an 'acc. absolute;' and translated, *takes thought regarding*, or, *for his own advantage*.

[5] The plural form of 'chár,' transl., '*all four*.'

[6] Fem. past part. of 'karna'

[7] 'Hamoṇ-ko,' understood.

[8] Doubled to express 'distribution.'

[9] 3rd pers. sing. subj. of 'lena.'

[10] '*Regarding which.*'

jánte ho, kih meri ghiza hai; raha[1] chautha ḥissah; so[2] maiṇ nahíṇ jánta, tum tínoṇ meṇ, us-ko kyúṇkar taḳsím karúṇ;[3] is-se[4] bihtar hai, kih us-ko bhi apne hi sarf meṇ lá,úṇ.' Yih kah-kar, sher, chároṇ ḥisse chaṭ-kar, gaya; aur sab ke sab, muṇh dekhte ke dekhte,[5] rah-ga,e.

Ḥásil:—Zabardast ke sáth sájha karne meṇ, hameshah nuḳsán hota.

8. Bheṛiya aur Sáras.

Ek bheṛiye ke gale meṇ ittifáḳ-se haḍḍi aṭak ga,i. Harchand kháṇsi aur bahuteri ubká,i,áṇ líṇ,[6] magar haḍḍi na nikli; par[7] na nikli. Majbúr hokar, sáras ke pás gaya aur kaha:—kih 'yár! ham tum donoṇ[8] ek jangal meṇ rahte haiṇ; is wakt ḥaḳḳ-i-hamsáyah[9] ada karo; mere halaḳ meṇ haḍḍi aṭak ga,i hai, aur ján par bani hai;[10] mihrbáni kar-ke, apni lambi gardan-se is-ko nikál-lo, aur yih kám main tum-se muft bhi nahíṇ cháhta; jo tum kahoge, so dúṇga.' Sáras rázi ho-gaya; aur bheṛiye ke ḥalaḳ meṇ apni lambi gardan ḍálkar, haḍḍi-ko khaṭ-se alag nikál-liya.

Chand roz ke bád, bheṛiya shikár kar-ke gorkhar láya; aur darya-kináre[11] baiṭhkar, kháne laga. Sáras-ne dekha, aur

---

1 '*There remained.*'
2 '*As to it.*'
3 '*I do not know—among you three—it—how I can divide.*'
4 '*Than this.*'
5 A phrase, equivalent to 'looking dejectedly in each other's faces.'
6 Fem. 3rd pers. plur. past tense 'lena;' agreeing with 'ubká,i,áṇ.
7 '*Still*'
8 'Ham tum donoṇ,' a phrase, '*both of us.*'
9 Adj. following noun; in imitation of the Persian.
10 See 'banna,' '*is settling on my life.*' i.e., '*is threatening,*' *&c.*
11 Acc. of place; without prep.

bahut khush-ámad se, pás já-kar, kaha:—Kih 'áj maiṇ, bhúkha húṇ, gosht ka ek ṭukṛa mujhe bhi do.' Bheṛiye-ne ta,ammul kiya. Sáras ne—dabi zabán se—haḍḍi ka nikálna[1] yád-diláya. To, bheṛiye-ne kaha:—'A,i aḥmaḳ! yih inám kya kam tha,[2] kih tu, mere ḥalaḳ se, teri gardan, saḥíḥ-ṣalámat nikál-kar, le-gaya.'[3]

Ḥásil:—Zálim aur múzi ádmi ke sáth sulúk-karna,[1] aur bihtari ki ummed rakhna[1] ná-dáni hai. Dunya ke log iḥsán-ko jald bhúl-játe haiṇ; zarúrat meṇ[4] ádmi jo waadah karta hai,[5] kamtar us-ko púra-karta hai.

9. Saudágarán[6] aur Faujdár-Ṣáḥib.

Laṛá,i ke waḳt meṇ, do saudágarán, achchhe kapṛe pahin-kar, apne mál ke sáth, ráste meṇ chale-játe the. Ittifáḳan, un-ko chár sipáhi,án mile; aur un bad-bakht saudágaroṇ ka sab mál lúṭ-kar, bhág-ga,e. Saudágarán, láchár hokar, fauj-dár-sáḥib ke pás dauṛe, aur apni bad-ḳismat ka ḥál bayán kiya.[7] Hákim-ne un-se púchha, kih, 'jis-waḳt un sipáhi,oṇ ne tum-hára mál lúṭ-liya, us-waḳt tum log, yih kapṛa oṛhe,[8] játe the?' Unhoṇ-ne jawáb diya, kih 'Háṇ! sáḥib.' Tab faujdár-ne kaha:—kih, 'is-se khúb maalúm hai, kih we shakhs mere ádmi nahíṇ haiṇ; lekin dushman ke log haiṇ; agar mere

---

[1] Verbal Noun.

[2] 'Yih inám kya kám tha.' idiomatic; lit. *this gift (of) what use was (it)*, viz., *that, &c.*, equivalent to *is it nothing that, &c.*

[3] 'Le-gaya' (from 'le-jána') govs. 'gardan.'

[4] '*In necessity*;' i.e., '*under a strain, or compulsion.*'

[5] Transl.:—*The man who makes a promise under compulsion, seldom fulfils it.* English idiom of Relative Pronoun.

[6] 'An,' the Persian plural. See page 73.

[7] 'Unhoṇ-ne' understood. Transl.:—*They stated the circumstances of their misfortune.*

[8] Past part. Plur. 'oṛhna' *to put on clothes*; agreeing with 'tum log.'

ádmi hote, to, yih achchha kapṛa kabhi nahíṇ chhoṛ-dete: Khuda ka shukr hai, kih tum-ko mere ádmi nahíṇ mile the.'

Bolte, bolte faujdár-sáhib-ne apne logoṇ-ko ishárah diya; aur jab saudágarán, údás hokar, phire[1] játe the, tab faujdár ke ádmi,oṇ-ne un-ke kapṛe utár-di,e, jis-se we be-nasíb saudágarán khálí jáṇghie meṇ apne ghar-ko pahuṇche.

10. Maut Joru aur Gá,e ki.

Ek basti meṇ ek kisán rahta tha, aur sab kám bahut nek-námi o diyánat-se kiya-karta[2] tha. Is-liye, us-se aur gáṇw-wáloṇ-se,[3] bahut dosti thi. Bad-nasíbi-se, us-ka kám achchhi taraḥ nahíṇ chala. Pahle, us ki gá,e mar-ga,i; tab us ki joru. Is wajhe-se, bahut gham-gín aur dil-gír hú,a; kyúṇ-ki, dúsri gá,e mol-lene ke wáste, rúpíye nahíṇ the; aur is-ki joru har dam ghar ke kám meṇ madadgár rahi thi.

Is áfat meṇ, gáṇw-wáloṇ-ne, us-ke dil bahláne ke wáste, bahut koshish ki. Ek shakhs-ne kaha, kih, 'Are! bhá,i! kyúṇ rote ho? tum achchhe jawán ho; tum-ko jald dúsri joru milegi; dekho, to, meri beṭi bahut khúbsúrat laṛki hai, maiṇ tum-ko use khushi-se dúṇga.' Dúsre-ne, apni bahin ke báre meṇ, wohi bát kahi. Tísre-ne apni bhánji ka ḥál batáya.

Ákhir ko, kisán-ne jawáb diya, kih, 'is gáṇw meṇ, joru ki maut bihtar hai, gá,e ki maut se.[4] Bahut ádmi mujhe

---

[1] Similar to 'oṛhe;' here agreeing with 'saudágarán.'

[2] 'Kiya karna,' *to be in the habit of doing a thing;* it is the same as our idiom with 'always.'

[3] 'Us-se aur gaṇw-wáloṇ se,' *with him and with the villagers;* or, *between him and the villagers.* Notice this idiom; it occurs frequently. Notice also that in Hindústáni, you say '*I and you,*' *&c.*, not '*you and I.*' 'ham-se tum-se,' *between you and me;* 'Ego et rex meus.'

[4] Transl.:—*The death of a wife is better than, &c.*

dúsri joru dene ko taiyár haiṇ; ko,i shakhs mujhe dúsri gá,e dena ḳabúl nahíṇ karta.'

11. 'Insáf Karna Hoga.'

Paṭne ke zile ki ek basti meṇ, ek lohár, ba-nám Rám Gopál, rahta tha. Wuh bahut hoshyár kárígar tha; lekin, fazúl kharchi ke sabab se, hameshah tangi se guzrán kiya karta[1] tha. Ek rát, ráh meṇ usko ek saudágar mila; us-ko lohár-ne ján se már-ḍála, aur mál chorá-liya. Magar yih wuḳu chhipa nahíṇ raha. Gáṇw ke mahtoṇ-ne, zamíṇdár ke pás já-kar, púchha, kih 'ḥuzúr! kya marzi hai? hákimán ko is ki[2] ittila ki[3]-jáwe,[4] ya nahíṇ?'[5]

Ittifákan, zamíṇdár se,[6] aur Ràm Gopál se,[6] málguzári ki bábat, takrár thi; is liye zamíṇdár-ne mahtoṇ ko ḥukm diya, kih 'us wuḳu ki[7] khabar ḥákim logoṇ ko do.' Pas, chaukídár-ne, tháne meṇ já-kar, apna izhár likwá-díya. Is-par, dárogha sáḥib, ma,i tín chár barḳandáz, sar-zamín par áya, aur tadáruk karne laga

Chúṇkih Rám Gopál gharíb tha, thána-wáloṇ ko rázi nahíṇ kar-saka.[8] Pas, un logoṇ-ne Rám Gopál ko, ma,i subút, ḥákim ke pás chálán kiya. Tajwíz ke bád, ḥákim-ne fármáya, kih 'us kam-bakht-ko pháṇsi do.'

Jab is ḥukm ki khabar gáṇw-wáloṇ ke pás pahuṇchi, niháyat afsurdah hú,e; aur bole, 'agàr ham-logoṇ ke lohár-ko

---

[1] 'Kiya-karna,' *to continually do a thing; to keep doing it.*

[2] Because 'ittila' is fem.

[3] Fem. p. part. 'karna.'

[4] Passive.

[5] The local Indian squire is generally consulted as to whether a crime is to be reported to the authorities or not.

[6] Notice this idiom 'se...se,' *between* A. and B. See preceding Story.

[7] Because 'khabar' is fem.

[8] Alluding to the venality which some people attribute to the police.

pháṇsi deṇge, to, hamáraṇ kám kis-taraḥ se chalega? hamáre hal aur gáṛi,áṇ kaun marammat karega? Bhúkh se mar-já-eṇge.'

Fikrmand ho-kar, ḥákim ke pás ga,e, aur apna ḥál bayán-kiya, aur darkẖást ki,[1] kih ḥákim mausúf lohár-ko kẖalás kareṇ. Ḥákim-ne nahíṇ ḳabúl kiya, aur kaha kih, '*insáf karna hoga.*'

Gáṇwár-log báhar ga,e; aur, pípal ke gáchh ke níche tambáku píte, píte, mashwarah karne lage. Ákẖir-ko ḥákim ke pás phir á,e, aur bole:—"Gẖaríb-parwar! ḥuzúr ki bát durust hai: 'insáf karna hoga'; lekin, insáf nahíṇ hai kih ham be-ḳusúr ádmi sab bhúkh se mar-já,eṇ; gáṇw chhoṭá hai, aur is meṇ sirf ek lohár rahta hai; magar do júláhe haiṇ; hamáre kám ke wáste, ek júláhah bas hai; un donoṇ meṇ se, ek shakẖs le-kar, pháṇsi díjiye; is taur se insáf hoga."

Jab is bát-ko bhi ḥákim-ne nahíṇ manzúr kiya, basti-wále chale-ga,e; aur ápas meṇ bole:—'Bhá,i! bhá,i! kal-yug[2] hai, dunya[3] meṇ insáf nahíṇ hai.'

12. KACHHÚA AUR KHARGOSH.

Báb Auwal.

Ek kachhúe-ko safar darpesh tha. Is ki just-o-ju hú,i,[4] kih 'ko,i sáthi mile,[5] to safar karúṇ.' Ittifáḳ se, ek kẖargosh bhi usi taraf-ko jáne-wála tha. Kachhúe-ne kaha: kih 'miyáṇ

---

[1] Fem. past *tense* of 'karna.'

[2] The black era, *i. e.*, the evil days.

[3] The reader will have noticed that 'dunya' is a word of which the 'a' does not change into 'e'; so also 'darya,' *a river.*

[4] '*His search was,*' *i.e.*, he was enquiring.

[5] Subj. understand 'mujh-ko,' transl., '*Could any companion be found.*'

khargosh ! á,o ! ham tum sáth-chaleṇ.'[1] Khargosh be ikhtiyár haṇsa, aur kaha :—'Abe ! aḥmaḳ ! Kaháṇ[2] *tu* bhadda, phaph-sa, reng reng-kar, pahároṇ meṇ[3] ek bálisht zamín[4] chalta hai, aur kaháṇ *maiṇ*, bijli ki mánind lapakta húṇ, hawa ki tarah uṛta húṇ ;—bhala ! mera aur tera kya sáth ?' Kuchhúe ne kaha :—'yih saḥíḥ hai ; magar manzil par (Khuda-ne cháha) ap se áge hi pahuṇchúṇga. Yaḳín na ho, to shart bándh-líjiye.[5] Chunánchih, yih shart hú,i, kih jo háre, us-ke kán káṭe-já,eṇ.'[6]

13. Kachhúa aur Khargosh.

Báb Doyam.

Kachhúa, áhistah, áhistah, apni chál chalne laga. Khargosh, do chhaláṇgoṇ meṇ, nazar-se gháib ho gaya.[7] Thoṛi dúr áge já-kar, khargosh-ne socha, kih, 'jitna maiṇ chal-chuka húṇ,—shám tak,'[8] to, kachhúe ko, yaháṇ-ána mushkil hai ;

---

[1] Imperative, *let you (and) me go together.*

[2] Here begins a long sentence. Its purport is : where *you*, being such and such, do such and such ; and where *I* do such and such. The sentence ends with a break-off at 'uṛta húṅ,' and resumes : 'well ! mera aur tera ' '*as to your (affairs) and mine,*' 'kya sáth (hai).' '*What (is there) in common.*''

[3] *In the 'pahars'* or *watches*, transl., '*in the 24 hours.*'

[4] Ek bálisht zamín : apposition : '*a span of ground.*'

[5] The sense is :—' I (the tortoise) am sure to reach the journey's end before you (the hare),—for God so wills it,—but if you think this doubtful, then have a bet on it.'

[6] Passive.

[7] '*Became vanished from sight,*' '*was out of sight.*'

[8] 'Tak' here (and often) expresses the idea of a time not yet arrived; the mind being directed to the interval between now and then. The sense here is that the hare thinks that he has now gone so far that it will be difficult for the tortoise to reach the spot, ' shám tak, ' even by evening.

maiṇ jaldi kyúṇ karúṇ? lá,o![1] so-[2] rahúṇ, Khargosh árám-se so-[4]raha. Kachhúa, baṛi der ke bád, ghisarta, ghisarta, áya. Dekha, to, ḥaríf paṛa[3] sota hai. Chup-ke chal-diya. Baṛi rát ga,i, khargosh jága; to, kachhúa nazar na' áya.[4] Áp hi áp kahne laga[5]:—'Alláh! re![6] sust ḳadam! miyáṇ kachhúe ab-tak tashríf nahíṇ lá,e.[7] Khair! chaleṇ! sará,e meṇ rát-ko raheṇ; kal, jo[8] miyáṇ kachhúa yaháṇ á,ega, to jáeṇge.'

Joṇ sará,e meṇ ḳadam rakha, dekha to kachhúa maujúd hai. Khargosh-ko dekhte hi, kachhúa lapka, kih 'lá,iye, Ḥazrat! kán!'[9] Khargosh, dum dabá-kar, aisa bhága, kih áj tak, kánoṇ ke ḍar ke máre, bhága,-bhága-phirta hai.[10]

ḤÁSIL:—Kaisa-hi[11] ásán kuchh kám ho, jab uska íhtimám nahíṇ kiya-játa,[12] to mushkil ho-játa. Kund-zihn, miḥnati laṛke, zahín laṛkoṇ-ko hará-dete haiṇ. Dushman-ko ḥaḳír nahíṇ samajhna cháhiye. Ghurúr, kamál ḥásil-karne se, rokta hai; waghairah.

---

1 As interj. '*take it so.*'

2 Stem of 'sona,' *to sleep*: 'so-rahna,' *to remain sleeping*.

3 '*Lain down*,' or, as we say, 'lying down.'

4 *Was*, or, *had not come in sight*.

5 *He began to say to himself*.

6 *God Almighty!*

7 See page 76, section 17.

8 *When*: or, *if*.

9 '*Bring (me) oh! Your Excellency!—Your Ears!*' (The mock polite.)

10 Thus do Orientals account for the timorous movements of rabbits and hares.

11 'Kaisa-hi,' '*however*.'

12 Passive Voice.

14. KHÚRSHÍDI BEGAM.

The following extract is taken from an excellent modern novel called "Fisánah-e-Khúrshídi," *i.e.*, "The Story of Khúrshídi"—a Muḥammadan lady of rank. The author is the well-known Saiyid Afzal-ud-dín Aḥmad. In this book, English as well as native characters are introduced. It recommends itself by the simplicity of its style, by its freedom from all coarseness, and by the attempt which it makes to render Natives and Europeans better acquainted with each other than they at present are. This extract consists mainly of a dialogue between the English lady of the piece (Miss Thompson) and Khúrshídi's father.

Mis Támsan shahr-i-Landan ke baṛe saudágar ki beṭi thi. Apne báp ke sáth Hindústán á,íṇ.[1] Us-wakt in[1] ka sinn bís baras ka tha; chálís baras tak, Hindústán meṇ rahíṇ.[1] Aṭhárah zabánoṇ se wáḳif thíṇ.[1] Laṛkoṇ ke paṛháne ka niháyat shauḳ tha. L'illáh,[2] logoṇ-ko paṛháti thíṇ.[1]

[Then begins the dialogue.]

NAWWÁB.—Maiṇ áp se, kya kahúṇ? Áp to[3] jánti hi[3] haiṇ, kih ham-logoṇ ke yaháṇ auratoṇ ki taalím ki—kya ḥálat hai.[4] Auwal, ko,i aurat paṛhi, likhi[5] milti[6] nahíṇ, jo púri taraḥ se taalím de;[7] dúsre, yaháṇ ki má,eṇ[8] aisi ajhal o ná-parwah hoti haiṇ, kih is taraf kuchh khiyál hi[3] nahíṇ karti

---

[1] Pronouns and verbs *plural*, out of respect to the lady.

[2] Arabic, '*for the love of God.*'

[3] Idiomatic strengthening particles. Transl. as best suits your English: or leave untranslated.

[4] Begin with 'kya ḥálat hai;' and go on '*of the education of the women resident-with us-people.*' Trace the application of the rules for 'ka,' 'ke,' 'ki,' by also translating '*you know our people's women's education's condition—what it is.*'

[5] '*Read-written,*' i.e., '*who can read and write.*'

[6] Understand 'hamoṇ-ko.'

[7] Subj. 'dena.'

[8] Plur. of 'ma,' *mother.*

haiṇ;—maiṇ akela kya kar-sakta húṇ? Kidhar dekhúṇ, kidhar na dekhúṇ? mujh-ko, umúr-i-dunyáwi se, itni furṣat kaháṇ hogi, kih k͟hud apni laṛki-ko taalím dúṇ? [1]

MISS T.—Is meṇ shakk nahíṇ hai, kih yaháṇ ki auratеṇ bil-kull jáhil aur aksar an-paṛh[2] haiṇ; is-liye aulád ki taalím achhi nahíṇ hoti hai. Lekin, agar ko,i *aurat* aisi lá,iḳ[3] nahíṇ milti thi, to, áp ke yaháṇ *maulavi* to[4] haiṇ, un hi[4] se taalím dilwá,i hoti.[5]

NAWWÁB.—Yih bhi nahíṇ ho-sakta,—do wajhoṇ se:—ek to yih, kih jab laṛki syáni hú,i, to, maulavi ke sámne nahíṇ já-sakti; dúsri,[6] kih hamáre yaháṇ ke maulavi bhi aḳl ke putle hote haiṇ; taríḳah paṛháne ka, achchha nahíṇ jánte haiṇ.

MISS T.—Sach hai! Áp durust farmáte haiṇ;[7] lekin, ḳusúr mu,áf![8] is-meṇ áp ki[9] bhi kuchh khata hai: maiṇ sálha[10] sál se yaháṇ húṇ, aur áp-ne mujh-ko ittila nahíṇ di.[11]

NAWWÁB.—Maiṇ kahne hi ko tha:[12] lekin l'illah bura na mániega.[13] Áp jánti hoṇgi, kih yaháṇ ki auratеṇ kis ḳadr

---

1 Subj. 'dena.'

2 'A' or 'an' *negative*, as in Greek; 'paṛh' from 'paṛhna;' 'an-paṛh,' *unread; illiterate.*

3 Understand 'hamoṇ-ko.'

4 Idiomatic strengthening particles. Transl. as best suits your English: or leave untranslated.

5 See page 17, section 16.

6 Fem. because 'wajh' which is fem. is understood.

7 'Farmána,' *to order;* but used of any utterance by a great man.

8 *Excuse fault,'* i.e., 'you will excuse my saying,' &c.

9 '*Áp ki k͟hata,*' 'ki' is used because 'k͟hata' is fem.

10 'Ha' is the Persian plural of neuter nouns; as 'án' is of masc. nouns, transl., '*years on years.*'

11 Past tense *fem.* of 'dena,' 'ittila' being fem.

12 'Was on telling,' *i.e.*, 'was about tell you.'

13 An unusual form; got by adding 'ga' of the future to the respectful imperative; the word is from 'mánna.'

nákis-ul-akl[1] aur muta,assib haiṇ. Chunánchih, jab maiṇ-ne apni bíbi se, áp ka zikr kiya, to wuh kahne lagíṇ, kih áp meri laṛki-ko Kristán baná-ḍáleṇgíṇ.

MISS T.—Taubáh! yih kya guft-o-gu hai! Áp dekhiye to! maiṇ un logoṇ-ko kis-taraḥ miláti húṇ! Mujh-ko chúṇkih áp-se dili-dosti hai, is-liye maiṇ dil-o-ján se áp ki laṛkí ko taalím dúṇgi.

* * * * * * * * * *

NAWWÁB.—Ab áp Khurshídi begam-ko apni laṛki samjhiye; aur jis-taraḥ munásib samjhiye, is-ko taalím díjiye.

MISS T.—Áp khátir-jamah rakhiye; áp ki laṛki bahut zahín aur hoshyár haiṇ; aisi laṛki to ḳismatoṇ se milti hai;[2] jald ilm o hunar se wáḳif ho-já,egi.

15. KHURSHÍDI BEGAM.

SECOND EXTRACT FROM THE SAME WORK.

The young lady has progressed with her education so well that her drawing gains the prize at the Calcutta Exhibition; the Viceroy makes a speech; the young lady's father being present. She herself, however, has not yet so far advanced in English manners as to allow her pretty face to be seen.

THE VICEROY'S SPEECH.

Maiṇ niháyat khushi se, is bát-ko kahta húṇ, kih yih naḳshah, kih mere háth meṇ hai, is ikzibíshan (E.) meṇ umdah-tarín[3] naḳshah hai; balki, kam aise dekhne meṇ áte

---

[1] 'Ul' is the Arabic '*of the.*'

[2] 'Milna' is here used as a fully personal verb. In this sense it means '*to be mixed up with*' or *associated with*,' '*to be allied to*' or the like. Translate, '*such a girl is sure to have a good destiny before her*,' but don't fail to analyse the clause literally.

[3] Persian superlative; see page 74, section 9.

haiṇ[1] (táli,áṇ). Maiṇ bahut khush hú,a, is amr se, kih áp log meri rá,i se ittifáḳ karte haiṇ, aur is naḳshe-ko aur naḳshoṇ par[2]—tarjíḥ deté haiṇ. Mujh-ko ziyádah khushi iṣ bát ki hai, kih yih naḳshah ek Hindústán ki laṛki ke háth se banáya hú,a hai. (suno ! suno !) Is laṛki ka sinn pandrah ya solah baras ka hai; lekin is kam-sinn meṇ, wuh bát kar-dekhá,i—kih jis-se ham log maḥz ná-wáḳif the. Is laṛki-ne *yih*[3] bát sábit-kar-di, kih Hindústán ki laṛki,áṇ bhi aḳl o dánist meṇ Inglistán ki laṛki,oṇ se,[4] kisi taraḥ kam nahíṇ haiṇ (khushi). Agar aisi hi taalím, Hindústán ki kull laṛki-oṇ ko, ho, to phir ko,i ádmi, in logoṇ par, haṇs-na-sake. Yih laṛki maḥz jáhil aur gum-nám rahti; agar hamáre lá,iḳ aur mu,azzaz dost, Nawáb——Bahádur, C. S. I.[5] is rishtah-e-ta,assub-ko na' toṛte,[6] aur apni beṭi ki taalím is taraḥ se na' karte.[6] Khuda kare, ki har báp-ki aisi hi laṛki ho; aur har laṛki-ko aisa hi báp mile. (ḥúra E.). Maiṇ Mis Támsan ki baṛi taaríf karta húṇ, kih unhoṇ-ne[7] is miḥnat o shafaḳat se—is laṛki-ko ilm o hunar sikhláya—jis ka natíjah sab par záhir hú,a.

Ab maiṇ is taḳrír-ko khatm karta húṇ; aur áfsos ke sáth karta húṇ, kih mu,áfiḳ rasm Hindústán ke, wuh laṛki yaháṇ nahíṇ á-sakti. Nahíṇ-to, maiṇ khud, apne háth se yih

---

[1] '*Few such* (pictures) *come into seeing*,' i.e., before one.

[2] '*On*,' or '*over other pictures*:' a form of the comparative degree.

[3] Namely, the 'bát' foreshadowed in the preceding sentence, and now about to be stated; a very common form of Hindústáni composition.

[4] 'Se' of *comparison*. See page 74, section 8.

[5] Companion of the Star of India, a British, not a native title of honour.

[6] See page 17, section 16.

[7] 'Unhoṇ-ne,' *she*.

meḍal (E.) us-ke zeb-i-gulu[1] karta. Lekin, maiṇ ummed karta húṇ, kih Nawwáb——aur Mis Támsan yih medal us laṛki-ko pahiná-deṇge, aur meri taraf se bahut mubárakbád deṇge (táḷi,áṇ táli,áṇ).

1 '*Her ornament of neck.*' See page 52, *Note 1*; also page 17, section 16.

GLOSSARY OF USEFUL WORDS.

PART I.

HINDU'STA'NI-ENGLISH.

NOTE.

It is hoped that the following Glossary contains every word which occurs in the Vocabularies, Exercises, and "The Reader,"—except those intentionally omitted, namely, English words which have crept into the language, and the 'numerals' which are given on pages 64 and 103. Numerals which occur in the Exercises or "The Reader" are, however, given.

There are also thousands of words given which do not occur in the earlier part of the book.

The following Table shows the sequence of the letters, not only as the Head-Letters of the Glossary; but *throughout the columns.* Thus all words in 'Kat' are exhausted before you find 'Kaṭ,' &c., and so with other letters which are different and yet similar, as 'd;' and "ḍ;" 'h,' and 'ḥ.'

TABLE.

A.	B.	CH.	D.	Ḍ.	E.
F.	G.	GH.	H.	Ḥ.	I.
J.	K.	Ḳ.	KH.	L.	M.
N.	O.	P.	R.	Ṛ.	S.
SH.	T.	Ṭ.	U.	V.	W.
Y.	Z.				

The general arrangement is to give the *shortest* word—Noun, Adjective or other word—as a 'Head-word;' and to range under it, longer words connected with the same subject. The 'head-word' is not, as a rule, reprinted; but is represented by a short line. Ex.:—Dúkán (f.), *a shop.* –dár, *a shop-keeper.* –dári, *shop-keeping.* Occasionally, the 'head-word' changes before additions can be made. In such cases the short line represents the 'head-word' down to the last permanent consonant, which consonant is repeated in that part of the new word which is printed. Ex.:—Azurdah, *grieved.* –dagi, *grief.*

Contractions are used as follows:—

i. The ordinary grammatical ones; as 'Adj.' *Adjective;* 'Adv.' *Adverb, &c.* 'Sing.' *Singular;* 'Pl.' *Plural;* 'trans.' *transitive;* 'intr.' *intransitive*, and so on.

ii. Compound Verbs ending in '*karna*' and '*dena*' are very common. So these auxiliaries are shown by –'k' and 'd' respectively.

iii. When the meaning of *words following a 'head-word'* is easily to be understood from the English of the 'head-word,' the words which follow are left untranslated. They are marked 'A.' if Adjectives; 'Adv.' if Adverbs; 'N.' if Nouns; and 'V.' if Verbs. Ex.:—Azurdah, *grieved,* N. –dagi, which *must* mean '*grief.*' Fikr, *anxiety; care.* A. –mand. Shuru, *a beginning.* V. –k.

iv. (p.) ... indicates a Persian word not in use in its simple form; but common in derivatives from it.

v. 'Persian' ...indicates that a phrase, though *Persian*, is in common use in Hindústáni.

vi. (m.) Stands for *masculine;* (f.) for *feminine;* (a.) shows that a word (e g., *light*) is *an adjective*, not a *noun;* (n.) means that a word (e.g., *light*) is *a noun* and not *an adjective;* (n.a.), means that the word is both *a noun and an adjective.*

vii. (M.)...indicates that the word is to be used only concerning things *Muḥammadan.*

viii. (H.)...the same as regards things *Hindu.*

ix. (L.B.)...means that the word is current chiefly or wholly, in *Lower Bengal* only.

x. (E.)...Stands for *English;* 'compos,' for *composition;* 'Lit.' for *literally;* 'fig.' *for figuratively.*

xi. The long word 'Muḥammadan' is generally contracted *Muḥam.*

Masculine Nouns ending in any of the feminine terminations are marked (m.)

Feminine Nouns ending in anything except the recognised feminine terminations are marked (f.) See Page 8, Section 13.

GLOSSARY OF USEFUL WORDS.

Hindústáni-English

A.

A *or* an, *a negative prefix*, e.g. an-paṛh (*See* 'paṛhna'), *illiterate*.

Ab, *now ; at present*. –tak, *till now*.

Áb (p.), *water*. –dár, *a servant who attends to the wines, &c.* –o-hawa (f.), *climate*.

Ábád, *cultivated ; peopled*. -i, *cultivated land*.

Abe, *an interj. expressing scorn*.

Abr, *a cloud*. abri, *clouded*.

Ábru (f.), *dignity ; respect ; inspired*.

Abru (f.), *the eyebrow*.

Abwáb (pl. of 'báb.'), *chapters ; readings ; columns ; entries in detail in columns ; hence, payments ; cesses, &c.*

Achchha, *good ; well*. Also *as interj.* achhá,i, *goodness*. achchhi-tarah, *in good style ; carefully*.

Ada, *payment*, V. –k.

Adálat, *a court of justice*.

Ádat, *custom ; habit*.

Ádha (n. a.), *a half ; half*.

Ádil, *just ; equitable*.

Ádmi, *a human being ; a man ; a woman*. –yat, *humanity ; the human species*.

Adrak, *green ginger ; preserved ginger*.

Áfat, *a calamity*.

Áfrín, *bravo !*

Afsánah, *a story ; tale ; romance*.

Afsos, *sadness ; a pity*. Also [*as interj.*

Afsurdah, *grieved; sad.* N. -dagi.

Áftáb, *the sun.*

Áftábah, *a water-jug; a ewer.*

Ág (f.), *fire.* -dán, *a fire-stand.*

Agar, *if.* -chih, *although.*

Áge, *in front; forward.* -baṛhána, (*trans.*) *to start; move forward.* -chalna; -j., *to go in front.* -píchhe, *in single file.*

Áhar, *a natural reservoir of water.*

Áhistah, *slowly.*

Aḥd-o-paimán, *mutual agreement.*

Aḥmaḳ (n. a.), *a fool; foolish. folly.* -i.

Aib, *fault; blemish.* -lagána, *to impute blame to; to cast discredit on.*

Á,ín, *law; order; rule.*

Á,ínah, *a looking-glass.*

Aisa, *like this; such a...; thus; to such a degree.*

Áj, *to-day.* -kal, (lit. *to-day–to-morrow*), *the present time.*

Ajá,ib, *wonders; wonderful things.*

Á-jána, *to arrive.*

Ajhal, *very ignorant.*

Ajíb, *wonderful.*

Ajúbah, *wonderful.*

Akár; akárath, *fruitless; in vain.*

Akela, *alone.*

Aks, *reflection* (e.g., in water.)

Aksar, *frequently; generally.*

Áḳa, *an owner; master.*

Aḳl, (f.), *sense; wisdom.* A. --mand.

Áḵẖir, *the end.* -ko, *at last; lastly.*

Aḵẖroṭ, *a walnut.*

Alag, *separate; separately.*

Aláhdah, *separately.*

Aláḳah, *jurisdiction; relationship,* or *connection, with a person or thing.* -ḳa-dár, *a person in charge of an* 'aláḳah.'

Ala-s-sabáh, *early in the morning.*

Albattah, *for certain; certainly.*

Álim, *learned.*

Alláh (M.), *God.* -re! (interj.) *God Almighty.*

Almás, *a diamond.*

Álo, *light* (n.)

Álu, *a potatoe.*

Ám, *a mango.* Also, *common; vulgar.* Adv. umúman.

Ámad-o-raft, *coming-and-going; intercourse.*

Ambár, *a heap; stock; store.*

Ámín, *Amen!*

Amín, *a deputy; a commissioner.*

Amír (pl. umara), *a nobleman; an 'Amir.'*

Amr (pl. umúr), *any business, matter, or affair.*

Amrúd, *guava* (fruit).

Ánah, $\frac{1}{16}$ *of a 'rúpi.'*

Áná-jána, *to come-and-go.*

Anannás, *a pine-apple.*

Anár, *a pomegranate.*

Andar, *within; inside.*

Andeshah, *anxiety; thought.*

Andha, *blind.*

Andhera (n. a.), *darkness; dark.*

Anḍa, *an egg.*

Angrez, *an Englishman.* -i, *English.*

Angúr, *a grape; grapes.*

Angúṭhi, *a ring.*

Anjír (f.), *a fig.*

Ánkh (f.), *an eye.*

Añ-paṛh, *illiterate.* (*See* paṛhna.)

Anṭa, *a ball.* -ghar, *a billiard-room; the club.*

Áp, *Your Honor.* Áp-hi-áp, *by,* or, *to oneself.* Ápas meṇ, *among themselves.*

Apna. *See page* 30.

Á-pahunchna, *to arrive; to have arrived.*

Aráf, *purgatory.*

Árá,ish, *ornamentation.*

Árám, *ease; comfort.* -kursi, *an easy-chair.*

Are! *hey, you!*

Aṛhái, *two and a half.*

Arkán-i-daulat, *the Pillars of the State,* i.e., *the nobles.*

Arsah, *a space of time.*

Arz (f.), *petition; request; what I want to say.* V.-k.

Árzu, *wish; desire.* A.-mand.

Asa, *a stick; cane.*

Asar, *impression.*

Asámi, *a tenant; a client; a debtor; a dependent; a prisoner.* Also, *agency; substitution.*

Ásán, *easy.* N. -i.

Asbáb, *goods and effects.*

Asl, *root; origin.* –i, *radical; real.* aslan, *by no means.* aslan-mutlakan, *by no manner of means.*

A'smán; *the sky.*

Astabal, *a stable.*

A'stín (f.), *a sleeve.*

A'tish, *or* átash (p.), *fire.* –bázi, *fireworks.* –khánah, *a fire-place; a grate.*

A'ṭa, *flour.*

Aṭakna; aṭak–jána, *to be stopped; to stick.*

Aṭṭhárah, *eighteen; a large number.*

Aṭkána; aṭká-d, *to stop; detain.*

Aulád, *offspring; descendants.*

Auliya, *the saints.*

Aur, *and; also; more.* –ek, *one more.* –do, *two more,* and so on. –kuchh, *some more; any more.* –kya, *what more? what else? what more do you want?*

Aurat, *a woman.*

Auwal, *the first; first.* –aṇ, *in the first place.*

A'wáz (f.), *the voice; a cry.*

A'yaḥ, *a female attendant.*

A',yindah (n. a.), *the future; future.*

A'zád, *free; solitary; independent.*

Azíz, *dear; precious.* –rakhna, *to value; esteem.*

A'zurdah, *grieved; sad.* N. –dagi.

B.

Ba (*a prefix*), *at; with; by,* e.g. –múјib, *according to.* –nisbat, *respecting; about.* (prep.) –nisbat is ki, *compared with this.* –sar, *at,* or *to a head,* or *end,* –sar ána, *to reach an end.* –sar–k., *to bring to an end; to pass time.* –taraf, *aside; apart.* –taur, *by way of; as being,* and so on.

Baad, *or* bád (ke.), *after; (of time.)*

Baaze, *several.*

Báb, *a chapter; heading.*

Bába, *a father; an old man.* In L. B., *a child.* –log, *the children* (L. B.)

Bábat (ki.), *concerning.*

Bachcha, *a child; a young specimen of any animal; e.g., a pup, a kitten, &c.*

Bachhra, *a calf.*

Bachna; bach-jána, *to be saved; to escape.* bachána; bachá-d., *to save; rescue; protect.*

Bad, *bad.* N.–i. –aḳl, *defective common-sense.* Adj. –aḳli. –bakh̲t, *unfortunate; wretched.* –bu (f.), *a bad smell.* –ḳismat, *bad luck; misfortune.* –nám, *evil repute; slander; abuse.* –nasíbi, *misfortune.* –shakl, *ill-formed; unshapely.* –súrat, *ugly.* –súrati, *ugliness.* –zát, *of low caste; villanous.* –záti, *villainy; vice.*

Bád (ke.). *See* 'Baad.'

Bád (p.), *wind.*

Badal, *exchange.* As prep. (ke.), *in exchange for.* –lena, *to take in exchange; to exchange.* –na, *to change; alter.* Badla, (also as prep. 'ke badle,') same as 'badal.'

Bádám, *almonds.*

Badan, *the body.*

Bádsháh (M.), *a king.* –i, *the royal state.*

Bá,en, *on*, or, *to the left hand.*

Bág (f.), *a bridle.*

Bágh, *a tiger.*

Bág̲h̲; bág̲h̲án; bág̲h̲íchah, *a garden.*

Bag̲h̲al, *the arm-pit; side; direction.*

Bahádur (*a title*), '*Bahádur.*' –i, *bravery; swagger.*

Báham, *together.*

Bahánah, *a pretence; pretext.*

Bahangi, *a pole on which burdens are carried.* –ḍák, *the parcel-post.*

Báhar (Adv.), *outside.* As prep. (ke.) *out.* –jána, *to go out.*

Bahár (f.), *spring; beauty.*

Bahin, *a sister.*

Bahlána, *to amuse; cheer one up.*

Bahna, *to flow.*

Bahra, *deaf.*

Bahut, *much; very; sufficient.* –achchha! *all right! very well!* –era, (a.) *very much*, or *very many.*

Bá,i, *a native lady; a dancing-girl.*

Bail, *an ox.* –gáṛi, *an ox-cart.*

Bá,is (ke), *by reason of.*

Baiṭhna, *to sit; sit down.*

Bája, *a musical instrument.* bajána, *to play on ditto.* bàjna, *to be played on ; to sound.* (*intr.*) *See page* 67.

Bajá-lána, *to perform ; carry through.*

Bak-bak, *chattering.* V –k.

Bakri, *a goat.*

Báḳi, *what remains over.*

Bakh̲íl, *a miser.* -i, *stinginess.*

Bakh̲shna, *to give a present.* N.–bakh̲shish.

Bál, *the hair.* –wal, *a barber.*

Baland. *See* 'Buland.'

Bál-bachche, *children.*

Báligh̲, *one who has attained majority.* -a (f.), *marriageable.*

Bálish, *a pillow.*

Bálisht, *a span.*

Balkih, *on the other hand ; nay ! nay, more !*

Ballam, *a spear.*

Bálṭi, *a tent-can, or bucket.*

Bálu, *sand.*

Bam, *the pole of a carriage.*

Banána, *to form ; construct.* baná-ḍálna, *to convert one thing into another.*

Banát, *broad-cloth.*

Band, *closed.* V.–k. band-o-bast (m.), *arrangements.*

Bandah ; bandi, a *servant ; dependant ; slave.* –dagi, *service ; attachment to a person.*

Bandar, *a monkey.*

Bándh, *a closing ; an embankment.* –na ; –d. ; –kar-d. *to close ; fasten ; tie.*

Bandúḳ (f.), *a musket.*

Báng (f.), *a noise ; shout.* V. –d.

Banna, *to be made.* baná-rahna, *to remain waiting.*

Ban-paṛna, *to succeed ; be able to do.*

Báṇs, *a bamboo.*

Bánṭna, *to divide.* bánṭ-lena, *to divide and take.*

Báp, *a father.* báp-báp ; *and* bápre-bápre ! *See page* 56.

Bar (p.), *on ; upon.* Much used in compos.

Baṛa, *great.* As adv., *very.* baṛa- sáḥib, *the head of a house, firm, &c.*

Barábar, *breast to breast ; equal ; 'all the same.'*

Bárah, *twelve.* –singa, *having twelve tines ; a stag.*

Barámdah, *a verandah.*

Bárán (p.). *rain.* –i kurti, *a great-coat.*

Baras, *a year.*
Barasna, *to rain.*
Bar-bád-d, *to squander.* –hona, *to be sacrificed* or *lost.*
Barchhi, *a spear.*
Báre (ke.), *in the matter of.*
Barf, *snow; ice.* –páni, *iced water.*
Barga, *a rafter.*
Barham; barham-darham, *confused; entangled.*
Bárík, *fine in texture.*
Bárish, *rain.*
Barkandáz, (*lightning throwing*), *a police constable; a guard; a watchman.*
Bar-khást, *removing; dismissing; adjourning,* V. –k.; kar-d.
Barsát, *rain.* –i kapre, *waterproofs.*
Bartan, *a plate; dish.*
Bárút, *gun-powder.*
Bar-wakt, *up to time; punctual.*
Barha,i, *a carpenter.*
Barhána (*trans.*) *to advance; increase.* barhna; barh-j. (*intr.*) *to advance; increase.*
Bas, *enough; 'that'll do.'*
Básan, *a dish; a bowl.*
Bastah, *a bundle.*
Basti, *a village.*
Bat; battakh, *a duck.*
Bát, *word; affair; news; business.* –chít, *conversation.*
Batána *or* batlána, *to point out; show.*
Batás (L. B.), *wind.*
Batti, *a wick;* also, *a light; candle; lamp.*
Bat-khara, *a weight for weighing with.*
Bater, *quail.*
Batwára, *dividing property into shares.*
Báwar, *belief; trust.* –chi, *a cook.* –chi-khánah, *a kitchen.*
Bayán, *a statement.* V.–k.
Báz, *a hawk.*
Báz (adv.), *back.* –rakhna, *to restrain; keep back.*
Bázár, *a market; bazaar.*
Báze (*See* Baaze), *several.*
Bázu, *the arm.*
Be (prefix), *without.* –fikr, *without care.* –gánah, *strange; foreign.* –ikhtiyár, *without power of control.* –hosh, *senseless;* also, *in a swoon.* –húdah, *absurd; ridiculous.* –ján, *lifeless.* –jigar (*without liver*), *cowardly.* –karár, *restless.*

-ḳiyám, *unstable.* -ḳusúr, *without blame.* -khabar, (*without news,*) *careless.* -nasíb, *destitute of good luck.* tarah, *beyond the proper manner; improperly.* -sabab, *without a reason.* -shakk, *beyond a doubt.* -sharm, *shameless.* -táb, *weak; faint.* -wuḳúf, *foolish; stupid.* N. -wuḳúfi.

Bechna, *to sell*

Bel, *the 'bel'-fruit.*

Bheṇṭ, *a meeting with a person.*

Besh, *more; sufficient.* -i, *excess; surplus.* -ḳimat, *high-priced.*

Beṭa, *a son.* Beṭi, *a daughter.*

Bhadda, *dull; stupid.*

Bhágna; bhág-jána; bhága-jána, *to flee; escape.*

Bhagwat, *the religious book of the Hindus.*

Bhá,i, *a brother; relation.*

Bhaiṇsa; bhaiṇs, *male* and *female buffalo.*

Bhál, *or* bhálu, *a bear.*

Bhala, *good.* bhalá,i, *goodness.*

Bhánja, *a sister's son.*

Bhánji, *a sister's daughter.*

Bhár, *a load.* -i, *heavy.*

Bhara; bhar-púr, *full.*

Bharna, *to fill.*

Bhát (m.), *cooked rice.*

Bhaṭṭi, *a still.*

Bhauṇkna, *to bark.*

Bhed, *secrecy.*

Bhejna; bhej-d., *to send.*

Bheṛa; bheṛi, *a ram, a sheep.* bheṛi ka gosht, *mutton.*

Bheṛiya, *a wolf.*

Bhi, *also* (*after a noun or other word.*)

Bhíga, *a measure of area, varying in different places.*

Bhínga, *wet.*

Bhor (f.), *the dawn.* -ko, *at dawn; early.*

Bhúkh (f.), *hunger.* A. -a.

Bhúl, *an error.* -na; -jána, *to commit an error; to forget.*

Bhúsi, *chaff.* (lit.)

Bhút, *a ghost; a demon.*

Bhuṭṭa, *Indian corn.*

Bíbi, *a native married lady;* also applied to *a female,—European, or of the mixed race,—working in the country,* e.g., *as keeper of a boarding-house.*

Bích (ke.), *between; among.*

Bicháli, *straw.*

Bichhána, *to spread.*

Bichhauna, *bedding.*

Bigaṛ-jána, *to go wrong; get out of order; become alienated.*

Bih (p.), *good.* –tar, *better,* –tarín (p.), *the best.* –tari, *improvement.*

Bihisht, *heaven.* –i, *a water-carrier.*

Bíj, *seed.*

Bijli, *lightning.* V.–hona.

Bikna, *to be sold.* (*See* bechna.)

Bi'l,[1] (*Arabic prefix,*) *in; on.* bi-l-faur (*on the heat*) *instantly.* bi-l-fel, *in fact; on the fact; instantly.* bi-l-kull, *on the whole; entirely.* bi-l-aks, *on the contrary.*

Bil, *the burrow of an animal.*

Bila (*Arabic prep.*), *without,* (*i.e. devoid of.*)

Billi, *a cat.*

Bímár, *sick.* N–i.

Biphe, *Thursday.*

Birni, *a wasp; a bee.*

Bís, *twenty.* –i, *a score.*

Bítjána (*intr.*), *to pass.* (of time.)

Biṭhána; biṭhá-d, *to seat.*

Bo,á,i, *sowing.*

Bodna, *to coax; wheedle.*

Bogla, *a crane.* (bird.)

Bojh; bojha, *a load.* bojhna, *to load.*

Bolna, *to say; speak; tell.*

Bona, *to sow.*

Bora, *a sack.*

Boṛa, *a bean.*

Bosah, *a kiss.* V. –d.

Brihispat, *Thursday.*

Bu (f.), *scent; smell.*

Budh, *Wednesday.*

Buḍḍha, *old.* Also, *an old man.* buḍḍhi; buṛhiya, *an old woman.* –pan, *old age.*

Bújhna, *to understand.* bujhána; bujhá-d, *to explain.* Also, *to extinguish a light.*

Bukhár, *fever.*

Bukhl, *stinginess.*

Buland, *lofty.*

Bulbul, *a 'bulbul.'* (bird.)

Bura, *bad.* burá,i (n.), *evil.* bura-jánna, *to consider bad.*

Búṛha, búṛhi, buṛhiya, *same as* 'buḍḍha,' &c.

Butá-d, *to extinguish a light.*

---

[1] Pronounce as plain 'bil.'

CH.

Chábi, *a key*.

Chábuk, *a whip*.

Chabútrah, *a platform; a 'chabútrah,'* generally of masonry: used in gardens for enjoying the air.

Chha-chhúndar, *a musk-rat*.

Chádar (f.), *a sheet; table cloth*, or *cover*.

Chá,e, *tea*. chá-dán, *a tea-caddy*. chá-pochi, *a tea pot*.

Cháha, *snipe*.

Chahárum, *the fourth part*.

Cháhiye. *See page* 18, *section* 20.

Cháhna, *to wish; desire*.

Chákar, *a servant*.

Chakki, *a wheel*.

Chál (f.), chál-chalan, *habit; behaviour*.

Chálák, *clever; too clever*.—i, *cleverness; sharpness; device*.

Chálán, *a despatch note;* -kar-d, *to despatch*.

Chalána, *to set in motion; despatch*.

Chális, *forty*.

Chalna; chalá-jána; chal-d., *to go; proceed; move off*. Also of affairs, *to prosper*.

Chammach; chamchah, *a spoon*.

Cham-gádaṛ, *a bat*. (animal.)

Chamṛa, *skin; leather*.

Chana, *gram*. (for horses.)

Chand, *several; a few*.

Chánd, *the moon*.

Changul, *a claw*.

Chapáti, *a thin flour-cake; a scone; a 'chapatty.'*

Chaprás, *a badge*.—i, *a messenger; a 'chaprassy.'*

Chár, *four*; oblique cases cháron.—pá,i, *a four poster; a bed*.

Chára, *a seedling*.

Charána (*trans.*), *to graze*.

Charkh, *a wheel*.

Charna (*inter.*), *to feed; graze*.

Chaṛhána; chaṛhá-d., *to cause to ascend*.

Chaṛhna; chaṛh-jána, *to ascend*.

Chashm, *an eye*.

Chashmah, *spectacles; a spring of water*.

Chaṭá,i, *a floor-mat*.

Chaṭán (f.), *a slab of stone*.

Cháṭna, *to lick; lick-up*.

Chaṭni, *'chutnee.'*

Chau, *four* (in compos.), chauk, *a square in a town.* chauki, *a watch-post; a chair.* chaukídár, *a watchman.* chaukona, *four-cornered.* chauras, *on all four sides.* chaurástah, *a place where four roads meet, &c., &c.*

Chaudah, *fourteen.* –roz, *a fortnight.*

Chaukaṭh (f.), *a door-frame.*

Chauṛa, *broad.* N. –chauṛá,i.

Chauṛi, *a fly-flicker.*

Chautha, *the fourth.*

Cháwal, *uncooked rice.*

Chela, *the disciple of a religious teacher.*

Cheṛa, *a domestic slave.*

Chhágul, *a goat.*

Chhaláng, *a leap.* V. –na.

Chhánna (*trans.*), *to pass through a strainer.*

Chhápa, *printed.* V. –k.

Chhappar (f.), *a roof; a thatch.*

Chharra, *shot.* (for a gun.)

Chhat, *a roof; house-covering; ceiling.*

Chháta, *an umbrella; a sunshade.*

Chháti, *the breast.*

Chháuni, *military lines; barracks.*

Chhed, *a hole.* V. –na.

Chhekna (*trans.*), *to stop; check.*

Chheṛ-chháṛ, *the act of annoying.*

Chhi-chhi (interj.), *nasty! ugly!*

Chhilka, *a shell; the rind; parings.*

Chhínkna, *to sneeze.*

Chhín-lena; *to snatch; rob; carry-off.*

Chhipkali, *a lizard.*

Chhiṛakna, *to sprinkle.*

Chhitáṇk, *a 'chiṭák,'* $\frac{1}{16}$ *of a 'ser.'*

Chhokra; chhokṛi, *a boy; a girl.*

Chhoṛna; chhoṛ-d.; chhoṛ-jána, *to let go; release; dismiss.*

Chhoṭa, *small.* N. –chhoṭá,i.

Chhúna, *to touch; to finger.*

Chhuri, *a knife.*

Chhúṭna; chhúṭ-jána, *to escape; slip through the fingers.*

Chihrah, *the face.*

Chikna, *oil ; grease ; oiled ; polished ; smooth.*

Chíl, *a kite.* (bird.)

Chillána, *to scream.*

Chilam, *the part of a native pipe* ('hukkah') *in which the fire and the tobacco are placed.*

Chingári, *a spark.*

Chingri, *shrimps.*

Chíni, *brown sugar.*

Chír ; chíra, *a cut ; incision ; dissection.* V. chírna.

Chirágh, *a native lamp.*

Chiriya, *a bird.*

Chíta, *a leopard.*

Chitthi, *a letter ; a note.*

Chíz (f.), *a thing of any kind.*

Chob, *a post ; a mace.* –dár, *a mace-bearer.*

Chonch (f.), *the bill* or *beak,* (of a bird.)

Chor, *a thief.* –ána ; *to steal.* N. –i.

Chúha, *a mouse.*

Chukna. *See page* 18, *sec.* 23.

Chúlha, *a fire-place ; a stove.*

Chumkárna, *to coax ; wheedle.*

Chúna, *lime.*

Chúna, *to leak ; drop.*

Chunánchih, *in such manner that ; accordingly ; thus ; for example.*

Chúnti, *an ant.*

Chup, *silent.* –rahna, *to remain* or *become silent.*

Chúr, *dust ; atoms ; crumbs.*

Chúra, *dry grain prepared for eating.*

Churána ; churá-lena, *to steal.*

Chútar, *the buttocks.*

Chúnkih, *in as much as.*

D.

Daba, *low ; depressed.* dabána ; dabá-d., *to depress ; lower ; crush down ; squeeze.*

Dádni, *an advance of money.*

Dafah, *a time. See page* 65, *sec.* 6.

Dafn, *burial.* V. –k.

Daftar ; –khánah, *an office-room.*

Dágh, *a spot ; a stain.*

Daghábázi, *deception ; fraud.*

Dahánah, *a* (horse's) *bit.*

Dahi (m.), *curd.*

Dáhine, *on,* or *to, the right-hand.*

Dahshat, *fear.*
Dá,i, *a wet-nurse.*
Dakhan, *the South.*
Dál, *a kind of pea; 'dál.'* -bhát, *cooked 'dál' and rice.*
Dálán, *a hall.*
Dalíl, *proof.*
Dam, *breath.* Also, *a moment.*
Dám, *price.*
Dámád, *a son-in-law.*
Dáman, *a skirt.* -i-koh, *the base of a mountain.*
Dána, *wise; learned.*
Dánah, *grain; a grain.*
Dánist, *wisdom; knowledge.*
Ḍanḍ *or* ḍanḍa, *a stick; a blow with a stick.*
Dánt, *or* dant, *a tooth.*
Dar (p.), *in,* as in dar-miyán, *in the midst.* dar-pesh, *in front, &c.*
Darak͟ht, *a tree.*
Darbán, *a gate* or *hall-porter.*
Darbár, *an audience-hall; an audience; a levee; a 'darbár.'*
Dár-chíni, *cinnamon.*
Dard, *pain.* -khána, *to feel pain.*
Darham-barham, *confused.*
Dari, *a native carpet; a 'durry.'*
Darya, *a river; the sea.*
Darj, *mention; entry.* V. -k.
Dark͟hást, *a petition; request.* V. -k.
Darma, *a mat.*
Darmáha, *monthly wages.*
Darobast, *the whole of anything.*
Darog͟h, *falsehood.* -go, *a liar.* -go,i, *falsehood.*
Dárog͟hah, *a superior police officer; a 'daroga.'*
Darwázah, *a door.*
Daryáft, *enquiry.* V. -k.
Darzan, *a needle.*
Darzi, *a tailor.*
Dáṛhi, *a beard.*
Das, *ten.*
Dast, *the hand; diarrhœa.* -ánah, *a glove.* -k͟hatt, *a signature.*
Dastár (f.), *a turban.*
Dastúr, *what is customary; the 'dastoor.'* -i, *customary perquisites; discount; 'dastoori.'*
Daulat, *wealth.* A. -mand.
Dauṛna, *to run.*
Dawa (f.), *medicine.*
Dawa, *or* dawi (m.) (*vulg.* dábi), *a claim; suit.* V.-k. dawídár, *a claimant; one who supports any side of a question.*

Dawat, *an invitation; a feast.*

Dawát, *an inkstand.* -ḳalam, *writing materials.*

Degchah, *or* degchi, *a copper-cooking pot.*

Dekhna, *to see; look at.*

Dena; de-d., *to give.*

Der, *or* deri (f.), *delay.* V. -k.

Des, *or* desh, *one's country.*

Devi, *a goddess.* devasthán, *a consecrated place.*

Dhamkána, *to snub; threaten.*

Dhamki, *snubbing; silencing.* V. -d.

Dhan, *wealth.* A. -i.

Dhán, *rice growing,* or *in the husk.*

Dharam, *virtue.* -avatár, *Incarnation of Virtue* (a form of address.)

Dhauṇki, *bellows.* dhauṇkna, *to use bellows.*

Dhobi; dhobin, *washerman; washerwoman.*

Dhona; dho-d., *to wash.*

Dhú,áṇ, *smoke.* -kash, *a steam-boat.*

Dhúp, *sun-shine; sun-heat.*

Dih(pl. dihát), *town; village; land appertaining thereto.*

Dikhána; dikhlána, *to show; to point out.*

Diḳḳ, *trouble; annoyance.* V. -k.

Dil, *the heart.*-gír, *sad; grieved.* -i-dosti, *the heart of friendship.* -kusha, *heart-expanding* (as wine.) -k͟húsh, *happy.* -o ján se, *with heart and soul.* -se, *heartily.*

Diléna; dilá-d.; dilwána; dilwá-d., *to cause to give.*

Dimág͟h, *the brain; conceit; pride.*

Din, *a day.* -bhar, *all day.*

Dín, *religion.* -dár, *religiously inclined.*

Ḍíṇgi, *a kind of boat; a* [' *dhingy.*'

Díp, *a lamp.* Also, *an island.*

Dí-roz (Persian), *yesterday.*

Dímak, *a white ant.*

Díwár, *or* díwál (f.), *a wall.*

Díwán, *a Minister of State.* -i, *relating to Civil Justice.*

Diyánat, *honesty; good-faith.* -dár, *conscientious.* N.-dári.

Do, *two.* Also, *imperat. of* dena, *to give.*

Dohar (f.), *double-cloth.*

Do-latti, *a kick.* V. -márna, *or* jháṛna.

Ḍol, *swinging.* -i, *a swinging article:* e.g., *a litter; a hanging meat-safe, &c.* V. -na.

Donoṇ, *both;* i.e., *two things or persons.*

Dost, *a friend.* -ánah, *friendly.* -i, *friendship.*

Doyum, *the second.*

Dozakh (f.), *hell.*

Du,a (f.), *benediction.*

Dúb-ghás (f.), *a grass much liked by horses.*

Dúdh, *milk.* -ya pathar, *an opal.*

Duhá,i (interj.), *justice! [mercy!*

Duhra, *or* dohra, *double.* V. duhrána.

Dúkán (f.), *a shop.* -dár, *a shop-keeper.* -dári, *shop-keeping.*

Dukh, *pain; distress.* A. [dukhit.

Duldul, *a hedge-hog.*

Dum, *a tail.* -chi, *a crupper-strap.*

Dunga, *a side-dish.*

Dunya (f.), *the world; the universe.* dunyávi, *relating to the world.*

Dúr (f.), *distance; distant.* dúr; dúr ho! *be off!* -andesh, *provident.* -andeshi, *foresight.* bín (f.), *a telescope; a 'glass.'* -k., *to remove; place at a distance.*

Durbal, *weak; infirm.*

Durust, *right; correct.* -k., *to arrange; put right.*

Dushman, *an enemy.* -i, *enmity.*

Dushwár, *difficult.*

Dúsra, *a second* (thing); *a different* (thing).

Ḍ.

Ḍák (f.), *a station,* e.g., *for relief of post-horses, or runners; the post* (letters, &c.) -chauki, *the changing-station.* -ghar, *the post-office.* -munshi, *the post-master.* -piyádah, *the postal runner.* -ṭikaṭ (F.), *a postage stamp.* -wála, *the postman.* -meṇ ḍálna, rakhna, *or* dena, *to post.*

Ḍáka, *an attack by robbers.* -paṛna, *to rob.*

Ḍakait, *a member of a gang of robbers; a 'dacoit.'* -i, *gang-robbery; 'dacoity.'*

Ḍál (f.), *a branch.* [‘*dolly.*’

Ḍáli, *a present of fruit; a*

Ḍálna; ḍál-d., *to throw down.*

Ḍánḍ, *an oar.*

Ḍank (f.), *a sting.* V. – márna.

Ḍar, *fear.* –na, *to fear.* –ána, *to frighten.*

Ḍáyan, *a witch.*

Ḍera, *a tent.* –k., *to encamp.*

Ḍeṛh, *one and a half; a good deal.*

Ḍhakna, *a lid; a cover.* Also as V. *to put on a cover.*

Ḍhál (f.), *a shield; a target; a slope.*

Ḍhela, *a clod.*

Ḍhíla, *slack.* Also, *remiss.*

Ḍhúṇḍna, *to search-for.*

Ḍubána; ḍubá-d., *to submerge; lower; depress.*

Ḍúbna; ḍúb-jána, *to sink; be drowned; be ruined.*

E.

Ek, *one; a* or *an.* –a-ek; -báragi, *suddenly.* –dam, *instantly; this instant.* –sáth, *together.*

Eṛi, *the heel.*

Ewaz, *a substitute; exchange.*

F.

Fá,idah, *profit; advantage.* A. –damand.

Fajr(f.), *dawn; early morning.*

Faḳat, *only; ‘finis.’*

Faḳír, *a Muham: mendicant.*

Fánús (f), *a lamp-shade.*

Farághat, *leisure; repose; prosperity.*

Farámosh, *forgetful.* N. –i. V. –k.

Fard (f.), *a sheet; a ply; a fold.*

Fareb, *deceit.* -d., *to deceive.* –khána, *to be deceived.*

Farḳ, *difference; consequence,* (as in the phrase, ‘ *it's of no consequence.*’)

Farmán; *an order; edict.* –a, *to issue ditto;* also used of any utterance by a person of rank.

Farsh, *a carpet.* farrásh, *one who attends to the carpets.*

Faryád (f.), *a complaint*, (e.g., in Court.)–i, *a complainant.*

Farzand, *a son.*

Fasád, *strife ; rebellion.*

Fasl (.) *crop.* (in the fields.)

Fatḥ (f.), *victory.*

Fatwa, *a decree of a judge.*

Fauj (f.), *an army.* –dár, *a commander.* –dári, *relating to Criminal Justice.*

Faulád, *steel.*

Fazúl, *excessive ; surplus.* –kharchi, *extravagance.*

Fi (Arabic), *each ; 'per ;' in.* fil-jumlah, *in the total.* fil-ḥál, *in the present ; immediately.* fil-ḥaḳíḳat, *in truth.* fil-wáḳe, *in reality ; as matters really stand, &c.*

Fidwi, *a servant ; a retainer.* –yat, *fidelity.*

Fihrist, *a list; an index.*

Fikr (f.), *thought ; anxiety.* A. –mand. V. –mandhona.

Fíl, *an elephant.* –bán, *an elephant-driver.*

Firishtah (pl. –tagán), *an Angel.*

Fírozah, *turquois.*

Fisánah, *a story; tale ; romance.*

Fulánah, *a certain one.*

Fursat, *leisure ; opportunity.*

G.

Gáchh, *a tree.*

Gaddi, *a cushion ; a throne.*

Gadha ; gadhi, *an ass* (male and female.)

Gáh, *time ; place.* Much used in compos. *e.g.*, 'shikárgáh,' *hunting ground.*

Gahra, *deep.* N. gahrá,i.

Gájar, *a carrot.* gajarah, *carrots.*

Gál, *the cheek.*

Gala, *the throat.* –band, *a neck-tie.*

Gáli, *abuse.* V. –d.

Gális, *braces.* (for pants.)

Gána, *to sing.*

Ganḍa, *four* (things), *looked on as a unit.*

Gandh (f.), *odour ; perfume.* gandah, *fetid.* gandi, *a certain badly-smelling insect, a 'gundy.'*

Gandak, *a rhinoceros.*

Ganj, *a mart.* (The 'gunge' of Anglo-Hind.)

Gánja, *hemp,* as used for intoxication. A decoction of this plant gives the drink known as 'bháng.'

Gánṭh, *a knot.* V. -baná-d.

Gánw, *a village.* ganwár; gánw-wála, *a villager.*

Gá,o, *or* gá,e, *a cow.* gá,o-sálah, *a cow-shed.*

Garaj, *thunder.* V. -na.

Gard (f.), *dust.* A. -a.

Gardan (f.), *the neck.*

Garm, *warm; hot.* N. -i.

Garh, *a fort; a steep place.*

Gári, *a carriage; a cart.* -bán, *a driver.*

Gárna, *to fix in the ground; to plant.*

Gaṭhri (*vulg.*, giṭhri,) *a bundle.*

Gawáh, *a witness.* -i, *evidence.*

Gaz, *a yard* (measure.); *a rod; a ramrod.*

Gehún, *wheat.*

Ghabrána, *to be confused; put out; puzzled.* Also *trans.*

Ghám, *sun-shine; sun-glare.*

Ghanṭa, *a bell; an hour.*

Ghá,o, *a sore.*

Ghar, *a house.* -ámi, *a thatcher.*

Ghara, *an earthen pot.*

Ghari, *about* 20 *minutes:* Also, *an English hour; a watch; a clock.*

Ghás (f.), *grass.*

Ghát, *a mountain-pass; steps, &c., down to a river; a ferry.* -wál, *a guardian of a pass.* -wála, *a ferry-man.*

Ghaṭi, *trade-loss.*

Gher, *all round.* -k., *to surround.*

Ghi (m.), *native butter.*

Ghisarna, *to creep; crawl.*

Ghoṛa, *a horse.* ghoṛi, *a mare.*

Ghulna, *to melt* (*intr.*) ghulána, *to melt* (*trans.*)

Ghúnṭ, *a gulp; draft.* V. -na.

Ghusna, *to enter.*

Gídaṛ, *a jackal.*

Gidh, *a vulture.*

Gilehri, *a squirrel.*

Girán, *important; weighty.*

Girána; girá-d, *to cause to fall; to throw down.*

Gird (ke), *around; round.*

Giriftár, *or* giriftah. *captive; arrested.* -hona, *to be in arrest.* -k., *to arrest.*

Girja, *a church*, otherwise 'grija;' probably Portuguese.

Girna; gir-paṛna, *to fall.*

Gít, *a song.*

Go,ála, *a cow-herd; the milkman.*

Gobar, *cow-dung.* Much used as fuel.

God; godi, *the lap.*

Go,indah, *a spy; informer.*

Gojar, *a centipede.*

Go-kih, *let it be said that; given that; granted; even though.*

Gol, *round.* gola,[1] *a granary; a store-house.* goli, *a ball; a bullet.* –mirch (*round*, i.e.) *black pepper.*

Gond, *gum.*

Gor, *a grave.* –istán, *a burial-ground.*

Gora, *fair-complexioned; a European of inferior rank; a European soldier.* gore-log, *Europeans.* goroṇ ki palṭan, *a European regiment.*

Gor-khar (an animal, probably) *the wild-ass.*

Gosh, *an ear* (of the body.)

Goshah, *a corner.*

Gosht, *flesh.*

Grám, *a village.* (L B.)

Gúda, *the marrow.*

Gúdaṛ, *rags; rubbish.*

Guḍḍi, *a (boy's) kite.*

Guft-o-gu (f.), *conversation.*

Guhár (f.), *tumult; noise; outbreak.* –i, *a rioter.*

Gul, *a rose,* –áb, *rose-water.* –áb-phúl, *a rose-bush,* or *rose flowers.* –istán, *a place where roses are cultivated.* Also, *the name of a celebrated Persian book.* –zár, *a garden of roses.* (lit. or fig.)

Gulu, *same as 'gala.'*

Gum, *lost.* –k., *to lose.* –ho-jána, *to be lost.* –nám, *nameless; obscure; lost to fame.*

Gumán, *guess; fancy.* V. –k.

Gumáshtah, *a steward.*[2]

Gumbaz, *a dome.*

Gunáh, *a fault; sin.* –gár, *a transgressor.* –gári, *sinful doing.*

Gúṇga, *silent; dumb.*

---

[1] Generally built in a circular form.

[2] Not applicable to a *ship* steward.

Guroh (f.), *a crowd.*

Guru, *a Hindu teacher.*

Gùstákh, *impudent.* N. -i.

Guzárna (*trans.*), *to pass ; convey.* guzarna ; guzar-jána (*intr.*), *to pass ; pass-over.* guzar-gháṭ, *a ferry.*

Guzashtah, *past ; last* (as in 'last year.')

Guzrán (f.), *mode* or *means of livelihood.*

Gh.

Ghaflat, *negligence.*

Gháib, *out of sight ; vanished.*

Ghair, *foreign ; strange ; different.* As a prefix, *wanting, deficient.* e.g., ghair-ḥázir, *absent.* ghair-mumkin, *impossible.*

Ghalat, *error ; oversight.*

Ghalíchah, *a carpet.*

Ghallah, *corn ; produce.*

Ghamm, *sorrow.* A. -gín.

Gharaz (f.), *design ; aim ; object.* As adv., *in short.*

Gharíb, *poor ; humble ; tame.* -log, *the poor.* -parwar, *Nourisher of the Poor !* (a form of address.)

Gházi, *a slayer of an infidel.*

Ghiláf, *covering-slip,* e.g., *a 'case' for a pillow.*

Ghiza, *ordinary diet.*

Ghol, *or* ghúl, *a crowd ; pressing.* -mál (L. B.), *confusion ; a row.*

Ghulám, *a servant ; a slave.*

Ghulel, *a bow from which pellets are shot ; a 'catapult.'*

Ghurúr, *pride.*

Ghussah, *grief ; anger.*

Ghusse, *in a rage.*

Ghusl (f.), *a bath.* -khánah, *a bath-room.* Also, *the W. C.*-k., *to bathe.*

H. (a light Aspirate.)

Haḍḍi, *a bone.*

Há,e, *alas !*

Haftah, *a week.*

Ḥaizah, *cholera.*

Hal, *or* hál, *a plough.* V. -jotna.

Halákat, *death.*

Haldi, *turmeric.*

Hál-kamra, *a drawing-room.*

Halka, *light* (not heavy.)

Halkah, *an area of jurisdiction.*

Ham, *we ; us.* Also, *together;* Much used in compos. *e.g.*, ham-ráh, *a fellow-traveller.* ham-ráhi, *travelling together.* ham-sáyah (*same shade*); *neighbourly; friendly.*

Hameshah, *always.*

Háṇ, *yes.*

Hangámah, *a riot.*

Háṇkna, *to drive.*

Háṇṛi, *a pot.* –bartan, *cooking utensils.*

Háṇs, *a swan.*

Haṇsi, *laughter.* haṇsna, *to laugh.*

Haṇsli, *an ornamental hoop for the neck.*

Hanoz, *yet ; still* (of time.)

Har, *each ; every.* –ek, *each one ; everyone.* –kárah, *a man of all work ; a messenger.*

Haran, *or* hiran, *a stag ; a deer.*

Harchand, *although.*

Hárna, *to lose* (e.g. a bet.) hará-d., *to lose to one.*

Háth, *the hand; a cubit.* –ána *to reach.* –ḍálna, *to seize.*

Hatheli, *the palm of the hand.*

Háthi, *an elephant.*

Hatiyár, *tools ; weapons.*

Háṭ, a fair.

Haṭána ; haṭá-d., *to drive back ; repel.*

Haṭna ; haṭ-jána, *to clear out of one's way ; to step aside.*

Hawa (f.), *the air.* –khána, *to take the air ; go a walk, drive, &c.*

Hazár, *a thousand.*

Hezam, *firewood.*

Hi (a particle of emphasis, often untranslateable), *very ; this very...; just this, &c.*

Hibah, *a formal gift* or *grant.*

Hiba-námah, *a deed of ditto.*

Hijrah, *the flight of Muḥammad to Madina, A.D. 622, whence begins the Muḥam : era.*

Hilna, *to shake* (*intr*) ; hilána ; hilá-d. (*trans.*)

Hindu, *a dark-skinned man.* –stán, *Upper India.*-stáni *relating to Hindu matters,* e.g., *language,*

Híra, *a diamond.*

Hona, *to be; to occur; to take place.* ho-jána, *to become.*

Hosh, *sense; 'common sense.'* -yár, *careful; prudent; skilled.* N. -yári.

Hunar, *skill.* A. -mand.

Hunḍi, *a native Bill of Exchange, a 'hundee.'*

Ḥ. (a strong Aspirate.)

Ḥadd, *a boundary.*

Ḥaiwán, *an animal.*

Ḥajjám, *a barber.*

Ḥájat, *want; necessity; restraint.*

Ḥáji, *one who has made the Pilgrimage to Mecca.*

Ḥajj, *the pilgrimage to Mecca.*

Ḥákim, *a ruler; a judge.*

Ḥakím, *a native physician; a wise man.*

Ḥakír, *base; contemptible.* -jánna, *or* samajhna, *to hold in contempt; despise.*

Ḥaḳḳ, *one's rights.* ḥaḳíḳat, *the very truth.* ḥaḳíḳi, *really true.* ḥaḳíḳi bhá,i, &c., *a full brother, &c.*

Ḥál, (pl. Ḥálát,) *state; condition; facts of the case.* ḥálan, *presently.*

Ḥalaf, *an oath.* (e.g., in Court.) ḥalfan, *on oath.*

Ḥalaḳ, *the throat.*

Ḥalál, *according to law; lawful.* -k., *to kill according to prescribed form* (as by cutting the throat); *to cut the throat.*

Ḥalwá,i, *a sweet-meat seller.*

Ḥaml,[1] *a burden.* ḥammál,[1] *a porter.* ḥámilah, *pregnant.*

Ḥamlah, *an attack; onset.*

Ḥarakat, *a movement,* e.g., *of the body.*

Ḥaram, *or* ḥarám, *unlawful; forbidden.* -zádah, *base-born; a scoundrel.*

Ḥarf, *a letter.* (*of the Alphabet.*)

Ḥaríf, *an opponent.*

Ḥásil, *acquiring; accomplishment of an object; the 'moral' of a story.* V. -k.

---

[1] Not used in Lower Bengal.

Ḥasrat, *desire ; regret ; grief.*
Ḥawálah, *charge ; responsibility ; custody.*
Ḥaya (f.), *modesty ; shame.*
Ḥázir, *present.* –i, *presence ; the family 'presence' at breakfast ; breakfast*[1]
Ḥazrat, *dignity ;* also *as a title of high respect.* –ísa, *Jesus.*
Ḥikáyat, *history ; story ; narration.* V. –k.
Ḥikmat, *wisdom ; skill ; device.*
Ḥílah, *a stratagem ; a trick.*
Ḥisáb, *an account in figures.*
Ḥissah, *one's share ; a portion.* –dár, *a partner.*
Ḥudúd, *boundaries* (pl. of ḥadd.)
Ḥukm, *an order.* ḥukúmat, *sovereignty ; power.*
Ḥuḳḳah, *a native pipe ; a 'hookah.'*
Ḥuḳúḳ, *rights.* (pl. of ḥaḳḳ.)
Ḥurúf, *letters of the Alphabet.* (pl. of ḥarf.)
Ḥuzúr, *presence ; appearance ; court ; Your Honour !*

I.

Iba (f.), *a cloak.*
Ibárat, *composition ; writing.*
Iblís, *the devil.*
Ibtida, *the beginning.*
Íd, *a religious festival ; especially the festival in honour of Abraham sacrificing his son Ishmáil.*
Iflás, *poverty.*
Ihtimám (f.), *diligence ; necessary application.*
Iḥtirám, *the act of showing respect.*
Iḥtiráz, *abstinence ; control of the passions.*
Iḥsán, *benevolence.* –mandi, *gratitude.*
Ijárah, *a lease ; a farm.*
Ijázat, *permission ; favour.*
Ikhaṭṭa, *together.*
Iḳbál, *good fortune ; favour.*
Iḳlím, *clime ; country.*
Iḳrár, *agreement ; confession.*
Ikhtiláf, *discrepancy.* (pl. -át)
Ikhtiyár, *power ; authority ; option.*
Iláhi, *divine.*

---

[1] Called 'Náshta' in Western India.

Iltifát, *friendliness.*

Iltimás (f.), *petitioning; beseeching.*

Imám, *a religious Muham: leader.*

Imárat, *a public building.*

Imli, *tamarind.*

Im-roz (Persian), *to-day.*

Im sál (Persian), *this year.*

Imtiḥán, *an examination.*

Inám, *a present; a favour.*

Indára, *a large well.*

Indúr, *a rat.*

Inglistán, *England.*

Insáf, *justice.*

Insán, *a human being.* –iyat, *humanity,* i.e., *the human race.*

I'ṇṭ (f.), *a brick.*

Intiḳál, *transport; change; death.*

Intizám, *good arrangement; management.*

Irádah, *intention; purpose.*

Iráf, *purgatory.*

Is, *inflected form of* yih. *See page* 30.

Isfanj, *a sponge.*

Islám, *the Muham: religion.* –i, *appertaining to ditto.*

Is-liye, *on this account.*

Ism, *a name.* (pl. asámi, q.v.)

Istabal, *a stable.*

Istífa, *full performance; resigning service; abandonment.*

Istimál, *use.* V. –k.

Istibágh, *baptism.*

Istimrári, *permanent; fixed.* –band-o-bast, *the Permanent Settlement of Bengal.*

Istri, a *smoothing iron.*

Is-waḳt, *at this time; now.*

Isbárah, *a hint; a signal.*

Ishtihár, *a public advertisement.*

Ishwar (H.), *God.*

Itiráz, *displeasure; refusal.*

Itna, *this much.* itne meṇ, *in the meantime.*

Itr, *essence.* (Anglicé, '*otto.*')

Itibár; itimád, *confidence; belief in one.* V. –k.

Ittifáḳ, *agreement; equality; union; chance.* –hona, *to happen; to be in agreement.* –k., *to bring into agreement; to agree with.* –an, *by chance; it so happened that.*

Ittila (f.), *announcement; publication of news; an 'information' lodged before a public officer.*

Itwár, *Sunday.*

Izhár, *deposition; statement.*

Izzat, *honour; respect due to one; estimation in which one is held.*

J.

Jab, *when.* –tak, *or* talak, *till when.* *See page* 104.

Jabr, *oppression.* Adv. jabran.

Jabṛa, *the jaw.*

Jádu, *conjuring ; a 'ghost.'*

Já-e-phal, *nutmeg.*

Jagah (f.), *a place ; room.*

Jagána ; jagá-d. (*trans.*), *to awaken.*

Jágna (*intr.*), *to waken.* jágta, *awake.*

Jahán, *wherever.* *See page* 104 ; *the universe.* –dídah. (*having seen the world*) ; *experienced.*

Jahannam (f.), *Hell.*

Jáhil, *ignorant.* N. –i.

Jai, *victory.*

Ja,i, *oats.*

Já,iz, *just ; proper ; fair.*

Jal, *water.*

Jál, *a net.*

Jál, *forged.*

Jála, *a cobweb.*

Jalána ; jalá-d., *to set on fire.*

Jald, *quickly.* –i, *speed.*

Jalna, *to be on fire.*

Jamá,at, *an assembly.*

Jámah, *cloth.* Much used in compos. *e.g.*, mom-jámah, *wax-cloth.*

Jama, *a collection ; a gathering ; the total of an account.* –bandi, *the rent-roll of an estate.* –kharch, *a credit and debit account.* –dár, *a native officer of army or police ; a head man of any body,* e.g., *coolies.* –wásil-báki, *a statement of claims collections and arrears.*

Jamna ; jam-jána, *to congeal.*

Ján, *life ; soul.* –kani, *anguish of soul.* –se márna, *to kill.* –nisár, *self-sacrificing.* –war, *an animal.*

Jána, *to go ; proceed.* jáne-dena, *to allow to go.*

Janáb ; –áli, *titles of respect.* as '*Your Worship.*'

Janam, *birth.* –din, *birth-day.*

Jánch, *testing; trying.* V. –na.

Jang (f.), *war.*

Jangal, *forest ; high-grass land ; scrub ; 'jungle.'* A. jangli, *waste ; wild ; savage ; 'jungly.'*

Jángh, *the thigh.* –ia, *short (wearing) drawers.*

Jánna, *to know.* ján-bújh-kar, *knowingly ; intentionally.*

Jannat, *Paradise.*

Jánib (f.), *side ; part.* —dár, *a partizan.* —dári, *taking one's side.*

Janúb, *the South.*

Jaṛ, *a root ; roots.*

Jaráhat, *a wound.*

Jarímánah, *or* jurmánah, *a fine.* V.—lena.

Jáṛa, *the cold ; the cold weather.*

Jásús, *a spy.* –i, *spying.*

Jauhar, *a gem.* –*i, a jeweller.*

Jaun. *See page* 104.

Jauz, *a nut*

Jawán, *young, a youth.* –i, [*youth.*

Jazírah, *an island.*

Jel-khánah, *a jail.* (half E.)

Jhagṛa, *a quarrel.* V. jhagaṛna ; –k.

Jhálar, *a fringe.*

Jhanḍa, *a flag.*

Jháṛ, ; jháṛi, *underwood.*

Jháṛan, *a duster.*

Jháṛna, *to sweep ; dust.*

Jháṛu, *a broom.*

Jhaṭ-paṭ (adv.), *this instant.*

Jhíl, *a shallow lake ; a marsh.*

Jhilmili, *the venetians.*

Jhoṇk, *a push.* V.–jhoṇkna ; jhoṇk-d.

Jhopṛi, *a cottage.*

Jhukna ; jhuk-janá, *to be* or *become awry* or *crooked.*

Jhúl, *a covering for an animal ; horse-cloth, &c.*

Jhulána (*trans.*), *to swing.* jhúlna (*intr.*), *to swing.* jhúla-jhúli, *swinging ; see-saw.*

Jhúṭh, *or* júṭha, *false ; untrue.* jhúṭh, *falsehood.*

Ji, *life ; soul ; spirit.*

Ji, *or* Ji háṇ, *yes.*

Jíbh (f.), *the tongue.*

Jidhar. *See page* 104.

Jigar, *the vitals ; the liver.*

Jihád, *a Muham : religious war.*

Jihat (ki.), *on accouut of.*

Jin, *oblique case, pl. of* jò. *See page* 33.

Jína, *to live ; be alive.*

Jins, *kinds ; sorts ; goods ; merchandise.*

Jis, *oblique case, sing. of* jo. *See page* 33.

Js-ḳadar. *See page* 104. jis-taraf, *in whatever direction.* jis-taraḥ, *in whatever manner.* jis-waḳt. *See page* 104.

Jism, *the body.*

Jítna, *to win.*

Jitna. *See page* 104.

Jo, jo ko,i, jo-kuchh. *See page* 33.

Jo, *if.*

Jo,ár, *Indian corn.*

Jogi ; jogin, *a Hindu asectic,* (*male and female.*)

Joṇ, *when ; as soon as.*

Joṇk, *a leech.*

Joru, *a wife.*

Joṛi, *a pair.* –gaṛi, *the carriage and pair.*

Jotna, *to yoke ; to plough.*

Joṭ, *one thing of a pair ; a 'match ;' harness 'traces.'*

Jú,a, *a yoke ; a die ; dice ; gambling.* –khelna, *to gamble.*

Juba, *young.* jub-ráj, *a prince.*

Juda. *separate.* V. –k.

Júláhah, *a weaver.*

Jumah, *Friday.*

Jurm, *a crime ; offence.*

Just-o-ju (f.), *search.* V. –k.

Júta ; júti, *a shoe ; shoes.*

Juz, *a portion of any thing.*

K.

Ka. *See page* 5.

Kab, *when ?*

Kabáb. *sliced meat roasted on skewers,* –i, *suitable for roasting.*

Kabhi, *ever,* –kabhi, *now and then* .-nahíṇ, *never.*

Kachahri, *an office ; a court-house.*

Kachhúa, *a tortoise.*

Ka i, *some ; several.*

Kaffárat, *repentance ; atonement.*

Káfi, *enough ;* kifáyat, *sufficiency.*

Kaghaz, *paper.*

Kahna, *to say ; speak ; tell.*

Kahíṇ, *somewhere ; anywhere ; anyhow.* As in such phrases as 'it were *anyhow* better, &c.'

Kae, *how many.?*

Kaisa, *what sort of a ? what like ? how ?* –hi, *however.* As in such phrases as '*however difficult.*'

Kaj, *crooked.*

Kal, *yesterday ; to-morrow.*

Kal, *an engine ; a machine.*

Kála, *black.* kal-yug,' *the black age ; i.e., the present age of the world.* –páni, *the open sea.*

Kalá,i, *a kind of vetch.*

Kaleja, *liver. (organ of body).*

Kam, *deficient.* Much used in compos. e.g., kam-aḳl, *of deficient sense.* kam-aḳli, *want of sense.* kam-bakht, *unfortunate.* kam-sinn, *of tender age.* kam-arz, *of narrow breadth.* –i, *deficiency; failure.* kam-kar-dena, *to lessen.*

Kám, *business; use; wish; desire* –ána, *to be serviceable.* –yáb, *prosperous.* N.-yábi.

Kamál, *perfection.*

Kamán, *an (archer's) bow.* –dár, *an archer.*

Kamar, *the waist.* -band, *a waist-cloth.*

Kámil, *perfect.*

Kamínah, *base; low.*

Kammal; kamli, *a blanket.*

Kamra; kamara, *a room.*

Kán, *the ear.*

Kána, *blind of one eye.*

Kanghi, *a comb.*

Káṇṭa, *a thorn; a spur; a fork.*

Káṇdha, *the shoulder.*

Kapás, *undressed cotton.*

Kapṛa, *cloth.* kapṛe, *clothes.*

Kár, *work; business.* kár-bár, *trade; trafficking.* –khánah, *a place of business.* –igar, *a workman.*

Kar-dekhlána, *to make plain; demonstrate.*

Kári-bhát, *curry and rice.*

Karna, *to do; make; effect; accomplish.*

Karoṛ, *ten millions.*

Kaṛwa, *strong (as liquors tea, &c.)*

Kasna, *to tighten; pull.*

Kásht, *one's cultivation.* -kár, *a cultivator.*

Kátib, *a scribe; a writer.*

Káṭ, *a cut.* –na; –ḍálna, *to cut.* kaṭna, *to be cut.*

Kaṭhal, *the jack-fruit.*

Kaṭora, *a brass cup.*

Kaṭṭha, *a 'cottah.' (land measure.)*

Kauwa, *a crow.*

Ke. *See page* 5.

Kela, *plantains.*

Khaiṇchna, *or* khíṇchna *or* khíchna; *to draw* (burden or picture); *to pull.*

Khajúr, *dates;* –gáchh, *the date-palm.*

Khambha, *a post; a pillar*

Kháṇa, *food; dinner.* Also, V. *to eat.* Also, *to suffer; undergo.*

Kháṇsna, *to cough.* kháṇsi, *coughing; a cough.*

Khári-miṭṭi, *chalk*

Kharkhara, *rough; a curry-comb.*

Khaṛa, *erect; standing.* -hona, *to be,* or *become standing.* -karna, *to set up; make straight,* -rahna, *to stand; remain standing; wait; stop (intr.)*

Khát, *a pit; the gullet.*

Khata (f.), *fault; defect.*

Kháta-bahi, *an account book.*

Kháṭ; khaṭiya, *a wooden bed-frame.*

Khaṭmal, *a bug.*

Khel, *play.* -gáh, *play-ground.* -áṛi, *frolics.* -na, *to play.*

Khet, *a field.* -i, *cultivation.* kheti karna, *to cultivate.*

Khilána, *to feed. (trans.)*

Khiṛki, *a window.*

Khodna, *to dig.*

Khoj, *search.* khojna; khoj-karna, *to search for.*

Kholna; khol-d. *to open; unfasten; untie.* khol-bandi, *taking off a horse's shoes, paring the hoofs; and putting the shoes on again.*

Khona, *to lose.* kho-jána, *to be lost; 'go a missing.'*

Khujlána, *to itch; to scratch.*

Khula, *open; fair (as* weather.) -din, *a fine day.* khulna; khul-jana, *to be* or *become open; to clear.* (e.g., *after rain.*)

Khúṇṭi, *a peg.* (e.g., *for a tent-rope.*)

Ki. *See pages 5 and 22.*

Kih, *that (of narration).* Also, *as relative pronoun, often preceded by* 'jo.' 'kih na,' *or not.*

Kíchaṛ, *mud.*

Kidhar, *whither?*

Kíl, *a plug; peg; pin; bolt.*

Kínah, *spite; malice* Adj. kínawár.

Kinárah, *river-bank; sea-shore; edge.*

Kiráni, *a native clerk.*

Kíṛa, *a worm; insect; maggot.*

Kisán, *a cultivator.*

Kishmish, *raisins.*

Kishti, *a boat; vessel; tray.*

Kismis (E.), *Christmas.*

Kitáb (f.), *a book.*

Kitna, *how many? how much?*

Kiwáṛ (m.), *a door ; door-way.*

Kiya-karna, *to be in the habit of doing a thing ; to keep on doing it.*

Ko. *See pages* 5 *and* 7.

Kobi, *cabbage.*

Kochbán, *a coachman.*

Koh, *a Mountain.* –i-núr, *The Mountain of Light.*

Kohásah, *fog ; mist.*

Ko,i. *See page* 38. ko,i, na ko,i, *some one or other.* ko,i, nahíṇ, *no one.* ko,i hai, *is there any one there ?* (used in India instead of a bell.)

Ko,ilah, *charcoal ; coals.*

Kolu, *an oilman ; the caste of an oilman.*

Kona, *a corner* or *angle.*

Kori, *or* kúri, *a score.* (*i.e.*, 20.)

Koṛa, *a native whip.*

Kos, *a distance of about* 2 *miles.*

Koshish, *an attempt.* V. –k.

Kotáh, *short in stature, &c.*

Kotwál, *a chief police officer of city, town, or market.*

Koṭhi, *or* kúṭhi, *a masonry house.*

Kú,a, *a well.*

Kubṛa, *hump-backed.*

Kúch, *a march.* V. –k.

Kúchah, *a lane.*

Kuchh. *See page* 38. kuchh se kuchh, *from this thing to that.* kuchh na kuchh, *some little ; somewhat.*

Kudál, *or* kudáli, *a spade.*

Kúd, *a leap.* V. –na.

Kuftah, *rissole.*

Kull (adj.), *the whole ; all the.* –yat, *entirely.*

Kulchah, *a cake.*

Kumhár, *a potter.*

Kumhír, *an alligator.*

Kunji, *a key.*

Kuṇwar, *a prince.*

Kurah, *a globe ; sphere.* –i-k͟hák, *the terrestrial globe.*

Kúṛa, *rubbish.*

Kuredna, *to scratch.* kured-rahna, *to continue scratching.*

Kursi, *a chair.*

Kurti, *a coat.*

Kutta, *a dog.* kutiya, *a pup.*

Kya. *See page* 33. –bát, *See page* 56.

Kyúṇ, *why ? wherefore ?*–kih, *because.* –kar, *how ?* kyúṇ na ho, *why not ?*

Ḳ.

Ḳabálah, *a deed of sale.*

Ḳábil, *capable ; competent.* N. –íyat.

Ḳabúl or ḳubúl, *consent.* –iyat, *a document expressing consent ; a counterpart.* ḳabúl karna, *to consent.*

Ḳabzah, *grip ; power.*

Ḳadam, *a step ; pace.* V. –k.

Ḳadar, *worth.* –karna, *to value ; appreciate.*

Ḳadd, *stature.*

Ḳadím, *ancient.*

Ḳafilah, *a caravan.*

Ḳaḥwah, *coffee.*

Ḳai, *vomiting.*

Ḳaid, *fetters ; imprisonment.* –karna, *to imprison.* –i, *a prisoner.*

Ḳá,im, *erect ; firm ; stable.*

Ḳaisar, *an Emperor ; an Empress.* –i-Hind. *The Empress of India.*

Ḳainchi, *scissors.*

Ḳala,i, *tin ; the tinning of cooking vessels, &c.*

Ḳalam, *a reed ; a pen.* –tarásh, *a pen-knife.*

Ḳamís (f.), *a shirt ; a chemise.*

Ḳarár, *rest ; stability.* –i, *firm ; the firm land.* –dád, *a deed of settlement ; of a dispute,* or other matter.

Ḳaríb, *about.* ḳaríb tha kih, &c., *it was on the point of, &c.* (e.g., *being settled.*)

Ḳarz, or ḳarzah, *a loan ; a debt.* ḳarz-dár, *one in debt.*

Ḳasam (f.), *an oath.* (e.g., *in Courts*) –khána, *to take the oath.*

Ḳatrah, *a drop.*

Ḳatl, *killing.* V. –k. –amd, *wilful murder.* –insán, *homicide.*

Ḳaul-o-ḳarár, *agreement ; bargain ; stipulations.*

Ḳaum, *a tribe ; sect ; family ; brotherhood.*

Ḳawi, *strong ; solid.*

Ḳaza, *fate ; destiny ; death.*

Ḳázi, *a Muḥam : Judge.*

Ḳiblah, *the sacred point in Mecca, to which Muḥam : turn when praying.*

Ḳilah, *a fort.*

Ḳímat, *price.* –i, *valuable.*

Ḳaná,at, *contentment.*

Ḳism, *kind ; sort.*

Ḳismat, *fate ; destiny ; what falls to your lot,* or *share.*

Ḳissah, *a story ; a tale.*

Ḳist, *an instalment; 'Quarter-day.'* -bandi, *a settlement for periodical payments.*

Ḳiyámat, *the Resurrection.*

Ḳiyás, *thought; guess; 'idea.'* V. -k.

Ḳiyási, *conjectural.*

Kristán (E.), *a Christian.*

Ḳudrat, *omnipotence.*

Ḳufl, *a lock.* (e.g., *of a box.*)

Ḳuli, *a labourer; a 'coolie.'*

Ḳurah, *lots.* -ḍálna, *to cast lots.*

Ḳurán, *the religious book of the Muḥam:*

Ḳusúr, *a fault.*

Ḳúwat, *power; authority.*

Kh.

Khabar (f.), *news;* -dár, *careful; take care?* -dári, *care; caution.*

Khachchar, *a mule.*

Khafa, *angry; 'huffed.'* N. -gi.

Khafíf, *light; trivial.*

Khair, *well. See page* 56. *Note* 1. -iyat, *welfare.*

Khairát, *deeds of charity.*

Khák (f.), *earth; dust.*

Khalal, *interruption; noise.*

Khalás, *release; freedom, free.* V. -k. -hona.

Khalási, *a general out-door servant, who attends to tents, &c., a 'Klashy.'*

Kháli, *empty.* Adv. *only.*

Khalífah, *a fencing master; a prince; a 'caliph.'*

Khámosh, *silent.* N. -i.

Khán (*a title*), *Khan.* Also, Khán Bahádur. khán-sámán (*lord of your property,* i.e.), *the butler.*

Khánah, *a room; a place where work is done; or things are kept,* e.g., lohár-khánah, *a black-smith's shop.* murghi-khánah, *a hen-house.* Much used as last word in compos.

Khándán, *a family; a household.*

Khár, *a thorn.*

Kharáb, *bad.* N. -i.

Kharásh, *scraping; scratching; a scratch.* V. -na.

Kharbúzah, *a melon.*

Kharch, *expenditure.*

Kharíf, (f.), *autumn; the second harvest.*

Kharíd, *purchasing*-farokht, *buying and selling.*

Khárij, *excluded; cut off.* -karna, *to exclude, &c.* -hona, *to be excluded, &c.*

Kharítah, *a purse; a bag; the covering of a letter sent in ceremonious style;* hence, *the letter itself.*

Khar-khara, *snoring.* V. -na.

Khasam, *a husband.*

Khas-khas, *a scented grass, used —wetted—for door-screens.*

Kháss, *pure; noble; reserved to one's self.* -kamra, *a private sitting-room.* -mahál, *land reserved by Government.* -o-ám, *the 'classes and the masses.'*

Khata, *fault; defect.*

Khatam, *the end.* V. -karna, (*trans.*) -hona, (*intr.*)

Khátir (f.), *the heart; the soul.* -jama, *peace of mind.* khátir-jama rakhna, *to preserve peace of mind; to feel assured.*

Khatt, *a letter; a note.* Plur., Khutút.

Khátún (M.), *a female title.*

Khauf, *fear; danger.*

Khazánah, *a treasure-house; treasure; applied also to water stored for irrigation.* khazánchi, *a treasurer.*

Khidmat, *service.* -gár, *a servant, especially a table-servant.*

Khilál, *a tooth-pick.*

Khilat, *a dress of honor.*

Khímah, *a tent.* -gáh, *encamping-ground.*

Khiráj, *tribute; revenue.* -lagána, *to tax.*

Khiyál, '*idea;*' *notion; recollection; thought.* V.-k. *See page* 110. *Note* 2.

Khúb, *good; excellent. Also as interj.* -súrat, *beautiful.* -súrati, *beauty.*

Khud, *self; by,* or *of him, her, its, self;* or *themselves.* -gharaz, *self-seeking.*

Khuda, God. khudáwand, *lord; master. See page* 56 *Note* 2.

Khún, *blood; murder.*

Khurák (f.), *food.* -i, *an allowance of food* or *money*

Khurshíd, *the sun* (*hence* 'Khurshídi Begam.' *See page* 122.)

Khusús, *affair; business.*–an, *especially; particularly.*

Khush, *pleased; satisfied.* Much used as first word in compos. e.g. –áwáz, *sweet-voiced.* –ámad (f.), *fawning approach; flattery.* –bu (f.), *a sweet-smell.* –ḥál, *in happy circumstances.* dil, *pleased at heart.* –go, *pleasant of speech.* –numa, *neat; pretty; pleasant.* –taba, *jocularity.* –zabán, *honey-tongued.* N. khushi, *pleasure; satisfaction; one's will and pleasure.*

Khushk, *dry; withered.* –i, *drought; the dry land.* as Adv., *by land* (not by water.)

Khwáb[1] (f.), *a dream; sleep*

Khwáh... khwáh, *either ... or; take it this way, or take it that way.*

Khwáhish, *desire; wish.*

L.

La, (*prefix.*) *destitute of;* e.g., lá-jawáb, *without an answer;* lá-chár, *helpless.* –khiráj, *rent-free.* lá-parwáh, *without care.* lá-wáris, *without an heir, &c.*

Lab, *a lip.* lab-á-lab, *brimful.*

Labádah, *a cloak.*

Lád (f.), *a load.* –na, *to load.* ladna, *to be ladened.*

Lagám (f.), *a bridle.*

Lagána; lagá-dena, *to apply one thing to another; to cause to touch; to moor, &c.*

Lagna; lag-jána, (*intr.*) *to touch; meet; fit.* lagna, *means also to begin.*

Lahsan, *garlic.* –iya, *cat's eye.*

Laḥzah, *a second* (*of time.*)

Lá,iḳ, *suitable; fit; capable.*

Laimún, *a lemon;* more commonly called '*lemu.*'

Lajána, *to be ashamed; to blush; to put to shame.*

Lajja, *shame; modesty.*

Lákh, *100,000.* (In India, printed '1,00,000.') Also, *sealing-wax.*

---

[1] When a 'w' follows a consonant it is to be very faintly sounded. The letter has been omitted in some words, where it has practically ceased to affect the pronunciation.

Lakṛi, *wood; firewood; a walking stick; any kind of (playing) bat or stick.*

LákshＬáh, *lac.*

Lál, *red.* -kágh̲az, *blotting-paper.*

Lálach (f.), *avarice.* Adj. lálchi.

Lamba, *long; tall.*

Lána, *or* le-ána, *to bring.*

Langa, *naked.*

Langar, *an anchor.*

Langṛa, *lame,* N. langṛá,i.

Lapakna, *to flash; rush; pounce up.*

Lapeṭna, *to roll-up.*

Larzah, *trembling; the ague.* V. larazna.

Laṛá,i, *quarrel; battle.* V. -karna; laṛna.

Laṛka, *a boy.* laṛki, *a girl.*

Laṛakpan, *childhood.*

Lashkar (f.), *an army.*

Lát, *a kick.* V. -márna.

Latíf, *fine; subtle.* latífah, *a witticism; a joke.*

Láṭhi, *a cudgel; a heavy stick.* laṭhiál, *a club-man.*

Laṭkána; laṭká-dena, *to hang-up; to suspend.*

Lau, *a flame.*

Lázim, *proper; fitting.*

Lazza, *a bright flame.*

Le,i, *paste; batter.*

Le-jána, *to take away.*

Ḷekha, *a writing.* -bahi, *a writing-book; an account-book.*

Lekin, *but; still.*

Lemu, *a lemon.*

Lena; le-lena, *to take; accept.*

Lep, *plaster.* (for walls, &c.)

Leṭna, *to lie down; to rest.*

Líchi, *or* líchu (*a fruit*), *leechee.*

Lifáfah, *an envelope.*

L'illah (Arabic), *for the sake of God.*

Likhna; likh-dena, *to write.* likhána; likhá-dena, *to cause to be written.* likh-wána; likwá-dena, *to cause to be written by a third person.* likh-lena, *to take down in writing.*

Lípna, *to plaster.* lipna, *to be plastered.* lipt, *plastered.*

Liyáḳat, *ability.*

Liye (ke.), *for the sake of.*

Log, *people.*

Loha, *iron.* lohár, *a black-smith.* -band, *iron-bound.*

Lohu, *blood.*

Lomṛi, *a fox.*

Loṭa, *a native brass-pot; a 'lota.'*

Loṭna, *to wallow.*

Lúbán, *incense.*

Lughat, *a dictionary.*

Lutf, *courtesy.*

Lúṭ, *robbery; 'loot.'* -na; lúṭ-lena, *to rob.* luṭna, *to be robbed.*

M.

Ma, *a mother.*

Maalúm, *evident; known.*

Maani, *meaning; drift.*

Maamúl, *the custom; what is customary.*–i, *in accordance with routine.*

Maazúl, *deposed; discharged from office; dismissed.*

Ma-báda, (Persian.) *may it not be! God forbid.*

Má-báp, *parents; a benefactor.*

Mablagh, *a sum of money.*

Machán, *a raised platform.*

Machchhar, *a musquito.*

Machhli, *fish.*

Madad (f.), *help.*—gár, *helping; a help-mate.* V.–d.

Mádah, *female; a female.*

Máddah, *any matter; affair.*

Madh, *honey.*

Mádiyán, *a mare.*

Madrasah, a *Muḥam; college.*

Magar, *but.* Also, a *crocodile.*

Magas (f.), *a fly.*

Magra, *cross; 'grumpy.'*

Maghrib, *the West.*

Maghrúr, *proud.* N.–i.

Maghz, *the brain; pride; a kernal.*

Máh, *the moon; a month.*

Maha, (in compos.) *great.* Hence, Mahárája; Mahárání (titles.) mahá-naddi, *the great river.* mahá-jan, (*the great person,*) *a money-lender; a banker; a merchant.*–jani, *the business of a 'mahájan.'*

Mahábat, *awe; majesty.*

Mahant, *a Hindu priest.*

Maháwat (*vulg.* mahout), *an elephant-driver.*

Máhi, *a fish.*

Mahínah, *a month.*

Mahṇga, *high-priced.*

Mahtoṇ, *a village headman.*

Maḥabbat, *love; friendship.*

Maḥall, *a section of a house; a storey.*

Maḥáll, (plur. of maḥall and of maḥallah) *streets; sections of towns, &c.; land, or other sources of revenue reserved to Government. a* 'mehal.' *See* 'Kháss.'

Maḥallah, *a ward of a town.*

Maḥbúb, *a loved one.* –Adj. –ah. –i, *amiability; sweetness.*

Maḥbús, *imprisoned.*

Maḥsúl, *a tax; duty; postage.*

Maḥz, *pure.* Adv. *merely.*

Ma,i, (Arabic prep.), *along with.*

Maida, *flour.*

Maidán, *a plain; a 'maidan.'*

Maila, *dirty.*

Maiṇ, *I.*

Maina, (bird.) *a 'maina.'*

Májara, *the circumstances which occurred.*

Majbúr, *forced; constrained.* N.–i.

Majlis (f.), *an assembly; conference.*

Majma, *an assembly.*–khiláf ḳánún, *an unlawful assembly.*

Makán, *a dwelling; a place; a house.*

Makkhan, *butter.*

Makkhi, *a fly.*

Makṛa, *a spider.*

Maḳám, *a dwelling-place; resting-place; lodging; halting-ground.*

Maḳdúr, *within the limits of possibility; power.* –bhar, *to the full extent of possibility.*

Mál, *goods; property; merchandize.* mál-o-mata, *goods and effects.* mál-guzár, *a rent-payer; a tenant.* málguzári, *the paying of rent; rent.* málik, *a master; owner; lord.* málik-ána, *a payment made to an owner out of possession.* mál-khánah, *a store-house.* máliyat, *wealth.*

Malá,i, *cream.*

Malak, *an Angel.*

Máli, *a gardener.*

Malik, *a King; a Chief.*–ah, *a Queen.*

Málish, *rubbing.* V.–k.

Mal-mal, *muslin.*

Malna, *to rub; to chafe.*

Mámu, *a maternal uncle.*

Man, *the mind; intention.*

Man, *a 'maund.'* = *about* 80 *lbs.*

Manádi, *a proclamation.*

Máṇda, *tired.* N. máṇdagi.

Mangal, *Tuesday.*

Máṇgna; máṇg-lena, *to ask for; want.* mangwána; mangwá-dena, *to procure.* máṇg-lena, *to borrow.*

Máni, *a hindrance; obstacle.*

Mánind (f.), *resemblance.* As prep. (with 'ki'), *like; as.*

Manjan, *tooth-powder,* or *paste.*

Mánna, *to obey; respect; allow; confide in; believe; hold as; attend to.*

Manzil (f.), *a stage of a journey.*

Manzúr, *approved; permitted.*

Máp, *the measure of a thing.* –na, *to measure.*

Már, *beating.* márá-mári, *mutual assault.* már-pít, *an assault.* V. márna, (*which means also to kill*). már-d., *to beat.* mar-ḍálna, *to kill.*

Marammat, *repairing; repairs.* V. –k.

Máre (ke.), *by reason of.*

Mard, *a man; a husband.* –ánah, *brave.* –nagi, *bravery; manliness.*

Márifat (ki.), *by the agency of.*

Marḥúm, *one who has found the mercy of death; the deceased; 'the late.'*

Marna; mar-jána, *to die.*

Martabah, *step; degree; rank.*

Mártol, *or* mártaul, *a hammer.*

Marzi, *wish; will; 'pleasure.*

Masahri, *musquito-curtains.*

Masálah, *spices; solder.*

Masíḥa, *The Messiah.*

Masjid (f.), *a mosque.*

Maskharah, *a jester.*

Masalan, *for example.*

Masnad (f.), *the throne.*

Mast, *lustful; drunk.* N. –i.

Mastisa, *a half-caste.*

Mastúl, *a mast.*

Mashál, *a torch.* –chi, *a torch-bearer; a scullion.*

Mashghúl, *busy; occupied.*

Mashhúr, *celebrated; well-known.*

Mashk (f.), (*vulg.* mashak), *the leather bag used by the 'bihishti,' for carrying water.*

Mashriḳ, *the East.*

Mat, *not,* (with the imper. mood.)

Matlab, *intention; meaning.*

Matrúkah, *property; especially as left by a deceased person.*

Matwála, *a drunkard.*

Maṭh, *a Hindu temple.*

Maṭar, *peas.*

Mauj (f.), *a wave.*

Maujúd, *present; at hand.*

Mauḳúf, *postponed; put off; stopped.* (as an allowance.)

Maulavi, *a Muham: learned man; a 'Moulvi.'*

Mausam, *or* mausim, *a season of the year; weather.*

Mausúf, *afore-said.*

Maut (f.), *death.*

Mauza, *a parish; the village and the village lands.*

Mazah, *taste; flavour.*

Mazbút, *firm; solid.* N.-i.

Mazdúr, *a daily labourer.* -i, *his daily pay; the work of a labourer.*

Mazhab, *religion.*

Mazkúr, *afore-said.*

Mazmúm, *sense; meaning; the contents of a book.*

Mekh (f.), *a peg,* (e. g., *for a tent;*) *a nail.*

Mela, *a fair; a 'mela.'*

Meṇ, *in; into.*

Mez (f.), *a table.*

Mí,ád, *the period allowed for doing anything.* –i, *limited to a specified time.*

Midah, *the stomach.*

Mihín, *fine in texture; subtle.*

Mihmán, *a guest.* –dár, *a host.* –dári, *hospitality.*

Mihrbán, *kind; condescending.* N. –i.

Miḥnat, *labour.* -i, *laborious.* –ánah, *wages.*

Mihtar, *or* mehtar, *a sweeper. If female,* mihtráni.

Milki, *a landowner; often used for* milkíyat, *landed property held in one's own right.*

Milna, as 3rd personal verb, *See page* 50; as fully personal verb, *to be mixed up,* or *associated with.* milána; milá-dena, (*trans.*) *to mix; adjust; fit; match a pattern,* and the like. mili-julí, *on the best of terms.*

Minár, *a minaret.*

Mír, *a Muḥam. title.*

Mirch, *or* mircha, *pepper.*

Mirgi, *epilepsy.*

Mirza, *a Muḥam. title.*

Miskín, *poor; humble.*

Misl (f.), *a file of papers.*

Misr, *Egypt.* misri, *Egyptian,* hence applied to *crystallised sugar*, as coming from Egypt.

Mistar, *a guide for writing straight by; a ruler.*

Mistiri, *or* mistri, (*supposed by some to be the English 'mister'*) *a head workman; a workman.*

Míṭha, *sweet.* –páni, *lemonade.* miṭhá,i, *sweet-meats.*

Míṭṭha, *a kiss;*[1] *sweet.*

Miṭṭi, *earth.*

Miyáṇ, *a word of respectful or friendly address, or reference to one.*

Mizáj, *temperament; health.*

Mízán (f.), *a balance; scales.*

Mlecha, *an unclean person,* i.e., *any one not a Hindu.*

Mochi, *a cobbler; a currier.*

Modi, *a grain-shop-keeper; a grocer.*

Mohr, *or* mor, *a peacock.*

Mol, *purchasing. V.* –lena.

Mom, *wax.* –batti, *a wax-candle.*–raug͟han, *polishing-paste; varnish; grease.* –i, *waxen.*

Moṛha, *a footstool.*

Moti (m.), *a pearl.*

Moṭa, *fat; coarse.* N. –i.

Moze, *boots;* used also for *stockings; socks.*

Mu,áf, *forgiven.* V. –k. N. –i.

Mu,áfiḳ (ke.), *conformably to.*

Mu,aiyan, *fixed; stationed.*

Mu,ámalah, *any affair; business.*

Mu,azzaz. *honoured; esteemed.*

Mubárak, *happy; fortunate.* –bád (Persian, '*may it be fortunate*') *congratulations; compliments; 'blessing.'* –bádi, *the act of congratulating, &c.*

Mublag͟h, *or* mablag͟h, *a sum of money.*

Múchh (f.), *mustachios.*

Mudda,á-alaih, (*plur.* mudda,á-alaihim), *a defendant in a suit.*

Mudák͟halat, *entry on land, &c.*

Mudda,i, *a plaintiff in a suit.*

Muddat, *time; space.*

Mufassil, *in detail; the counties in contrast with the metropolis.*

---

[1]Ayahs use the corrupted English, 'Kissi.'

Muflis, *poor; wretched.* N. –i.

Muft, *gratis.*

Mufti, *a Muḥam: law-officer.*

Mug͟hal, *a 'Mogul.'*

Muhr (f.), *a seal; an obsolete gold coin.*

Muhri, *a drain.*

Muḥáfiz, *a defender; a record-keeper.*

Muḥarram, *forbidden; sacred. The first month of the Muḥam: year. 'The muḥarram' festival.*

Muḳábalah, *the comparing of* e. g., *draft with fair copy; attack; onset,* V. –k.

Muḳarrar, *fixed; enduring.* –i, *a fixed land tenure.* –idár, *the holder of such.*

Muk͟hálif, *disagreeing; conflicting; an opponent.* –at, *variance; discrepancy; plur.* muk͟hálifát.

Muk͟htár, *exalted; an attorney.*

Muláḥazah, *viewing; inspection.* V. –k.

Malá,i, *cream.*

Mulá,im, *soft; tender.*

Muláḳát, *a visit.* V. –k.

Mulázim, *a servant.*

Múli, *radish.*

Mulk (Anglo-Hind., moolook), *a country.*

Mulla, *a Muḥam: lawyer* or *doctor.*

Multavi, *put off; adjourned.*

Mumkin, *possible.*

Munásib, *suitable; right; proper.*

Muṇh, *the mouth; the face.*

Muníb, *a patron; a master.*

Munshi, *a Muḥam: teacher of languages; a writer; a head-clerk.*

Murabba, *pickled; preserved; jam.*

Murabbi, *a teacher; director; guardian.*

Murád (f.), *wish; intention.*

Murattab, *arranged; put in order; prepared.*

Murdah, *dead; a corpse.*

Murdár, *polluted; carrion.*

Murg͟h, *a cock,* murg͟hi, *a hen.* murg͟h-ábi, *water-fowl.* murg͟hi-k͟hánah, *a hen-house.*

Musáfir, *a traveller.*

Musawwir, *a painter; a sculptor.*

Musalmán; muslim, *a Musalman.* fem. -i.

Musíbat, *adversity.*

Músíḳi, *music.*

Mushkil, *difficult.* -át, *difficulty; difficulties.*

Musht, *the fist.*

Mushwarah, *consultation.*

Muta,aiyan, *posted; fixed.*

Muta,ammil, *meditative.*

Muta,assib, *bigotted.*

Mutábiḳ (ke,), *according to.*

Mutafarriḳ, *miscellaneous.*

Mutarjim, *a translator.*

Mutasaddi, *an accountant.*

Mutawalli, *a guardian of a mosque, &c.*

Mutlaḳ, *or* matlaḳ, '*at all,*' e.g., mutlaḳ nahíṇ, *not at all.*

Muṭṭhi, *the fist; a handful.*

Muyassar, *available; ready to hand.*

Muzá,iḳah, *importance,* e.g., 'kuchh muzá,iḳah nahíṇ, *it's of no consequence.*

Múzi, *importunate; troublesome; vexatious.*

N.

Na, *no; not.* Much used as prefix. -dáni, *want of wisdom.* -durust, *not right; out of order; incorrect.* -iḥsánmandi, *ingratitude.* -ḳis, *worthless.* -ḳis-ul-aḳl, *of no mental calibre.*-khún-(blood.) *the nail of man or animals.* -maalúm, *unknown.* -pasand, *disagreeable; not approved.* -rást, *unjust; unrighteous.* táḳat, *without strength.* -wáḳif, *uninformed.* -yih, -wuh, *neither this nor that.*

Nabz (f.), *the pulse.* -dekhna, *to feel the pulse.*

Nách (*f.*), *a native dance.* V. -na, *or* -k.

Nadámat, *repentance.*

Naddi, *a river.*

Nafa, *profit.*

Nafs, *the soul; the spirit.*

Nág, *a snake.*

Nágáh, *suddenly.*

Nagar (as last part of word *e.g.*, Aḥmad-nagar), *a city; a town.*

Nahána (*intr.*), *to bathe.*

Nahr (f.), *a canal.*

Náhi, *no! not so! you're not to do that.*

Nahíṇ, *not.* -to, *if not then; otherwise.*

Ná,ib, *a deputy; an agent; a subordinate*, e.g., -gumáshtah, *an under steward.* -paṭwári, *a subordinate 'paṭwári'* (i.e., *collector of rents.*)

Najíb, *noble.*

Nák (f.), *the nose.*

Naḳl (f.), *a story; a copy.* -navís, *a copyist.*

Naḳshah, *a drawing; a model; a design; a map; a plan; a chart.*

Nál, *a horse-shoe.* -bandi, *shoeing a horse.* V. -bandi-k. -kholna, *to take off the shoes.*

Nála, *a ditch; a 'nullah.'*

Nálán, *wailing.*

Nálish, *a complaint (of wrong.)*

Nám, *a name; fame; character.* -burdah, *the above-named.*—war, *famous.*

Námah (as last part of word), *a writing,* e.g., hibah-námah, *a deed of gift.*

Namak (*vulg.* nimak,) *salt.* -dán, *a salt-cellar.* -ka chammach, *a salt-spoon.*

Namáz (f.), *prayer.* V. -parhna.

Namdah, *a coarse woollen covering; a pad, used as under saddle-cloth, &c.*

Namúnah, *a pattern; a sample.*

Nána, *a mother's father.*

Ná,o (f.), *a boat; a ship.*

Náp (f.), same as Máp. q.v.

Nápit, *a barber.*

Nar, *a male; male.*

Nárikel, *or* náriyal, *a cocoanut.*

Nárangi, *an orange.*

Narm, *soft* (lit. and fig.). N.-i.

Nas (f.), *a vein; a sinew.*

Nasíb, *good fortune; lot in life.*

Nasíḥat, *advice; good counsel.* V. -k. *and* -d.

Nasr, *an eagle.*

Nashah, *intoxication.*

Náshpáti, *a pear.*

Náshtah *breakfast.*

Nashtar (f.), *a lancet.*

Natthi, *an official string* or *file of papers.*

Náti, *a daughter's son.*

Natíjah, *the necessary result* (e.g., of an argument); *upshot; end of the matter.*

Nau, *young; new; fresh.* -jawán, *a youth.* -jawáni, *youth.* -roz, *New Year's Day.*

Naubat, *time ; turn.*

Naukar, *a servant.* –log, *the servants.* –i, *service.*

Nawáḥ, *district ; neighbourhood.*

Nawwáb, *or* Núwáb, (pl. of Ná,ib.) (*Anglicé*, 'Nabob,') *a viceroy ; a governor ; a Nawáb.*

Naya, *new.*

Nazámat, *the criminal department of Government.* –adálat, *the criminal court of a judge.*

Nazar (f.), *a look.* –k, *to take a look ; cast an eye upon.*

Názim, *a governor.*

Názir, *a superintendent ;* (especially) *a sheriff* or *head bailiff.* nazárat, *the department superintended by such.*

Nazdík (Adj.) *near ; neighbouring.* Also as prep. with (ke.) –i, *neighbourhood.*

Nazr, *an offering from an inferior to a superior ; a 'nuzzur.'*

Ne. *See page* 5. *Also page* 19, *section* 25.

Nek, *good ; of good repute.* N. –nám, *and* –námi.

Nibedan, *prayer,* e.g., *for redress.*

Nícha (adj.). *low ; under.* –k., *to lower.* níche (ke), *below.*

Nigáh (f.), *look ; regard.* –rakhna, *to watch one.* –báni, *custody ; charge.*

Niimat, *joy ; delight.*

Niháyat, *the extremity.* Adv. *extremely.*

Nikalna ; nikal-jána, *to go out ; get out.*

Nikálna ; nikál-d., *to put out ; turn out,* (e.g.. from one's presence). nikál-lena, *to extract.*

Nikáḥ, *marriage.* V. –k.

Níl ; níla, *blue ; indigo.* níl-gá,o, (*blue cow*) (an animal), *a 'neel-gai.'* níl-koṭhi, *an indigo-factory.* níl-koṭhi ka sáḥib, *an Indigo Planter.*

Nílám, *an auction* –k., *to sell by auction.*

Ním, *half ;* Also, *a kind of tree ; a 'Neem-tree.'* –roz, *midday.*

Nínd, *sleep.* V. –lena. A. –i.

Nir, a prefix, *like 'un' in English.*

Nirauni, *weeding.* V. –k.

Nirkh (*vulg.* nirrik), *the market-rate.*

Nisár, *largesse; donation; sacrifice of one's self.* V. -k.

Nisbat, *the relation of one thing to another,* iṣ ki nisbat, *in comparison with this.*

Nisf, *the half; half.* (n. a.)

Nishán; nishánah, *a mark; a signal.*

Niwár, *cotton-belting; obstruction.*

Níyat, *intention; aim.*

Nizám, *good arrangement; a governor; 'The Nizám,'* (e.g., of Ḥaidarábád.)

Nok (f.), *a beak; an end; a point.*

Nona, *or* núna (adj.), *salt,* -páni, *salt-water.*

Nujúm, *astrology.* -i, *the art of ditto.* Also, *an astrologer.*

Nuḳsán, *loss; injury.* -pahuṉchána, *to cause ditto.*

Numá,ish, *appearance; show; from.*

Núr, *light; brightness.* Hence 'Koh-i-núr,' *The Mountain of Light.*

Nuskhah, *a recipé; a medical prescription.*

O.

O (Persian), *and.*

Ojha, *a wizard; a magician.*

Ola-píra, *cholera.*

Olti, *eaves.*

Oṛhna, *to put on clothes; to cover one's self up.* as N. *a covering-cloth,* e.g., *a blanket.*

Os, *dew.*

Osárah, *a verandah.*

Oṭ, *shade; protection.* -k., *to protect; conceal.* -hona, *to lie concealed.*

P.

Pa[1], *a leg; a foot.* -e-jámah, *sleeping drawers.* -e-khánah, *a privy.* -o-dán, *a foot-stool.* -posh, *a slipper,* pai-dal, *on foot.*

Pachchham, *the West.*

[1] Takes many forms, as pá,e, pá,i, páṉw, pá,o; páya, Pl. pá,oṉ.

Pádsháh, *a king.* -i, *sovereignty; a kingdom.*

Pádri,[1] *minister; a priest.*

Pag, *a foot.* -ḍanḍi, *a foot-path* -ḍanḍi-lena, *to track.*

Págal, *a fool; a lunatic.* '*a poggle.*' -khánah, *a lunatic asylum.*

Pagṛi, *a turban.* *See page* 95.

Pahalwán, *a wrestler; a swash-buckler.*

Pahar. *See page* 67. *Sect.* 3.

Paháṛ, *a mountain.*

Pahchánna. *to recognize; to know one.*

Pahinna, *to put on clothes.*

Pahiya (m.), *a wheel.*

Pahuṇchna, *to arrive.* pahuṇchána; pahuṇchá-d., *to escort; cause to arrive.*

Pái, *a 'pie,'* $\frac{1}{12}$ *of an 'ánah.'*

Paida, *born.* -hona, *to be born.* -ish, *birth.* -wár, *produce; 'yield.'*

Paighám, *a message; evangel.* -ghambar, *a messenger; an apostle; especially Muḥammad.*

Paihla, *or* pahle, *first; the first; in the first place.*

Paik, *a runner; a messenger.*

Paimán, *a promise.*

Paimá,ish, *measurement of land.* V. -k.

Pairna, *to swim.* pairák, *a swimmer.*

Paisa, *a coin,* = 3 '*pái.*' paise, *money; 'change.'*

Paiṭhna, *to enter.*

Páji, *contemptible; mean.*

Pák; pákízah, *clean; pure.* N. -i; -ízagi.

Pakaṛna, *to seize; to catch.* pakaṛ-le-jána, *to seize and carry off.*

Pakka, *also,* pukhtah, *ripe; cooked; thorough; done in the best manner; e.g.,* pakka rásta, *a metalled road.* The *converse* word is 'kachcha.' The '*pucca*' and '*catcha*' of Anglo-Hind.

Pakána (*trans.*), *to cook.* pakna (*intr.*), *to cook; to grow ripe.* pakwána, *to cause to be cooked.*

Pakhál, *a large bag for water carried in pairs on bullocks.*

Palak (f.), *the eye-lid.*

---

[1] Not Hindústáni.

Palang, *a bed.*

Palás, *the cotton-tree.* Hence 'Plassey.'

Pálki, *a palanquin ; a 'palki,'* –wála, *a palki-carrier.*

Pálna, *to rear ; bring-up ; cherish.* palna, *to be reared, &c.* pálak, *one who rears, brings up, &c.*

Palṭan (f.), *a regiment.*

Pán, *betel (chewed by natives.)*

Pána, *to get ; obtain.*

Panáh (f.), *shelter ; protection.* Used as form of address, e.g., jaháṇ-panáh ! *Protector of the Universe!*

Páṇch, *five.* pancháyat, *a village-council of* (nominally) *five members.* panch, *a member of the village-council.*

Pandrah, *fifteen.*

Panḍit, *a learned Hindu.*

Páni (m.), *water ; rain.* –h., *to rain.*

Panír (f.), *cheese.*

Panj, (Persian,) *five.* –áb, (*the* 5 *waters*) *The 'Punjaub.'* –ah, *a claw.*

Páṇjar, *the side (of the body).*

Panjari, *a rib.*

Pankha, *a fan ; a 'punkha.'* –wala, *a punkha-puller.*

Panna, *an emerald.*

Panseri, *a measure,* or *weight of* 5 *'sers.'*

Pá,o, *a quarter ; one-fourth.*

Páp, *sin.*

Par, *on ; upon, at.* As particle, *still ; for all that.* As N. *a feather.*

Pár (ke.), *over ; across.* V.-k., *to cross.*–hona, *to be across.* (e. g., *a river.*) As N. *a shore ; a bank.*

Parb, *a religious holiday.*

Parchah, *a fragment ; a scrap.*

Pardah, *a curtain ; curtains.* –nishín, *remaining behind the curtain ;* (applied to ladies who do not go out.)

Pardeshı, *foreign.*

Pareshán, *distressed ; vexed ; worried.* N. –i.

Parganah, *a local division ; a 'purgunnah.'*

Parhez, (f.), *abstinence ; moderation*

Pari-roz, (Persian,) *next-day.*

Paros, *neighbourhood.* –i, *a neighbour.*

Parsoṇ, *the day after tomorrow ; the day before yesterday.* *See page* 69.

Parwáh, *matter ; consequence.*

Parwánah, *a written order from one in authority.*

Parwar, a *patron, as in* 'gharíb-parwar!' *Patron of the Poor!*

Parwasti, *cherishing; supplying means of livelihood.* V.–k.

Páṛa, *a quarter of a town; a beat.* -wála, a *watchman of ditto.*

Paṛhána, *to teach.*

Paṛhna, *to read; to learn.*

Paṛna, *to fall; be down.* (e.g. *with sickness.*) paṛa, *down; fallen.*

Paṛti, *land 'resting'; waste-land.*

Pas, *then; therefore; consequently; so.*

Pás (ke.), *beside, near,* or *by one.* –ana, *or* jána, *to go near,* or *up to.*

Pásbán, *a patrol.* -i, *patrolling.*

Páse, *dice.*

Pasínah, *perspiration.*

Pásh-pásh, *smashed; in morsels.* –ho-jána, *to be smashed; to go to pieces.*

Pashemán, *repentant.*

Pashm (f.), *wool.*

Pata, *signs; indications; traces; a person's address.*

Patthar, *a stone; hail.* –ka ko,ila, *coals.*

Patla, *thin; meagre.*

Pattar, *a leaf.*

Páṭ, *a 'breadth' of cloth; a flap; a board.* Also, *tow.*

Paṭakna; paṭak-d., *to dash against; to throw to the ground.*

Paṭána, *to irrigate.*

Paṭna, *a district, and also a city in Lower Bengal; 'Patna.'*

Paṭpaṭ, *the sound of beating; beating.*

Paṭṭa, *a deed of lease.*

Paṭṭi, *a plaster; a bandage.* Also, *a demarcated section of land.*

Paṭwári, *a village rent-collector.*

Paṭel, *beating; a village magnate so called.*

Paune. *See pages* 64 *and* 67.

Pauti, *a small basket.*

Pech, *a twist; a turn.* –dár, *twisted.* –kash, *a screw-driver.* –táb, *restlessness; 'the fidgets.'* –ish, *contortion; stomach-ache.* V. –na.

Peru, *a turkey.*

Peṛ, *a tree.*

Pesh, *in front; facing.* -áb, *urine.* -ah, *one's trade; business.* -áni, *the forehead.* -gi, *an advance of money.* -kár, *a clerk who lays business before his superior.* -tar, *formerly; at an earlier time* V.-k., *to bring forward any matter for attention; to place before one.*

Peshwa, *a Mahraṭṭa Minister; 'The Peishwa;' a guide.*

Peṭ, *the belly.* -i, *a waistband.* also, *a trunk; a box.*

Phailána (*trans.*) phailna, (*intr.*) *to spread abroad,* (*as news, &c.*)

Phal, *fruit.* (lit. and fig.) -dár, *fruitful.*

Pháṇk (f.), *a slice; a 'cut.'*

Pháṇsi, *a loop; noose.* -d., *to execute by hanging.*

Phaphsa, *blown-out; swollen.*

Phaphola, *a blister;* dil ka-, *soreness of mind.*

Pharsa, *an axe.*

Pháṛna; pháṛ-d, (*trans.*) *to tear,* pháṛa hú,a, *torn.*

Pháṭak, *an outer-gate.*

Phaṭna, phaṭ-jána, (*intr.*) *to tear; to burst; to break.*

Pheṇkna; pheṇk-d., *to throw; to throw down.*

Phephṛe, *the lungs.*

Pher, *or* phir, *back; again.* -ána, *to come back.* -jána, *to go back.* pheri-k., *to exercise horses.*

Phirta-phirta, *wandering about.*

Phir. *See* 'Pher.'

Phúl, *a flower; flowers.* -a, *swollen.* -dán, *a flower-vase.* -jána, *to swell.* -kobi, *a cauliflower.* -na, *to blossom; flower; be in robust health.* phul-wári; phúl-bágh; phúl-baghán, (I..B.) *a flower-garden.* phul-jhaṛi, *a kind of fire-work.* phul-kári, *an ornamental cloth studded with bright metal.*

Phúṇk, *blowing with the mouth.* V. -na.

Phuslána, *to wheedle; coax; deceive.*

Phúṭna, *to be broken.* phúṭa, *broken.* phúṭa páni, *boiling water.*

Píchhe, *behind.* also, prep. (ke). pichháṛi, *the hinder parts; ropes for fastening horses by the hind legs.* pichhla, *the hindermost; the last.*

Pichkári, *a squirt; a syringe.*

Pidar, (Persian,) *a father.*

Pík (f.), *saliva caused by chewing betel-nut.* -dán; *a spittoon.*

Píl, *an elephant.* -bán, *his driver.* -khánah, *his stable.*

Pilána, (*trans.*) *to give water.*

Pilá,o, (*a kind of food.*) 'pillaw.'

Pilla, *a pup.*

Pillu, *a worm.*

Pína, (*trans.* and *intr.*) *to drink.* Also, (*trans.*) *to smoke.*

Pindli, *the calf of the leg.*

Pinjra, *a cage; a trap.*

Pípa, *a cask; a barrel; a 'pipe.'*

Pípal, *a 'peepal' tree.*

Pír (M.), *an old man; a religious man; a saint.* -ka roz, *Monday.*

Pirich, *a saucer.*

Pírozah, *turquoise.*

Píru. *See* 'Peru.'

Pisar, (Persian,) *a son; a boy.*

Písna, *to grind.* pisna, *to be ground.*

Pistah, *pistachio-nut.*

Pissu, *a flea.*

Pit, *or* pith, *bile.*

Pítal, *brass.*

Pitára, *a travelling-box.* (of special make.)

Pítna, *to beat; to assault.* pitna, *to be beaten, &c.*

Piyádah, *a messenger.*

Piyálah, *a cup.*

Pyár (f.), *affection.* -a, *dear; loved.* -k., *to caress; fondle.*

Piyáz, *an onion.*

Poddár, *a money-changer.*

Ponchhna; ponchh-d., *to dust; to clean.*

Post, *rind; skin.* Also, *the poppy-plant.* -i, *one who uses opium.*

Poshák (f.), *clothing.*

Pota, *a son's son.* poti, *a son's daughter*

Prán, *life; soul; sweetheart.*

Prasansa, *praise.*

Prem (f.), *love.* -ságar, "*The Ocean of Love,*" (*a book so called.*)

Prít, *love; friendship.*

Prithi, *the earth.* -náth, *Lord of the Universe.*

Púchhna, *to ask a question.*

Pudínah, *mint.*

Púja (H.), *worship.* -ri, *a priest.* V. -k.

Pukárna, (*intr.*) *to shout.* (*trans.*) *to call one by shouting.*

Pukhtah. *See* 'Pakka.'

Pul, *a bridge.* –bandi, *a contribution for making or maintaining bridges.*

Pulá,o. *See* 'Pilá,o.'

Puanḍa, *a parcel; a bundle.*

Púṇji, *capital used in trade.*

Púr, *a town; a city.* only as termination, *e.g.*, Nágpúr.

Púra, *complete; full.* –k., *to do in a complete manner; fulfil; finish.*

Púrab, *the East.*

Púrán; puránah, *certain quasi-religious books of the Hindús.*

Purána, *old; ancient.*

Purush, *a human being.*

Pusht, *a generation; ancestry* –ba–, *from generation to generation.*

Putli, *a doll; an image.*

R.

Rabi, *the Sun.* –bár, *Sunday.*

Rabi, *the spring-crop.*

Radd, *rejection; refutation; vomiting.* –badal, *argumentation; wrangling.* –i-jawáb, *a rejoinder to an answer.* –námah, *a deed of abandonment.* V. –k.

Rafa, *repairing; making up a dispute.* V. –k. rafa-námah, *a deed settling a dispute.*

Raftah-raftah, *gradually,* (from Persian 'raftan,' *to go.*)

Rag (f.), *a vein; a sinew.*

Raged (f.), *pursuit.* V. –na.

Ráh, *or* rah (*f.*), *a road.* ráhzan, *a highway robber.* ráh-zani, *highway robbery.*

Rahá,i, *or* rihá,i, *release.* V.–k.

Ráḥat, *repose; peace.*

Rahn, *or* rihn, *a pledge; a pawn.*

Rahna, *to dwell; to remain.* rahne-d., *to leave; let alone.* rah-jána, *to remain waiting.*

Raḥm; raḥmat, *pity; mercy.* A. raḥmán.

Rá,i, *opinion; advice.* Also, *mustard.*

Ra,ís, *a chief; a nobleman.*

Ra,íyat, (plur. ri,áya.) *a peasant; a 'ryot;' a subject.*

Ráj (H.), *rule; a kingdom.* --a, *a 'Rája.'* -- háns, *a goose.*

Ráj, *or* ráj-mistri, *a mason.*

Rikáb (f.), *a stirrup.* --díwál, *stirrup-leathers.*

Rakhna; *to put; to place; keep beside one.* rakh-d., *to put a thing down.*

Rákshas, *an Evil Spirit.*

Rám; Rám-Rám (H.), *God.*

Ramazán, *the Muham: 'Lent.'*

Ramnah, *an open plain; a park.*

Rána (H.), *a prince;* ráni, *a queen; a 'Ránee.'*

Randi, *a wench; a woman.*[1]

Rang (f.), *colour; paint.* --i, *chintz.* --rez, *a dyer.* -sáz, *a house-painter.* --d., *to dye; to paint.* --ín, *dyed; coloured.*

Ranj; ranjish, *grief; bitterness of spirit.* A. ranjídah.

Rás (f.), *driving-reins.*

Ras, *juice.*

Rasad, *provinder.*

Rasm (f.), *law; custom.* rasmi, *according to ditto.*

Rassi, *a rope.*

Rást, *just; true; sincere.* N. --i.

Rásta, *a road.*

Rasú,i, *cooking; cooked food.*

Rashíd, *wise.*

Rát, *night.*

Ratan (f.), *a jewel.*

Rath, *a chariot; a religious processional car.*

Ratti, *a weight by which jewels are weighed.*

Rátib, *food-allowance. (for an animal.)*

Raughan, *polish; oil; harness-paste.*

Rawádár, *one who gives his consent to anything.*

Rawán, *flowing.* Also, *soul; life.*

Rawánah, *a pass; a permit; despatch of goods.* --k., *to despatch.*

Ráz, *a secret.*

Raza (f.), razámandi, *consent.*

Razá, i, *a bed-cover; a quilt.*

Rázi, *satisfied; 'agreeable.'* --k., *to satisfy; appease.* --i-námah, *a deed expressing satisfaction of a claim.*

---

[1] *Not* a respectful word.

Reg (f.), *sand.*

Reṇgna ; reṇg-reṇg. –k., *to creep.*

Reṇkna, *to bray.*

Resham, *silk.* reshmi, *of silk.*

Ret (f.), *sand.* –i, *a file.* V.–na.

Rezah, *a scrap ; a crumb.*

Ri,áya. *See* 'Ra,íyat.'

Ríchh, *a bear.*

Rís (f.), *anger.* - k., *to enrage.*

Rísh (f.), *a beard.*

Rishi (H.), *a sage.*

Rishtah, *relationship ; a thread on which papers, &c., are strung.*

Rishwat, *a bribe.* –d., *to give a bribe.* –khána, *or* lena, *to take a bribe.*

Rít ; ríti, *the custom.*

Rog, *sickness : disease.*

Rohu, *a fish so called.*

Rokaṛ (f.), *prompt payment.* –bahi, *a cash-account book.*

Rokna (*trans.*), *to stop ; check ; hem-in.*

Rona, *to weep.*

Roṛa, *small stones ; gravel.*

Roshan, *or* raushan, *clear ; bright.* N. roshná,i, which means also, *blacking ; ink.*

Roṭi, *bread.*

Roz, *a day.* –ba–, *day by day.* –ána, *daily.* –gár, *daily earnings ; service ; means of livelihood ; daily pay* –ínah, *daily pay.* –námchah, *a diary.* –i,maidáṇ, *the day of battle.*

Rozah, *a fast.* V. –rakhna.

Ru, *the face,* –ba-kár, *or* –ba-kári, *a writing by which a matter is laid before one ; a 'roobacarry.'* –ba–, *face to face.* –e-dád (f.), *a written statement of facts.* –mál,[1] *a handkerchief.* –posh,[2] *hidden.* –posh hona, *to be concealed ; to hide one's self.*

Rúḥ, *the soul ; the spirit.*

Rú,i, *cotton.*

Ruju, *a turning* or *appealing to one ; making a matter over to one.* V. -k.

Rukh, *the cheek.*

Rukhsat, *permission to go ; leave ; discharge.* –d., *to grant permission to go.* –hona, *to be allowed to go ; to depart.* –lena, *to take one's leave,* or *discharge ; to depart.* [*page* 70.

Rúpa, *silver.* rúpíya. *See*

---

[1] See 'Malna.'

[2] From the Persian 'poshídan,' *to cover ; clothe ; hide.*

Ṛ.

No word begins with this letter.

S.

Note.—There are three 'S's' in Hindústáni; but their sounds are so much alike that they have not been distinguished in this book.

Sa, (adj.) (after a noun) *like*, e.g., bandar-sa, *monkey-like.* (after an adj.) '*-ish;*' '*pretty;*' '*rather.*' e.g., ek baṛa-sa ghar, *a pretty large house.*

Sab; *all; the whole; often used to give a plural sense to words which have no plural Nom.* -ke-, *an emphatic form of* 'sab.' -ko,i, *every one.* -kuchh, *everything.* Oblique Pl. sabhoṇ.

Sabab, *cause; reason.*

Sabere, *in the morning.*

Sábiḳ, *relating to past time.*

Sábit, *firm; established.* -kar-d., *to establish, or make good a point.* -hona, *to be established, &c.*

Sabr, *patience.* -k., *to have patience; to wait a little.* A. sábir.

Sábúṇ, *or* sábun, *soap.* -dán, *a soap-dish.*

Subút, *firmness; stability; establishment by evidence.*

Sabz, (Adj.) *green.* -i, *verdure; vegetables.*

Sach; sachha, *true; honest; upright.* N. sachhá,i.

Sáda, *plain; unadorned.* Also *artless.*

Saḍmah, *a shock; a blow.*

Sáf; safa, *clean.* (lit. or fig.). safá.i, *cleanness; the clearing of one's character; defence.*

Safar, *a journey.* V. -k

Saff-i-jang (f.), *battle-order.*

Sag, (Persian,) *a dog.*

Ság, *spinach;* '*ság.*'

Ságu, *sago.*

Ságar, *the Ocean.*

Ságún, *teak-wood.*

Sahi, (interj.) *true! quite so!*

Sáḥib, sáḥibah. *See pages* 24 *and* 26. –i-k͟hánah, *the master*, (or *mistress*) *of the house.*

Saḥíḥ, *accurate ; just ; just the thing* –k., *to correct ; to sign.*–salámat, *safe and well.*

Saḥn, *a court-yard.*

Sai, *or* sau, *one hundred.*

Sá,il, *a petitioner.*

Sailáb, *an inundation.*

Sair, *a walk ; a journey.* –k., *to take a walk, &c.*

Sá,ís, *a groom.*

Sáj, *adornment ; equipment ; harness.* V. (*trans.*) –na ; -lagána ; -lagá-d. V. (*intr.*) sajna.

Sájha, *companionship ; partnership.* sájhi, *a companion, &c.*

Sákin, *an inhabitant.*

Sakna. *See page* 18, *Sect.* 22.

Sukúnat, *one's 'parish ;' domicile.* [*difficult*, N. –i.

Sak͟ht, *hard.* (lit. or fig.) ;

Sak͟hi, *liberal ; open-handed.*

Sál, *a tree so called.*

Sál, (Persian,) *a year.* (*plur.* sálha.) –ánah, *yearly.*

Saláḥ, *peace ; concord ; good advice.* V. –d. *and* lena.

Salám, *compliments ; an obeisance*, –k., *or* d., *to salute.* –d., *or* bolna, *to send one's compliments.*

Salámat, *safety ; preservation ;* as adv., *safely.*

Salámi, *money paid on a lease being granted, or the like.*

Sális, *an arbitrator.* –i, *arbitration.*

Salís, *easy.* N. –i.

Salotar, *a farrier ; a 'vet.'* –i, *the profession of ditto.*

Sálu, *coarse red cloth.*

Sálús, *The Trinity.*

Samá,at, *the hearing*, e.g., *of a case in Court.*

Samajh (f.), *understanding.* V. –na ; –meṇ lena, *to understand.* samjhána, *to explain.*

Saman, *jasmine.*

Samán, *level ; equal ; alike.*

Sámán, *furniture ; equipage.*

Sambat, *a special era so called.*

Sámbar, *a kind of elk.*

Sombár, *Monday.*

Samet, *with ; along with.*

Sámne (adv.) *in front ; opposite.* also, as prep. (ke.). –wála, *what is opposite.*

Samundar, *the Ocean.*

San, *the year*, (*in dating.*)

Sanad (f.), *a royal, or other deed of grant; a letter of appointment.*

Sandal, *sandal-wood.*

Sáṇḍ, *a bull.*

Sang, *a stone.* –ín, *stony; arduous; serious.* (as a crime.)

Sáni, (Persian,) *second.*

Sanibár, *Saturday.*

Saníchar, *Saturday.*

Sáṇp, *a snake.*

Sáṇs (f.), *the breath.* –ṭúṭna, *to break,* i.e., *lose one's breath.*

Sanyási, *a Hindu devotee.*

Sar, *or* sir, *the head; the top; the point; starting-point.* sar-ba-sar, *entirely.* sar-dard, *headache.* sardár, *a headman.* sar-i-nau, *quite new; fresh.* sar-i-ráh (f.), *the centre of the road.* –k., *to execute; succeed; get on; make head with.* sar-zamín (f.), *the place at which any event occurred.*

Sára, *the whole; all the...*

Sará,e (f.), *an abode; an inn; a halting-place; a shelter.*

Saṛak (f.), *a public road.*

Sar-anjám, *apparatus; necessary things.*

Sáras, *a crane* (*bird*).

Sarásari; sarsari, (adj.) *all round about; summary.*

Sard (adj.), *cold;* N. –i., *cold; a cold.*

Saresh, *glue.*

Sarf, *expenditure; use.* V.–k. –meṇ lána, *to bring into one's use.*

Sarfaráz, *exalted; noble.*

Sare, '*per.*' (e.g., per yard.)

Sári, *a wrapper worn by native females.*

Sirkah, *vinegar.*

Sarkár, *the Government; a Superintendent.* A. –i.

Sar-o-kár, *business; relation which one thing bears to another.*

Sar-posh, *a covering-cloth,* (e.g., *a tea-cosy*); *a lid.*

Sarráf, *a banker; a 'shroff.'*

Sarrishtah, *a record-office, or the like.* -dár, *head of the same.*

Sáṛhe. *See page* 64.

Sás, *a mother-in-law.*

Sasta, *cheap.* N. –ti.

Satána, *to vex; to annoy.*

Satar (f.), *a line.*

Sáth (ke.), *with ; along with.* –jána, *or* chalna, *to accompany.* –i, *a companion.*

Sati, *a widow who burns herself on her husband's pyre. a 'suttee.'*

Sattu, *a kind of flour.*

Satún, *or* sutún, *a pillar.*

Saṭána ; saṭá-d., *to join ; to place two things beside each.*

Saṭna ; saṭ-jána, *to stick ; to adhere.* saṭa hú,a, *stuck together ; contiguous.*

Sau *See* 'Sai.'

Sauda ; saudágari, *trade.* saudágar, *a trader.*

Sawál, *or* suwál, *a question ; a petition in Court.* V. –k.

Sawár, *mounted ; a horseman.* N. –i, *riding ;* A. –i, *relating to riding.* sawáṛi ghoṛa, *a riding horse.* –h., *to be mounted ; to ride.*

Sawere, *early morning.*

Sáyah, *shade ; shadow.* sáyabán, *any structure for the purposes of shade ;* e.g., *a verandah.*

Sáz, *equipments ; harness.* –ka ghoṛa, *a harness-stand.*

Saza (f.), *one's deserts ; punishment.* –d, *to punish.*

Se, *from ; with ; by means of ; ago ; since ; than.*

Seb, *an apple.*

Seṇkna, *to toast ; to warm at the fire.*

Ser, *a weight of about* 2 *lbs.*

Sih (p.), *three.* –pahar, *the third watch ; the afternoon.*

Sídha ; *straight ; in order.* V. –k.

Sifárish, *recommendation.* V. –k.

Sijil, *a seal ; a register ; a decree.* V. –k.

Síkhna, *to learn.* sikhána ; sikhlána ; sikhlá-d., *to teach.*

Síkh (f.), *a spit.*

Silái, *sewing.* V. –k.

Silli, *a hone ; a strop.*

Silsilah, *a chain ; a sequence.*

Sína, *to sew.*

Sínah, *the bosom.*

Síng (f.), *a horn.*

Siṇgár, *ornament ; dress.*–mez. *a dressing-table.* V. –na.

Singh, *a lion ; used also as a name.*

Sinn, *one's age.*

Sipáhi, *a foot-soldier ; a 'sepoy.'*

Sir. *See* 'Sar.'

Siráj, *a lamp; the Sun.*

Sirf, *only.*

Síṛhi, *a ladder; steps; a staircase.*

Sísa, *lead.*

Sít (n.), *cold.* A. –al. sítal-páṭi, *a cool kind of mat for sleeping on.*

Sitárah, *a star.*

Sítla, *small-pox.*

Síṭh, *or* síṭhi, *refuse of plant* (e.g., indigo) *after manufacture; of betel* or *tobacco, &c., after being chewed.*

Síṭi, *whistling.* V. –bajána.

Siwa, *or* siwá,e (adv.), *more;* as prep. (ke.), *besides; in addition to.*

Siwánah, *a boundary line.*

Siyáh, *black.* –i, *blacking; ink.*

Siyána, *grown-up.*

So. *See page* 104. Also *stem of* 'sona.' *q.v.*

Soch, *meditation; thought.* -na, *to think; take thought about.*

Sohán, *a file* (tool).

Sojh, *straightness.* A. -a.

Sokna, *to absorb.*

Solah, *sixteen.*

Solah-ṭopi, *a pith-hat.*

Sona, *gold.* A. sone ka. sonár, *a gold-smith.*

Sona, *to lie down; to sleep.* so-rahna, *to continue sleeping.*

Soṇṭa, *a club; a pestle.*

Sonṭh, *dry ginger.*

Stán, *a suffix meaning 'place,'* e.g., 'gulistán,' *a place of roses.*

Sthír, *firm; fixed.*

Stri, *a woman.* –dhan, *the private property of a woman.*

Súbah, *a province.*-badár, *a governor; a native military officer; a sergeant.*

Subh (f.), *the morning; in the morning.*

Subuk (adj.), *light.* (not heavy.) (lit. or fig.).

Súd, *interest on money; profit.*

Sufed, *white.* N. –i.

Sú,i, *a needle.* –tága, *a needle and thread.*

Súkhna (*intr.*), *to dry.* rúkhána; súkhá-d. (*trans.*), *to dry.* A. súkha.

Sukhan, *speech; language; business; affairs.*

Sulḥ, *peace of mind; concord.* –námah, *a deed settling a dispute.*

Sultán, *a 'Sultan.'* saltanat, *dominion; power.*

Sulúk, *good behaviour.* V. –k.

Súṇghna, *to sniff; to smell.*

Sunni, *lawful; the orthodox party among the Muḥam: opposed to 'Shíah.'*

Sunna, *to hear; listen to; obey.* sunána; suná-d., *to cause to hear; read over to one.*

Supári, *areca*, or *betel-nut.*

Supurd, *entrusting.* V. –k.

Suráḥi, *a porous water-bottle; a goblet.*

Surágh, *search; traces.*

Súraj, *the Sun.*

Súrákh, *a hole.*

Súrat, *shape; form.*

Surkh, *red.* –i, *redness; brick-dust.*

Surmah, *antimony.*

Sust, *lazy; out of sorts;* of a watch, *slow.* N. –i.

Sút, *thread.* –i, *made of thread; Hence.* 'ek-súti;' 'do-súti,' &c., *in describing cloth.*

Suthra, *clean; tidy; nice.*

Sutli, *thread; string.*

Sh.

Shab (f.), *night.*–i-máh, (*night of the moon*), *moonlight.* –nam, *dew.* –o roz, *night and day,* or *by* ditto. –chirágh, *a fire-fly; a glow-worm.*

Shábásh, *bravo! well done!*

Shabd, *a sound; a noise; a vocable.*

Shádi, *rejoicing; marriage.* V. –k.

Shaft-álu, *a peach.*

Shafḳat, *condolence; kindness; sympathy.*

Shágird, *a pupil; a scholar.*

Sháh, *an Emperor.* –i, *imperial; royalty.* –an-sháh, *King of Kings* (i.e., the Emperor of Persia). –zádah, *a prince; of princely birth.* fem., –zádi.

Shahad, *honey.* –ki makkhi, *a bee.*

Shahádat, *evidence.*

Sháhid, *a witness.*

Shahr, *a city; a town.*

Shaikh, *a 'Shekh.'* (*title*).

Shaitán, *Satan.*

Shakar, *sugar;* in compos: *sweet.* e.g. –lab, *sweet-lipped.*

Shakk, *doubt.* V. –k.

Shakl (f.), *shape; form*

Shákh (f.), *a branch.*

Shakhs, *an individual.*

Shál (f.), *a shawl.*

Shalgham, *turnips.* [*evening.*

Shám (f.), *evening.* –ko, *at*

Sháma, *a nightingale.*

Shamál, *the North.*

Shámil, *along with; put along with.* –k., *to put one thing up along with another.*

Shámiyánah, *a large tent; a canopy.*

Shams, *the Sun.* (*Arabic.*)

Shamsher (f.), a *scimitar.*

Shán, *dignity; state; nature.*

Sharáb (f.), *wine.*

Shara, *Muham: law.*

Sharákat, *partnership.*

Sharárat, *vice.*

Sharbat, '*sherbet.*'

Sharíf, *noble.*

Sharífah, *a custard-apple.*

Sharík, *a partner.*

Sharm (f.); -indagi, *shame; modesty.* A. sharmindah. sharmána (*intr.*), *to feel abashed.* sharm-sár, *bashful.*

Shart, *a stipulation; agreement; wager.*

Shast, *aim.* (*with gun, &c.*) V. –k.

Shástr (f.), *the sacred books of the Hindus.*

Shatranj, *chess.* –i, *a large carpet.*

Shauk, *one's favourite pursuit;* '*hobby.*' (Anglo-Hind., 'shok.')

Sháyad, (Persian,) (*it may be*); *perhaps.*

Sher, *a tiger.* –ni, *a tigress* –babar, *a lion.*

Shikam, *the belly.*

Shikár, *hunting; shooting; game* (*alive or dead*). –i, *a hunter; appertaining to sport.* e.g. –i kutta, *a hound.*

Shikastah, *broken; running-hand-writing.* –háli, *broken fortune.*

Shíl, *nature; quality; deportment.*

Shírín, *sweet; gentle.* (lit. and fig.) –zabán, *sweet-tongued; eloquent.* N. –zabáni.

Shíshah, *glass; a phial.* –she ka, *made of glass.*

Shít (n.), *cold.* –kál, *the cold weather.*

Shitáb, *haste ; speed.* Adv. –i.

Shokh, *forward ; impudent.* N. –i.

Shor, *noise ; row.*

Shorah, *marshy-land ; salt-petre.*

Shorba, (*vulg.* súrwa,) *soup.*

Shubhah, *doubt.*

Shubh, *happy ; fortunate.*

Shuja, *brave.* –já,at, *bravery.*

Shukr, *gratitude ; thanks.* –guzár, *grateful.* –guzári *expressing gratitude.*

Shulah, *a flame.*

Shumár, *counting.* V. –k.

Shuru (f.), *a beginning.* V. –k.

Shutur, *a camel.* –bán, *a camel-driver.*

T.

There are two soft 't's' in Hindústáṇi, but their sounds are so similar, that you have not been troubled to distinguish them.

Ta, *up to* (of time) tá-kih, *until ; in order to ; to the end that.*

Ta,ajjub, *surprise ; admiration.* V. –k.

Ta,ála (M.), *Almighty God.*

Taalím (f.), *instruction.* V –d.

Ta,alluḳ, *or* ta,alluḳah, *connection ; association ; a territorial division ; an estate ; a 'talook.'* ta,alluḳ-dár, *the owner of a ta,alluḳ.*

Taamíl, *putting in force ; carrying out.* V. –k.

Ta,ammul, *meditation.* V. –k.

Taaríf (f.), *praising ; praise ; a definition.* V. –k. Also, *a table of rates, a 'tariff.'*

Ta,assub, *prejudice ; bigotry.*

Tab, *then* –tak, *up to a time indicated. See page* 104.

Tab, *or* tap, *fever.*

Tabi ; tabíyat, *disposition ; temperament ; health.*

Tábi, *subordinate.* –dár, *a subordinate ; an adherent.* –dári, *subordination ; allegiance.*

Tabíb, *a physician.*

Tabassum, *a smile.*

Tad, *then ; next.* –antar, *after that.*

Tadáruk (f.), *retaliation ; preparation for ditto, as by getting up evidence in a case in Court ; investigation.*

Tadbír (f.), *deliberation ; advice ; plan.*

Tafarruj (f.), *recreation.* V. -k.

Tafáwut, *distance; delay.* V.-k.

Tafsíl (f.), *details.* -k., *to give in detail.* -bolna, *to tell at length.* -an, *in detail.*

Taghmah, *a medal ; a uniform ; a property-mark.*

Tahán. *See page* 104.

Tahkík, *or* tahkíkát, *enquiry ; investigation.* V. -k.

Tahsíl (f.), *collection of rents; a revenue area ; profits,* or *collections generally.* -dár, *a collector of rents, &c.* -dári, *his area of work.*

Tá,íd, *corroboration ; assistance ; an apprentice.*

Taiyár, *ready.* N. -i.

Taisa. *See page* 104.

Táj, *a crown.* -dár, *a prince.*

Tajwíz (f.), *investigation ; trial* (e.g. in Court.) *result of trial.* -V. -k.

Ták (f.), *look ; glance ; aim.*

Tak, *up to* (*time,* or *place*).

Takalluf, *ceremony.*

Tákíd, *pressing ; urging ;* or *reminding one.* V. -k.

Takyah, *a pillow.*

Takrár (f.), *reiteration ; dispute.* -i, *contentious ; quarrelsome ; disputed.*

Taklíf (f.), *ceremony ; trouble; inconvenience.* V. -d.

Tákna (*trans.*), *to observe ; to watch.* takna (*intr.*)

Ták (f.), *a niche.*

Tákat, *strength ; ability.*

Takáza, *a dunning of one.*

Takdír (f.), *fate ; predestination.*

Takrír (f.), *recital ; oration ; detailed statement.* V. -k.

Taksím (f.), *division of property, &c., by shares.* V. -k. *and* lena,

Taksír (f.), *a fault ; a crime* A. -mand ; -wár.

Takhfíf, *making light of anything.*

Takhmínan, *by guess ; approximately.*

Takht, *a throne.*

Takhtah, *a board ; a plank ; a shelf ; a plot of land.* -posh, *a low wooden platform for sitting on cross-legged.* -nard, *backgammon.*

Tál, *a lake.* Also, *a kind of palm tree.* Also, *same as* 'táli,' *q.v.*

Tála, *a padlock ; a key.*

Táláb (f.), *or* talá,o, *an artificial water-pond.*

Talab, *sending for one; desire.* Also, *pay; salary.* –k., *to send for one.* –d., *to give one one's pay.* –ánah, *fees for summoning; daily allowance while waiting.*

Talaffuz, *pronunciation.*

Talak, *same as* 'tak,' *q. v.*

Taláḳ, *divorce.*

Talásh, *search* V. –k.

Talá,o, *same, as* 'táláb,' *q.v.*

Tale (ke), *under.*

Táli, *a key.* Also, *clapping the hands.* –áṇ, *applause by clapping.*

Tálíḳah, *a list; a schedule.*

Tálu, *the palate; lampas.*

Talwár (f.), *a sword.*

Tamáchuh, *a slap.*

Tamám, *whole; entire.* –k., *to complete.*

Tamassuk, *a bond for money borrowed.*

Táma; támba; *or* támra, *copper.*

Tamásha, *an entertainment; a show, a fête.*

Tamátu, *tomatoes.*

Tambáku, *tobacco.* –pína, *to smoke ditto.*

Tambu, *a tent.*

Tamsíl (f.), *comparison; a parable; an illustration.*

Tan-durust, *in good health.* N. –i

Tang, *narrow; too tight.* N. –i. means, also, *poverty.*

Táṇga, *a hill-cart; a 'tongah.'*

Tankhwáh (f.), *wages; salary.*

Tánna (L.B.), *to pull; stretch.*

Táṇt, *a loom.* –i, *a weaver.*

Tanúr, *an oven.*

Tap (f.), *heat; fever.* tápna. *to warm one's self.*

Tapish, *heat* (lit. or fig.); *affliction.*

Tar, *moist; wet.* –á,i, *moist land at base of mountains; 'The Terai.'*

Tár, *string; wire; the telegraph.* –ghar, *the telegraph-office.* –ki khabar, *or* chiṭṭhi, *telegraphic news; a telegram.*

Tára, *a star.*

Taraddud, *perplexity.*

Taraf (f.), *side; direction.* Also, *as prep.* (ki.) –dár, *a partizan.* –dári, *partizanship.* –sáni, *the second par ty n uit; the defendant.*

Taraḥ (f.), *mode; manner.* Also as prep. (ki.), *like.*

Taraḳḳi, *promotion; advancement.* –pána, *to get ditto.*

Tarásh (n.), *cutting.* V. –k. *or* –na.

Tarázu, *a weighing machine.*

Taríḳah, *mode; manner.*

Táríkh (f.), *a date,* (e.g. of a letter.)

Tarjíh, *superiority.* –rakhna, *to gain superiority.* –d., *to assign preference.*

Tarjamah, *a translation.* –mán, *a translator.*

Tarkári, *moist vegetables.*

Tarsoṇ, *on the fourth day.* (backwards or forwards.)

Tartíb (f.), *good order, arrangement.* –k., *to set in order.* Adv. –i.

Taṛka, *the dawn.*

Tásh, *the cards; a game with cards.* –ki mez, *a card-table.*

Tasar, *a kind of silk; 'tusser.'*

Tasarruf, *use; enjoyment; expenditure; waste.* V. –k.

Tasbíh (f.), *praising God by a certain formula; a rosary.*

Tasdíḳ (f.), *verification.* V.–k.

Taskín (f.), *comfort; consolation.*

Tasmah, *a leather thong.*

Taswír (f.), *a picture.*

Tashaffi, *a feeling of satisfaction; satisfaction.*

Tashríf, *honour conferred.* *See page* 76. *Sect.* 17.

Tatíl, *rendering waste* or *useless; a vacation; a holiday.*

Ṭaṭolna, *to grope.*

Tau, *then;* –bhi, *even then; even in such circumstances.*

Taubah, *repentance; penance.* As interj., *what a shame!* i.e., *matter for repentance.*

Tauliyah, *a towel.*

Taun. *See page* 104.

Taur, *mode; manner.*

Tauret, *or* taurát, *the Old Testament.*

Tawaḳḳuf, *delay; wasting time.* V. –k.

Tawelah, *a tethering-rope; a stable; a cattle-pen.*

Tawíz, *having recourse to God; an amulet.*

Tázah, *fresh; green; young.* N. –zagi.

Tazím (f.), *the act of honouring one.*

Tel, *oil.* –batti, *an oiled-wick; a lamp; a night-light.* –i, *an oil-man.*

Tez; tez-rau, *swift.* N.–i. tez nahíṇ, *slow.* tez-zihn, *sharp-witted.*

Thaili, *a bag; a nose-bag.*

Thaka, *tired.* thakána, *to weary.*

Tháli, *a brass platter so called.*

Thambha, *a pillar; a post.*

Thámna (*trans.*), *to stop; to check.*

Thán, '*a piece,*' or *web of cloth;* also, *a stall.*

Thánah, *a police station.* –dár, *an officer in charge of a* '*thánah.*'

Thápa, or thápi, *the sound of beating; a mallet; a bat.*

Thoṛa, *a little.* –thoṛa, *a very little.*

Thúk, *spittle.* V. –na.

Tidhar. *See page* 104.

Tiffin,[1] *lunch;* '*tiffin.*'

Tifl, *a child.*

Tijárat, *trade; trading.*

Tilak, *the dedication mark on a Hindu's forehead.*

Tilli, *the spleen.*

Tín, *three.* Obl. cases, 'tínoṇ.'

Tipá, i, *a small table; a teapoy.*

Ṭipári, *Cape-gooseberry.*

Tír (m.), *an arrow.*

Tirchha, *bent; crooked; awry.*

Tísra, *the third.*

Tishnah, *thirsty.* N. –nagi.

Títa, *bitter.* –pani, *tonic-water.*

Titna (*co-relative*), *so many; so much.*

To. *See page* 47. *Note* 1.

Tol; taul, *the weight of a thing.* tola, *the weight of a rupi.* taulna, *to weigh.*

Ṭonṭa, *a cartridge.*

Top, *a cannon.* –k̲h̲ánah, *the artillery-lines.*

Top, *a grove; a* '*tope.*'

Toṛna; toṛ-d., *to break; tear; destroy.* toṛ-rahna, *to continue breaking.*

Toshah, *valuables.* –k̲h̲ánah, *a treasure-house.*

Toshak (f.), *a mattress; bedding.*

Tota; toti, *a parrot.* (m. f.)

Tu, *thou.*

---

[1] This word is derived from an Arabic oot, "fan," meaning *enjoyment.*

Túfán (m.), *a storm.* A.-í.

Tufúliyat, *childhood.*

Tuhmat, *an accusation.* V. -lagána.

Tujh, *inflected sing. of 'tu.'*

Tukhm, *a seed; a seed-stone.*

Túl, *length.* also, *long.*

Tul, *like; similar.*

Tulna, *to be weighed.*

Tulsi, *sacred basil.*

Tum, *ye; you.* Also, *in Obliq: cases.*

Tund, *sharp; active; fierce.* Often used in compos. e.g. -zihn, *sharp-witted; clever.*

Turat, *at once.*

Turk, *a Turk.* A. -i, 'Turki' also means *a certain kind of horse.*

Tursh, *harsh; sour.* (lit. or fig.)

Ṭ.

Ṭálna, *to be evasive.* ṭálá-ṭoli. *evasiveness; beating about the bush.*

Ṭáng (f.), *the leg.* -na; -d., *to give a leg; to hang up.*

Ṭáṅga, *or* ṭáṅgi, *an axe.*

Ṭápa, *a coop;* Anglo-Hind., *a 'topper.'*

Ṭappál,[1] *the letter, &c. post; the post-office.*

Ṭáṭ, *coarse canvas; 'gunny.'*

Ṭaṭolna (*intr.*), *to grope; feel.*

Ṭaṭṭi, *a screen; a privy.*

Ṭaṭṭu, *a pony; a 'tatt.'*

Ṭeṛha, *not straight.*

Ṭhag, *a garotter; a 'thug.'*

Ṭhaharna, *to remain; stop; wait.* ṭhahrána, *to detain.*

Ṭhákur, *a divinity; an emblem of ditto; a Brahman.* Also, *common as a name among the Brahman class.* -áni, fem. of 'Ṭhákur.' -bári, *a Hindu place of worship.*

Ṭhanḍa (Adj.), *cold.* N. -i.

Ṭhaṭṭha, *a jest.* ṭhaṭhol, *a jester.* ṭhaṭholi, *jesting,* ṭhaṭholna, *to jest.*

Ṭhelna, *to push.*

Ṭiḍḍi, *a locust; a grass-hopper.*

---

[1] Not used in L. B.

Ṭhík ; ṭhík-ṭhák, *exact ; perfectly right.* ṭhikána, *one's address ; trace whereby to find a thing ; certainty.*

Ṭhíka, *hire ; lease ; contract.* -gáṛi, *a hired carriage.* -dár, *the holder of a lease ; a contractor.*

Ṭhokar (f.), *a blow ; a knock.* ṭhokna, *to strike.* -khána, *to get a blow,* or *knock.*

Ṭhuḍḍi, *the inch.*

Ṭikli, *a wafer.*

Ṭikṭikki, *a lizard.*

Ṭíp (f.), *a note of hand ; an I. O. U.*

Ṭokri, *a basket.*

Ṭola, *a quarter of a town.*

Ṭukṛa, *a piece ; a morsel.*

Ṭúngna, *to peck.*

Ṭúṭa, *broken.*

U.

Ubálna (*trans.*), *to boil.* ubalna, (*intr.*)

Ubká, i, *vomiting ; straining.* V.-k. *and* lena.

Uchhal, *leaping.* V.-na.

Udás, *grieved.* N. -i.

Udhar, *thither ; on the far side ; over there.*

Ugál, *spit.* -dán, *a spittoon.*

Ukháṛna, *to uproot.*

Ulaṭ, *the act of upsetting.* -na (*trans.* and *intr.*), *to upset,* or *be upset.*-d., *to upset.* -pulaṭ, *upside down.*

Ullu, *an owl.*

Ulṭána, *to upset: turn upside down.* ulṭa, *reversed ; turned upside down.* ulṭa,-pulṭa, *upside down ; in confusion.*

Umdah, *excellent ; noble.*

Ummed(f.), *hope.* A. -wár, *which is also used as a noun meaning one hoping for an appointment, &c.*

Ummúmat, *maternity.*

Umr (f.), *one's age.*

Umúr (Pl. of 'amr.'), *affairs ; business.*

U'n, *wool.* un, *inflected plur. of* 'wuh.'

U'ṇcha, *high.* N. -i.

Ungli, *a finger.*

Ungul, *the thumb.*

U'ṇṭ, *a camel.*

U'par, *above ; up ; high up ;* As prep. (ke.)

Urdu (f.), *a market; a camp. a name of the Hindústáni language, as formed by the mixing of various races in market and camp.*

Uṛna; úṛ-jána (*intr.*), *to fly.* uṛána; uṛá-d. (*trans.*), *to fly; to squander.*

Usárah, *a portico; a verandah.*

Us, *inflected, sing. of 'wuh.'* -ḳadar. *See page* 104. -waḳt, *at that time; then.*

Usturah, *a razor.*

Utárna; utár-d. *to break down; to tear off; to strip off.* utarna, *to come down; to descend.*

Uthla, *shallow.* V. -i.

Uttar, *the North.*

Uṭhna, *to rise.* uṭh-jána, *to rise and go.* uṭhána; uṭhá-d, *to raise.*

Uzr, *an excuse.* -k., *to excuse.*

V.

Words in which W is sounded like V are nearly all derived from Saṇskrit, and would not be of use to you. But you should know the word '*Ved*' or '*Veda,*' the general name of the Sacred Books of the Hindus—*the 'Veds.'*

W.

Waadah, *a promise.* V. -k.

Wá,e-wá,e, *woe is me!*

Wafa, *fulfilling a promise; integrity.*

Waghairah, *et cætera.*

Waháṇ, *there:* may be followed by ka, ko, se, tak, &c. like a noun.

Wahhábi, *a follower of Abd-l-'Wahháb,' a Muḥam: teacher of the last century.*

Waḥíd, *alone; unique.*

Waisa, *like that; so. See page,* 104. -hi, *in that very manner just like that.*

Wajab, *a span.* (*of the hand.*)

Wajh (f.), *reason; cause.*

Wájib, *or* wájibi, *right; proper.* wájibát, *proper accessories; necessary things.*

Wakíl, *or* Vakíl, *an ambassador; representative; attorney.* wakálat-námah, *a power of Attorney.*

Waḳf, *a Muḥam: religious endowment.*

Wáḳifíyat, *experience; knowledge.*

Wáḳif, *aware; informed; acquainted with.* –hona, *to be,* or *become ditto.* –k., *to inform, &c.*

Waḳt, *time.* –ba–, *from time to time.* –ná–, *occasionally.*

Wála-wáli. *See page* 73, 7.

Wali (M.), *a holy man.*

Wápas, *back; behind; returning.* –ána, *to come back.* –d., *to give back.* –hona, *to be back.* –rakhna, *to keep back.*

Wálid, *a father.*–ah, *a mother.*

Waraḳ, *a leaf of a book,* or *of a tree.*

Wárid (Adj.), *approaching; arriving; present.* V.–hona.

Wáris, *an heir.* Pl. –án.

Warna, *and if not; if this be not so; otherwise.*

Wasíḳah, *firmness; solidity; a bond; a written agreement.*

Wásil, *joined together; collected.* –báḳi, *a statement of collections and arrears.* –át, *accounts; mesne-profits.*

Wasílah, *means used to accomplish any object.*

Wasíyat, *one's last 'will.'*

Wáste (ke.), *for the sake of; for.*

Watan, *one's native country.*

Wazír, *a minister; a 'Vizier.'*

Wazn, *weight.* (lit. *or* fig.) V. –k. –i, *heavy.*

We, *they; those.* Nom. Pl. of '*wuh.*'

Wiláyat, *foreign lands.* –i, *foreign; European; English.* –i páni, *soda water.*

Wírán, *depopulated; waste; a desert.*

Wohi, *that very.* wohín, *thus; in this manner.*

Wujúd, *existence; substance; essence; invention. See* 'Bá-wujúd.'

Wuh, *he; she; it; that.*

Wuḳu, *an occurrence; an event.* Pl. wáḳiyát.

Wuḳúf, *experience.*

Wusúl, *collection of rents, &c.* V. –k.

Y.

Ya, *or.* ya...ya, *either...or.*

Yád (f.), *recollection.* V. -k. -dásht, *a memorandum.* -dilána (*trans.*), *to remind.*

Yaháṇ, *here.* Also used with ka, ko, se, &c. as a noun. As prep. (ke.). *See page* 44. -ána, *to arrive.*

Yahúd, *a Jew.* -in, *a Jewess.*

Yaḳín, *certain.* -jánna, *to know for certain.* N. -i.

Yáḳút, *a ruby.*

Yakh (f.), *ice.*

Yane, *namely ; that is to say ; 'I mean.'*

Yár, *a friend.* -i, *friendship.*

Yatím, *an orphan.* -i, *-cy.*

Yáwah, *idle talk ; nonsense.*

Ye, *they ; these.* Nom., Pl. of '*yih.*'

Yih, *he ; she ; it ; this.* -, *this, very.*

Yogi, *also* jogi, *a Hindu ascetic.*

Yoṇ, *thus, in this manner.* -hiṇ, *in this very manner.* Also, *by chance ; casually.*

Yug, *a cycle of time.*

Z.

There are four 'Z's' in Hindústáni, but their sounds are so similar that you have not been troubled to distinguish them.

Zabán (f.), *the tongue ; a language.* -i, *orally.*

Zabar, *superior in position.* -dast,[1] *powerful ; oppressive.* N. -dasti. V. -dast hona. -dasti k.

Zabḥ, *sacrifice.* -k., *to kill an animal as prescribed by law,* i.e., *by cutting the throat.*

Zábitah, *ordinance ; law ; established custom.*

Zabt, *confiscation.* V. -k.

Zabún, *bad ; wicked.*

Zahín, *sharp-witted.*

Záhir, *evident ; clear.* -hona, *to be evident.* -k., *to make evident ; to demonstrate.* Adv. -an.

---

[1] 'Dast,' *the hand.* V. *ante.*

Zahr, *poison* ; -álúdah,*poisoned* (as food.).-íla, *poisonous.*

Zaḥmat, *anxiety ; pains.*

Za,íf, *frail ; infirm.*

Zakhm, *a wound.* A. --i, *means also a wounded person.*

Zálim, *an oppressor.* A. -i.

Zamán ; zamánah, *any time ; an epoch* or *age of the World.*

Zámin, *bail.* zamánat, *suretyship.*

Zamín (f.), *land.* -dár, *a landed proprietor.* -dári, *landed-property.*

Zamurrad, *or* zumarrad, *an emerald.*

Zan (p.), *a woman.* -áni, *appertaining to women.*-ánah, *the female apartment* .

Zanakh, *the chin.*

Zang, *rust.* -khúrdah, *rusty.* -pakaṛna, (*rust has seized this ;*) *equal to,* '*this has turned rusty.*'

Zánu, *the knee.*

Zanjír (f.), *a chain.*

Zar, *gold.*

Zarar, *hurt ; injury.* -khafíf, *trivial injury.* -shadíd, *serious injury.*

Zarb (f.) *a blow.*

Zard (Adj.), *yellow.* N. -i.

Zarrah (f.), *a little ; a morsel.*

Zarúr, *necessary.* -at, *necessity ; time of difficulty.*

Zát, *caste.*

Zaujah, *a wife.*

Zer (p.), *under.* -band, *a martingale.* -tajwíz, *under enquiry.*

Zewar ; zewarát, *jewels.*

Zidd, *perversity ; spite.* V. -k. A. -i.

Zikr, *remembrance ; mention.* V. -k.

Zila ; *a district ; a country.*

Zimmah, *charge ; keeping ; responsibility.*

Zín (f.), *a saddle.* V. -bándhna ; bándh-d. -posh, *a saddle-cloth.*

Zindah, *alive,* -dagi ;-dagáni *life ; being alive.*

Ziyádah, *more ; too much.* dat, *increment.*

Ziyáfat, *a feast.* V. -d.

Ziyán, *loss.*

Zor ; zori, *force ; strength.* -áwar ; -mand, *strong ; oppressive.* -d., *to assist ; to strengthen.* -k., *to strain ; to force ; to oppress.*

Zúd, *quick ; swift.* also as adv.

Zuf, *or* zof, *bodily frailty.*

Zuhr, *the turn of the day at noon; noon.*

Zukám, *a cold in the head.*

Zulál, *pure; limpid; wholesome.*

Zulf (f.), *curly hair.*

Zulm, *oppression.* A. -i.

GLOSSARY OF USEFUL WORDS

PART II.

ENGLISH-HINDÚSTÁNI.

NOTE.

THE contractions used in the English-Hindústáni part of this Glossary are the same as those used in the first part, with one addition, *viz.* (v. n.), which means 'Verbal Noun.' *See page* 15. *Sect.* 17.

The 'head-word' is generally the shortest word from which longer words are derived. Thus under 'Art' you will find 'Artificer.'

Always look for the Noun first, (if there be a noun,) *e.g.*, for 'Advice,' not for 'Advise.'

As, within the space available, all synonyms cannot be given, if you cannot find the precise word wanted, try another of a similar meaning— Note also that as *familiar* words are given, you should lock for such; as for '*Delay*,' not for '*Procrastination*.'

A double use is made of the short line; first, *associated with English*, it represents the head English word, (or so much of it as is wanted,) *e.g.*, 'accurate,' '-acy;' secondly, *associated with the Hindústáni*, it refers to the preceding word or words, *e.g.*, 'affirmation,' iḳrár; izhár. V. -k., means that you may use 'karna' with both 'iḳrár' and 'izhár,' for the English 'to affirm.' When one verb is not applicable to a string of nouns, the string is broken, the verb applicable to the nouns up to that point is shown *within brackets*; the nouns are then resumed; other appropriate verbs being given in their proper places.

English *within brackets* indicates the precise shade of meaning of the word being dealt with.

Nouns of an abstract sense do not often occur in the common Hindústáni. Few therefore are given here. The abstract idea of *an act* is generally expressed by the Verbal Noun, *e.g.*, chup-rahna bihtar hai bak-bak karne-se, "*silence is better than chattering*;" and the abstract idea of *a person* is expressed by a clause with 'jo'—or by the humble 'wála,' *e.g.*, Jo insáf karta hai, wuh Khuda-ko pasand hai, "*The Doer of Justice is pleasing to God.*"

GLOSSARY OF USEFUL WORDS.

ENGLISH–HINDÚSTÁNI.

A.

A, *or* an. *See page* 9. *Note.*

Abandon, *chhoṛ-d.; tark-k.*

Abetment, *madad* (f.); *iánat.* V. *-d.* –tor, *madadgár.*

Abide. *See* 'Live,' 'Remain.'

Ability, *ḳábilíyat; maḳdúr.*

Able, *ḳábil.* to be–, *sakna.* *See page* 18. *Sect.* 22.

Above (adv.), *úpar.* (prep.), *ke úpar.*

Absent, *ghair-ḥázir.* N. *–i.* V. *–hona.*

Absorb, *sokhna; sokh-jána.*

Abstinence, *parhez* (f.), V. *-k.; nahíṇ karna.*

Abstract, *khulásah.* V. *–k.;* (as essence), *nikál-d.*

Absurd, *be-húdah.* N. *–dagi.*

Abuse, *gáli.* V. *-d.*

Academy, *madrasah.*

Accede to, *ḳabúl-* (or *ḳubúl-*) *k.; manzúr-k.*

Accelerate, *jaldi-karána.* N. *jaldi.*

Accept, *lena; le-lena; pasand -k.; ḳabúl-k.* A. *pasand; pasandídah; achchha.* –ance, *lena* (as v.n.).

Access, *ráh* (f.); *rásta.* of fever, *ámad* (f.).

Accident, *ittifáḳ.* by –, *ittifáḳan.*

Accompany, *sáth-jána; hamráhi-k.*

Accomplish, *tamám-k.; púra-k.; taamíl-k.;* –ed, (done), *tamám,* &c. (learned), *álim; kámil; árástah.*

According to, *ḥasb; ba-mújib; ke mu,áfiḳ.*

Account (in figures), *ḥisáb. to* do–, *–k.*, or *likhna.* to take–, *–lena.* to keep –, *–rakhna.* –ant, *mutasaddi* –book, *–ki bahi.* (in words) *bayán; bát; ḳissah; ḥikáyat.* V–*k.*

Accurate, *ṭhík; durust; achchhá.* –acy, *siḥḥat.*

Accusation, *tuhmat.* (V. *la-gána*); *nálish.* (V. *–k*) –er, *faryádi; mudda,i.*

Accustomed, I am, *yih mera dastúr hai*, or other phrase.

Acknowledgment, *iḳrár; ḳabúl-k.* (v.n.). V. *–k.* deed of–, *iḳrár-námah.* (receipt), '*rasíd.*' (E.).

Acquaint, *khabar-d.; ágáh-k; wáḳif-k.* –ed (with any matter.) *wáḳif; ágáh; maiṇ jánta húṇ.* –ance, *dost; yár; bhá,i.* –ance-ship, *ján-pahchán; dosti.*

Acquire, *pána; ḥásil-k.; jama-k.; milna.* *See page* 50, *Note* 1. -sition, *ḥásil; jo ḥásil hú,a.*

Acquittance (in Court), *kha-lás; rihá,i.* V. *–kar-d.* (of an account), '*rasíd*'; (E.); *fárigh-khatti.* V. *–d.*

Across, *pár; us pár.*

Act, *fel; amr; amal.* -tion, *kám.* V. *karna.*

Active, *tez; chálák.* –ity, *chusti; cháláki.*

Add, *lagá-d.* (figures), *jama-k.*

Address (speech), *taḳrír* (f.); *arz* (f.); *baḥs* (f.); *nibedan.* V. *–k.* (of letter, &c.,) *ṭhikána.*

Adhere, *lagna; lag-jána; saṭna; saṭ-jána.*

Adjacent, *nazdík; ḳaríb.*

Admiration, *ajab; ta,ajjub.* V. *–k.* -able, *ajíb; khúb; achchha.*

Admit (to presence), *áne-d.* (agree to), *ḳabúl-k.; iḳrár-k.* –mission, *iḳrár.*

Adorn, *sajána.* –ment, *árá,ish; siṇgár.*

Advance, *baṛhá,o.* V. (*trans.*), *áge baṛhána; chalána.* (*intr.*), *chalna; áge jána.* (of money), *dádni.* –ment in life, *taraḳḳi.* V. *–d.* and *pána.*

Advantage, *fá,idah.* –ous, *fá,idamand.*

Advertisement, *ishtihár.* V. *–jári-k.*

Advice, *saláḥ* (f.); *maslaḥat.* V. *–d.*

Affair, *bát; amr; kám; wuḳu.*

Affect, *asar.* V. *-k.; lagna.*

Affection, *pyár; muḥabbat.*

Affirmation, *iḳrár; izhár.* V. *-k.; kahna.*

Affliction, *ghamm; ázurdagi; taklíf* (f.). -ed, *ghamgín; ázurdah; dil-sokhtah.* V. *satána; taklíf-d.*

Afford, *de-sakna.*

Afoot, *paidal; pá,oṇ-pá,oṇ.*

After (time), *ke baad; ke píchhe.* (place), *ke píchhe:* (adv.), *píchhe.* -wards, *is ke baad; tab.* -noon, *do pahar ke baad; sih-pahar.*

Again, *phir; pher.* - and-, *ber-ber; aksar.*

Against (*e.g.*, a stone), *par.* (adverse), *se khiláf.*

Age, *umr* (f.); *sinn.* (period), *waḳt; zamánah; yug.* old-, *buṛhápa.*

Agent, *ná,ib; gumáshtah; kartah; kár-pardáz.* (for law business), *vakíl; mukhtár.* -cy, *gumáshtagari; vakíli.*

Agree to, *ḳabúl-k; rázi-hona.* -able, *khush; pasand; mu,áfiḳ.* -ably to, *ḥasb; ba-mújib; ke mu,áfiḳ.* -ment, *shart; ḳaul-o-ḳarár; aḥd-o-paimán.* -(in writing), *saṭṭa; sarkhatt.* ...*námah*, added to word expressing the nature of the agreement; as *sulḥ-námah*, an agreement for peace, *e.g.*, in a litigation.

Aid, *madad* (f.). V. *-d.*

Aim (at mark), *shast.* V. *-k.* (intention), *matlab; irádah; ḳasd; níyat; gharaz* (f.).

Air, *hawa* (f.). to take the-, *hawa kháṇa.*

Alarm, *ḍar* (f.). V.*-dikhláṇa.*

Alike, *eksáṇ; ek ḳism ka; barábar.*

All, *sab; sab ke sab; kull; tamám.* -right! *bahut achchha!; bahut khúb!*

Allegation, *bát; bayán; arz* (f.). V. *-k.; kahna.*

Alligator, *magar; ghaṛiyál; kumhír.*

Allow, use '*dena*,' and the verb of that which is allowed, e.g., *us-ne ham-ko áne diya hai*, he has allowed me to come. When equivalent to 'give,' (I *allow* you ten rupees a month), also use '*dena*.'

Allude to, *zikr-k.* N. *zikr.*

Almonds, *bádám.*

Alms, *khairát.* V. *-d.*

Alone, *akela ; ekla ; tanha ; mujarrad.*

Along (*e.g.*, the street,) *meṉ; par.*-with, *ek sáth ; kesáth.*

Aloud, *zor se,* or *baland awáz se.*

Already, *ab-hi ;* with *chukna*, e.g., I have *already* spoken, *maiṉ bol-chuka húṉ.*

Also, *aur ; bhi.*

Alternate. *See page* 69.

Although, *agar-chih ; har-chand.*

Always, *hameshah ; aksar.*

Am, *húṉ.*

Amendment, *bihtari ; du-rusti ; tarmím.* V. *-k.*

Amiable, *azíz ; sháyastah.* -bility, *sháyastagi.*

Among ; amidst, *ke bích.* -themselves, *ápas meṉ.*

Amount, *jumlah ; jama.*

Amuse, *bahlána ; khush-k.* -ment, *támásha ; khela-kheli.*

Analysis, *tafsíl ; tafrík.* V. *-k.*

Ancestor, *jadd ; báp-dáda ; múris.* -try, *jaddíyat.*

Anchor, *langar.* V. (to cast,) *-ḍálna.* (to heave), *-uṭhána.*

Ancient, *ḳadím ; agla ; purána.*

And, *aur ; wa ; o.*

Angel, *firistah.*(*Pl.* *-ta gán.*) ; *malak.*

Anger, *ghussah ; khafgi ; rís,* (f.). A. *ghusse ; khafa.* V. *-hona.*

Animal, *jánwar ; ḥaiwán.*

Animosity, *adáwat ; dush-mani.*

Announcement, *khabar,* (f.) ; *ittila* (f.). V. *-d.*

Annoyance, *dikḳ ; taklíf* (f.). V. *-d.; satána.*

Another, (an additional thing,) *aur ek.* (a different thing), *dúsra.*

Answer, *jawáb,* V. *-d.* (*to 'do,'*) *ṭhík-hona ; achchha-hona.* (liable to answer), *jawáb-dihi.*

Ant, *chyúṉṭi.* (red.) *beṉbúṭ.* (white.) *dímak.*

Antimony, *surmah.*

Antipathy, *zidd ; nafrat ; chiṛh* (f.).

Antiquity, *awá,il ; agle-wakt.*

Anxiety, *fikr* (f.) ; *andeshah ; taraddud.* A. *fikrmand ; mutafakkir.* V. *fikrmand, &c. hona.*

Any. *See page* 38. –where, *kahín.* –how, *kisi tarah ; jis - tarah ban - parega.* –more, *aur kuchh.*

Apart, *juda ; alag ; ek taraf.* –ment, *kothri ; kamra.* (for females), *zanánah.* (for males), *mardánah.*

Apology, *uzr.* V. *–k.*

Apostle, *rasúl ; paighambar.* (the latter referring, *par excellence*, to Muhammad.)

Apparatus, *sáz; sáz-o-sámán; saranjám ; chíz sab.*

Apparent, *záhir ; maalúm ; sáf.* to be–, *–hona.* to make–, *–k.*

Appearance, *súrat ; shakl* (f.).

Append, *jorna ; lagá-d. ; shámil-k.* –age, *láhik.* –ix, *tatimmah.*

Apple, *seb.*

Applicable, *lá,ik ; munásib.*

Apply (one thing to another), *lagána ; lagá-d. ; milána ; milá-d.* (as to study), *mihnat, tandihi,* or *ihtimám-k. ; dil-lagá-d.* –plication, (of one thing to another,) *ek chíz dúsri ko lagá-d.* (v.n.). (diligence,) *mihnat ; tandihi ; ihtimám.*

Appointment, *kám ; naukari.* V. *kisi ko kám, &c. d. ; tayín-k ; nám-zad-k.* –ed, *muta,aiyan ; mansúb.*

Apprehend (with mind), *samajhna ; samajh men lena ; bújhna.* –hension, *samajh,* (f.) ; *bújh,* (f.) ; *hosh ; akl* (f.) *See* 'Arrest.'

Approach, *nazdík,* or *sámne,* or *pás ána ; wárid hona.*

Approve, *pasand-k. ; manzúr-k.* –al, *manzúri.*

Apricot, *khúbáni,* or *khobáni.*

Arbitration, *sálisi ; panchdyat.* V. *–k.* –tor, *salís ; panch.*

Arch (n.), *mihráb.* V. *–banána.*

Archer, *kamán-dár ; tír-andáz.* –ery, *kamán-dári ; tír-andázi.*

Ardour, *garmi ; dil-sozi ; zahmat ; mihnat.* filled with–, *garm ; dil-soz ; mihnati.*

Arduous, *sakht ; mushkil ; sangín ; wazani.*

Are. *See page* 15. *Sect.* 11.

Area, *maidán ; jagah.*(court) *saḥn.*

Areca-nut, *supári*, *pán.*

Arise, *uṭhna ; uṭh-jána.* (begin,) *shurú-k.* (come up, *e.g.*, for attention,) *bar-pá-hona ; pesh-hona.*

Arm, *bázu; háth.*–pit, *baghal,* (f.). (of sea, or river), *sota.*

Arms, *hathiyár ; ḥarbe.*

Army, *fauj* (f.) ; *lashkar* (m.).

Around, *har taraf ; cháron taraf;chauras.*prep.*ke gird.*

Arrangement, *tartíb; intizám; band-o-bast.* (m.). V. *–k. ; ṭhík-k. ; durust-k.*

Arrears, *báḳi ; jo báḳi hai ; báḳiyát.*

Arrest, *pakaṛna ; pakaṛ-lena,* or *le-jána ; giriftár-k.* in arrest, *giriftár-hú,a ; ḳaid-hú,a ; pakṛa gaya.*

Arrive, *pahunchna ; á-pahunchna ; ána ; á-jána ; ḥázir-hona,* or *ána ; tashríf lána.* *See page* 76. *Sect.* 17. *wárid-hona.* –al, *ámad* (f.). *dar-ámad* (f.). and with the verbs used as v. n. –e.g., 'on his arrival,' *us-ke áne ke waḳt.*

Arrow, *tír* (m.).

Art, *hunar ; ilm ; kám.* –ful, *ḥílah-báz ; shokh.* –fully, *fann se.* –less, *sídha ; sachcha,* –ifice, *ḥílah.* –ificer, *kárígar.* –ist, *musawwir.*

Artichoke, *háṭichok.* (E.).

Artillery, the, *top-khánah.*

As. *See page* 104. (like.) *ki mánind ; ke mu,áfiḳ ; chunánchih.* '*he gives orders* as *a master*, málik *kar* (from 'karna,') ḥukum deta hai 'as if' is best translated by 'like,' e.g., *he speaks* as if *he were a great man,* –he speaks 'like,' or 'in the manner of' 'a great man,' 'baṛe ádmi *ke taur se* bolta hai, or, baṛa ádmi *kar* bolta hai.' As far as, as long as, &c. *See* corresponding phrases at page 104. as often as...so often, *jai-ber...tai-ber.* '*that* as well as *this*,' wuh, *aur* yih *bhi.*

Ascend, *chaṛhna ; chaṛh jána.* N. *únchi zamín* (f.).

Ascertainment, *daryáft ; taḥḳíḳ.* V. *–k. ; khabar lána ; púchhna.*

Ascribe, *lagá-d.*

Ashamed, *sharmindah; lajit.* to be–, *–hona; sharmána; sharm-khána; lajána.*

Ashes, *rákh.*

Ask, (a question.) *púchhna; sawál-k.* (for something.) *mángna; cháhna.*

Asparagus, *sparugras.* (E.).

Aspec, *aspik.* (E.).

Aspire, *árzu rakhna.* –ation, *álí-himmat.*

Ass, *gadha.* (f. *gadhí*); *khar.*

Assault, *hamlah; már-pít.* V–*k.*

Assembly, –blage, *jamá,at; majmú,ah; majlis; amboh.* (unlawful) *majma khiláf kánún.* (riotous) *guhár.* V. (*trans.*), *jama-k.* (*intr.*), *jama-hona.*

Assent. *See* 'Agree to.'

Assert. *See* 'Say.'

Assist. *See* 'Aid.' –tant, *madad-gár.*

Associate, *sharík; rafík.* to –with. *mel-rakhna; sáth-rahna; suhbat-rakhna.*

Assume (take), *lena; le-lena.* (for argument's sake,) *farz-k.* (airs), *itrána.*

Assure, *kahna; yakín karána.* –ance, *yakín; khátir-jama.* –edly, *albattah.*

Astonishment, *tahaiyur.* V. *kisí ko tahaiyur-k.* –ed, *ghábra.* –ing, *ajúbah; ajíb.*

Astrology, *nujúm.* –ger, *nujúmí.*

At, (a person's,) *ke pás; ke yahán.* (place,) *men.* (time,) *ko.* –all events, *ba har súrat.* -first, *awwalan; paihle.* –hand, *ke pás; ke nazdík; muyassar.* –home. *ghar men.* –last, *ákhir; ákhir ko; ákhir-ul-amr,* –least, *kam se kam.* –leisure, e.g., *ab mujh-ko fursat hai.* –length, (in detail,) *mufassalan.* (See, 'at last.') –most, *bahut se bahut.* –pleasure, *marzí ke mu,áfik.* –present, *ab; is wakt.* –random; *ittifák-se; be-taur; be-thikána.* –times, *kabhi-kabhi.* –work, *kám men; mashghúl.*–the worst, *sab se burí hálat men.*

Attach, *lagána; lagá-d; jorna.* –ment (as a friend), *tarafdárí; mail.* (a joining), *jor.* (seize, by process of law, or otherwise), *zabt-k.*

Attack. *See* 'Assault.'

Attain, *pána ; milna* (*See page* 50. *Note* 1.) *ḥásil-k.* -ment, (of wish,) *kámyábi.* (acquisition), *ḥásil.* (learning), *ilm ; dánist ; hunar.*

Attempt, *koshish.* V. *-k.*

Attendance, *ḥáziri, khidmat ;* (in hopes of employment), *ummedwári.* -tion, *khabardári ; sucheti.* -tive, *khabardár ; suchet.* to give attention, *khabardári-k. ; dil-lagána.* to attend on one, *kisi ki khidmat-k.* with attention, *khabardári se ; surt se.*

Attestation, *tasdíḳ* (f.) ; *shahádat.* V. *-k.*

Attorney, *vakíl ; mukhtár ; ná,ib.* power of–, *vakálat-námah ; mukhtár-námah.*

Auction, *nílám.* V. *-k.* to send to–, *nílám meṇ d.*, or *ḍálna.*

Audience, *darbár ; majlis.* -hall (public), *díwán-i-ámm.* (private), *díwán-i-khάss.* to grant an–, *díwán-i-ámm* (or *khάss*) *meṇ mulá-ḳát farmána,*

Augment, *baṛhána ; ziyádah-k.* -ation, *ziyádat.*

Aunt, (paternal,) *phúphi.* (maternal), *mausi.*

Author, *musannif.*

Authority, *ikhtiyár ; maḳdúr ; ḥukúmat.* -ise, *ijázat-d.*

Autumn, *kharíf.* A. *kharífi.* —crop, *kharíf.*

Avail of, *kám-lena.* -able, *kám ka.* of no avail, *kuchh kám ka nahíṇ.*

Avarice, *lálach,* (m.) ; *bukhl ;* (f.) ; *hirs,* (f.) A. *lálchi.*

Avenge, *intiḳám lena.*

Averse (*kuchh chiz se*), *mukhálif.* V. *-hona.* -sion, *nafrat.*

Await, *rahna ; kisi ke wáste sabr-k.*

Award (v.) *dilána.* (n.) *fatwa ; ḥukm.*

Aware, *wáḳif.* to be–, *wáḳif-hona.* to make–, *-k.*

Away. *See* 'Absent.'

Awaken, (*trans.*) *jagána ; jagá-d.* (*intr.*), *jágna.* awake, *jágta ; bedár.* wide-awake, (fig.) *hoshyár ; chálák.*

Awe, (n.,) *ḍar* (m.). (v.) *ḍar dikhlána.* -ful, *haul-nák.*

Awning, *shámiyánah.*

Axe, *ṭáṇga ; kulháṛi.*

Azure, *ásmáni.*

B.

Babe, baby, *bachchah ; bachchah miyáṇ ; laṛka ;* (fem.) *laṛki ; bába* (L. B.).

Bachelor, *mukhlis ; mujarrad ; ko,ára.*

Back (v. *trans.*), *píchhe-k. ; haṭá-d.* (v. *intr.*), *haṭ jána ; haṭna.* to give–, *wápas-d.* to keep–, *rokna ; báz-rakhna.* (n.) *píṭh,* (f.). (adv.) *pher ; píchhe ; báz.*

Bacon, *bekam.* (E.).

Bad, *kharáb ; bura ; bad* (last much used in compos.) –ly, *kharáb ; kharáb taur se.*

Badge, *chaprás.* wearer of a–, *chaprási.*

Bag, *thaili ; kísah ; kharítah.* for water (small), *mashk.* (large), *pakhál.* –gage, *chízbast,* (f.).

Bail, *zámini.* –or, *zámin.* –iff, *názir.*

Bake, *pakána.* –er, *roṭi-wála.* –house, *tanúr-khánah.*

Balance, (for weighing,) (n.), *tarázu.* (unpaid,) *báḳi ; báḳiyát.* (excess,) *fázil.*

Bald, *ganja.* –ness, *ganj.*

Ball, *goli ; gend ; anṭa.* –of thread, &c., *baṭṭa.* (dance), *nách,* (f.). a fancy –, *púdṛinách.* (half E.).

Bamboo, *báṇs.*

Band, (of people,) *guroh.* (m.), (music,) *bája.* (for waist,) *kamar-band.* (for neck,) *gala-band,* or *gulu-band.* –age, *paṭṭi.*

Bank, (river, &c.,) *pár ; kinárah* (money,) *koṭhi ; bank.*[1] (E.). –er, *sarráf ; sáhúkár ; mahájan.*

Barber, *bárwal* (E.); *ḥajjám ; nápit.*

Bare, (naked,) *langa,* or *nanga.* (plain,) *sáda ; khálí.* to lay–, *kholna ; dekhne-d.* –faced, *be-sharm.*

Bargain, *shart ; ḳaul-o-ḳarár.* V. *–bándhna ; –bándhlena ; –k.*

Barley, *jau.* (for table,) *báṛli.* (E.).

Barouche, *baṛúsh-gáṛi.* (half E.).

Barracks, *chháuni ; láins* (E.).

Barrel, *pípa.*

---

[1] Preserve your Hindústáni pronunciation of the short 'a.

Barren, -land, *zamín jis-se fasl nahíṇ milti hai.*

Base (n.), *bunyád*, (f.). (adj.), *bad-zát; páji.* (of coin,) *mekhi.*

Bashful. *See* 'Ashamed.'

Basil, *tulsi.*

Basin, *básan.* (metal,) *chilamchi.*

Basket, *ṭokri.* work–, *pauti.*

Bat, (beast,) *chamgádaṛ.* (playing,) *thápi; lakṛi.*

Battle, *laṛá,i; jang.* (f.). V. *-k.; laṛna.* –array, *saff-i-jang.*

Bazaar, *bázár.*

Be, *hona;* (for Passive Voice), *jána.* –it so, *so hi ho.*

Beach. *See* 'Bank.'

Bead, *dánah.* a string of–, *mála.*

Beak, *choṇch; nok.* (f.).

Beam, (large,) *laṭṭha;* (small,) *barga.*

Bean, *boṛa; lobiya.*

Bear (v.). *See* 'Carry.' (endure,) *bardásht-k.* –fruit, *phalna; phal-d.* –pain, *dard uṭhána.* –children, *janna.* –young, *biyána.* –witness, *gawáhi*, or *shahádat-d.* 'bearer.' *See page* 35, *See* 'Carrier.' (animal), *ríchh; bhál; bhálu.*

Beard, *dáṛhi; rísh* (f.).

Beast, *jánwar; ḥaiwán.*

Beat, *márna; píṭna; ṭhokna;* (in contest,) *jítna,* (*i.e.*, to win,) (*e.g.*, a drum,) *bajána.* –ing, *már; már-már; mára-mári; már-píṭ.* to be beaten, *már-khána.*

Beautiful, *khúb-súrat.* N. *-i.*

Because, *kyúṇkih.*[1]

Become, *ho-jána* (suit,) *achchha-lagna; lá,iḳ-hona.*

Bed, *palang.* –stead, *chárpá,i; khâṭ; khaṭiyah.* (for flowers,) *takhtah.* (of river,) *peṭ.* –clothes, *bichhâwan; oṛhne ka kapṛa.* –ding, *bichhauna.* to make the–, *palang taiyár-k.* to spread –ding, *bichhauna bichhána.* –room, *sone ka kamra.*

Bee, *zambúr; shahd ki makkhi.*

Beef, *bíf-gosht.* (half E.).

Beer, *bír-sharáb*, (f.), (half E.).

---

[1] The idiom often is as follows: *Eng.* 'Because it is raining, I shall not go out.' *Hind.* 'It is raining, therefore (*is sabab se*), I shall not go out.

Before, (adv.) (person *or* place,) *sámne ; pás ; áge.* (time,) *áge ; paihle ; pesh-tar.* (prep.), *ke sámne ; ke pás ; ke áge ; ḥuzúr meṇ.*

Beg, *mángna ; iltimás-k.* (alms,) *bhíkh - mángna.* –gar, *bhikári.* 'I – your pardon,' *mu,áf kíjiye.*

Begin, *lagna ; shurú-k.*–ning, *shurū. ; ibtida.* (f.) from beginning to end, *kull ; tamám ; sar-á-sar ; sar-á-pá.*

Behalf (on – of,) *ke wáste ; ke liye.*

Behave, *nibáhna.* N. *chál-chalan.*

Behind, (adv.) *píchhe.* (prep.) *ke píchhe.*

Being, (a human,) *ádmi ; insán.*

Belief, *báwar ; itimád ; itibár.* V. *–k. ; mánna.* (religious) *mazhab ; ímán.*

Bell, *ghanṭa.*

Bellows, *dhauṇkni.* V. *dhauṇkna.*

Belly, *peṭ ; shikam.* to fill the–, (*i.e.*, to satisfy one,) *peṭ bharna.* –ache, *pech-ish.*

Belong, by the genitive, e.g., *yih ghoṛa mera hai.*

Beloved, *pyára ; maḥbúb.*

Below, (adv.) *níche.* (prep.) *ke niche ; ke tale.*

Belt, *band* (as last part in compos.) ; *peṭi ; belaṭ.* (E.).

Bench, *chauki.* of Justices, '*binch.*' (E.).

Bend(n.), *ṭeṛhá,i; pech.* V. *–k.* A. *ṭeṛha ; kaj ; báṇka.*

Beneath. *See* 'Below.'

Benediction, *du,a* (f.).

Benefactor, *má-báp; murabbi.*

Benefit, *fá,idah ; nafa ; iḥsán.*

Benevolence, *khair-khwáhi ; iltifát ; shafaḳat ; iḥsán.*

Beseech. *See* 'Beg.'

Beside, besides, (near,) *ke pás ; ke nazdík ; ke yaháṇ.* (except,) *ke siwa.* (in addition to,) *aláwah is ke ; is ke siwa ; is-par yih bhi hai.*

Best, *sab se achchha,* to do one's–, *maḳdúr bhar kám-k.* to make the – of it, *bure bhale nibáhna,* or *lena.*

Bestow, *de-d. ; bakhshna ; bakhshish-d.*

Bet, *shart.* V.–*baná-lena.*

Betel, *supári*, or *supyári*. as chewed by natives, *pán*. a dealer in–, *tamboli*. -box, *pán-dán*.

Better, *bihtar* ; *us-se achchha*. V. *kisi ki bihtari-k*.

Between. *See* 'Among.'

Beware. *See* 'Acquainted.'

Beyond, *ke báhar* ; *us taraf*. (*e.g*, the sea,) *pár*.

Bible, *baibal*. (E.).

Bid, *kahna* ; *ḥukm-d*. –good day, &c. *khair-bád* or *mubárak-bád kahna* (n.) (at auction,) *ḍák*. (to bid at auction) *ḍák-k*., or *bolna*.

Big, *baṛa* ; *buzurg*. (fat,) *moṭa*. N. *baṛá,i* ; *moṭá,i*.

Bigoted, *muta,assib*.

Bile, *pith*, or *pit*.

Bill. *See* 'Beak' *and* 'Account.' –of exchange, *hunḍi*.

Billiards, *anṭa-khel*. –room, *anṭa-ghar*.

Bind, *bándhna* ; *bándh-d*. –ing of a book, *jild-bandi*.

Bird, *chiṛiya*. –cage, *pinjra*. –lime, *lása*.

Birth, *janam*. –day, *–din*.

Biscuit, *biskit*. (E.).

Bishop, *láṭ pádṛi sáḥib*.

Bit, *ṭukṛa* ; *zarrah* (f.); *thoṛa-sa* (for horse,) *dahánah*.

Bite, *káṭa*. V. *dáṇt se káṭna*. (as hot things,) *lagna*.

Bitter, *títa* ; *kaṛwa* ; *tez*. –ness, *talkhi*.

Black, *kála* ; *siyáh*. –ness, *siyáhi*. V. *kála-k*. –ant, *chyúṇti*. –guard, *bad-zát*. smith, *lohár*. –ing, *siyáhi* ; *roshná,i*. pepper, *gol-mirch*.

Blame, *ilzám* ; *malámat*. V.–*k*. less, *be-ḳusúr* ; *nirdosh*.

Blanket, *kammal*, (f.). *kamli*.

Blaze, *lau* ; *lahar* ; *shulah*. V. *lahrána*.

Bleed, (*trans*.), *fasd-kholna* ; *lohu lena*.(*intr*.),*lohu girna*.

Blemish, *aib*, (f.) ; *khata* ; *dágh*. A. *dághi*. V. *dághi-k*.

Blessing, *du,a*, (f.). A. *mubárak*. V. *–d*.

Blind (adj.), *andha* ; *kor*.–of one eye, *kána*, V. *andhera-k*. –ness, *kori* ; *ná-bini*.

Blind (n.), *pardah*.

Blister, *phaphola*.

Block, *kundah*. –head, *aḥmaḳ* ; *be-wuḳúf*.

Blood, *khún* ; *lohu*. –y, *khún-álúdah*. –less, *be-khún*.

Blossom, *phúl*. V. *-bahar ána*.

Blot, *dágh*. -ed, *dághi*. V. *-k*. -ting-paper, *lál-kághaz*.

Blow (n.), *zarb* (f.); *ṭhokar*, (f.); *ghúsa*. (V.) (as wind,) *chalna*; *bahna* -with the mouth, *phúṇkna*; *phúṇk-d*. -over, (as a storm,) *sáf hona*; *khulna*. to - an instrument, *bajána*. to give a-, *See* 'Beat.'

Blue, *níl*; *níla*.

Blunt, *kund*. N. *-i*.

Blush, *khijlat*. V. *-k*. at the first-, *dekhte hú,e*.

Boar, *jangli sú,ar*.

Board, *takhtah*. (assembly), '*boraḍ*.' (E.).

Boasting, *láf-zaní*. V. *-k*. a -er, *láf-zan*.

Boat, *kishti*; *ná,o* (f.); with their various kinds, as '*bajra*'; '*panso,i*'; '*ḍeṇghi*,' &c. -man, *malláḥ*. head ditto, *máṇjhi*.

Body (human,) *badan*; *jism*. (of men.) *See* 'Assembly.'

Boil (*trans*.), *ubálna*; (*intr*.), *khaulna*; *ubalna*. -ing water, *garm páni*. servants say, *phúṭa páni*. N. *phaphola*.

Bold, *mardánah*; *shuja*. -ness, *mardánagi*; *ausán*, (f.); *shujá,at*. (in a bad sense,) *shokh*. N. *shokhi*.

Bolster, *baṛa takiyah*. -up, *madad-d*.

Bolt (n.), *belna*; *ṭheki*. V. *-lagána*. as, e.g., a horse. *bhágna*; *bhág-jána*.

Bond (fetter,) *ḳaid* (f.). (to secure debt,) *tamassuk*.

Bone, *haḍḍi*; *háṛ*.

Book, *kitáb*, (f.); *bahi*. -shelves, *-ka takhtah*. binder, *jild-band*. -binding, *jild-bandi*.

Boot, *búṭ*. (E.); *mozah*. -lace, *búṭ ka fítah*.

Border, *kinárah*. (of a writing,) *ḥáshiyah*.

Bore (v.), *chhedna*. (annoy,) *satána*; *diḳḳ-k*. -er, *barmah*.

Born, to be, *paida-hona*.

Borrow, *máng-lena*; *ḳarz-lena*. -er, *mustair*.

Bosom, *sínah*.

Both (two), *donoṇ*. both and, *See page* 46.

Bottle, *botal*, (f.),(E.). *shíshah*.

Bough. *See* 'Branch'

Bound (leap,) *kúdna ; uchhalna*. N. *kúd ; uchhal*. (enclose,) *ḥadd* (f.) (or, plur.) *ḥudúd-d*, or *lagána*. A. *pá-band*. -ed, *ghera ; maḥdúd*.

Bow (for arrows,) *kamán ; dhanuk* (f.). (for pellets,) *ghulel* (f.). to use a–, *-k*. (salutation,) *salám*. V. *-k*.

Bowl, *boli* (E.); *piyálah ; kaṭora*. finger–, *háth-boli*.

Box, *sandúḳ ; sandúḳ-chah ; bakas*. (E.). (trunk,) *peti*. tin-box of a particular shape for clothes, &c., *piṭárah*. ...*dán*. *See page* 41. a small –, *e.g.*, for snuff, a single ring, &c., *ḍibiya*. *See* 'Blow.'

Boy, *chhokṛa ; laṛka*. In Bombay and Madras, '*boy*' is used in calling one's personal servant; never so in Bengal. -hood, *laṛakpan*. -ish, *chhokṛa-sa*.

Bracelet, called by endless names; a general word is, *bázu-band*.

Braces, *gális*.

Bracket, *brákiṭ*. (E.).

Braid, *gundhan*.

Brain, *maghz; dimágh*. -less, *be-wuḳúf*.

Bran, *bhúsi*.

Branch, *shákh ; ḍál* (f.). (of river,) *sota*. (of a subject,) *juz ; báb*.

Brandy, *bráṇḍi-sharáb* (f.).

Brass, *pítal*. of–, *-ka*. -platter, *tháli*. -vessels (generally), *tháli-loṭa*.

Brave. *See* 'Bold.' *diláwar ; diler*. -ery, *diláwari, dileri*.

Bravo! *shábásh ; bahut achchha!*

Brawn, *barán*. (E.).

Bray, *reṇkna*.

Bread, *roṭi ; nán* (f.). (food generally,) *khána*.

Breadth, *chauṛá,i ; araz*.

Break (*trans.*), *toṛna ; toṛ-d.; phárna*. (*intr.*), *ṭúṭ-jána*. -open, *toṛna ; toṛ-d* -away, *bhág-jána*. -off, *barkhást-k*. of day, *bhor ; baṛi fajr ; taṛka ; subḥ; ala-s-sabáḥ*. broken, *ṭúṭa ; ṭuṭa hú,a*. -fast, *ḥáziri ; náshtah*. V. *-lena ; -khána*.

Breast, *chháti ; sínah*.

Breath, *dam ; sáṇs*. to be out of–, *dam-ṭúṭna*. to draw–, *-lena*.

Breeches, *jáṅghia ; brichis.* (E.).

Bribe, *rishwat ; ghús.* to give a–, *–d.* to accept a– *–lena,* or *–khána.*

Brick, *iṇṭ,* (f.) ; *khisht.*

Bridge, *pul.* V. *–banána.* tolls for construction of–, *–bandi.*

Bridle, *lagám* (f.) V. *–lagá-d.*

Brief ; briefly, *mukhtasar.* a–, *intikháb.*

Bright, *sáf ; raushan.* V. *–k.* –ness, *raushani.*

Bring, *lána ; le-ána ; lete-ána.* –about, *baná-lána.* –in, *házir lána ; házir-kar-d.; áne-d.; yaháṇ-lána.* –over, *is taraf lána.* –up, *pálna ; parwarish-k.*

Broad, *chauṛa ; aríz.* N. *chaurá,i ; araz.* –cloth, *báṇát.*

Brocade, *kamkhwáb.*

Broker, *dallál.*

Brooch, *baṛoch.* (E.).

Broom, *jháṛu.*

Broth, *shorba.*

Brother, *bhá,i ; barádar.* –hood, *barádari.* –ly, *barádarána.*

Brougham, *band-gáṛi.*

Brow (of face,) *abru.* (of a hill,) *lab.*

Brown, *barún.* (E.).

Brush, *See* 'Broom.' (hair, clothes,) *brúsh,* (E.) V. *–d.,* or *lagá-d. See page* 96. (sweep,) *jháṛna ; jháṛ-d.* –wood, *jháṛ ; jháṛi.*

Bucket, *ḍolchi ; bálṭi.*

Buffalo, *bhaiṇsa.* f. *–si.*

Buffoon, *maskharah.*

Bug, *khaṭ-mal.*

Build, *banána ; bándhna ; uṭhána.* –ing, *ghar ; makán, koṭhi ; imárat.*

Bull, *nar-gá,o ; sáṇḍ,* or *sáṇṛ.*

Bullet, *goli.*

Bullock, *bail.* –cart, *–gáṛi.*

Bunch, *guchchha.*

Bundle, *gaṭhri ; bastah ; chíz-bastah ; moṭ.* (*e.g.*, of grass,) *bojha.*

Burden (n.), *bojha.* V. *bojhna.*

Burial, *kafan-dafan,* (f.). V. *–k. ; miṭṭi-d.* –ground, *goristán ; kabristán.*

Burn (n.), *sokhtah.* (v. *trans.*,) *jalána ; jalá-d.; ág-lagá-d.* (*intr.*), *jalna.*

Burst (*intr.*), *phúṭna ; phaṭ-jána.* (*trans.*), *toṛna ; pháṛna.*

Bush, *jhár*; *gáchh*. rose–, *gul-áb-phúl*.

Business, *kám; kár; kár bár; kár-o-bár*. (trade,) *tijárat*. (profession,) *peshah*. V. –*k*.

Busy, *kám meṇ; mashghúl*.

But, *lekin; magar*. (only,) *sirf; kháli*, e.g., there is nothing but books here, *yaháṇ sirf* (or, *kháli*) *kitábeṇ haiṇ*.

Butcher, *kassáb*. V. *katl-k.; zabh-k*.

Butler, *khánsámáṇ*.

Butter, *makkhan*, (native,) *ghi* (m.). –man, *makkhan-wála*.

Butterfly, *titli*.

Buttocks, *chútar*.

Button, *ghundi; butám*. (E.), –hole, *múndi*.

Buy, *mól-lena; kharíd-k*. –ing and selling, *kharíd-farokht* –er, *kharídár*.

Buzz, *bhin-bhinána*. –ing, *bhin-bhináhaṭ*.

By, *se*. –me, *mere pás*. by hundreds, *sau, sau hokar*. –one's self, *áp hi áp*, or *áp-se*. –chance, *ittifákan*. –all means, *har tarah se*. –no means, *hargiz na*. –and,– *thoṛi ghaṛi ke baad*. -heart, *yád se*. year by year, *sál-ba-sál*.

C.

Cab, *ṭhika-gáṛi* –man, -*wála*.

Cabbage, *kobi*.

Cage, *pinjra*

Cake, *kulchah; kek*. (E.).

Calamity, *áfat; musíbat*.

Calendar, *jantri*.

Calf, *bachhṛa*. –of leg, *pindli*.

Calico, *kaṭan kapṛa; márkín* (i.e., 'American.')

Call (one), *bulána; bulá-lena; talab-k*. (shout), *pukárna; áwáz-d*. N. *áwáz*, (f.); *báng*. (visit,) *mulákát*. V. –*k*.

Camel, *úṇṭ; shutur*. –driver, *shutur-bán*.

Camp, *khímah*[1]-*gáh; jis jagah khíme khaṛe hú,e haiṇ*.

Camphor, *káfúr*.

Can, *See page* 18, *Sect*. 22. *ána*, (of what a person is able to do, e.g., *ham ko likhna áta hai*, I can write.)

[1] Pronounced also '*Khaimah*.'

Canal, *nahr.* (f.).
Candle, *mom-batti* ; *kandíl.* (*not* E.). –stick, *shama-dán.*
Cannon, *top* –ball, *top ki goli.*
Canvas, *ṭáṭ.*
Cap, *ṭopi.*
Capable. *See* 'Able.'
Caper (n.), *kabar* (f.) ; *kepar* (E.). (v.) *uchhalna.* N. *uchhal.*
Capital (in trade,) *púnji.* Adj. *achchha* ; *bahut achchha* ; *umdah.*
Capon, *pekan.* *See page* 84.
Captain, *sirdár* ; *kaptán sáhib.*
Caravan, *kárwán* ; *káfilah.*
Card, *ṭikaṭ* (E.). playing–, *tásh.* –board, *kaṭ.*
Care (anxiety,) *fikr* (f.) ; *andeshah* ; *tarraddud* ; Adj. *fikr-mand.* V. *fikrmand-hona.* (guardianship.) *amánat* ; *hifázat* ; *zimmah.* V. (to take care of a thing,) *apne pás rakhna* ; *hifázat meṉ rakhna.* (caution,) *khabardári*, Adj. *khabardár.* V. *khabardár-hona.* –less, *gháfil.* N. *ghaflat.* (free from care,) *be-khabar.* N. *be-khabardári.*
Caress, *nawázish.* V. *pyár-k.*
Carpenter, *baṛha,i.* –try, *najjári.*
Carpet, *dari* ; *farsh* ; *shatranji* ; *ghálíchah,* or *kálíchah.*
Carriage. *See page* 90. stage–, *ḍák-gáṛi.*
Carry, *uṭhána* ; *úṭhá-ke-le-jána.* –into effect, *ba-sar-lána* ; *ba-ja lána* ; *nibáhna.* –ier, *kuli* ; *bardár* ; *hammál* ;[1] *moṭiya.*
Cart, *gáṛi.* bullock–, *bail-gáṛi.* –load, *gáṛi ka bojha* ; *gáṛi ki khep.*
Case (covering,) *ghiláf.* (box,) *sandúk.* *See page* 41, '*dán.*' (in Court,) *mukaddamah* ; *nálish.* the facts of the–, *hál* ; *asl hál* ; *májara.* one's–, (i.e. what he has to say,) *guzárish* ; *arz* (f.), *nibedon.*
Cash, *paise* ; *rúpiye.* ready–*nakd-rúpiye* ; –book, *khátabahi* ; *hisáb ki bahi.* –ier, *khazánchi.*

---

[1] Not in use in Bengal.

Cask, *pípa.*

Cast. *See* 'Throw.'

Cat, *billi.*

Catalogue, *fihrist.*

Catch, *pakarna*; *pakar-lena.* -cold, *sardi khána.* to be caught, *pakra-jána.*

Caterpillar, *jhánjha.*

Cattle, *maweshi*; *ga,e-goru.*

Cauliflower, *phúl-kobi.*

Cause, *sabab*; *wajh,* (f.). V. *karána*; *kará-d.* without-, *be-sabab.*

Caution. *See* 'Care.'

Cease (*trans.*), *maukúf-k.*; *band-k.* (*intr.*), same words and *hona*; *ho-jána.*

Celery, *silari* (E.).

Cent, per, *saikra,* e.g. *pánch rúpiye saikra,* 5 per cent.

Centipede, *gojar.*

Centre, *markaz*; *bíchon bích.* in the-, *bích men.*

Ceremony, *takaluf*; *taklíf* (f.).

Certain (sure,) *yakín.* N. -*i.* V. -*hona.* (settled,) *mukarrar*; *ká,im.* V. these words and *hona.* 'a certain person' *fulánah*; *fulánah shakhs.* -ly, *albattah*; *be-shak*; *zarúr.* -ify, *sábit-k.*; *tahkík-k.*

Certificate, *sifárish ka khatt*; '*sartifikat* (E.).

Chaff, *bhúsi.*

Chain, *zanjír.* (f.). V. *lagá-d.*

Chair, *kursi*; *chauki.* -man, (of a meeting,) *sar-i-majlis.*

Chalk, *khári-matti.*

Chamber, *kamra*; *kothri.*

Chamois-leather, *sábari.*

Chance, *ittifák.* V. -*se hona.* by-, *ittifákan.*

Change, *tabdíl*; *badl*; *badlá. badli.* V. (*trans.*) -*k.* (*intr.*) -*hona.*

Channel, *nála*; *sota*; *khál.*

Character, *chál-chalan.* good-*nek-nám.* bad-, *bad-nám.* a bad character (person,) *bad-maásh.* (letter,) *harf,* pl. *hurúf.*

Charcoal, *ko,ila.*

Charge (keeping,) *amánat*; *hifázat*; *nigáhbáni.* V, (*trans.*) -*men rakhna.* (*intr.*) -*men hona.* (attack,) *hamlah.* V. -*k.* (accusation,) *ilzám.* V. -*lagá-d.* charge in an account, *hisáb men likhna.*

Charity, *khairát*; *lutf* (f.). -able, *khairáti*; *faiyáz*; *sakhi.*

Chase (sport), *shikár*. V.–*k*. (pursuit), *raged ; khader*. V. *ragedna ; khedna*.

Chattering, *bak-bak ; káṇ-káṇ*. V. –*k*.

Cheap, *sasta ; manda ; kam-ḳímat*. –ness, *sasti ; kam-ḳímati*.

Cheating, *fareb ; daghá-bázi*. V. –*k*. one who cheats, *daghá-báz*.

Check, *áhiste-k ; rokna ; aṭkána*.

Cheek, *gál ; rukh*.

Cheer (amuse, &c.) *bahlána ; khush-k*. –ful, *khush ; khush-dil ; khush-ru ; be-fikr*. –fulness, *khush-tab,i*. (applaud,) *khushi-khushi-bolna*. (by clapping,) *táli,án-k*. cheers, *khushi-khushi ; 'húra'* (E.).

Cheese, *panír* (m.). –monger, –*farosh*.

Chess. *shatranj*. to play–, –*khelna*. –board, –*bisát*. –man, *muhrah*.

Chest. *See* 'Box.'–of drawers, *dráj* (E.). (of body,) *chháti*.

Chew, *chábna ; chabána*.

Chief, (n.) *sardár*. (a.) *paihla ; awwal*.

Child, *bachchah ; laṛka, laṛki ; tifl ; bába* (L.B.) –hood, *laṛakpan ; tufúliyat*. –less *be-auládd ; lá-wáris*. –dren, *laṛke-log ; bába-log*, (L.B.).

Chin, *ṭhuḍḍi ; zanakh*.

Chintz, *rangi*.

Chisel, *ṭáṇki*.

Choose, *lena ; cháhna ; pa-sand-k*. N. (what pleases,) *jo pasand hai* (option,) *ikhtiyár ; marzi ; khushi*.

Cholera, *haizah ; ola-píṛa*.

Chop, (v.) *káṭna ; ṭukṛa-ṭukṛa kar-d*. (n.) *cháp*. (E.). –per, *báwarchi-kháne ki chhuri*.

Christ, *Hazrat-I'sa*. –ian, *ísawi* –ianity. *I'sá-i-maz-hab*. –mas, *baṛa din ; kismis*. (E.). a Christian, *Krisṭán* (E.).

Church, *girja*, or *grija*.

Cinnamon, *dár-chíni*.

Circle, *ghera ; dá,irah*. (of jurisdiction.) *ḥalḳah ; alá-ḳah ; parganah ; zila* : and many other territorial words—'i' added to the title of an officer often means his jurisdiction, e.g., '*zamíndári*,' the territory of a zamíndár, and so on.

Circumstance, *jel ; amal ; amr ; ḥál ; asl ḥal ; wáḳi,-át ; jo hú,a hai.* –tial, *mufassalan ; tafsíl-wár.*

City, *shahr* ; (as last part in compos:) '*nagar*' and '*púr.*' –izen, *shahr meṇ rahne-wála.*

Civil, *su-shíl.* –ity, *sulúk ; nek-chalan.* –ization, *tahzíb-i-akhláḳ.*

Claim, *dawa.* (f.) ; as formulated,) *darkhwást ; arz ;* (f.) *sawál.* V. *–k* –ant, *dawádár.* (in Court,) *mudda,i.*

Claret, *lál-sharáb* (f.) ; *kalárat* (E.).

Class, *ḳism.* (rank,) *darjah.* (of Railway, or School,) *kalás.* (E.). –ification, *tartíb.* –ify, *tartíb-k.*

Clause, *dafah ; jumlah.*

Claw, *changul ; ná-khun.*

Clay, *gil* (f.), *chikni miṭṭi.*

Clean (adj.), *sáf ; safa.* (v.) *sáf-k.* -liness, *safá,i ; pakízagi.*

Clear, *sáf ; shaffáf.* (obvious,) *sáf ; maalúm ; sáf maalúm ; záhir.* V. *sáf-k.*

Cleave, *phárna ; chírna.* --er, *See* 'Axe' --to one, *lagá rahna ; ke pás rahna.*

Clerk, *kiráni ; kátib ; nawísandah ;* as last part of word ... *navís*, e.g., *naḳl-navís*, a copying-clerk.

Clever, *chálák ; hoshyár*, N.--*i*-

Climate, *áb-o-hawa*, (f.).

Cloak (n.), *iba* (f.) ; *labádah.* (v.) *chhipána.* (adj.) *chhipa-hú,a.*

Clock, *ghaṛi.* *See page* 67.

Clod, *ḍhela.*

Close, (v.), *band-k.*(n.) *ákhir*, or *akhír*, (near,) *nazdík ; ke pás.*--ed, *band.*

Closet, *koṭhri.* the W. C. *ghusl-khánah ; pá-e-khánah ; já-e-zarúr.*

Cloth, *kapṛa.* table--, *mez ki chádar ; dastar-khwán.* web of--, *thán.* cotton--, *nan-kláṭh ;*[1] *katán-kapṛa.* woollen--, *bánáṭ.* to lay the--, *mez lagána*, or *taiyár-k.* clothes, *kapṛe.* night--, *rát ke kapṛe. See page* 95. Clothe (v.), *kapṛe pahinna ; oṛhna.*

---

[1] This is an attempt at the English, 'long-cloth.'

Cloud, *abr; badli; megh.* -y, *abri.*

Clove, *karanful.*

Club, *láṭhi; chob; sonṭa.* -man, *láṭhiál.*

Coal, *ko,ila.*

Coarse, *moṭa.* N. *moṭá,i* (fig.) *be-hunar; be-adab.*

Coast, *kinárah; pár.* V.- *kináre par chalna.*

Coat, *kurti.*

Coax, *phusláná; chumkárna.*

Cobbler, *mochi.*

Cob-web, *makṛi ka jála.*

Cock, *murgh.* (of a gun,) *ghoṛa* (v.) *-khaṛa-k.*

Cockroach, *til-chaṭṭa.*

Coco, *koko* (E.).

Coffee, *kahwah; káfi* (E.).

Coffin, *sandúk,* (v.) *-men rakhna.*

Coin, *paise; rúpiye.* V. *-banána.* false-, *mekhi rúpiye.*

Cold (adj.), *sard; ṭhanḍha; sítal.* (n.) *sardi; ṭhanḍhá,i.* -in the head, *zukám.* V. *-ṭhanḍha-k.* to be-, *ṭhanḍha hona.*

Collar, *kálar* (E.).-of a coat, &c., *girebán.*

Colleague, *rafík; sharík.*

Collection, *jama; jamíyat.* V. *-jama-k.* -of dues, *wasúl.* V. *-k.* -tor, (of a district,) *kàlekṭar sáhib.* (generally,) *tahsíldár; sazáwal.*

College, *madrasah.*

Colonel, *karnail* (E.) *sáhib.*

Colour (n.) *rang.* (f.), V. *-d.* -en, *rangín.*

Column, *sitún; khamba.*

Comb, *kanghi.* V. *-d.* or *lagá-d.*

Come, *ána; á-jána; tashríf lána.* (*See page* 76. *Sect.* 17.) -about, *ho-jána.* -back, *phir-ána.* -out, *báhar-ána; nikalna; nikalána.* -to one's self, *hosh men ána.*

Comfort, *tasalli; tashaffi; taskín* (f.); *khushi.* V. *-d.*; *bahlána.*

Command, *hukm.* V. *-d.* -er, *hákim; sardár.* with special names for various commanders, e.g., *fauj-dár,* a military -er; *kila-dár,* a -er of a fort, and so on, down to *jama-dár,* headman of any small body, military or other.

Commence. *See* 'Begin.'

Commendation, *sifárish.* (praise,) *taaríf* (f.). V. *-d.*

Commerce, *saudágari ; tijárat; kharíd-farokht; mahájani.*

Commit (do.), *karna.* (entrust to,) *hawále meṇ rakhna ; hawálah-k.; supurd-k.; amánat meṇ rakhna.* commission, (e.g. of an offence,) with 'karna,' as v.n.

Common, *ámm.* -ly, *umúman; aksar.* held in-, *ijmáli ; mushtarak.* a-, *maidán ; parti zamín* (f).

Companion, *sáthi ; rafík ; ham-ráhi.* -ship, *rifákat.*

Company. *See* 'Assembly.' The East India Company, *Kampani Bahádur.*

Compare, *milána ; mukábalah-k.* -atively, *ba nisbat is ki.* -ison, (act of,) *mukábalah-k.* as v.n.

Compel, use '*zor-se,* or *zabar-dasti se,*' with appropriate verb.

Competent. *See* 'Able.'

Complaint(in words,) *nálish ; nála.* V. *-k.* (sickness,) *bímári ; rog.* complainant (in Court,) *faryádi; mudda,i.*

Complete, *tamám.* V. *-k.* -tion, *-k.* as v.n. -ly *tamám ; kull ; bil-kull ; sar-a-pa.*

Comprehend, *samajhna ; samajh meṇ lána.* -sion, *samajh* (f.) ; *hosh ; akl* (f.).

Conceal, *chhipána.* to be -ed, *rúposh-hona.* -ment, *rúposhi.*

Conclude *See* 'Close.'

Condemn (disapprove,) *ná-pasand-k.* (sentence,) *hukm -d.* -nation, *sazá ka hukm.*

Conduct, *sulúk ; chál-chalan.* V. *pahunchá-d.*

Confectioner, *haiwá,i.* -ery, *mithái.*

Confession, *ikrár ; kubúl.* V. *-k.* (person who admits,) *ká,il.*

Confine (by bounds,) *hadd-lagá-d.* (imprison,) *kaid-k.* -ment, *kaid ; giriftári.*

Confirmation, *subút.* V. *-kar-d. ; sábit-k.*

Conflict. *See* 'Battle'

Conform to, *hukm ke mu,áfik kám k.* ; *mánna.* -bly to, *hasb* ; *ke mu,áfik ; ba-mújib.*

Confound (*trans.*), *ghabrána.* be –ed, *ghabrána.* Adj. *ghábra.* –(one thing with another,) *milá-d.* –fusion, *gol-mál* (L. B.); *be-tartíbi.* (of mind,) *ghabráhaṭ.*

Congeal, *jamna ; jam-jána.*

Congratulations, *mubárak-bádí.* V. –*k.*

Conjuring, *jádu.* V. –*k.* –er, –*gar.* *See* 'Beseech.'

Connection, *alákah; sar-o-kár.* V. –*rakhna.* *See* 'Relation.'

Conscience, *dil ; khátir.* –cious, *rást ; sachcha ; sádiḳ.* –ciousness, *rásti. sachá,i ; sádiḳi.*

Consent. *See* 'Agree.'

Consequence, *natíjah ; máḥasal.* *See page,* 99.

Consideration, (thought,) *soch* (f.); *khayál; tadbír* (f). V. –*k.* (dignity.) *martabah.* –ately, *tadbír-se ; bújh-ke.*

Consign. *See* 'Commit.' –ment, *mál ; chalán* (f.).

Consist of, –*ka hona ;* –*se hona.*

Consolation. *See* 'Comfort.'

Constancy, *ḳá,imi ; mazbúti ; istiḳrár* A. *ḳá,im, mazbút.* V. *hona,* (with the Adjs.) –tly, *hameshah ; aksar.*

Construct, *banána ; baná-d.* –tion, *imárat.*

Consultation, *maslahat.* (v. –*k.*) *saláḥ* (f.). V. –*lena.*

Contain, by phrase, e.g. *is sandúḳ meṇ misri hai,* in this box is sugar = this box contains sugar. contents, *is meṇ jo kuchh hai.* table of contents, *fihrist.* –of a book, *mazmún.*

Contemplation, *muláḥazah.* (mental,) *ta,ammul.* V. –*k.; dekhna.* –tive, *mutafakkir.*

Contemptible, *ḥaḳír ; páji,* –temn, *ḥaḳír jánna.* tempt, *ḥiḳárat.*

Contention, *jhagṛa ; laṛá,i.* V. –*k.* A. *jhagṛálu; ziddi.*

Contentedness, *razámandi.* A. *rázi ; khush.* V. *rázi,* or *khush hona.*

Continue, *rahna.* (to keep doing a thing,) *rahna,* *added to stem.*

Contract, *shart ; ḳaul-o-ḳarár ; aḥd-o-paimán.* V. –*k. ; bándh-lena.* –debt, *ḳarz-lena ; ḳarz-dár hona.* (e.g. in business,) *ṭhíka.* V. –*lena.* –or, *ṭhíká-dár.*

Contradict, *bar-khiláf kahna.*

Contrary to, *mukhálif.* –riness, *zidd* (f.); *aks; addáwat.*

Contusion, *choṭ; ṭhokar* (f.).

Convenient, *mu,áfiḳ; durust; achchha; ṭhík.* to be–, *hona.*

Conversation, *bát-chít; guft-o-gu* (f.). V. *–k.*

Convey, *le-jána; pahuṇchá-d.* See 'Carriage.' deed of –ance, *námah* (following the word expressing the kind of conveyance, e.g. *hibah-námah,* a deed of conveyance by gift.)

Convict (n.), *ḳaidi; mulzim.* V. *ek shakhs ko mujrim sábit-k.*

Cook (n.), *báwarchi.* –room, *–khánah.* (v.), *pakána.* -ing, *rasú,i.* See page 87.

Cool. See 'Cold.'

Copy, *naḳl* (f.) V *–k.* ist, *–navís.* (as last part in compos.).

Cord, *rassi; sutli.* V. *–lagá-d; se bándh-d.*

Coriander, *dhaniya* (f.).

Cork, *ḍhaṭha; ṭheṇṭhi;* '*kág.*' (E.). V. *d.* –screw. *kág kholne ka pech.* [Servants use only the word '*kág.*']

Corn, *anáj; ghallah; dánah.* a grain of– *dánah.* –field, *fasl ka khet.*

Corpse, *lásh* (f.); *murdah.*

Correct, *saḥíḥ; ṭhík; durust.* V. *–k.* See 'Punish.' –ly, *ṭhík.*

Correspond (match,) *milna; mil-jána; eksán,* or *ṭhík* or *barábar hona.* N. *mu,áfaḳat.* (by letter,) *khatt,* or *khutút likhna.* N. *khatt-khutút; khatt-kitábat.*

Cost (n.), *dám; ḳímat.* V. *itni ḳímat ka hona.* –ly, *ḳímati; besh-ḳímat.*

Cotton, *rú,i; pumbah; kapás.* –tree, *kapás,* or *símal gáchh.*

Couch, *kauch* (E.). See 'Bed.'

Cover, *sar-posh; ḍhakna; chapni.* V. *–d.; lagá-d.* –ing (according to its kind, e.g.), *kammal* (m.) or *kamli,* a blanket; *rizá,i,* a quilt; *chádar* (f.), a sheet, &c.; *oṛhne ki chíz.*

Covetousness, *lálach; ḥirs,* (f.) V. *–k.* A. *lálchi.*

Cough, *khánsi.* V. *–k.*

Council. See 'Assembly.'

Counsel. See 'Advice.' (lawyer,) *kausili sáḥib* (E.).

Count, *ginna ; shumár-k.* –ing, *shumár-k.*, as v.n. ; *ḥisáb-k.* –ing-house, *daftar-khánah ; áfis.* (E).

Country (a.), *mulk.* native–, *watan; des.* (not the town,) *dihát ; mufassal.* –man, *gaṉwár.* (co-patriot,) *ham-watan ; des-bhá,i.*

Courage. *See* 'Brave.'

Court (yard,) *saḥan.* (King's,) (public,) *díwán-i-ámm.* (private,) *díwán-i-kháss.* (of Justice) (civil,) *díwání-adálat.* (criminal,) *fauj-dárí-adálat.* V. (none ; natives do not 'court,' they employ a broker, called '*ghaṭak.*')

Cousin, *bhá,i ; bahin*, with descriptive words before them, *viz* : father's brother's son, *chachera–.* mother's ditto, *mamera–.* father's sister's son, *phu-phera–.* mother's ditto, *mausera–.* So, '*chacheri bahin,*' *&c.*, if the cousin be female.

Cow, *gá,e*, or *gá,o ; goru.* –dung, *gobar.* –herd, *or* –keeper, *go,ála.* (f.) *go,álin.* –shed, *gá,o-sála*, or *go-sála.*

Coward, *ná-mard.* –ly, *be-jigar.* –liness, *be-jigari.* *See* 'Jigar.'

Crack, *phát.* V. (*trans.*) *phárna ; phár-d.* (*intr.*) *phat-jána.*

Crane (bird,) *sáras ; ghoṉgla.* (machine,) *charkh ; kal.*

Creak (v.), *charcharána.*

Cream, *malá,i.*

Creature. *See* 'Being.'

Credit, &c. *See* 'Believe,' &c.

Creep, *ríngna*, or *rengna ; reng-reng-k.*

Crime, *jurm ; gunáh*, –inal (n.a.), *mujrim ; gunáh-gár.* *See* 'Court.'

Croak, *ghoṉ-ghoṉ-k.*

Crocodile, *magar ; kúmhír ; nihang ; ghariyál.*

Crooked, *ṭeṛha ; tirchha ; bánka ; kaj.*

Crop (of field,) *fasl*, (f.) ; *ghallah ; paidáwár.*

Cross (adj.), *magra; sarkash.* V. (e.g., a river,) *pár-k.* (e.g., two sticks,) *áṛa-lagána.* road, *chau-rásta.*

Crow (voice,) *báng.* (f). V. *-d.* (bird,) *kauwa ; kág.*

Crowd, *guroh ; amboh.*
Crown, *táj.* V. *-rakhna.* -lands. *khdss mahdll.*
Cruel, *be-rahm.* -ty. *-i.*
Cruet, *sirkah-dán.*
Crumb, *chúr ; rezah ; tukra.*
Crush, *dabána ; dabá-d.*
Crust, *chhilka.* (of bread,) *post.*
Cry (weep,) *rona.* (out,) *pukárna ; chilldna.* (up,) *taaríf-d.* N. *pukár ; báng* (f.) ; *áwaz* (f.) ; *shor.*
Cubit, *háth.*
Cucumber, *khíra.* (native,) *pindol ; palwal.*
Cudgel, *láthi.* V. *-chalána ; -se márna.*
Cultivate, *kheti-k.* -tion, (fields,) *kheti ; kásht.* -tor, *kásht-kár ; kisán ra,íyat.* -ed land, *ábádi.* -tion, (of mind,) *tahzíb-i-nafs.*
Cup, *piyálah ; katora.* -board, *almárí.*
Curd, *dahi,* (m.)
Cure (medicine,) *iláj* (f.) ; *dawa,* (f.). (recovery,) *shifa ; durusti.* V. *durust,* or *achchha-k.* -ed, *bhala.*
Curl, of hair, *zulf,* (f.). V. *pechtáb-d.*
Currier, *chamár.*
Curry, *kári.*
Curtain, *pardah ;* (mosquito,) *musahri.*
Cushion, *gaddi; kúshan,* (E.).
Custard, *kastad,* (E.) ; *fálú-dah.* -apple, *sharífah.*
Custom, *dastúr ; riwáj ; maamúl.* (tribute,) *khiráj : mahsúl; tikkas,* (i.e., 'tax.') -house, *parmit-ghar.* (half E.). -ary, *dastúr ke mú,áfik; hasb zábitah.*-ary discount, *dastúri.*
Cut, *kát ; chíra.* V. *kátna ; chírna ; taráshna.* -cut, *káta hú,a.* a -ting, (of plant,) *kalam.*
Cycle, *yug.*
Cypress, *saro,* or *sarv.*

D.

Damage, *nuksán ; ziyán ; zarar.* V. *-k.;* *-pahunch-ána.*
Damp, *tar ; bhínga.* V. *bhingá-d.* -ness, *tari ; tará,i ; bhingá,i.*

Dance, *nách*, (f.), (fancy,) *púdṛi-nách*. V. *-na*.

Danger, *khatrah*. –ous, *khatar-nák*. to run into –, *khatre meṇ ána*.

Dare, *himmat-rakhna*. N. *dileri*. Adv. *dileri se*.

Dark, *aṇdhera ; tárík*. –ness, *aṇdhera*. V. *-k*.

Darning, *rafu*. V. *-k*.

Dash (assault,) *paṭak*. V. *-d*. (down), *ḍál-d*. (at,) *lapakna*.

Date (time,) *tárikh*, (f.), V. *-d*. –d, *markúm*. (fruit,) *khajúr*.

Daughter, *beṭi ; dukhtar*. –in-law, *bahu*.

Dawn, *subḥ ; bhor ; taṛka ; baṛi fajr*.

Day, *din ; roz*. –by–, *roz-ba-roz*. daily, *har roz*. ; (as adj.) *rozínah*. daily pay, *rozínah*. a fine–, *khula*, or *achchha din*. a bad–, *páni ka din*. to–, *áj*. in these days, *áj-kal*. –book, *roz-nám-chah*. –break, *See* 'Dawn.' –labourer, *mazdúr*. daily bread, *khána-pína*.

Deaf, *bahra*. –ness, *bahrá,i*.

Dear (price,) *mahṇga ; besh-ķímat*. N. *besh-ķímati*. (affection,) *pyára*. papa! dear! *bába ján*. dearest mamma, *amma ján*. my dear! *meri ján*. Oh! dear! *há,e. há,e!* to hold dear, *pyár-k*. or *rakhna*.

Death, *maut*, (f.) ; *maran ; intiķál*.

Debate, *baḥs*, (f.). V. *-k*.

Debt, *ķarz* ; –or, *ķarz-dár*. to be, or get in to–, *ķarz-lena : ķarz-dár hona*.

Decayed, *saṛa ; purána*.

Decanter, '*kanṭar*.' (E.) ; *sharáb ki suráḥi*.

Deceased, *marḥúm ; muta-waffa*.

Deceive. *See* 'Cheat.'

Decision, (e.g., of a case,) *ḥukm ; faisalah ; farmán* V. *-d*. 'I have decided to go to Calcutta,' *mera ķasd hai kih maiṇ Kalkatta já,úṇ*.

Declaration, *bát ; bayán ; izhár*. V. *-k*. ; *kahna* (as v.n.).

Decline (slope,) *ḍhál*. (f.). *See* 'Refuse.'

Decrease. *kami*, V. *-k*. and *hona*.

Decree. *See* 'Decide'

Deed, *kám ; fel ; amr.* –in writing. *námah*, as last part of word, e.g., *hiba-námah*, a deed of gift. Various kinds have different names, e.g., *ḳabálah*, a deed of sale ; *sanad* (f.), a deed of royal, or other grant of favour ; *paṭṭa*, a deed of lease ; *ḳabúlyat*, an acceptance of a lease. &c., &c. A general word is *dast-áwez*, (f.).

Deep, *gaihra ; amíḳ.* V. *–k.* N. *gaihrá,i.*

Deer, *hiran*, or *haran.*

Defeat, *hazímat.* V. *–d.* to be defeated, *–khána.*

Defect, *ḳusúr ; k͟hata ; aib.* A. *náḳis.*

Defend, *bachána ; bachá-d.* (in Court,) *jawáb-d.* (one's character,) *uzr-k.* defence, *bachá,o ; ḥifázat ; jawáb ; uzr.* –dant, *muda,á-alaine ; faríḳ sáni.*

Defer, *mauḳúf-k ; multavi rakhna.*

Deficiency. *See* 'Decrease.'

Definition, *taaríf*, (f.). V. *–k.*

Defraud. *See* 'Cheat.'

Defy, *dhamkána ; dhamki-d.*

Degree, *martabah ; darjah.* by degrees, *raftah-raftah ; ḳadam-ba-ḳadam.*

Delay, *der*, or *deri ; tawaḳ-ḳuf.* V. *–k.* (*trans.*) *rokna.*

Deliberation, *ta,ammul.* V. *–k.* Adv. *–se ; tadbír se ; soch karke.*

Delicious, *latíf ; lazíz ; k͟hush-mazah.* a – cacy, *lazzat ; niimat ki chíz.*

Delight, *k͟hushi.* V. *–k.*–ful, or –ed, *k͟hush ; dil-k͟hush.*

Deliverance, *k͟halási ; rehá,i.* V. *–d.*

Demand. *See* 'Ask.'

Demon, *rákshas ; bhút ; jinn ; baitál.*

Demonstration, *subút.* V.*-kar-d.* ; *–kar-diklána ; záhir-k.*

Denial, *inkár.* V. *-k.*

Departure, *rawánagi ; chalá-jána*, as v.n. V. *jána ; chalá-jána ; uṭh-jána ; ruk͟hsat lena ; tashríf le-jána.* *See* page 76.

Dependent (a), *tábi.* ('on,' *se.*) (n.) *–dar.* –dence, *tábi-dári.* This depends on my pleasure, *yih meri k͟hwáhish par mauḳúf hai.*

Deponent, *ḳá,il.*

Deposit, *amánat; giraw.* V. *rakhna; sipurd-k.*

Deposition, *bát; bayán; izhár.* (V. *-k.*) on oath,) *shahádat; gawáhi.* V. *-d.*

Depress, *dabána; dabá-d.* (in mind), *afsurdah-k.* -ed, *afsurdah.*

Deprive of, *le-jána; chhín-lena.* N. *nuksán; ziyan.*

Deputy, *wakíl,* or *vakíl; gumáshtah; ná,ib.* V. *bhejna.*

Descend, *utarna; níche-ána.*

Description, *bayán; taaríf* (f). V. *-k; -d.* (sort,) *kism.*

Desert (n.) *bayábán; jangal.* (a.) *wírán.* V. *See* 'Abandon.'

Design, *See* 'Intention.' 'Drawing.'

Desire, *khwáhish; murád,* (f.) *árzu; jo main cháhta hún, so.* V. *cháhna.* A. *arzúmand; mushták.*

Despatch (speed), *jaldi; shitábi.* (of e.g. goods,) *chalán; rawánagi.* V. *chalán-kar-d.; bhej-d.*

Despise, *hakír-jánna.* N. *hikárat.*

Despot, *zálim.*-ic, *mustakill,* -ism, *zulm.*

Dessert, *mewa; farút,* (E.).

Destiny, *kismat; kaza,* (f.); *takdír.*

Destitute, *gharíb; be-makdúr;* and almost any noun preceded by '*be*'; *bila,* (Arabic prep.) -tion, *iflás.*

Destroy, *kharáb-kar-d; nuksán-kar-d.* N. *nuksáni; kharábi.*

Detail, *tafsíl,* (f.) V. *-d.;* or. *bolna.* Adv. *-wár. mufassal.* V. *-kahna.* Adv. *-lan.*

Detention, *ruká,o; atká,o.* V. *rokna; báz-rakhna; atkána.*

Determination. *See* 'Decision.'

Devil, *iblís; shaitán.* A. *shaitán-ka.*

Device, *hikmat; tadbír,* (f.); *bandobast; taur.* V. *-pána-nikálna; batlána; karna.*

Devotion, (piety,) *ibádat; namáz,* (f.). (to one,) *fid-wíyat.* V. *dena.*

Devout, *musalli; khuda-tars.*[1]

Dew, *shabnam.* (A. *i.*) *os.*

---

[1] From Persian, 'tarsídan,' *to fear.*

Dialogue. *See* 'Conversation.'

Diamond, *almás ; híra.*

Diarrhœa, *dast.*

Diary, *roz–námchah.*

Dice, *páse.* V. *–khelna.*

Diction, *ibárat ; bol-chál.* –ary, *lughat.*

Die (expire,) *marna ; mar-jána ; intiḳál hona.*

Difference, *farḳ.* –ent, *ná-mu,áfiḳ ; dúsre ḳism ka.* a different ... , *dúsra.* V. *dúsre ḳism ka hona.* (quarrel,) *ḳaziyah ; jhagṛa.* V. *–k.*

Difficult, *mushkil ; dushwár ; sakht.* V. *–hona.* –y, *mushkilát ; dushwári ; ish-kál.* Adv. *ishkál-se.*

Dig, *khodna.* –up, (e.g. plants,) *ukháṛna.* --ger, *bel-dár.*

Dignity, *ḳadr ; darjah ; izzat.* --nified, *shán-dár.* V. *ḥur-mat-d.*

Diligence, *ihtimám ; tandihi; miḥnat.* A. *miḥnati.* V.*–k.*; (with adj.).*–hona.* Adv.*–se.*

Dinner, *khána.* V. *–khána.* dining-room, *kháne ka kamra.* dining-table, *kháne ki mez.*

Direction (order,) *ḥukm.* (V. *–d.*) (way,) *ráh* (f.) ; *taraf.* (V. *batlána.*) (of letter,) *ṭhikána.* V. *lagá–d.*

Dirty, *maila.* V. *–k.* and *hona.* N. *mail.*

Disagreement. *See* 'Difference.'

Disallow, *ná-manzúr-k.* (and so with many other words in 'dis;' place 'na' before the affirmative word.)

Disaster, *áfat ; musíbat ; bad-bakhti.* A. *bad-bakht.*

Discern, *dekhna ; samajhna.* –ment, *aḳl,* (f.) ; *hosh, zihn; cháláki.*

Discharge (freedom,) *khalás ;* (V. *–k.*) *rihá,i.* V. *–kar-d.* (dismissal,) *jawáb ; rukh-sat.* V. *–d.* –ed, *barkhást ; maazúl.* (of an account.) *rasíd,* (E.). *dákhilah.*

Disclose, *kah-dena ; iḳrár-k ; záhir-k.*

Discount, *baṭṭa; dastúri.*V.*–d.*

Discourse, *baḥs,* (f.) ; *waz.* V.*–k.* *See* 'Converse.'

Discovery, *daryáft.* V. *–k.* ; *ḍhúnḍhna.*

Discretion, *aḳl,* (f.) ; *imtiyáz.* A. *aḳlmand.*

Disdain, *ḥiḳárat*. V. *ḥaḳír-jánna*. -ful, *maghrúr*.
Disease, *rog; bímári*. -ed, *rogi; bímár*.
Disfavour, *ná-iltifáti*.
Disgrace, *be-ḥurmati; taḥḳír; be-izzati*. V. *-k*. ed, *be-ḥurmat; be-izzat*. -ful, *ná-shá,istah; kharáb*.
Dish,[1] *bartan*. side-, *dúṇga*.
Dishonest, *bad-diyánat*; (N. *-i*.); *be-ímán*.
Dismiss. *See* 'Discharge.'
Dismount, *utarna*.
Disobedient, *sar-kash; muṇh-zor*. N. *-i*. V. *nahíṇ mánna*.
Disorder, *be-tartíbi*. in --, *darham-barham*.
Dispel, *haṭá-d.; bhagá-d.; uṛá-d*.
Display. *See* 'Show.'
Displease, *ná-khush-k.; ná-pasand-hona*.-sure, *khafagi; ná-khushi*.
Dispose, of. *See* 'Sell.' also, 'Arrange.' --al, *ikhtiyár*. -ition, *mizáj; tabí,at*. (arrangement,) *intizám; band-o-bast*. --ed (in order,) *murattab*.
Dispute, *ḳaziyah; jhagṛa*. V. -k.
Dissatisfied, *ná-ráz; ná-khush; khafa*. -faction, *ná-khushi; khafagi*.
Dissect, *chírna; káṭna*.
Dissipate, *uṛá-d*.
Dissolve (*intr.*) *galna*. (*trans*. *galána*.
Distance. *dúri; tafáwut; fásilah*. A. *dúr*.
Distant. *See* 'Separate.'
Distinction. *See* 'Difference.' (rank,) *martabah; shán*. a person of-, *shán-dár*.
Distress; *tasdi; taklíf; tangi; dukh*. V. *-d.; satána*. --ed, *ázurdah; af-surdah; ghamgín*.
District, *nawáḥ; nazdíki* (technical,) *zila*.
Disturbance, *khalal; ghul; shor; hangámah*. V. *-k*.
Ditch, *nála; paghár*.
Ditto, *aizan*.
Dive, *ḍubki márna; ḍúbna*. -er, *ghotah-már*.
Diverse, *baaze; ka'i-ka'i*.-ify, *baazi taraḥ kám-k.; adal-badal-k*.

[1] The English 'dis' is used by servants to mean the *Pièce de résistance*.

Divert, *khush-k.; bahlána.* (turn aside,) *pher-d.* –ion, *khushi; tamásha.*

Divide, *báṇṭna; bánṭ-lena.* --sion, *taksím,* (f.); *hissah;* (of family property,) *baṭwára.* V. *-k.*

Divine, *bújhna; samajhna.* A. *iláhi.*

Divorce, *talák.* V. --*d.*

Do, *karna; ba-já-lána; taamíl-k.* See 'Deed.' --er, *karne-wála.*

Doctor, (if of English training;), *ḍákṭar sáhib.* (if native,) *tabíb; hakím; baid.* (in learning,) *maulavi,* (M.) *panḍit,* (H.). See 'Cure.'

Dog, *kutta; sag.* –cart, *ṭamṭam.* (Not Hindústáni.)

Doll, *putli.*

Don't, *mat karo; nahíṇ!*

Door, *darwázah; khiṛki.* outer–, *pháṭak.* out of doors, *báhar.* indoors, *bhítar.* –keeper, *darbán.*

Double, *dohra.* V. *dohrána.*

Doubt, *shakk; shubhah.* V. –*k.* and *rakhna.* A. *sáf nahíṇ; shakk ki bát.* (subject to –, or suspicion,) *mushtabah.* –less, *be shakk; be-shubhah.*

Down, downward, *níche; tale,* (prep) *ke.* –.

Dozen, *bárah; ek-darjan.* (E.)

Drain, (off,) *sukhána.* (strain,) *chhánna.*

Draw (load, or picture,) *khaiṇchna.* a–ing, *nakshah.* –ing-room, *hál-kamra.*

Drawers (body,) *jánghiya; sul-dráj* (E. in some formation,) (chest of,) *dráj.* (E.).

Dress. See 'Clothes.' –ing-case, *siṇgár-dán.* --glass, *á,ínah.* –table, *siṇgár-mez.*

Dream, *khwáb.* V. –*dekhna.*

Drink (according to its kind, as '*páni, sharáb, &c.* See page 93). V. *pína.*

Drive, *háṇkna.* --in (a nail,) *márna.* --er, *gáṛíbán; kochbán.* (half E)

Drop, (down,) (*intr.*) *girna; gir-paṛna.* (let –,) *girána; girá-d.* (as water,) *chúna; ṭapakna.* N. *katrah.* (a very little.) *zarrah-sa.*

Drown (*intr.*) *ḍúbna; ḍúb-jána.* (*trans.*) *ḍubána.*

Drum, *ḍhol.* V. –*bajána.* --mer, –*iya.*

Drunk, *mast ; mat-wála ; nashe-meṇ.* –ard, *matwála.* –enness, *masti ; nashah.*

Dry, *k͟hushk ; súkha.* V. *sukhána ; sukhá-d.* –land, *k͟hushki.*

Duck, *bat ; battak͟h.* (brahmani,) *chakwa, chakwi.*

Due, to be, by various phrases, e.g., *mujh-ko das rúpiye pána hai,* or *áte haiṇ ; ham-ko das rúpiye dena, hoga.* my dues, *mera pá,ona ; mera ḥaḳḳ.*

Dull (intellect,) *kund-zihn.* (sad,) *afsurdah.* (weather,) *abri.* –ard, *kund-zihn ádmi ; aḥmaḳ.*

Dumb, *gúṇga ; chup.* V. *gúṇga hona ; chup rahna.* --ness, *gungá,i.*

Dung, *guh,* (f.), goats –, *mengni.* cow –, *gobar,* horse--, *líd,* (f.), --hill, *kura.*

During, *meṇ ; ke bích ; jabtak ...tabtak.* *See page* 104.

Dust, *gard.* A. --*a ; alúdah.* V. *poṇchh-d. ; jhárna.* --er, *jháran.*

Duty, *kám ; jo wájib o-muná sib hai ; wájibi kám.* (tax,) *maḥsúl.*

Dwell, *rahna ; búd-o-básh-k.; maḳám-k.*–ing-house, *ghar ; makán ; koṭhi.*

Dynasty, *k͟handán-sháhi.*

E.

Each, *har-ek ; ek-ek.* *See page* 40. --other, *ek-dígar.* on --side, *donoṇ taraf.*

Ear, *kán ; gosh.* (of corn,) *bál ; báli.*--rings, *bála ; báli.*

Early. *See* 'Dawn.'

Earth, *miṭṭi ; k͟hák* (world,) *dunya* (f.) ; *álam* --en, *miṭṭi ka.*

Ease, *árám ; ráḥat fará-g͟hat ; fursat.* at ease, *árám meṇ* --sy, *ásán ; salís.* N. *ásáni ; salísi.* --ily, *ásáni-se ; ba-k͟húbi.*

East, *púrab ; mashriḳ.*

Eat, *khána.* give to – *khilána.*

Eaves, *olti.*

Ebb, (of tide,) *bháṭha.* V. *–hona.*

Ebony, *ábnús.*

Eclipse, (of sun,) *súraj-grahan.* (of moon,) *chánd-grahan.*

Edge, (e.g., of knife,) *dhár.* (of cloth, the sea, &c.) *kinárah.* a stiff – (as in matting), *kor.*

Edifice, *imárat.*

Education, *taalím,* (f.) ; *tarbiyat; tahzíb,*(f.)V.*taalím-d.*

Effect, *asar ; natíjah.* to produce an --, *karna ; karána; anjám-k ; asar-k.* my words produced no effect, *meri báton se kuchh asar nahín tha.*--ive, *kám ka; kár-gar ; mu,assir.*

Effects, *mál ; mál-o-mata ; asbáb ; chízen ; chíz sab.*

Effort, *koshish.* make an,--*k.*

Egg, *anda ; baizah.*[1] --cup, --*dán.* --spoon, *ande ka chammach.* eggs and bacon, *ande bekam* (E.).

Either. *See page* 46.

Eject. *See* 'Expel.'

Elapse, *bít-jána; guzar-jána.*

Elbow, *kuhni; baghal.*

Elegant, *latíf ; suthra; khushnuma.* --gance, *latáfat.*

Elephant, *háthi ; píl,* or *fíl.* --driver, *maháwat ; pílbán.* --shed, *píl-khánah.*

Eloquence, *fasáhat.* A. *fasíh.*

Else, (otherwise,) *nahín to,* (additional,) *aur.* e.g., anywhere else. *aur kahín.* what else, *aur kya?* who else is there? *aur kaun hai?*

Embankment, *bándh,* (f.). V. --*banána.*

Embezzlement, *tasarruf ; khiyánat.* V. --*k.*

Embroidery, *chikan-dozi.*--ed cloth, *got laga hú,a kapra.*

Emerald, *zamurrad; panna.*

Emetic, *kai ki dawa.*

Emperor, *kaisar ; sháh–an-sháh ; sultán.* The Empress of India, *Kaisar-i-Hind.*

Empire, *ráj ; bádsháhi ; saltanat.*

Employ, *khidmat men lena ; kám-d.* (oneself,) *mashghúl-hona.*--er, *málik ; áka; muníb.* --ment, *kám ; naukari ; kárbár ; rozgár.*

Empty, *khálí.* V. --*k.* ; *sab chíz nikálna.*--iness, *khulu.* --handed, *khálí-háth.*

Enable, *madad-d ; ijázat-d.*

Enact, *farmána.* --ment, *farmán ; hukm ; á,ín.*

---

[1] Used in Western and North-Western India. The word is Persian.

Encamp, *dera-k.*; *makám-k.* –ment, *khaima-gáh*; *makám.*

Enclose, *ghera lagána.* --ure, by the word appropriate to the use of the place, e.g., *bágh*, a garden. *sahn*, a court-yard, &c.

Encouragement, *dilása.* V. --*d.*

End, *ákhir*; *khatm.* (of e.g., a stick,) *nok*, (f.). V. (*trans.*) *ba sar lána*; *ákhir-k*; *khatm-kar-d.* from beginning to--, *awwal se ákhir tak.* to no --, *be-fáidah.*

Endeavour. *See* 'Effort.'

Endurance, *bardásht*; *burd-bári*; *sabr*, (f.) V. --*k.* (to last,) *ab tak hona*, or *rahna.*

Enemy, *dushman.* enmity, *dushmani*; *adáwat.*

Engaged in. *See* 'Employ.'

Engine, *kal.* (railway,) *injin.* (E.).

England, *Inglistán.* A. *ang-rezi.*

Enjoin. *See* 'Command.'

Enjoy, *lahna*; *kuchh chíz se khush hona.* I enjoy good health, *maiṇ bahut tan-darust húṇ.*–ment, *khushí*; *ánand.*

Enlargement, *barhá,o.* V. *barhána*; *is-se bara-k.*

Enough, *bas*; *bahut.* (suffi-cient,) *káfi.* N. *kifáyat.*

Enraged, *ghusse.* V. --*k.*

Enter, *bhítar*, or *andar-ána*, or *jána*; *paithna*; *ghusna.* (in a book, &c.) *likhna*; *siyáhah-k.*; *mundaraj-k.* –trance, (passage,) *dar-wázah*, *ráh*, (f.), act of entering, *dakhl-k.* (v.n.).

Entertainment, *ziyáfat*; *khá-na*; *bara khána.* (amuse-ment,) *tamásha.* the act of entertaining, *mihmáni.* V. –*k.* --er, *mihmán-dár*; *dene-wála.*

Entire. *See* 'All.'

Environs, *gird-nawáh*; *jo cháron taraf hai*; *atráf.* (pl. of '*taraf.*')

Envy, *hasad*, (f.). V. --*k.* A. *hásid.*

Epilepsy, *mirghi.*

Epistle, *chitthi*; *khatt*; *rukah.*

Equal, *barábar*; *ek-sán*; *mu,fiák.* N. *barábari*; *mu,áfakat.*

Equipage, *sáz ; sámán.* V. *saz-o-sámán taiyár-k.*

Equity, *insáf ; jo rást-o-durust hai, so.* A. *rást ; ádil ; sachha.*

Era, *san ; tárikh.* (f.).

Erect, *sídha ; khaṛa.* V. *-k.* to be -, *-hona.* –ion, *imárat.*

Error, *ghalati ; khata ; bhúl ; chúk.* V. *-k. ; bhúlna ; bhúl-jána.* --roneous, *ghalat ; ná-durust.*

Escape, *bhág-jána,* as v.n. ; *firár ;* (from danger,) *bachá,o.* V. *bhág-jána ;* (danger,) *bach-jána ; chhúṭna ; chhúṭ-jána.*

Especial, *khusús ; kháss ;* Adv. *khusúsan.*

Essence, (scent,) *itr.* (of any matter,) *ain ; nafs ; máhiyat.* --tial, *zarúr.* the essentials, *zarúriyát.*

Estate, *milk ; milkíyat ; zamín,* (f.) with names according to kinds ; as *zamíndári ; ta,alluḳ ; muḳarrari, &c.* –given for support, *jágír,* or *já-e-gír.* --holder, *zamíndár ; ta,alluḳ-dár ; muḳarrari-dár ; jágír-dár, &c.*

Esteem, *azíz-rakhna ; ḳadr -k.* --timation, *ḳadr.* -ed, *azíz ; pyára.*

Et cætera, *waghairah.*

Europe, *wiláyat,* --ean, *wiláyati.* a European, *wiláyati ádmi ; gora.*

Evasion, *ṭála; ṭála-ṭoli.* V. *--k.*

Even. *See* 'Equal.' --if, *agar-chih.*

Evening, *shám,* (f.) ; *sáṇjh.* at--, *--ko.*

Event, *wuḳu.* at all events, *ba har súrat.* in the event of, *agar ; is ḥál meṇ, kih, &c.*

Ever, *kabhi ; hargiz.* what--, *jo kuchh.* who--, *jo ko,í.* when-, *jab ; jab-kih. jis-waḳt.* where--, *jaháṇ-kaháṇ.* –more, *hameshah.*

Every, (one,) *har ek ; sab ko,í.* (thing.) *sab kuchh ; sab,* followed by noun of person or thing spoken of. –where, *har-jagah; chároṇ taraf.*

Evident, *záhir, maalúm ; sáf.* Adv. *záhiran,* –ce, *shahádat ; gawáhi.*

Evil, (n.) *badi ; zabúni ; kharábi , kharáb kám ;*

bura, i, *bura* *kám.* (a.) *kharáb; bura; bad; zabún.* -doer, *jo-karta hai.*-hearted, *bad-kho; bad-dil.* -speaker, *bad-go.*[1] -speaking, *bad-go,i.*[1]

Ewer, *áftábah.*

Exact, *ṭhík; durust; achchha; saḥíḥ.* Adv. *ṭhík.* V. *See* 'Demand.' N. *durustagi.*

Exaltation, *baṛá,i; sarfarázi.* V. -*k.*; -*d.* -ed, *sarfaráz.*

Examination, *imtiḥán; jánch; tajwíz* (f.). V-*k.*; *jánchna; ázmána.* to be examined, *imtiḥán-d.* to examine into, *taḥḳíḳát-k.* to pass an-, -*se nikalta hona.*

Example, *masal* (f.). *tamsíl,* (f.). for-, *masalan.*

Exceed, *ziyádah-k.* excess, *ziyádat; fázil; jo báḳi hai.* excessive, (and as adv.) *nihdyat.*

Excellence, *kamál; tarjíḥ,* (f.). V. *kámil-hona; tarjíḥ-rakhna; nikalta-hona; sab se achchha-hona.* Your -cy! *ḥuzúr; janáb-áli!* A. *khúb; sab se achchha.* Adv. *achchhi taraḥ se.* Interj. *khúb! khúb! bahut achchha! shábásh!*

Exception, *mustasna.* V.-*k.*; *chhoṛ-d.*; *jáne-d.* prep. *ke siwa,* or *siwá-e; aláwah is-ke.* to take -to, *bura mánna.*

Exchange. *See* 'Change.'

Excise, *ábkári.*

Exclaim, *kahna;* (scream,) *pukárna; chilláua; baland áwáz se bolna; zor-se bolna; shor-k.* N. *bát; áwáz,* (f.); *shor; shorshár.*

Exclude, *báhar rakhna; nahíṇ áne-d.; mana-kar-d.* N. *roká,o.* also, better. by Verbs as v. n.

Excuse, *uzr; mu,áfi.* V. -(oneself) *uzr-k.* -(another) *mu,áf-k.* -ed, *mu,áf.* -able, *ḳábil-i-uzr.* without-, *be-uzr.*

Execute. *See* 'Do.' (by hanging,) *pháṇsi-d.* -tioner, *jallád.*

Exercise, (work,) *kám; miḥnat.* (using,) *istimal; muhá-*

---

[1] From the Persian, '*guftan,*' 'to say.' See also '*Guft-o-gu*'.

warah. (lesson,) *sabaḳ.* (by walking, &c.) *by the words which mean these.* (military,) *ḳawá,id.* to take–, *hawa khána* to– e. g. a horse, *pheri-k.*

Exhaust, (e.g.a bottle,) *kháli-k.* (resources,) *uṛá-d.*; *bar*[1]*-bád*[1]*-d.* (one's strength,) *thaka-k.* and *hona.* –ively, *púre taur se.*

Exhibition, *iksibíshan.* (E.). V. *dikhlána*; *dikhlá-d.*; *záhir-kar-d.*

Exist, *hona.* –tence, *zindagi.* (abstract,) *hona* as v.n. –ing, *maujúd*; *ḥál.* in the –ing circumstances, *ba ḥálát maujúdah.*

Expand, *kholna*; *phailána.* (as a flower,) *khulna*; *phúlna.* N. *khuli jagah.*

Expectation, *intizár,* (f.); *ummed,* (f.); *ummedwári.* V. *–k.* –tant, *also,* an –tant, *ummedwár.*

Expedient, *wájib*; *munásib*; *lázim.* N. with '*jo.*'

Expel, *nikál-d.* N. *ikhráj.*

Expenses, *kharj*; *kharjah.* (cost,) *ḳímat*; –ive, *besh ḳímat*; *ḳimati*; *mahnga.* –diture, *sarf.* V. *kharj-k.*; *sarf-k.*

Experience, *wáḳif-kári.* –ed, *wáḳif*; *hoshyár.* V. (e. g. pain,) *khána*; *uṭhána.*

Expert, *chálák*; *hoshyár.* N. *–i*; *–i.*

Explanation, *tashríḥ* (f.); *bayán* (of conduct,) *uzr*; *safá,i*; *jawáb.* V. *–d.*; *samjhána.*

Expose. *See* 'Show.'

Express, –ion. *See* 'Diction.' 'Say,' &c. –ly, *khusúsan*; *táḳíd-se.*

Extend. *See* 'Spread,' 'Expand.'

Extinguish, *bujhá-d*; *buṭá-d*; *ṭhandha-k.*

Extract. *See* 'Essence.' (e.g. from a book,) *muntakhab.* V. *nikál-lena.*

Extravagance, *fuzúl-kharji.* A. *fuzúl kharj.*

Extremity, *ákhirat.* (e.g., of a stick,) *nok.* (f.). *See* 'Distress.' –ely, *niháyat*

[1] See 'bar' and 'bad' in Glossary, Part I.

Eye, *áṇkh*; (f.); *chashm*. -brow, *abru*, (f.). -ball, *putli*, -lash, *palak*, (f.). -lid, *papoṭa*. -sight, *bíná,i*. -sore, *áṇkh ka káṇṭa*. -glass, *chashmah* (telescope, binoculars,) *dúrbín*. -witness, *chashm-díd*[1]*-gawáh*.

F.

Fable, *ḳissah*; *afsánah*; *naḳl*, (f.).

Face, *muṇh*; *chihrah*; *ru*. V. *samne-ána*; *muṇh pherna*. to make faces, *muṇh ṭeṛha-k*. -to-, *ru-ba-ru*. -ing, *ke sámne*.

Fact, *asl ḥál*; *ḥaḳíḳat*. in fact, *ḥaḳíḳat meṇ*.

Factory, *koṭhi*. indigo-, *níl*.-

Fade, *kumlána*.

Fail, (as stores,) *kam-hona*. (in any work,) *chúkna*. I have failed in my attempt, *maiṇ apni koshish meṇ ná-kám-yáb*[2] *hú,a*. -ure, *ná-kám-yábi*.[2]

Faint, (a.) *be-hosh*, (n.) *-i*. V.—*hona*. (as, e.g. ink,) *kam-numa*. -ness, *zuf*; *ná-táḳati*; *kam-zori*.-hearted, *buz-dil*.

Fair, (n.) *mela*; *háṭ* (a.) *gora*; *sufed*. (as weather,) *k͟hula*; *achchha*. -to see, *k͟húb-súrat*. -play, *rást-bázi*; *nek-kám* -ly, *rásti-se*.

Fairy, *pari*.

Faith, *ímán*. -ful, *-dár*. -ful-ness, *dári*. to put- in, *itimád-rakhna*. -fully, *-se*. -less, *be-ímán*; *bad-diyánat*.

Fall, (n.) *gir-paṛna*, v.n. (v.) *gir-paṛna*. cause to-, *girá-d*.

False, *jhúṭha*; *darog͟h*; *farebi*. -hood, *jhúṭh*. *See* 'Lie'.

Fame, *nám*; *nek-námi*. A. *námwar*; *mashhúr*.

Family, *k͟handán*; *barádari*; *ghar-ke-log*. of good-, *k͟handáni*. the children of the-, *laṛke-bále*.

---

[1] From the Persian '*didan*,' 'to see.'

[2] From the Persian, '*yáftan*,' 'to obtain.'

Famine, *kaht ; akál.*

Fan, *pankha.* (small,) *háth–,* (for fire,) *phúkni* (for flies,) *chaunri.* V. (if large,) *–khínchna ; tánna.* (L.B.) (if small,) *jhalna* or *dolána.*

Fancy, *khayál ; atkal.* V. *–k. ; atkalna.* A. *mutawahhim.*

Far, *dúr ; dúr-daráz.* thus–, *yahán tak*

Fare, (n.) *kiráya.* (person,) *–dár.* V. *chalna.* how are you faring? *áp ke pás sab kaisa chalta hai?* –well, *Khuda háfiz.* [1] to take farewell, *rukhsat lena.*

Farm, *jot ; kásht ; zamín ;* (f.) *chás ; khet ; khet-bári.* (of revenues,) *ijárah ; thíka.* –er, *kisán, &c.* See 'Cultivator.' –of revenues, *mustájir ; ijárah-dár ; thíká-dár.*

Farrier, *salotri ; nál-band.*

Farther, *aur áge.* (in addition,) *aláwah is-ke.* –est. *sab se dúr ; sab se pichhla.*

Fast, (n.) *rozah.* V. *–rakhna.* (a.) *tez.* –ness, *tezi.* (closed, secure,) *band ; band-hú,a ; sakht ; mazbút.* V. *band, sakht,* or *mazbút. –k.* N. *mazbúti.*

Fat, (a) *mota ; farbih ;* (n.) *charbi.* –ness, *motá,i.* V. *mota-k.*

Fate, *kaza,* (f.) ; *kismat.* fatal, *kátil ; sangháru.*

Father, *báp ; wálid ; pidar.* –ly, *pidarána.* –in-law, *susra ; sosur.* (L.B.)

Fault, *gunáh,* (f.) ; *kusúr ; taksír,* (f.) ; *khata,* (f.); *aib.* –ty, *taksír-wár.* (as work, &c.) *thík nahín ; achchha nahín.* –less, *be-kusúr.* (as work, &c.) *thík ; durust ; bahut achchha.*

Favour, (thing granted,) *inám.* (mental,) *ináyat ; iltifát.* (kindness,) *mihrbáni.* to grant a–, *inám-d. ; mihrbáni-k.* to be favourable to.) *ináyát-k. ; iltifát-rakhna.* –able, *mihrbán.* a – ite, *yár ; dost ; musáhib.* ably, *mihrbáni se ; dili-iltifát se.*

Fear, *dar,* (f.) ; *khauf dahshat ; tars.* V. *darna ;*

[1] Literally, (may) God (be your) keeper, as in our 'good-bye.'

ḍar-khána. -ful, (timorous,) *dahshat-nák.* (horrible,) *k͟hauf-nák.* -less, *be-k͟hauf; mardána.*

Feast. *See* 'Entertainment.'

Feather, *par.* -bed, *-ka bichhauna.*

Feature, *chihrah.*

Fee, (of office,) *rusúm.* (gratuity,) *bak͟hshish.*[1] V. *-d.*

Feeble, *kam-zor; durbal, za,íf.* N. *kam-zori; zuf.*

Feed, (eat,) *khána.* (another,) *khilána.*

Feel, (grope,) *ṭaṭolna.* (e.g. pain)...*khána; uṭhána.* (for one,) *riḳḳat-rakhna.* -ing, (sense of,) *lámisah.* fine feelings. *k͟hayálát.*

Feign, *makr kachhána.*

Fellow, (person,) *ádmi; shak͟hs; kas.* a certain-, *fulána.* (match,) *joṛa,* or *joṛi.* a fellow (e.g. traveller,) *ham,* added to appropriate noun. -ship, *ham-sari; sajhá,i.*

Female, *mádah.* a-, *aurat.*

Fence, *ghera.* V. *-lagána.; d.*

Ferry, *guzar-gháṭ.* -man, *gháṭ-mánjí* V. *pár-k.*

Fertile, *zar-k͟hez.* N. *-i.*

Fever, *tab; buk͟hár.* -ish, *garm.* to have-, *mujh-ko tab hai.*

Few, *chand; thoṛe.* -ness, *kami.*

Field, *khet; maidán; ramnah.*

Fig, *anjír.* (f.).

Fight. *See* 'Battle.'

Figure, (shape,) *shakl,* (f.); *súrat* (1,2,3,&c.) *hindasah.*

File, (tool,) *súhán.* V. *retna.* (of papers,) *nathi; misl.* (f.).

Fill, *bharna; bhar-d.; púra-k.* (a post,) *uhdah-rakhna.; fulána kám-k.*

Final, *ák͟hir; ák͟hiri.* -ly, *ák͟hir-ko; ák͟hir-ul-umr.*

Find, *milna* (*See page* 50); *pána.* -out, *daryáft-k.; púchhna.*

Fine, (n.) *jarímánah.* V. *-lena.* (a.) *mihín; bárík.* N. *báríki.* in fine, *alḳissah; ák͟hirash.*

---

[1] This word suffers much in Anglo-Hind. The author has seen it reduced to '*boxis.*' It is a Persian word, from '*bakhshídan,*' 'to give a present,' 'to reward.'

Finger, *ungli.* V. *chhúna.*
Finish, *tamám-k.*; *khatm-k.* –ed, *tamám hú,a*; *kámil*; *púra*; *ho-gaya.*
Fire, *ág.* (f.); *átish.* V. *–lagá-d.* –place, *átish-khánah.* –fly, *shab-chirágh.* –wood, *lakṛi*; *hezim,* (f.). –works, *átish-bázi.*
Firm, *sakht, mazbút*; *ká,im*; *karár.* V. *–k.* –ness, *sakhti*; *mazbúti*; –ly, *sakht*; *zor se*; *mazbút taur se.*
First, *paihla,* or, *pahla.* in the –place, *or,* time, *paihle.*
Fish, *machhli*; *máhi.*–monger, *machhli-wála*; *machhli-farosh.* V. *machhli-márna.* –er-man, *jaliya*; *máhi-gír.* –ery, *jalkar.*
Fist, *muṭṭhi*; *musht.* –icuffs, *mukká-mukki*; *márá-mári.*
Fit, (*intr.*) *achchha baiṭhna*; *ṭhík-lagna.* (*trans.*) *ṭhík k.,* or *lagána,* or *baiṭhána.* (a.) *ṭhík*; *durust.* (suitable,) *lá,ik.*
Fix. *See* 'Firm.' –in the ground, *gáṛna.*
Flag, *jhanḍa*; *nishán.*–stone, *chaṭán,* (f.). (v.) *ḍhíla,* or *sust ho-jána.*
Flame, *shulah*; *lau,* (f.); V. *shulah uṭhna* (fig.) *chamak-na*; *lapaṭna.*
Flannel, *flálen,* (E.); *dhus-sa.*
Flash. *See* 'Flame.' a '*flash*' e.g. of lightning, say, e.g. the lightning *flashes.*
Flat, *chapṭá.* N. *–á,i.* Adv. (plainly,) *saríhan.*
Flattery, *khush-ámad,* (f.). V. *–k.*; *phustána.* –er, with '*jo.*'
Flea, *pissu.*
Flee, *bhágna*; *bhág-jána*; *bhagá-jána*; *chal-jána*; *firár-hona.*
Flesh, *gosht.* –y, *moṭa*; *far-bih.*
Flight, *bhagel,* (f.); *firári.*
Flock, *gallah.*
Flog, *chábuk*[1] *se márna.*–ing, (by the operator,) *chábuk-bázi.* (as received,) *chábuk ki saza.*

---

[1] Vary '*chábuk,*' which means '*a whip,*' according to the instrument used. The cane ('*bet*') is generally used. In India, only criminals are flogged. Domestic and school discipline are unknown.

Floor, *zamín*, (f.). (storey,) *maḥallah*. –cloth, *dari ; farsh*.

Flour, *áṭa ; maidah ; sattu*.

Flourish, *achchhe ḥál meṇ hona ; phúlna*. (e.g. a stick,) *hiláná*.

Flow, (v.) *bahna ; jári-hona ; chalna*. –ing, *jári ; rawáṇ*. the –of the tide, *juwár*.

Flower, *phúl ; gul*. –garden, *phul-wári*. –pot, *gamlah ; jhári*. –y. *phúlphúla* ; (fig.) *rangín*. (speech,) *gul-fisháṇ*. V. *–na ; –d*.

Fly, *magas*, (f.) ; *makkhi*. (cab,) *ṭhíká-gáṛi*. (v.)(*intr.*) *uṛna ; uṛ-jána*. (*trans.*) *uṛána ; uṛá-d*.

Fodder, *ghás*, (f.) ; *chárah ; rasad*, (f.).

Foe. *See* 'Enemy.'

Fog, *kohása*. –gy, *dhundla*.

Fold, (for animals,) *beṛh ; bathán* ; or with '*khánah*, added to the name of the animal, e.g. *murghi-khánah*. (in cloth,) *tah*. (of a door, &c.), *palla*. two–, &c. *do-guna*. V. *lapeṭna ; tah-k*. with –ed hands, *háth-joṛ-kar-ke*.

Follow, *píchhe-ána* and *jána*. (a trade), *peshah-k*. –er, *píchhe-áne-wála*. (adherent,) *tábidár*.

Folly, *be-wuḳúfi ; aḥmaḳi ; ḥimáḳat*. A. *be-wuḳúf ; aḥmaḳ*.

Fond, *shá,iḳ ; má,il*. to be –of a person, *pyár-k. ; azíz-rakhna*. (of a thing,) *pasand-k*.

Fool, *aḥmaḳ*. V. *ḥimáḳat-k*. *See* 'Folly.' adv. *be-wuḳúfi-se*.

Foot, *páṇw*. (measure,) *fúṭ*. (E.). –man, *chob-dár ; piyádah*. –path, *pag-ḍanḍi*. –step, *ḳadam*. –stool, *moṛha ; ishṭúl*. (E.) ; *páo-dán*.

For, *ke wáste ; ke líye ; ko*. (because,) *chúṇkih*. –instance, *chunánchi ; masalan*.

Forbearance, *parhez*, (f.) ; *sabr*, (f.). V. *–k*.

Forbid, *mana-k*. which, may God–, *Khuda na kare*. N. *mana*.

Force, *zor*. (oppression,) *zulm*, (f.) ; *zabar-dasti*. V. *–k*. A. *zor-áwar*. Adv. *zor se, &c*. –ed, (constrained,) *majbúr*. N. *majbúri*.

Fore, (adv.) *áge ; agla ; sámne ; pesh*.

Fore-fathers, *jadā ; múrisán.* -finger, *shahádad ki úngli.* -foot, *agla-páṇw* -head, *pesháni.* -noon, *do pahar ke áge.* -go, *chhoṛ-d. ; jáne-d.*

Foreign, *pardeshi ; bideshi ; wiláyati.* -country, *pardes; wiláyat.* -er, *bidesi ádmi.*

Forest, *jangal ; ban.* (as in '*sundar-ban.*' '*the beautiful forest,*' The Soonderbunds.)

Forgetfulness, *bhúl,* (f.) ; *farámoshi.* V. *-k.; bhúlna ; bhúl-jána.* A. *farámoshgár.* -gotten, *farámosh.*

Forgiven, *mu,áf.* N. *-i.* V. *-k.* -er, with '*jo.*'

Fork, *káṇṭa.*

Form, *shakl,* (f.) ; *súrat.* V. *banána.* (bench,) *kursi ; takhtah ;* '*binsh.*' (E.).

Former, *peshtar ; agla ; pahla ; sábiḳ ;* -ly, *áge ; agle zamáne meṇ ; peshtar.*

Forsake, *chhoṛ-d. ; tyág-k.*

Fort, *ḳilah ; gaṛh.*

Forth, *áge.* and so-, *waghairah.* to go-, *báhar-jána.* to show-, *batlá-d. ; záhir-k.*

Fortnight, *chaudah roz ; do hafte.*

Fortune, (good, or bad,) *ḳismat.* (good,) *nasíb ; iḳbál.* (bad,) *bad ḳismat ; badbakhti. be-nasíbí.* (wealth,) *daulat ; mál.* A. *nek-bakht ; khush nasíb ; bhala ; daulatmand.* Adv. *nasíb-se ; nekbakhti-se.* to be -ate, adjs. with *hona.*

Forward, *áge.* (rude,) *shokh ; gustákh.* V. *chalán kar-d. ; rawánah kar-d ; áge bhej-d.*

Foundation, *bunyád,* (f.).

Fountain, *chashmah.*

Fourth-part, *chauthá-i ; pá,o.*

Fowl, *chiṛiya ;* (poultry,) *murgh ; murghi ;* (small,) *kharchah ;* (middle size,) *ním ;* (roast,) *kabáb.*

Fox, *lomṛi.*

Frame. *See* 'Make.' picture-, *ḍháṇcha.* door-, *chau-kaṭh,* (f.).

Fraud. *See* 'Deceive.'

Free, *khalás; ázád.* N. *khalási; rihá,i ázádagi.* V. *chhoṛ-d ; khalás kar-d. ; jáne-d.* adv. (e.g. with a freehand,) *kushádah*[1] *háth se.*

[1] From the Persian '*kushádan,*' 'to open.

Freeze, (*intr.*) *jam-jána.* (*trans.*) *barf meṉ rakhna ; jamá-ḍ.*

Frequent, (a.), *jo aksar hota hai.* –ly, *aksar.* (v.) *áná-jána ; ámad-o-raft-k.*

Fresh, *tázah ; nau.* –ness, *tázagi.*

Friday, *jumah ; shukr-wár.* (or *-bár.*).

Friend, *dost; yár.* –ship, *dosti.* –ly, *dostánah.*

Frighten, *ḍarána ; ḍar-dikh-lána* or *karna*, or *karána.*

Frock, *frák*, (E.). *kurti.* –coat, *frák kurti.*

Frog, *menḍak.*

From, *se ; az* (Persian).

Front. *See* 'Face,' 'Fore.'

Fruit, *mewah ; phal.* (results,) *natijah.* –erer, *mewah-farosh.* –ful, *phal-dár.*

Fry, *faṛái* (E.) *-kar-d.*–ing-pan, *faṛái-pán* (E.).

Fuel, *lakṛi; hezim,* (f.).

Fulfil, *adá-k.* &c. *See* 'Accomplish.'

Full, *púra ; bhara ; bhar-púr.* –grown, (of persons,) *siyána* Adv. *púre taur se ; tafsilan.*

Fun, *khushi ; khel ; tamásha.* –ny, *haṉsne ki bát.*

Fur, *pashm.*

Furious, *díwánah ; ghusse ; josh.* a –passion, *átish-bár ghussah.*

Furlough, *chhuṭṭi ; rukhsat.*

Furnish, (supply,) *pahuṉ-chá-d. ; bhej-d.* (e.g. a room,) *sajána ; siṉgár-k.*

Furniture, *sámán ; asbáb ; mez-chauki.*

Future, (n.a.), *áyindah.*

G.

Gain, *nafa ; munáfa ; fái-dah.* V. *-k.* (e.g. learning,) *ḥásil-k. ; jama-k.*

Gallop, (n.), *chhár-tag.* V. *dauṛna.*

Gamble, *jú,a khelna.* bler, *juwári.*

Game, *khel ; bázi* following the word for the kind of game, e.g. *átish-bázi*, games with fire, fireworks. (sport,) *shikár. See* 'Gamble.' *Also page* 88.

Garden. *bágh ; bághchah.* –er, *máli.*

Garlic, *lahsan.*

Garment, (according to its name.) –s, *kapṛe ; poshák*, (f.). *See pages* 34, 87 & 95.

Garrison, *ḳile ke log.*

Gate, *phátak.* –man, *darbán.*

Gather, *jama-k.* (flowers,) *toṛna.*

Gay, *khush ; khush-dil.* V. *hona.* N. *–i ; –i.*

Gaze, *dekhte rahna ; ghúrna.* N. *nigaráni.*

Gem, *jawáhir ; jauhar ; zewar.*

General, *ámm.* –ly, *umúman.*

Generation, *pusht.* from– to–, *pusht-ba-pusht.*

Generous, *sakhi ;* N. *sakháwat.*

Gentle, *narm ; gharíb.* (of birth,) *najíb ; ashráf ; asíl.* –man, *bhala ádmi.* gently, *áhistah.*

Get. *See* 'Acquire.' –you gone, *dúr ! ; dúr-ho !*

Ghost, *bhút See* 'Die.' 'Holy.'

Gift, *inám ; bakhshish.* (to a superior,) *nazr ; nazaránah ; salámi.* V. *–d.*

Gilding, *tilal.* –er, *kár.* gilt, *sunáhla.*

Gimlet, *barma.*

Ginger, (green, or preserved,) *adrak.* (dry,) *sonṭh.*

Girl, *laṛki ; chhokṛi.* (slave,) *bandi ; launḍi ; dási.* –ish, *laṛki-sa:*

Give, *dena ; de-d.* –up, *chhoṛ-d.* –way, *haṭna,* –er, *dene-wála. See* 'Gift.'

Glad, *khush ; khush dil.* V. *hona,* and *karna.* –ness, *khushi ; dil-khushi.* Adv. *khushi-se.*

Glass, *shíshah ; glás.* (E.), service of–, *glás sab.*[1] –of, *shíshe ka.*

Globe, *kurah.* A. *gol.*

Gloomy, *dhumla.* N. *–i.*

Glue, *saresh.* V. *–se joṛna.*

Glutton, *bisyár-khor.* –y, *–i.*

Gnat, *mas.*

Go, *jána ; chalna ; baṛhána ; ráh-lena.* –against, *kisi par jána.* –forward, *áge-jána,* or *chalna,* or *baṛhána.* –back, *pichhe jána, &c.* to let–, *chhoṛ-d.* –round about, *chakkar-karke jána.*

---

[1] See 'Sab' in Part I of this Glossary.

Goat, *chhágul; bakra,* (m.) *bakri,* (f.).

God, (Christian and M.) *Khuda; Khudá-ta,ála.* (M.) *Alláh.* (H.) *Ishwar; Parmeshwar; Bhagwán; Rám; Rám-Rám.* and many more, corresponding to *the attributes* of God. (as we say, 'The God of Love,' 'The God of Fire,' &c.). Religious figures are called '*but.*' Muḥammadans are forbidden to use them. -ly, *Khudá-tars.* -liness, *takwa.*

Gold, *sona; zar.* A. *sone ka; sonahla.* -smith, *sonár.*

Good, *achchha; bhala; khúb; nek.* -and bad, *bhala-bura.* a -deal, *khúb-kuchh.* a -while, *der tak.* a -way *kuchh dúr.* -for nothing, *ná-kára, kuchh kám ka nahíṇ.* -for, *kám ka,* a -many, *bahut-sa.* -morning, *sabá-ḥu-l-khair.* -evening, *shab ba-khair.* N. *achhá,i; bhalá,i; neki.* (kindness,) *mihrbáni.* to do-, *achhá,i, &c. k.* to make-. *See* 'Establish.'

Goods, *mál; asbáb; chíz sab.*

Goose, *ráj-háṇs.*

Gospels, the, *injíl.*

Government, *ḥukúmat; saltanat; amaldári.*

Governor, according to his rank, from *pádsháh,* to '*súbahdár*'; *ḥákim.* -General, *baṛa láṭ sáḥib.* lieutenant-, *láṭ sáḥib.* *See page* 78.

Gourd, *kadu.*

Grace, *ináyat.* to show-, *-k.* -ful, *sajíla.*

Gracious, *mihrbán; raḥím; shírín.* N. *i.* -ness, *mihrbáni.*

Graft, *kalam.* V. *lagána.*

Grain, *ghallah; anáj; dánah.* (a little,) *zarrah-sa.* (f.); *thoṛa-sa.*

Granary, *gola.*

Grand, *baṛa; umdah, buzurg; álíshán.* -eur, *baṛái; shaukat.* as applied to relatives: father's father, *dáda.* mother's father, *nána.* father's mother, *dádi.* mother's mother, *náni.* son's son, *pota.* son's daughter, *poti.* daughter's son, *náti.* daughter's daughter, *natni.*

Grape, grapes, *angúr.*

Grasp, *pakaṛna.* N. *ḳabzah; háth.*

Grass, *ghás*, (f.). (for horses,) *dúb-ghás.* –hopper, *ṭiḍḍi.*

Grate, *ragaṛ-k.*; *c̱haṛchaṛána.* N. *ragaṛ.* (for fire,) *átish-k̲h̲ánah; jhanjhári.*

Grateful, *iḥsánmand.* N. *–i.*

Gratify, *k̲h̲ush-k.* –itude, *shukr.* (expressing gratitude,) *shukr-guzári.*

Grave, (n.) *ḳabr; gor.* –yard, *–istán.* (a.) (in mind,) *fikrmand; udás; afsurdah.* (as an affair,) *sangín; wazani.*

Gravel, *roṛa; reg; kankar.*

Gravy, *áb-i-gosht; grevi.* (E.).

Gray, *sabsah*, flea-bitten–, *magasi.* (as hair,) *páka.*

Graze, (*intr.*) *charna.* (*trans.*) *charána.* one who tends cattle –ing, *charwáha.* –ing-ground, *paṛti zamín*, (f.); *chará-gáh.*

Grease, *charbi; chikná,i.* V. *–d.*

Great, *baṛa*, &c. *See* 'Grand.' a –deal, *bahut; ḍher.*

Green, *sabz.* (fresh,) *tázah; tar-o tázah.* –ness, *sabzi; tázagi.*

Gridiron, *gril-dán.* (half E.).

Grief, *g̲h̲amm; afsos; dukh; ranj.* A. *g̲h̲amgín; dukhit; ranjídah; ázurdah; udás.* V. (*trans.*) *bezár-k; izá-d; satána.* (*intr.*) *hona*, with the adjs.

Grind, *písna.* –stone, *chakki.* –ing –slab, *sil.*

Groan, *karáh; áh; nálah.* V. *–k.*; *kaharna.*

Grocer, *modi.*

Groom, *sá,is.* V. *ghoṛa ṭhanḍa-k.*; *g̲h̲oṛe-ko malna, sáf-k.* or other appropriate phrase.

Grove, *bág̲h̲; top.*

Ground, *zamín*, (f.) the surface of the–, *rú-i-zamin.* dry–, *k̲h̲ushki.* wet–, *tari; tará,i.* as in 'camping-ground,' &c., .. *gáh* as last part of word, *k̲h̲aima-gáh*, &c. (cause,) *sabab.* (origin,) *bunyád*, (f.); *jaṛ.* –less, *be-bunyád; be-sabab.* V. (as a boat,) *–par lag-jána; ṭhekna; ṭhek-jána.* (a case,) *is bunyád par arz karna, kih*, &c.

Grow, (*intr.*) *phalna; ugna; ána; á-jána; ho-jána.* (e.g.

in stature,) *baṛa hona; baṛhna.* (*trans.*) (e.g. vegetables,) *bona; ropna.* grown-up (persons,) *siyána.*

Grumble, *kuṛkuṛána; garajna.* N. *kuṛkuṛáhaṭ; garaj.*

Guava, *amrúd.*

Guarding, (n.) (as sentinel,) *pahra; nigáhbáni; pásbáni.* V. *-k.* one who guards, *pahra-wála; páṛa-wála nigáh-bán; chauki-dár.* to be on one's guard, *khabar-dár hona.*

Guardian, *ḥáfiz.* (of youth, &c.) *murabbi.* (of a minor,) *wali.* of (property,) *amánat-dár; chauki-dár.* (of a Muham. : religious trust,) *mutawalli.* (of a Hindu ditto,) *shewait,* (vulg. *shebait.*) -ship, *ḥifázat; amánat; zimmah.*

Guess, *ḳiyás; aṭkal.* V. *-k.; aṭkalna.* by-, *aṭkal-se; andázi.*

Guide, *ráh-numa; agwa.* (v.) *ráh batlána; pahunchá-d.*

Guile, *fareb; daghá-bázi; ḥílah; cháláki.* A. *farebi; ḥíla-báz.*

Guilt, *gunáh; ḳusúr.* A. *gunáh-gár; mujrim.* -less, *be-ḳusúr.*

Gulp, *ghúnṭ.* V. *-se kháma,* or *pína.*

Gum, *gond.* V. *-lagá-d.; dena.*

Gun, *bandúḳ,* (f.) -powder, *bárút.* shot for -, *chharra.* (cannon,) *top.* at -fire, *top ke waḳt.*

H.

Habit, *dastúr; maamúl.* a bad-, *buri ádat.* -ual, *jo aksar-hota hai.* -ually, *aksar; hameshah.*-of mind, *mizáj; kho.* See 'Dress.'

Hail, *patthar; ola.* V. *-paṛna.* interj. *mubáraḳ-bád!*

Hair, *bál; chúl.* -brush, *bál-ka brúsh* (E.). -dresser, *bálwal.* -less, *ganja; kora.* -y, *mú-e dár.* curling-, *zulf,* (f.).

Half, *ádha; nisf; ním.* V. *ádhiyána; nisfá-nisfi-k.* for 'half' in compos. : use '*adh,*' e.g. 'adh-bhara,' *half-full.* 'ním' is also used in this sense.

Hall, *dálán.* (of audience,) *díwán-i-ámm.*

Ham. *See page* 92.

Hammer, *mártol.* V. *–se márna.*

Hand, *háth ; dast.* of watch, *kánṭa ; sú,i.* at –, *taiyár ; muyassar ; murattab ; ke pás ; ke nazdík.* – in – *háthá-háthi.* –covering (gloves,) *dast-ánah.* –kerchief, *rú-mál.* –writing, *háth-likha.* –cuffs, *háth-kaṛí.*–ful, *muṭṭhí-bhar* (grip, power,) *ḳabzah.* (v.) *dena ; de-d.*

Handle, *dastah ; kaṛa.* (v.) *háth lagána ; pakaṛna ; chhúna.*

Handsome, *khúbsúrat.*

Hang, (*trans.*) *laṭkána ; laṭká-d.* (*intr.*) *laṭakna.* (execute,) *phánsi-d.* –man, *jallád.*

Happen, *hona ; ho-jána ; ána; pesh hona ; bar-pá hona.*

Happy, *khush ; khush-dil.* N. *–i. –i.* V. *–hona.*

Harass, *satána ; diḳḳ-k.* N. *diḳḳ ; tasdi.* (f.).

Hard, *sakht.* (lit. and fig.) N. *–i. See* 'Difficult.' –ly, *mushkil se.* There is *hardly* a man present, *kamtar ek ádmi ḥázir hai.*-ship. *See* 'Distress.' –dy, *mazbút ; sakht ; mardánah.*

Hare, *khar-gosh.*

Harm, *zarar ; taklíf ; tasdi,* (f.); *nuḳsán; ziyán.* V. *–k.; –pahuṇchá-d.* –ful, with '*jo,*' ; *muzirr.* –less, *ghair-muzirr ; be nuḳsán.*

Harness, *sáz.* (f.). –room, *–khánah.* –stand, *ka ghoṛa. See page* 90.

Harsh, *tursh ; khaṭṭa ; kaṛwa. See* 'Cruel.' 'Hard.' N. *turshi ; khaṭá,i.*

Harvest, (spring,) *rabí.* (autumn,) *kharíf.* (general word,) *fasl,* (f.).

Hash, (meat,) *hesh,* (E.); *ḳímah.* V. *–k.*

Haste, *shitáb,* or *shitábi ; jaldi.* V. *–k.* –en, *–karána; –kará-d.* Advs. *See page* 54. –y, (in temper,) *tund-kho.* N. *–i.*

Hate, *nafrat ; dushmani ; adáwat.* V. *–rakhna.* –ful, *bura ; zabún ; nafrat-angez.*

Have. *See page* 75. *Sect.* 13.

Hawk, *jurra*, (m.). *báz*, (f.).

Hawker. *See* 'Pedler.'

He, *yih ; wuh. See page* 30.

Head, *sar*, or *sir*. (so many cattle,) *rás*. (of corn,) *bál*. –ache, *sar ka dard*. –long, *be-tadbír*. –man, *sar-dár*. –quarters, *sadr maķám*. stall, *nuktah*. –strong, *muņh-zor*. N. *muņh-zori*, –y, *nasha-dár*. to make–, *sar-k*. (to lead,) *sardári-k.; sardár-hona*.

Health, *tan-durusti ; bhalá,i ; k͟hairiyat ; mizáj*. A. *tan-darust ; bhala ; k͟hair*. to be in good–, *tan-durust hona*. to be in bad–, *tan-durust nahíņ hona ; bímár hona ; kam-zor hona*.

Heap, (n.) *ḍher ; ambár*. (of people,) *guroh ; majma ; g͟hol*. *See* 'Collect.'

Hear, *sunna*. (obey,) *sunna ; mánna*. hearing, (e.g. a case in Court,) *samá,at*.

Heart, *dil*. (central part,) *mag͟hz ; gúda ; bhítar jo hai*. by–, *noķ zabán se*. hard –ed, *sang-dil*. soft –ed, *narm-dil*. –y, *dil-soz ; dil-garm*. –ily, *dil-o-ján se*. –less, *be-dil ; be-raḥm*. to take–, *himmat rakhna*.

Heat, *garmi ; tapish ; sozish*. (of sun,) *dhúp ; ghám*. (of temper,) *garmi ; tundi; josh ; átish*. V. *garm k*. *See* 'Hot.'

Heaven, *bihisht*. (paradise,) *jannat*.

Heavy, *bhári ; wazani ; giráņ*.

Hedge, (n.) *báŗh ; ghera ; iḥátah*. V. *–d. ; –lagána*. –hog, *dul-dul*.

Heel, *eŗi*.

Height. *See* 'High.'

Heir, *wáris*. Pl. *–án*.

Hell, *jahannam*, (f.). *dozak͟h*.

Help, *madad*, (f.); *iánat*, V. *–d*. –ful, *madad-gár*. –less, *lá-chár*. by God's help, *K͟huda cháhe ; ba-fazl-i-K͟huda*. a – mate, *madad-gár*.

Hemp, *san ; páṭ*. –plant, *gáņja*.

Hen, *murg͟hi*. –house, *–k͟hánah*.

Hence, (time,) *ke baad*. (place,) *yaháņ se*. (cause,) *is liye*.

Her, *is-ka ; us-ka. See page* 30. herself, *See page* 30. *Sect*. 7.

Here, *yahán; is jagah*, or *is jagah men*. –and there, *idhar-udhar*. –abouts, *kahín-yahín*. –after, *áyindah men*. –on, *or* –at, *is-par; is men; is-se. yih bát sun-kar*, or *bol-kar*.

Heron, *bagla*.

Hesitation, *pas-o-pesh; tálá-toli; deri*. (in speech,) *hichkich*. V. *–k*.

Hidden, *chhipá hú,a; rúposh*.

Hide, (*trans.*) *chhipána; rúposh-rakhna*. (*intr.*) *chhipá-hona; rúposh-hona* (n.) *chamra; khál*, (f.).

High, *úncha; baland*, or *buland*. N. *úunchá,i*. –bred, *asíl*. –in price, *mahnga; girán*. –minded, *áli-him-mat*. –in rank, *áli-shán*. –in spirit, *diler; himmati*. in the height of (anything,) *ain*[1]*-men*. –way, *ráh*, (f.); *sarak*. (f.). –way-man, *ráhzan*. –way robbery, *ráhzani*.

Hill, *pahár; únchi zamín*.

Him, *is, us; is-ko; us-ko*. *See page* 30.

Hinge, *chúl*.

Hint, (n.), *ishárah*. V. *–k*.

Hire, (fare in money.) *kiráya*. V. *–lena*. –r, *kiráya-dár*.

His, *is-ka; us-ka*. *See page* 30.

Hobby, *shauk*.

Hog, *sú,ar*. wild–, *jangli sú,ar*.

Hold. *See* 'Grasp.' –(contain.) reverse the sentence, say 'one ser of milk will go into this glass,' *is piyále men ek ser dúdh atta hai*. [*atna*, to get into a given space.] or you may say, *yih ek ser ka piyála hai* = this is a one ser glass, *i.e.* holds, or can contain, one ser. –one's tongue, *chup-rahna*. to –good, *rahna; thaharna*. –er, *dán*. *See page* 41.

Hole, *chhed*; (V. *–na*.) *súrákh*. (of an animal,) *bil*.

Holy, *musalli; Khudá-tars*. –iness, *takwa*. –day, *tatíl*. (religious,) *parb*, (vulg., '*parab*.') – war, *jihád*. –Ghost, *rúhu-l-láh*.

Home, *ghar; makán; kothi*. at–, *ghar men*. not at–, (lit.)

---

[1] Arabic for 'the eye.'

ghar meṇ nahíṇ. (fig.). *See page* 26. to go -, *ghar jána*.

Hone, *sillí*.

Honesty, *diyánat-dári*; *sachá,i*; *rásti*. A. *diyánat-dár*; *sachcha*; *rást*. -ly, by '*se*,' added to the nouns.

Honey, *shahd*.-comb, *chháta*.

Honour, (reputation,) *izzat*; (dignity,) *shán*; *sar-farázi*. (reverence,) *tazím*. your-, *ḥuzúr*. dress of-, *khilat*. V.-*tazím-k.*; *adab-k.* -able, *mu,azzaz*; *mutabar*.

Hook, *ankṛi*; *káṇṭa*. *húk*. (E). V.-*se pakaṛna*.

Hope, *ummed*, (f.). V. -*rakhna*. -ful, *also* one who is hoping for something, -*wár*. (expectancy,) -*wári*. -less, *be-ummed*.

Horn, *síng*; *shákh*. to draw in one's horns, *dum-dabána*.

Horse, *ghoṛa*; *asp*. -back, *ghoṛe par sawár*; *sawár ho-kar*. -dung, *líd*, (f.). -doctor, *salotar*. -man, *sawár*. -manship, *sawári*. -race, *ghuṛ-dauṛ*.

Hospitable, *mihmán-dár*. N. -*i*. -tal, *haspatál*, (E.); *shifá-khánah*.

Host, *mihmán-dár*; *sáḥib-i-khánah*. *See* 'Crowd.'

Hot, *garm*. the - weather *garmi ka mausam*.

Hound, *shikári kutta*.

Hour, *ghaṛi*. *See page* 67.-ly, (i. e. always,) *ghaṛi-ghaṛi*.

House. *See* 'Home.' -breaking, *sendh-chori*. -breaker, *sendhiya*. -hold, *khandán*. -holder, *sáḥib-i-khánah*. -keeping, *ghar ka intizám karna*; *khánah-dári*.

How? *kaisa*; *kis taraḥ*; *kyúṇ-kar*. -ever, *lekin*. -long, *kab-tak*. -often, *ka,e bár*; *kitne dafah* -many, *kitne*. -much, *kitna*. -do you do? *mizáj sharíf*; *áp ka mizáj kaisa hai?* however strong he may be, still, &c. *agarchih wuh bahut zor-áwar ho*, *taubhi*, &c.

Human, being, *ádmi*; *insán*. A. *insáni*. the -race, *insániyat*; *ádmiyat*. -mane, *raḥím*; *mihrbán*; *mulá,im*; *nek-kho*.

Humble, *gharíb*; *miskín*. N. -*i*; -*i*; *faro-tani*. to be- *hona*, with the adjs. (*trans.*) *níchá-k.*; *dabá-d.*

Humour. *See* 'Moist.' (wit,) *lutf; ṭhaṭṭha.* A. *latíf; ṭhaṭhol.* –ously, *latífe-se.* good–, *khush-ḥáli.* bad–, *bad-ḥáli;* in a bad–, *magra; ghusse.* to–, *ijázat-d.; dena.*

Hump, *kúbaṛ.* –backed, *kúbṛa.*

Hundred, *sau,* or *sai.* as a unit, *saikṛa.* 5 per cent. *fi saikṛe, pánch rúpiye.*

Hunger, *bhúkh.* (f.). A. *–a.* to be, *–hona.*

Hunt. (n.) *shikár.* V. *–k.* –sman, *–i.* –ing dog, *–i kutta.* –ground, *–gáh.* A. *shikári.*

Hurry. *See* 'Haste.'

Hurt. *See* 'Harm.'

Husband, *khasam; shauhar; mard.* *See* 'Cultivation.'

Hush! *chup; chup-raho; khámosh!* to –up, *chhipána.* –money, *rishwat.*

Husk. (n.) *chhilka; post.* V. *–utárna.*

Hut, *jhompṛi.*

I.

Ice, *barf,* (f.); *yakh,* (f.). V. *barf meṇ rakhna.* –d-water, *barf-páni.*

Idea, *khayál.* *See page* 110. A. *–i.*

Idiot, *págal; aḥmaḳ.*–ocy,–*i.* –tic, *aḥmaḳ ke taur par.*

Idle, (doing nothing,) *be-kár; be-kám; árám-meṇ* (lazy,) *sust; ḍhíla.* –ness, *árám; fursat; farághat.*(laziness,) *susti.* to be–, adjs. with *hona.*

Idol, *but.* –atry,*–parasti.*

If, *agar; jo.* *See page* 104.

Ignorant, *jáhil; ajhal; nádán; kam-aḳl.* –ce, *jáhili; ná-dáni; kam-aḳli,* (f.). adv. with '*se.*'

Ill, *bímár.* –ness, *–i.* *See* 'Bad.' –behaved, *bad-sulúk,* –behaviour, *bad-sulúki.* –disposition, *bad-kho; bad-tabí,at.*

Illegal,[1] *khiláf-ḳánún.* –ity, *jo khiláf-ḳánún hai.*

Illumination, *raushani; tanwír,* (f.). V. *–k.*

---

[1] For many negatives in 'il,' 'un,' 'im,' &c., use the affirmative and *nahíṇ;* or prefixes '*be,*' '*la*', '*ná,*' '*nir,*' *&c.*

Illustrious, *nám-war; nám-dár; mashhúr.* in compos: *jalíl.*

Image, *putla; putli.* (idol,) *but. See* 'Idol.'

Imagination, *khayál; tassawwur.* V. *-k.* -ary, *khayáli. See* 'Idea.'

Immediate, *maujúd; ḥázir; makhsús.* -ly, *bil-fel. See page* 54.

Immense. *See* 'Grand.'

Immodest, *be-sharm; be-ḥaya.* N. *be-sharmi, be-ḥayá,i.*

Immoral, *ná-maaḳúl; zabún.*

Impair, *ghaṭá-d.* to be -ed, *ghaṭna; bigaṛ-jána.*

Impatient, *be-sabr.* A. *-i.*

Impel, *chalána; chalá-d.*

Incapable, *ghair-ḳábil.*

Incense, (n.) *lúbán.* (v.) (make angry), *ghussa-k.*

Inch, *inshi,* (E.).

Incident, *kám; fel; amr; wuḳu; bát.*

Incite, *uṭhána; targhíb-d.* N. *targhíb,* (f.).

Inclination, *mail,* (f.); *raghbat; árzu,* (f.); *shauḳ.* I am inclined to think, *mera khayál yih hai, kih, &c.*

Include, *shámil-rakhna.* -ed, *shámil-kiya; sáth rakha.*

Income, *ámadani; má-ḥasal.*

Incomprehensible, *be-ḳiyás; ghair-mutasawwar; jo ko,i shakhs nahíṇ samjhe.*

Incorrect, *ná-durust, &c. See* 'Correct.'

Increase, (*trans.*) *baṛhána; ziyádah-k.* (*intr.*) *baṛhna; zidádah-h.* (n.) *izáfah; ziyádat.*

Indeed, *fil-wáḳe; ḥaḳíḳat meṇ.*

Independent, *mustaḳil; be-lagá,o; aláḥidah; khud-sar.* -ce, *ázádi; be-ta,alluḳi; khud-sari.*

India, *Hind.* -n, *Hindúi; Hindu.* -n corn, *bhuṭṭa.*

Indigo, *níl,* (f.). -factory, *-koṭhi.* -planter, *-ka sáḥib.*

Individual, (n.). *See* 'Being,' (a.) *ek; ek-ek.* -ly, *ek-ba-ek; farḳ-farḳ ho-ke.*

Indolent. *See* 'Idle.'

Industry. *See* 'Diligence.'

Infamous, *zabún; mayúb; baṛa kharáb.* N. *bad-námi; zabúni; kharábi.*

Infant. *See* 'Child.'

Infection, *saráyat.* V. *-k.*

Infidel, (one not a Muḥam :) *káfir*. (one not a Hindu,) *malechha*. –ity, *kufr*.

Infirm, (body,) *za,íf*. (body and other things,) *kam-zor; durbal; ná-táḳat; ná-tawán*. (of mind,) *mun-khárif*. –ity, (of body,) *zuf*, or *zof*. (of body, &c.,) *kam-zori; ná-tawáni; ná-mazbúti*. (of mind,) *in-khiráf*.

Inflame, *jalána; josh-k.*–mation, *josh; sozish; garmi*.

Influence, *asar; tásír*, (f.). V. *–k*.

Inform. *See* 'Tell.' an –ation in Court, *nálish; dawa*, (f.); *suwál*. –er, *go,indah*.

Ingratitude, *ná-iḥsánmandi*.

Ingress, *bhítaṛ jáne ki ráh*. (admission to presence,) *ḥuzúr meṇ ána*. (v.n.).

Inhabitant, *sákin; báshindah; rahne-wála*. *See* 'Live.'

Inherit, *wáris-hona*. –ance, *mírás*, (f.); *tarikah*, or *tarkah*. –or, *wáris*.

Inhuman, *be-raḥm, &c*. *See* 'Cruel.'

Iniquity, *páp; zabúni; burá,i*. A. *zabún; bura; kharáb*.

Injunction, *ḥukm; kahna*, (v.n.) V. *ḥukm-d.; kahna*.

Injury, *nuḳsán; ziyán*. (hurt,) *zarar*, (trivial ditto, *zarar-khafíf*. (serious ditto,) *zarar-shadíd*, or *sangín*. (wrong,) *ná-ḥaḳḳ; be-insáfi*. V.*—k.;–pahuṇchá-d.*–ious, *jis-se* (any of the nouns) *áta hai*.

Injustice, *be-insáfi.; ná-ḥaḳḳ*.

Ink, (black,) *siyáhi; roshná,i*. (red,) *surkhi*. –stand, *or* pen-and-ink, *dawát; ḳalam-dán*.

Inn, *sará,e*, (f.); *musáfir-khánah; ḍák-bangla; ḥotel*. (E.).

Innocent, *be-gunáh; sáf; pák*. N. *be-gunáhi; safá,i; páki; pakízagi*.

Inquiry, *púchhna*, (v.n.); *taḥ-ḳíḳát; daryáft; tadáruk*. V. the nouns and *karna*.

Insane. *See* 'Mad.'

Insect, *kíṛa; kirm*.

Insensible, *be-hosh; be-ḥawáss*. N. *–i; –i*.

Insert, *dákhil-k.; darj-k.; mundaraj-k.; zikr-k.* –ion, *indiráj*.

Inside, *bhítar; andar*.

Insight, *wukúf; hoshyári.*

Insist, *musirr-h.; zor se mángna*, or *cháhna*, or *kahna.* -ency, *bár-bár mángna, &c.* (v.n.).

Insolent, *gustákh; sar-kash.* N. *-i; -i.*

Inspect, *dekhna; muláhazah-k.* -ion, *takaiyud; nazar-andázi.*[1] -or, *mutamin; inshpektar-sáhib.*(half E.).

Instant, (n.) *lahzah; ek dam. See* 'Immediate.' This instant. *See page* 54.

Instead of, *ewaz men; ke badle.*

Instruct, *sikhána; sikhá-d.; sikhlána, sikhlá-d.; taalím-d.* N. *taalím*, (f.). -or, *jo sikháta hai; sikhak; munshi; pandit; guru.* -ive, *mufíd.*

Instrument, *álah; hathiyár. He was* instrumental *in, &c.*, us-ki *madad se*, &c.

Intellect, *akl*, (f.); *hosh; zihn.* A. *akli; zahín.*

Intelligence (of mind,) *See* 'Intellect,' (news.) *See* 'News.'

Intention, *kasd; irádah; murád*, (f.); *gharaz*, (f.); *matlab.* V. *-rakhna*, or, better, with *hona*, e.g. *mera kasd yih hai, kih, &c.* Adv. *kasdan; ján-bújh-ke.*

Intercourse, *ilákah; sarokár; ána-jáná*, (v.n.); *ámad-o-raft.* V. *kisi ke sáth-rakhna.* or, better, with *hona*, e.g. *mujh-se us-se kuchh-nahín hai*, 'I have nothing to do with that fellow.'

Interest, (of money,) *súd.* (with a person,) *kahá-suna; asar.* (share,) *hissah; sájha.* (in any matter,) *shauk; mail*, (f.) V. *-rakhna; dil-lagána.* self -ed, *gharaz-mand.* seeking one's own-, *khud-gharaz.*

Interpret, *samjhá-d. See* 'Translate.'

Interruption, *khalal; atká,o; rok.* V. *-k.; atká-d.; rokna.*

Interval, (time,) *arsah;* (space,) *fásilah.*

Interview. *See* 'Visit.'

---

[1] From the Persian '*andákhtan*' 'to throw;' a not uncommon termination. '*Andázi*' as adv., means 'approximately.'

Into, *meṇ ; ke bhítar ; ke andar.*

Intoxication, *nashah.* –ed, *nashe meṇ ; matwála.* V. *nashe meṇ hona ; matwála hona.*

Introduce, *mulákát-kara-d. ; házir-kar-d ; bhítar,* or *huzúr meṇ, lána.* –tion, *idkhál.* a letter of –tion, *sifárish ka khatt.*

Intrust, *supurd-kar-d. ; kisi ke pás rakhna, amánat meṇ rakhna.*

Invent, *nikálna ; pána.* –ion, *íjád,* (f.).

Inventory, *tálikah ; fihrist.*

Investigation. *See* 'Inquiry.'

Invisible, *ghá,ib ; ghair-mahsús.*

Invitation, *nyota.* V. *–bhejna.*

Involuntary, –rily, *–be-ikhtiyár.* N. *–í.*

Inundation, *sailáb,* (m.).

Iron, *loha.* of–, *lohe ka.* a smoothing –, *istri.* V. *–k.*

Irregular, *khiláf-dastúr.* N. *–í.* adv. *be-tartíbise.*

Irrigate, *paṭána.*–ion, *ábpáshi.*

Irritate, *satána ; dikk-k.* N. *chheṛ-chháṛ ; dikk.* –able, *ghussa.*

Island, *jazírah ; dwíp,* or *díp.*

Issue, (v. *trans.*) *jári-kar-d.* (*intr.*) *nikalna ; nikal-ána.* (n.) *natíjah ; ákibat.*

It, *yih ; wuh ;* its, *is-ka ; us-ka. See page* 30.

Itch, *khárisht ; khujli.* A. *khárishti.* V. *khujlána.*

Ivory, *háthi-dáṇt.*

J.

Jackal, *gídaṛ ; siyál.*

Jacket, *jákiṭ,* (E.); *kurtah,* or *kurti.*

Jail, *jel-khánah,* (half E.); *kaid-khánah.* –or, *jelar-sáhib,* (half E.).

Jam, *murabba ; jám.* (E.).

Jar, (vessel,) *ghaṛa ; jáṛ.* (E.). –ring sound, *kharkharáhaṭ.*

Jasmine, *saman.*

Jaw, *jabṛa.*

Jealous, *bad-zann,* N. *–í.*

Jelly, *jeli,* (E.).

Jest, *ṭhaṭṭha.* V. *–k.* –ing, *ṭhaṭholi,* –er, *ṭhaṭhol.* in–, *ṭhaṭholi ke taur se.*

Jesus Christ, *hazrat-ísa.*

Jew, *yahúd* (m.) ; *–in,* (f.).

Jewel, *gahna ; zewar ; jawáhir.* –er, *jauhari.* –box, with ...*dán.* *See page* 41.

Job, *kám ; tahal.*

Jockey, *sawár ; jáki*, (E.).

Jocoseness, *thatthe-bázi ; khush-tab,i.*

Join, (n.), *jor.* V. *–d.; jorna ; milá-d.* joint, (a.) *milá-hú,a.* (junction,) *jor.*

Joke. *See* 'Jest.'

Jolly. *See* 'Happy.' a –fellow, *yár-básh.*

Jot, *zarrah*, (f.) *thora-sa ; ek dánah.*

Journal, *roz-námchah.*

Journey, *safar; kúch.* V. *–k.* a day's–, *manzil.*

Joy. *See* 'Happy.'

Judge, *hákim ; jaj-sáhib*, (half E.). *sadr-ála sáhib ; munsif sáhib ; kázi sáhib.* (all these, except the first, are technical words.) –ment, (decision,) *faisalah ; fatwa ; hukm ; dikri*, (E). V. *–d.* (sense,) *akl*, (f.) ; *hosh ; samajh*, (f.). (to select,) *pasand-k.*

Judicious, *ákil ; dánishmand ; hoshyár.* –ness, *dánist ; akl*, (f.) ; *hosh.*

Jug, *kulhiya*, (f.) ; *piyála ; jag.* (E.).

Juice, *ras; páni; dúdh ; arak.*

Julep, *julláb.*

Jump, (n.) *kúd ; chhaláng*, (f.) ; *uchhál ; jast.* V. *–k. ; kúdna.*

Junction, &c., *See* 'Join.'

Jurisdiction, (power,) *hukm ; hukúmat ; amaldári ; ikhtiyár.* (territory,) *alákah ; zila, &c.* according to local divisions. a 'sub-division' of territorial–, *mahkamah*, –a word which really means '*a tribunal.*'

Jury (native village,) *panch ; pancháyat.* (in English courts,) *júri*, (E.). 'Gentlemen of the Jury,' *sáhib-án-júri.*

Just, *ádil; rást; sach ; sachcha; insáfi; insáf ka.* –ice, *insáf; hakk.* –ness, *rásti ; durusti.* (proper,) *munásib ; wájib ; ba-ja.* (at this moment,) *ab ; ab-tab.* –ify, *sáf*, or *safá,i-k; uzr-k.* adv. *rásti-se.*

Justle, *thelna ; dhakka-d* –tling, *–thel-pel kar-ke.*

K.

Keep, *rakhna ; apne pás rakhna.* (back,) *báz-rakhna ; rokna ; aṭkána.* (e.g. sheep.) *pálna.* He *keeps* two horses, *us ke pás do ghoṛe haiṇ.* –er, *rakhwál.* to –on doing a thing, use the stem of the principal verb, followed by *rahna.*

Kernal, *maghz ; gúda ; bhitari.*

Kettle, *ketli,* (E.); *tábah.* fish–, *machhli ki ketli.*

Key, *kunji ; cháoi ; táli.* bunch of keys, *–ka guchchha.* -hole, *–ka súrákh.*

Kick, *lát.* V. *–márna.* –ing and cuffing, *lát-mukki.*

Kill, *már-ḍálna ; ḳatl-k. khún-k.* (for food,) *zabḥ-k.; ḥalál-k.* –ing, *ḳatl ; khúṇrezi ;*[1] *zabḥ.*

Kind, (a.) *mihrbán ; shafiḳ.* –ness, *mihrbáni.* adv. *mihrbáni-se.* (sort,) *ḳism,* (f.)

Kindred. *See* 'Relations.'

King, (M.) *pádsháh,* or *bádsháh.* (H.), *rája ; mahárája.* –dom. *bádsháhi. saltanat ; ráj.* –ly, *sháhi.*

Kiss, (n.) *bosah ; miṭhi.* (v.) *bosah-d ; chúmna.* mutual –ing, *bosah-bázi.*

Kitchen, *báwarchi-khánah. See page* 87.

Kite, (bird,) *chíl.* (toy,) *guḍḍi.*

Kitten, *billi ka bachchah.*

Knee, *ghuṭna ; zánu.* to kneel, *do-zánu baiṭhna.*

Knife, *chhuri.* clasp–, *chakku.* pen–, *ḳalam-tarásh.*

Knock, (at a door,) *dhab-dhabána. See* 'Blow.' 'Strike.'

Knot, *gáṇṭh.* (fig. e.g. the marriage–,) *aḳd.*

Know, *jánna ; pahchánna ; wáḳif-hona ; khabar pána.* –ledge, *dánist ; ilm,* (f.); *wáḳfiyat.* –n, *maalúm. See page* 59. well-known, *mashhúr.* –ingly, *dídah-o-dánistah ;*[2] *ján-bújh-ke.*

---

[1] From the Persian, '*rekhtan,*' 'to pour out.'

[2] Persian; 'having seen and known;' '*dídan,*' 'to see.'

L.

Labour, *miḥnat.* (V. *-k.*) (A. *-i.*;) *ihtimám.* daily–, *mazdúri*; *roz-gár.* –er, *mazdúr*; *ḳuli.*

Lac, *lákh*; *láh.*

Lace, (embroidery,) *goṭa*; gold–, *kalábattúṇ*, for boot, &c. –, *fítah*; *ḍori*; *sutlí.*

Ladder, *síṛhi.*

Lady, *bíbi*; *khátún*; *begam*; *musammát*; *sáḥibah.* English title, *leḍi*[1]

Lake, *tál*; *tál-áb*, (m.); *talá,o.*

Lamb, *bheṛi ka bachchah.*

Lame, *langṛa.*–ness, *langṛá,i.*

Lamentation, *nálah.* V. *-k.*; *rona*; *chháti-piṭna.* –able, *ghamm-khez.*[2]

Lamp, (English,) *lamp.*[3] (native,) *chirágh*; *díp*; *siráj.* -black, *kájal*; *kajli.*

Lance, *ballam*; *barchhi.* –cet, *nashtar*, (f.). V. *chírna*; *nashtar márna.*

Land, *zamín*, (f.). –holder, *-dár.* –ed property, *-dári*; *milk*; *milkíyat.* the dry–, *khushki.* moist–, *tari.* by–, *khushki.* –lord, *málik*; *sáḥib-i-khánah.* V. (*trans.*) *utárna.* (*intr.*) *utarna. kináre tak á-jána.*

Lane, *gali*; *chhoṭi ráh.*

Language, *zabán*, (f.); *boli.* the common–, *chalni-boli.*

Lantern, *lalṭain* or *lanṭen* (both being attempts at the English word).

Large, *baṛa*; *buzurg*; *kaláṇ.* –ness, *baṛá,i.* –ly, *bahut-sa.* –esse, *nisár.*

Lash, (n.) *zarb.* whip–, *phúnd.* V. *chábuk*, *&c. se márna.*

Last, (a.) *sab se pichhla*; *ákhir.* e.g. –year, *guzashtah.* V. *ab tak rahna*, or *hona.* –ly, *ákhir-ul-amr.*

Late, *der.* –ness, *–i.* 'the late,' *marḥúm*; *mutawaffa.* (former,) *agla.* –ly, *thoṛe dinoṇ se.*

Laugh, *haṇsna.* –ter, *haṇsi.*

---

[1] You must ask for the '*ledi sáhibah*' (not the '*mem-sáhibah*,') if the lady has the title. *See page* 24.

[2] From the Persian, '*khezídan*,' 'to rise.'

[3] Pronounce, according to rule, like the English word 'lump.'

Law, (divine,) (M.) *shara*, (f.); (H.) *dharm-shástra*. (human,) *á,ín*, (m.); *ḳánún*. (custom,) *rasm*, (f.); *ḳá,idah; zábitah*. –court, *adálat*. (criminal), *fauj-dári*, civil, *díwáni*.) –ful, *já,iz; ḥasb ḳánún*. –less, *be-á,ín; á,ín ke khilaf*, –suit. *dawa*, (m.); *nálish; suwál; muḳaddamah*.

Lay, *rakhna; rakh-d. lagá-na; lagá-d*.

Lazy, *sust; ḍhíla; majhúl; káhil*. –iness, *susti; maj-húli; káhili*.

Lead, (n.) *sísa*. –en, *síse ka*.

Lead, (v.) *le-chalna; le-jána*. –er, *sar-dár*. to –the way, *áge chalna*. to –one's life, *guzrán-k*.

Leaf, *patta; waraḳ*. –of a book, *waraḳ*. –of a door, *palla*.

Lean, *dubla; patla*. –ness, *dublá,i*. V. *jhukna*. (to an opinion,) *máil-hona*.

Leap. *See* 'Jump.'

Learn, *síkhna; paṛhna*. –er, *shágird*. –ed, *álim; fázil*. –ng, *ilm*, (m.); *dánist*.

Lease, *ṭhíka; ijárah*. document expressing a –granted, *paṭṭa*, ditto –accepted, *ḳabúlyat*. V. *ṭhíka, ijárah* (or as the kind of lease may be) *dena*. to– e.g. a house, *kiráye-d*, or, *lena*. lessor of land, *málik*. lessee, *ṭhíkádár; ijárahdár; ra,íyat*, *&c.*, according to the kind of lessee. *See* Glossary Part I. *sub vocibus*.

Least, *sab se chhoṭa*. *See* 'At.

Leather, *chamṛa*. –n. *–ṛe ka*.

Leave, (n.) *ijázat*; (–to go,) *rukhsat; chhuṭṭi*. to take–, *–lena*. without–, *be-kahe-púchhe*. (v.) *chhoṛ-d*.

Leech, *joṇk*, (f.)

Leek, *gandana*.

Left, (over,) *báḳi*. (surplus,) *fázil; jo bacha hai*. on, *or* to the *left* hand, *bá,eṇ*.

Leg, and its parts. *See page* 63.

Leisure, *fursat; áram; fará-ghat*. at–, *–meṇ*. –ly, *dhíme-dhíme; áhiste-áhiste*.

Lemon, *lemu; lembu*. –ade, *míṭha-páni*.

Lend, *udhár*, or, *ḳarz*, or *mangni-d*. –er, with '*jo*.'

Length, *lambá,i; túl*, (time,) *arsah; muddat. See* 'At.' V. *lambá-k.*

Leopard, *chíta.*

Leprosy, *koṛh.* A. *koṛhi.*

Less, *kam; kamtar.* as suffix, '*be*' before the noun, e.g. *be-wuḳúf*, senseless. –en, *kam-kar-d.; ghaṭána.*

Lesson, *sabaḳ.*

Lest, e.g. be quiet, *lest* I be angry, *chup raho, nahín to main, &c.* don't speak, *lest* he hear, *mat bolo, zurúr sunega*, and so according to the analysed meaning in each use.

Let. *See* 'Lease.' (allow,) *dena*, following the inflected infin. of principal verb. e.g. *bhítar áne-do*, let him come in. or, more formal, *ijázat-d.; ḥukm-d.; farmána.*

Letter, (written,) *chiṭṭhi; ḵhatt; ruḳah.* (alphabet,) *ḥarf*, Pl. *ḥurúf.*

Lettuce, *salád*, (E.); *káhu.*

Levee, *darbár; jamá,at; majma; majlis.*

Level, *barábar; samán.* V. *-k.* N. *-i.*

Liable, *mákḫúz*, but best translated by the Persian suffix '*dih*,' or '*dihi*.' e.g. *jawáb-dih*, liable to answer, responsible; liable to punishment. *saza-wár*, –to sickness, error, &c. may be best translated by '*ana*,' or '*aksar ána*.' e.g. *us-ko zukám aksar áta hai.* or '*karna*.' e.g. *wuh hameshah ghalati karta hai.*

Liberal, *saḵhi; karím; faiz-baḵhsh.* –minded. *karím-un-nafs.* N. *saḵháwat; faiz*, (f.). –ly, *dil-khol-ke.*

Liberty. *See* 'Freedom.'

Library, *kutub-ḵhánah.*

Lick, *cháṭ.* V. *cháṭna.*

Lid, *ḍhakna; chapni; sarposh.*

Lie, (tell a,) *jhúṭh-kahna; darogh-bolna.* –ar, *darogh-go.*[1] –ying, *darogh-go,i.*

Lie, (down), *leṭna; sona.*

Life, *ján* (f.); *rúḥ*, (f.). (being alive, life-time,) *zindagi; zindagáni; ḥayát*, (f.).

---

[1] From the Persian, '*guftan*,' 'to speak." Hence also '*guft-o-gu*,' 'conversation;' '*go,indah*,' 'an informer,' or 'spy,' and many other words.

-less, *be-ján*; *mú,a-hú,a*. (fig.) *be-dil*; *afsurdah*; *udás*. to spend–, *guzrán-k*. –long, *umr-bhar*.

Lift, *uṭhána*; *uṭhá-d*.

Light, (not heavy,) *halka*; *subuk* (clear,) *sáf*; *raushan*; *ujála*. (fig.) *khafíf*. –ness, *halká,i*., (clearness,) *safá,i*; *raushani*; *ujála*. to lighten (e.g. a boat,) *halka-k*. -ning, *bijli*. V. *chamakna*. to light, *jalá-d*.

Like, (a.) *barábar*; *samán*; *ek ḳism ka*; *ki mánind*; *ke mu,áfiḳ*. to be – another thing, *yih is-se milta hai*. *See* Glossary, Part 1. 'Sa.' V. *cháhna*; *pasand-k.*; (be fond of,) *pyár-k*. –ly, *aghlab*. –ness, *mu,áfaḳat*; *saríkha*.

Lime, *chúna*. –kiln, *–e ki bhaṭṭhi*.

Limit. *See* 'Boundary,' 'Fence.'

Line, *satar*. –ing, *astar*.

Linen, *katán-kapṛa*.

Lion, *sher-babar*; *síngh*.

Lip, *lab*.

Liquor, *sharáb*, (f.). *See page* 34.

List, *fihrist*; *fard*, (f.); *táliḳah*.

Listen, *kán-lagána*; *sunna*.

Litter, *sawári*; *pálki*; *ḍoli*. (rubbish,) *kurkaṭ*.

Little, *chhoṭa*; *khurd*. a–, *thoṛa*; *zarrah-sa*; *kuchh-kuchh*.–better, *kuchh achchha*. –ness, (quantity,) *kami*. (size,) *chhoṭá,i*.

Live, *jína*; *zindah-hona*. -lihood, *guzrán*. means of –lihood, *rozi*; *rozgár*; *guzrán*. (to dwell,) *rahna*; *búd-o-básh-k*.[1]

Liver, (organ of body,) *jigar*; *kaleja*. (person living,) with '*jo*.'

Lizard, *ṭikṭiki*; *chhipkali*.

Load, (n.), *bojha*; *bharti*; *khep*, (f.). (v. *trans.*) *ládna*; *bharna*. (v. *intr.*) *ladna*. ladened, *bhara hú,a*.

Loaf, *ek roṭi*.

Lock, *ḳufl*. V. *–lagá-d.*; *–se band-k*.

Long, *lamba*; *daráz*; *túl-tawíl*. *See* 'Length.' –ago, *bahut dinoṉ se*; *agle zamáne meṉ*; the whole day–, *tamám din*; *din bhar*. as–as, *jab-*

[1] From the Persian, '*búdan*,' 'to be.'

tak, followed by '*tab-tak.*' *See page* 104. to –for, *cháhna ; raghbat*, or *khwáhish-rakhna.*

Look, (n.) *nazar*, (f.); *nigáh*, (f.). (v.) *dekhna.* –this way, *tákna.* (to keep an eye on,) *nazar*, or *nigáh rakhna.* to –out for, *intizár-k.* (to consider,) *ghaur-k.* he *looks* (well, &c.), (*achchha, &c.*) *maalúm hota hai.* his –fell on me, *us-ki nazar mujh-par pari.* –out, *khabar-dár hona.* –ing-glass, *á,ínah.*[1]

Loose, *khula.* (slack,) *dhíla.* V. *kholna ; khol-d.* to come–, *khul-jána.* to break–, *chhút-jána ; chhút-ke bhág-jána.*

Lord, *sáhib ; málik ; khudáwand ; khāwind ; huzúr.* to – it over one, *zulm-k.; zabar-dasti-k.*

Lose, *khona ; gum-k.* generally the passive form is used, viz., *gum-ho-jána.* (e.g. a bet,) *hárna ; hará-d.* loss, *nuksán ; ziyán ; zarar.* (in trade,) *ghati.* to be at a loss. *pareshán-hona, shakk men hona.*

Lot. *See* 'Fortune.' (die,) *kurah.* to cast lots, *kurah dálna.*

Loud, loudly, *baland áwáz se.* to call–, *pukárna.*

Love, *pyár*, (f.); *mail*, (f.); *yári.* (animal) –, *ishk.* V. *pyár-k.; azíz rakhna.* –ly, *khúbsúrat.* –liness, *khúbsúrati.* –ed, *pyára ; mahbúb.*

Louse, *jún.*

Low, *nícha.* (mean,) *kamínah*, also as noun, a mean person. (as voice,) *daba.* to–, *bambána.*[2] to lower, *niche-k.; dabá-d.* –liness. *gharíbi ; faro-tani.*

Luggage. *See* 'Goods.'

Lumbago, *kamar ka dard.*

Lump, *tukra.*

Lunch, *tiffin. See* Glossary, Part I.

Luxury, *aiyáshi ; khushi.* A. *aiyásh.*

Lying, (n.) *jhúth-múth.*

---

[1] Accent on first syllable.

[2] In India the cattle are very silent.

M.

Mace, (staff,) *chob ; sonṭa.* –bearer, *chob-dár.* (spice,) *basbásah ; masálah.*

Machine, *kal.*

Mad, *díwánah; págal; pagla.* –man, *págal ádmi.* –house, *págal-khánah.* –ness, *díwánagi ; be-hoshi.* –ly, *díwánah-sa,* –den, *díwánah-k.* (fig.) *ghusse-k. ; josh-k.; bad dimágh-k.*

Magistrate, *ḥákim ; majistreṭ sáḥib.*

Maid, *bákirah ; kú,ári.* –servant, *áyáh ; bánḍi ; launḍi.*

Mail, *ḍák; ṭappál.* *See page* 98.

Maintain. *See* 'Assert,' 'Live.' (rear,) *pálna ; parwasti-k.* N. *parwarish ; rozi ; khúráki ; khána-pína.*

Make, *banána ; baná-d.; karna ;* 'I made him come to me,' *usko mere pás áne par main-ne majbúr kiya.* e.g. –profit, *ḥáṣil-k. ; kám-ána ;* –progress, *ba-sir-k.* –sport, *ṭhaṭṭha-márna,* –away with, *uṛá-d.; bar-bád-k.* –haste, *jalḍi-k.* (n.) (shape,) *shakl,* (f.); *banáwat.* –er, *sáz,*[1] or *kár,*[2] *&c.* as last part in compos.

Male, *nar.*

Malice, *kínah ; bad-khoi.* A. *kínawár ; bad-khwáh.*

Man, *mard ; ádmi ; insán ; shakhs ; kas.* (at games,) *nard.* –kind, *ádmíyat insániyat ; bani-ádam.*[3] –hood, *jawáni ; mardi.* –liness, *mardánagi.* A. *mardánah.* –ly, *mard-sa ; mardánah.* –eating, *mardum-khor.*[4]

Management, *intizám ; band-o-bast,* (m.); *sar-ba-ráhi.* V. *–karna.; kisi taur se karna.* –er, *sarbaráh-kár ; kár-pardáz; manejar,* (E.).

Mange. *See* 'Itch.'

Mango, *ám.* –tree, *–gáchh.* –fish, *ṭapsi-machhlí.*

---

[1] From the Persian, '*sákhtan,*' to 'make.'

[2] This of course is from '*karna.*'

[3] 'Sons of Adam ;' he being common to Muham : and Christians.

[4] From the Persian, '*khurdan,*' 'to eat.'

Manifest, (a.) *záhir; maalúm; sáf.* V.—*k.; kar-dikhlána.* –o, *izhár-námah; súrat-ḥál.* –ly, *záhiran.*

Manner, *taur; taraḥ*, (f.); *taríḳah. See* 'Custom,' in this, (that) *manner, is,* (*us*) *taraḥ.* in what manner, *kis-taraḥ; kyúṉkar.* –ly, *susíl.* good –s, *ádáb; akhláḳ.*

Manufacture, *dast-kári.* –tory, *kár-khánah.*

Many, *bahut; ḍher; bahutere; bahut-se.* –a, *bahut-ek.* –times, *aksar; bár-bár.*

Map, *naḳshah.* V. –*khaiṉch-na; –taiyár-k.*

Marble, *sang marmar.*

March, (n.) *kúch.* V. –*k.*

Mare, *mádiyán; ghoṛi.*

Margin. *See* 'Edge.'

Mark, *dágh; nishán.* (trace,) *asar; alámat; surágh; pata.* V. to make a–, –*d.* to find –s of, –*dekhna; –pána.*

Market, (n.) *bázár,* (v. –*k.*;) *háṭ; chauk.* –rate, *nirkh; bhá,o.*

Marriage, *shádi; byáh; nikáḥ.* V. –*k.* –ied, (m.) *byáha,* (f.) *byáhi.*

Marsh, *jhíl,* (f.); *gil-áb,* (f.), –y, *tar; martúb.*

Martingale, *zer-band.*

Mason, *ráj; ráj-mistri.* –ry, *ráj ka kám.*

Mass. *See* 'Lump.'

Master, *málik, &c. See* 'Lord.'

Mat, *chaṭa,i; darma.* (V. –*lagá-d.*); for sleeping on, *sítal-páṭi.* –maker, *or* seller, *chaṭá,i-wála.*

Match, (n.) *joṛa; sáni.*[1] V. *joṛna; barábar-k.; milá-d.* –es, *dia-salá,i; mechis*[2] (E.). –less, *lá-sáni.*

Materials. *See* 'Apparatus.'

Matter, *máddah; jism.*[3] (affair,) *kám; bát; mu,á-malah.* no–, *kuchh parwáh nahíṉ; kuchh muzá,iḳah nahíṉ.* what's the–; *kya hú,a? kya hai?*

---

[1] Persian 'second,' or 'a second.' [2] This word means 'lamp-chips.'

[3] The Author knows no word really in common use for 'matter' in the abstract.

Mattress, *toshak*, (f.).
Mature, *pakka* ; *taiyár*.
Maund, *man*. *See page* 70.
May. *See page* 18.
Me. *See page* 29.
Meadow, *maidán* ; *ramnah* ; *khuli jagah*.
Meal, (flour,) *áṭa* ; *maidah* ; *sattu*. (food,) *khána*.
Mean, *páji* ; *kamínah*. –ness, *kamínagi*.
Meaning, *mani* ; *matlab* ; *mazmún*, to mean, with *hona*, e.g., what does this mean? *is-ke mani*, *&c. kya haiṇ ?*
Means. *See* 'Wealth.' (agency), *wasílah* ; *tadbír*, (f.). by no –, *hargiz nahíṇ*. by some – or other, *kuchh-taraḥ se* ; *kisi taur se*.
Meanwhile, meantime, in the, *is meṇ* ; *itne meṇ* ; *darmiyán is-ke*.
Measles, *pan-goṭi*.
Measure, (of a thing,) *máp* ; *náp*, (f.). –ing of land, *paimá,ish* ; *jaríb*. V. *–k.* ; *mápna*. *See page* 70.
Meat, (butcher's,) *gosht*. *See page* 91. *Note*. (generally,) *khána pína* ; *khurák*, (f.).
Medal, *meḍal*. (E.). *tamghah*.
Medicine, *dawa*, (f.) ; *dáru*.
Meditation, *ta,ammul*, (m.) ; *fikr*, (f.) ; *soch* ; *andeshah*. -tive, *muta,ammil* ; *muta-fakkir* ; *fikrmand* ; *soch meṇ*.
Meet, (v.) *milna*. *See page* 50. (assemble,) *jama-hona*. (as clothes.) *ṭhík-hona*, or *baiṭhna*. (a.). *See* 'Suitable.' a – ing, (of friends,) *mulákát* ; *bheṇṭ*. V. *–k.* ; *bheṇṭna*. *See* 'Assembly.'
Melon, *kharbúzah*.
Melt, (*intr.*) *galna* ; *gal-jána*. (*trans.*) *galána* ; *galá-d.*
Member, (of the body,) *azo* ; *juz*. (of a meeting,) *sáḥib-i-majlis* ; *membar*, (E.).
Memory, *yád*, (f.) ; *ḥifz*, (f.). –andum, *yád-dásht*.–book, *bayáz*, (f.). –rial, *yád-gár*.
Mending, *marammat* ; *rafa*. V. *–k.* –in health, *bhala* or *achchha hona*.
Mental, *dili* ; *dil ka*. –arithmetic, *zabáni ḥisáb* ; *zabáni jokha*. –ly, *ba-dil* ; *dil se*.
Mention, *zikr*, (m.) V. *–k.*
Merchant, *saudágar* ; *mahá-jan* ; *baniyá*. (travelling,)

baipári; bakas-wála. (half E.). –dize, sauda; mál; jins, (f.); chíz, (f.). See 'Trade.'

Mercy, rahm, (f.); mihrbáni. A. rahím; mihrbán. –fully with se. –iless, be-rahm. –ilessness, be-rahmi.

Merely, fakat; sirf; khálí.

Merit, kadar, (f.); liyákat. –torious, kadar ka.; khúb; achchha; wájib-i-ri, áyat. the merits of any matter, bhalebure; aslhál; wákiát.

Merry. See 'Happy.'

Message, khabar, (f.); bát; paighám. V. –d. or bhejna. –enger, chaprási; piyádah; pi,an.[1] (divine,) paigham-bar.[2]

Messiah, Masíha.

Metal, dhát, or dhátu.[3]

Mid, ádh; ním. –day, nímroz; do-pahar; zuhr. –night, ádhi-rát; do-pahar-rát.

Middle, bích; miyán. in the –bích men; bíchon-bích; dar-miyán.

Midwife, dá,i.

Might, (v.) sakna. page 22. (n.) See 'Power.'

Mild, gharíb; narm; narm-dil. N. –i.

Mile, míl; ádha-kos.

Military, the, lashkar. A. –i.

Milk, dúdh. A –ka. V. doh-na. –man, go,ála. –woman, go,álin.

Mill, chakki; ásya. oil–, kolhu. –stone, chakki; sang-i-ásya.

Millet, bájara.

Million, das lákh. ten millions, karor.

Mince, minsh; (E.). kímah. V. –k.

Mind, (n.) akl, (f.); hosh; zihn; rúh, (f.) V. yád-k.; liház-k.; ghaur-k. to put in –, yád diláná.

Minister, (of state,) díwán; wazír. (of church,) pádri-sáhib. See pages 52 and 77.

Minor, (n.) ná-bálígh. (a.) khurd; chhota; kam. –ity, kam-umri, (f.); kam-sini.

Minute, (n.) ek minat, (E.). (a.) See 'Small.'

---

[1] Not Hindústáni; probably Portuguese generally written 'peon.'

[2] Applied especially to Muhammad.

[3] Not often heard, as you generally name the metal.

Mirror, *á,ínah ; darpan.*
Mirth. *See* 'Joy.'
Misbehaviour, *bad-salúki.* (v. *-k.*) *bad chalani.* V – *hona.*
Miscarry, (fail,) *bigar-jána.* (as a letter,) *gum-ho-jána ; kho-jána.*
Miscellaneous, *har kism ka ; mutafarrik.*
Mischief, *badi ; nuksán.* to make –, *bigárna ; bigár-d.*
Misdeed, *bad-fel ; bad-kám.*
Miser, *bakhíl.* –liness, *bukhl,* (m.). –ly, *bukhl-se.*
Misery, *zillat ; bad-háli ; be-chúragi ; tangi.* –able, *zalíl ; bad-bakht ; be-nasíb.*
Misfortune, *bad-bakhti ; musíbat ; tabáhi.*
Mislead, *bhatkána ; ráh-bhulána.*
Mismanagement, *bad-intizámí.* V. *-k.*
Misplace, *be-tartíb-rakhna ; kisi dúsri jagah men rakhna.*
Miss, *mís sáhibah,* (half E.); *begam ;*[1] *sáhib-zádi.*
Miss, (v.) *chúkna ; chhorna ;* (*intr.*) *nahín lag-jána.* (n.) *chúk ; khata.*
Mist, *kuhásah.* –y, *dhundhla.*
Misunderstand, use *nahín* with 'Understand.'
Mix, *milána ; milá-d.* N. *milá,o.*
Moan. *See* 'Groan.'
Mode. *See* 'Manner.'
Model, *nakshah.* (v. *-k.*) (pattern,) *namúnah.*
Modesty, *sharm,* (f.); *haya,* (f.); A. *sharmandah ; lajíla.* –ly, *sharm se*
Moist, *bhínga ; tar ; síla ; gíla.* V. *-k. ; bhingá-d. ; silána.*
Molasses, *gur.*
Mole, (animal,) *kor-músh.*
Moment. *See* 'Instant.' a matter of–, *zarúri kám.*
Monarch. *See* 'King.'
Monday, *Sombár ; pír ka roz ; do shambah.* *See page* 66.
Money, *paise ; rúpíye.* a sum of–, *mablagh ; zar,* (m.). ready–, *nakd rúpíye.* –bag, *tora ; thaili.* -changer, *sarráf.* –lender, *mahájan.* –less, *tihi-dast ; kháli-háth.*
Mongoose, *newal.*
Monkey, *bandar.*

[1] '*Khúrshídi begam,*' (*See page* 122,) may be translated 'Miss Sunbeam.' *Khúrshíd* is a Persian word meaning the 'Sun.'

Month, *mahínah ; máh.*–ly, or, – by–, *máh-ba-máh.* –ly pay, *máhiyána; dar-máhah.*

Moon, *chánd ; máh.* *See* 'Eclipse.' –light, *chándni.* a –light night, *chándni rát ; shab-i-máh.* –beam, *chánd ki jot.*

More, *aur ; aur kuchh ; ziyádah.* the more ... the more, *jyoṇ-jyoṇ ... tyoṇ-tyoṇ.* the more ... the less, same phrase, with '*nahíṇ*' in the co-relative clause.

Mosque, *masjid*, (f.).

Mosquito, *machchhar.* –curtains, *masahri.*

Most, *beshtar ; sab se ziyádah.* Adv. *beshtar ; sab se aksar.*

Mother, *ma ; mádar ; wálidah.* step–, *sauteli ma.* a – who has had a son, *laṛkori.* –less, *be-mádar*, –ly, *má sa.* –tongue, *watani*[1] *zabán*, (f.).

Motion, *ḥarakat.*

Motive, *sabab ; bá,is ; matlab ; g͟haraz*, (f.).

Move, (*intr.*) *hilna ; ḍolna.* (*trans.*) *hilána ; ḍolána.* –on, *chalna; chalá-jána ; áge-baṛhána.* –off, *chal-d.* –ing, *rawáṇ ; chalta ; ḥarakat meṇ.* as last word in compos.:... *angez*, e.g. *rik̤k̤at-angez*, compassion-stirring.

Mount. *See* 'Ascend.'

Mourning, *g͟hamm.* V.- *k.* –ful, –*gín.* –fully. –*se.*

Mouse, *chúha ; músh.*– trap, –*dán.*

Mouth, *múṇh.* to make a–, *múṇh ṭeṛha-k.* – ful, a, *luk̤mah*, – of a river, *muhána.*

Much, *bahut ; bahutera.* too–, *ziyádah.* *See page* 104. so–so, that, &c., *is martabe ko, kih, &c.*

Mud, *kíchaṛ*, (f.) ; *gil*, (f.). *kádo.* – dy, *maila ; bahut kíchaṛ hai.*– wall, *miṭṭi ki díwár*, (f.); *kachchi-díwár*, (f.)

Mug, *mag.* (E.).

Mulberry, *tút.*

Multiply. *See* 'Increase.' (arithmetic), *joṛna.*

Multitude, *guroh*, (m.); *jamíyat; g͟hol*, (m.) ; *guhár*, (f.).

[1] '*Watan*' means one's fatherland.

Murder, *khún.* wilful–, *katl amd.* (homicide), *katl-i-insán.* V. *–k.; már-dálna.* –er, *khúni; kátil.* –ous, *khún-rez.* –ed, *maktúl.*

Muse,(v). *sochna; andeshah-k.*

Mushroom, *musharúm*, (E.); *chháta; dharti.*

Music, *musíki.* –cian, *mutrib.* –cal, *shírín.* –cal instrument, *bájá.* (with very many names for various kinds.)

Musk, *mushk.* –cat, *mushk-billi.* –rat, *chha-chúndar.*

Musket, *bandúk*, (f.).

Muslin, *mal-mal.*

Must. *See page* 18.

Mustache, *múchh*, (f.).

Musalman, *musalmán; muslim.* Pl. *muslimín.* fem. *musalmáni.* their religion, *islám.*

Mutiny, *balwa; bagháwat.* V. – *k.*

Mutton, *bheri ka gosht.*

My, *mera.* *See page* 30. *Sect.* 6.

Mystery, *ráz*, (m.); *bhed.* A. *ráz ka.*

N.

Nail, *preg.* V. *–d.; lagána.* (of man or beast,) *nákhun.*

Naked, *langa*, or *nanga.* N. *nangá,i.*

Name, *nám; ism.* V. *–d.* –less, *gum-nám; ná-maalúm.* –sake, *ham-nám.*

Napkin, *háth ka tauliyah; rú-mál.*

Narrow, (tight,) *sakra; tang.* (not broad,) *kam-arz.* –ness, *sakrá,i; kam-arazi.*

Nation,[1] *mulk; mulk ke log.*

Native, (a.) *mulk ka.* (n.) *sákin; bashandah.* –country, *watan; des.* –ity, *janam; paidá,ish.* natal, *janam ka.*

Natural, *ba-ádat; tabí-i.* nature (disposition.) *ádat; tabíat; mizáj; kho.*

Near, (prep.) *ke pás; ke nazdík; ke yahán; kane.* (a.) *nazdík; karíb; pás; yahán.* –ly, *karíb-karíb.* –ness, *nazdíki.* –(in blood), *bhá,i-bandi; barádari.*

---

[1] The European conception of a 'nation' does not, and never can, exist in India.

Neat, *suthra.* N. *suthrá,i.*
Necessaries. *See* 'Apparatus.' -ary, *zarúr; lázim; cháhiye. See page* 20. (privy,) *já-e zarúrat.* -ity, *zarúrat.* -arily, *zarúr; zarúratan.* -itous, *muḥtáj; gharíb; tang ḥál.*
Neck, *gardan,* (f.); *gala; gulu.* -cloth, *gulu-band.* -lace, *mála.*
Need, (v.) *cháhna; mujh-ko zarúr hai.* (n.) *zarúrat.* -ful, *zarúr; dar-kár.* -y, *gharíb; tang ḥál.*
Needle, (large,) *sú,a.* (common,) *sú,i; darzan.* eye of-, *náka.* -case, *sú,i-dán.* -work, *silá,i; sú,i ka kám.*
Neglect, (n.) *be-khabardári.* (carelessness,) *ghaflat.* V. *-k.; bhúlna; nahíṇ karna;* (a.) *gháfil; káhil; majhúl.* (with *hona,* these make verbs.) -fully, *ghaflat se.*
Negro, *ḥabshi.*
Neighbour, *parosi; ham-sáyah.* -hood, *nawáḥ; nazdíki; jagah; paros.* -ly, *ham-sáyah; barádarána.*
Neither...nor, *na yih...na wuh; na ek...na dígar; ko,i nahíṇ; donoṇ nahíṇ.*
Nephew, (brother's son,) *bhatíja.* (sister's son,) *bhánja.*
Nerve, *rag,* (f.); *nas,* (f.).
Nest, *ghoṇsla; áshiyána.*
Net, *jála; jál.*
Never, *kabhi nahíṇ.*-theless. *tau-bhi; tá-ham.*
New, *nau; naya.*(fresh,) *tázah.* -ness, *tázagi.* -year, *nau sál.* -Year's Day, *nau roz.*
News, *khabar,* (f.) *bát.* good-, *khush-khabari; achchhi bát.* bad-, *bad-khabár; kharáb bát.*-paper, *akhbár; khabar ka kághaz.*-writer, *khabar-navís.* without-, *be-khabar.*
Next, *jo píchhe hai; dúsra,* -time, *dúsre wakt.* -year, *áyandah-sál.*
Nice. *See* 'Neat.'
Niche, *ták,* (f.).
Niece, (brother's daughter,) *bhatíji.* (sister's daughter,) *bhánji.*
Night, *rát; shab,* (f.). to-, *áj rát ko.* by-, *rát ko.* last-, *kal rát ko.* a moon-light-, *chándni rát.* -and day, *shab-o-roz; rát-din.* -dress, *rát ka kapṛa.*

Nightingale, *shámah.*

Nip, *nochna.*

No, *nahín; náhi; na.* –one, *ko,i nahín.* nothing, *kuchh nahín.* –where, *kahín nahín.*

Noble, *sharíf; asíl; najíb.* –man, *mír; amír, &c.* (according to the title enjoyed.) –bility, *sharáfat; najábat.* the -bility, *arkán-i-daulat.* (*See page* 52); *umara,* (Pl. of *amír.*). of –birth, *najíb-zádah.*

Nobody, *ko,i nahín.* a –, *nákas; ná-chíz.*

Noise, *shor; áwáz,* (f.); *ghul.* to make a –, *–k.*

None, (person,) *ko,i nahín.* (things,) *kuchh nahín.*

Nonsense, *behúdah bát; yáwah.*

Noon, *do pahar.* (*See page* 67.); *do pahar din; zuhr.*

Noose, *phánsi.* V. *phánsna.*

Nor. *See* 'Neither.'

North, *uttar; shamál.*

Nose, *nák,* (f.).

Not. *See* 'No.'

Notification, *ishtihár; manádi.* V. *–jári-k.*

Notion, *khiyál; gumán.* to have a–. *–k.*

Nourish, *pálna; parwarish* or *parwasti k.* or *d.*

Now, *ab; is–wakt; bil–fel; hálan.* –a days, *áj-kal.*

Number, by the numeral applicable. The English word '*nambar*' is in common use; the natives not having our idiom. Thus, for '*number* 8.' they say 'the 8th.' Also, 'there was a great *number* of people present' *bahut log házir the.* *See* 'Count.'

Numerous. *See* 'Many.'

Nurse, (native,) *áyáh;*[1] (English,) *nass.*[2] (E.) wet–, *dá,i.*

Nut, *jauz.* wal–, *akhrot.*

Nutmeg, *já-e-phal.*

Nutriment, *ghiza; ghizá, iyat.*

---

[1] Probably Portuguese.

[2] That is, 'nurse.'

O.

Oar, *ḍánḍ.*

Oath, *ḳasam ; ḥalaf.* to take an–, *–khána.*

Obey, *mánna; sunna.* –dient, *ḥukm-bardár ; tábidár.* dience, *–í ; –í.*

Object, (thing,) *chíz,* (f.). (aim.) *See* 'Intention.' any object of pursuit, &c. *matma-i-nazar.*

Object, (v.) *ná-manzúr* or *ná-pasand-k.; itiráz-k.* N. *itiráz.*

Obliged, (compelled,) *maj-búr.* N. *–í.* V. *–k.* (favoured) *mamnún.* (v.). *mihrbáni-k.* (n.) *mihrbáni ; minnat.* under –gation, *minnat-dár,* (n.a.). –ing, *mihrbán ; nek-kẖo.*

Observation, (noticing,) *liḥáz; gẖaur; nazar-andázi.* V. *–k.; dekhna.* –er, *dekhnewála ; nigáh-báz* *See* 'Word.'

Obstinate, *sar-kash ; gardan-kash ; sakẖt ; magẖrúr.* N. *sar-kashi.* V. *–k.*

Obstruct, *rokna ; aṭak-kar-d. ; ṭhek-k* –ion, *rok ; ruká,o ; aṭak.* This road is –ed, *yih ráh band hai.*

Obtain. *See* 'Acquire.'

Obtuse. *See* 'Stupid.'

Obvious, *sáf; záhir; maalúm.* Adv. *sáf ; záhiran.*

Occasion, (time,) *waḳt.* (cause,) *sabab ; wajh,* (f.). (opportunity,) *waḳt ; mau-ḳa.* (need,) *kám ; zarúrat.* V. *See* 'Cause.' –ally, *kabhi-kabhi.*

Occupation, *kám ; dhandha ; peshah.* –pied, (busy,) *mash-gẖúl.* V. *hona ; fursat nahíṉ hai.*–pier, *dakẖl-kár; ḳábiz.* V. (e.g., a house,) *dakẖl-k. ; dakẖil-kár,* or *ḳábiz-hona ; kiráya-dár hona.*

Occur, *hona ; bar-pá-hona ; ittifáḳ-hona ; ána ; á-jána; pesh-ána.* –rence, *wuḳu*[1] *; fel ; kám.*

---

[1] The real pronunciation of this difficult word is that of a short, *closed* Italian 'o' in the first syllable ; very near the 'o,' in 'oration,' 'oku.' In Hindústáni 'ó,' 'ú,' 'v,' and 'w' are written with one and the same character. Short 'o s' do occur in Hindústáni, and also short 'e s ;' whatever the Grammarians may say. Thus you will often hear *mŏḥarrir, Mŏḥammad ; mĕhtar, mĕhrbán, &c., &c.,* and these sounds cannot be said to be *wrong.* *See page* 47, Note ii.

Ocean, *samundar; ságar; kála páni*, (m.).

Odour, *khush-bu*, (f.). Adj. *mu,attar*.

Of, *See pages* 5 *and* 73. of himself, *áp-se; khud; khud-ba-khud*.

Off, (distant,) *dúr;* to go–, (person,) *jána; chalá-jána*. (gun,) *chhuṭ jána*. interj. *dúr; dúr-dúr!*

Offence. *See* 'Crime.'

Offer. There is no corresponding idea in Hindústáni. Use such phrases as suit. e.g. He *offered* to help me, *mujh-ko madad dene ko taiyár tha*. He *offered* (or made an offer of) ten rupis for the cloth, *kapṛe ke wáste das rúpíye bola*, and so on. *See* 'Present.'

Office, (post,) *uhdah; kám; peshah; naukari; khidmat*. –room, *daftar; daftar-khánah; áfis*, (E.) servant thereof, *daftari*. –er, according to his work, from the 'ḥákim,' or '*head*,' down to the 'mihtar,' or *sweeper*. Some of these are as follow:—Chief subordinate, *saṛ-rishta-dár*. reader, *pesh-kár*. Writer, (native,) *muḥarrir;* (English,) *kiráni;* translator, *mutarjim*. Record-keeper, *muḥáfiz*. (all these, when you call for them, should get 'sáḥib' after their titles): the copyist *or* section-writer, *nakl-navís*. the messenger, for near work, *chaprási;* for distant work, *piyádah*. –cers of the army. *See page* 97.

Often, *aksar*. how–, *kae-bár?* so, *or* as–, *jai-bár, tai-bár*.

Oil, *tel; raughan; chikná,i*. hair–, *bál ka tel*, and so of other kinds of oil: kerosine–, *karshin*[1] (E.) *ka tel*. mustard–, *sarsoṇ ka tel*. castor–, *reṇṛi ka tel*. cocoanut–, *náriyal ka tel*. –man, *teli; kolu*, –press, *kolhu*.

Ointment, *marham; raughan*

Old, *purána; ḳadím*. –man, *buḍḍha*. –woman, *buḍḍhi; búṛhi*. –age, *buṛhápa*.

---

[1] This oil is now extensively used in Indian houses.

of–, *ḳadím meṇ; agle zamáne meṇ.* how – are you? *tumhára sinn kya hai?* a boy of ten years –, *das baras ka laṛka.*

Olive, *jal-páe.*

Omelet, *mamlet,* (E.).

Omnipotence, *ḳudrat.* A. *ḳadír.*

On, *par;* (lit. and fig.) *ke úpar.* – a person's side (as a friend,) *ki taraf.* – this account, *is-wáste.* – that day, *us-roz.* – this, *is-par; tab.* I shall reach – *or* by, the day after to-morrow, *parsoṇ tak.* – the contrary, *bil-aks; báwujúd is-ke.*

Once, *ek dafah; ek bár.* all at – (persons acting together.) *sab-mil-ke; ek sáth.* (ditto, suddenly,) *achának; nágáh; ṇágahánṇ.* – or twice, *do ek martabe.* –upon a time, *sábiḳ dinoṇ meṇ.*

One, *ek.* often followed by '*ṭho,*' an expletive, not to be translated, but equivalent to 'unit' –another, *ek-digar,* some–, *ko,i; ko,i ádmi.* a certain –, *fulánah; fulánah ádmi.* – by –, *ek-ek.* it is all –, *ek hi bát hai; kuchh farḳ nahíṇ hai.*

Onion, *piyáz.*

Only, *ek; ekla;* (merely,) *sirf; faḳat; kháli.*

Onward. *See* 'Advance.'

Open, (v.) *kholna; khol-d.* (a.) *khula.* –land, *maidán; khuli jagah.* *See* 'Liberal.' –ing, *ráh,* (f.); *bhítar jáne ki ráh; báhar áne ki ráh; nikás.* –ly, *záhiran; sab logoṇ ke sámne.*

Opinion, *rá,i* or *rá,e; khiyál;* I hold this –, *meri rá,i yih hai, kih, &c.*

Opium, (made,) *afyún.* (growing,) *post.* one who uses –, *afími; posti.*

Opportunity. *See* 'Occasion.'

Oppose. *See* 'Obstruct,' *mukhálif hona.* –ponent *mukhálif,* (also as an adj.), –position, *muzáḥamat; rok; rok-ṭok; aṭ-ká,o.* –posite, (adv.) *sámne;* (prep.). *ke sámne.*

Oppression, *zulm; zabardasti; sakhti.* V. –*k.* –or, *zálim.* –ive, *zabar-dast; sakht; sang-dil.* –ed, *mazlúm.* –ively, *jabran.*

Oral, *zabáni.* also adv.
Orange, *nárangi.*
Orator, *zabán-áwar.* –y, *–i.* --tion, *taḳrír*, (f.); *baḥs*, (f.).
Orchard, *bágh*; *baghán*, (L.B.).
Order. *See* 'Command' and 'Arrangement.' –ly officer, *arḍali*, (E.).
Ordinary, *maamúli*; *bázári*; *chalni*; *jo dastúr hai.*
Origin, *jaṛ*; *asl*; *bunyád*, (f.). –al, *asli*; *awwal.* –ally, *shuru se*; *ibtida se.* *See* 'Beginning.'
Ornament, *siṇgár*, (f.); *zeb*; *ára,ish*; *khush-numá,i.* V. *siṇgárna.* –al, *zeb-áwar*; *khush-numa.* –ed, *árás-tah*; *khúb-súrat.*
Ortolan, *bageri.*
Ostrich, *shutur-murgh.*
Other, (extra,) *aur-ek.* (different,) *dúsra*; *dígar.* *See* 'One.' some one or –, *ko,i na ko,i.* some thing or –, *kuchh*; *kuchh na kuchh.* –wise, *aur*; *aur taraḥ se.* –wise, *nahíṇ to.*
Oven, *tanúr.*
Over, *úpar.* (prep.) *ke úpar*; *par.* –and above, *is ke siwá,e*; *aláwah is ke*; *ziyádah*; *aur.* Verbs compounded with 'over,' must be translated according to their meaning, there being no corresponding prefix in Hindústáni, e.g., he went over (=across) the river, *darya ke us pár gaya.* he overcame (=removed) my scruples, *us-ne mera pas-o-pesh* (hesitation) *dabá diya.* –look, *mu,áf-k.* *See* 'Neglect.' –night, *rát ke waḳt*; *rát-ko.* –sight, *bhúl*; *chúk*, (f.); *ghalat.* –take, *á-jána*; *pás ána*; *ke pás pahuṇchna.* –turn, *ultána*; *ulṭá-d.*
Ought. *See page* 18. *Sect.* 21.
Our, *hamára*; *ham logoṇ ka.* with 'own.' *See page* 30. we --selves, *ham,tum*; *ham-donoṇ* (if only two.); *ham-sab*, (if more.). among –selves, *ápas men.*
Out, (adv.) *báhar.* (prep.) *ke báhar*, to go–, *báhar jána*; *nikal-jána*, (as fire,) *bujh-jána*, to give–, *kahna*; *záhir-kar-d.* to cry–, *pukár-na.* to put–, (as a light,) *bujá-d.*; *bujhá-d.* –of, (a

place, or a number,) *meṇ se.* (a material,) *se.* –of (e.g.) fear, *daṛ ke máre.* –of breath, *be-dam.* –of time, *be-wakt.* –of spirits, *udás; ghamgín.* get–, *dut! dúr! dúr-dúr!* –most, *sab-se dúr.* –let, *nikás; muhána.* –right, *púre púre taur se.*

Outrage, *zulm; be-ḥurmati; be-izzati.* V. *–k.*

Owe, (money,) *ḳarz rakhna; ḳarz-dár hona.* owing to, *se* or *ke sabab se*, e.g. *dhúp se*, owing to the heat.

Owl, *ullu.*

Own, (adj.) *See page* 30. (v.) (e.g. property,)...*rakhna; málik hona.* –er, *málik; ḳábiz; dakhl-kár; sáḥib-i...* e.g. *sáḥib-i-khánah.*

Ox, *ba,il.* –cart, *–gáṛi.*

P.

Pace, *ḳadam.* (V. *–k.*); *ḍeg.*

Pacify, *khush-k.; rázi-k.; ṭhanḍa-k.* N. use these as v.n.

Pack, (v.) *chíz sab band karna.* –et, *gaṭhṛi; pákiṭ,*(E.).

Pad, *gaddi; namdah.* V. *is meṇ rú,i* (or other material,) *dena.*

Padlock, *ḳufl; tála.*

Page, (of book,) *safḥah; warak.* (servant,) *khás; khás naukar.*

Pageant,–ry, *ḥasham; ḥashmat.*

Pail, *bálṭi.* milk–, *dohni.*

Pain, *dard,* (m.); *sozish; dukh:* to feel –, *–uṭhána; khána.* to cause–, *–d.* –ful, *dard ka; dard-angez.*–fully, *dard-se.* –s, *miḥnat; zaḥmat.* V. *–k.*; *–uṭhána.*

Paint, (n.) *rang,* (m.) (v.) (as an artist,) *khínchna,* (as an artificer,) *–d.*; *–lagána.* –er, (artist,) *musawwir.* (artificer,) *rang-rez.* –ed, *mankúsh; jis par rang diya gayá hai.*–ing,a, *taswír,* (f.). (the art of,) *taswír-kashi.*[2]

Pair. *See* 'Join.'

Palace, *rang-maḥal; ráj-báṛi.*

Palanquin, *pálki.* –bearer, *–wála; –bardár; bérar,* (E.).

Palate, *tálu.*

---

[1] *See page* 22. *Sects.* 32 and 31.

[2] From the Persian, '*kashídan,*' 'to draw.'

Pale, (face,) *zard ; píla.* (general word,) *halke rang ka.*

Palette, *rang ki takhti.*

Palm, (according to its kind, followed by '*gáchh*' tree,) date, *khajúr.* cocoanut, *náriyal.* arecanut, *supiyári.* plantain, *kela.*

Palsy, *sitang.*

Pan, *pán,* (E.); *tábah.* –cake, *pán-kek,* (E.).

Pane, *shishe ki takhti.*

Panel, *lakṛi ka takhtah.*

Pantaloon. *patlún,* (E.).

Panther, *chíta.*

Pantry, *khánsámán ka kamra.*

Paper, *kághaz.* blotting–, *lál–.* –biscuit, *papṛi.*

Parable, *tamsíl,* (f.); *masal,*(f.)

Paradise, *jannat ; firdaus,* (m.)

Paralysis, *lakwah.*

Parasol, *chháta.*

Pardon, *'afu ; mu,áfi.* V. *–d. ; uzr manzúr-k. ; mu,áf-k.* –me! *mu,áf kíjiye ; bura na mániega kih main, &c.* –ed, *mu-áf.*

Parent. *See* 'Father.' 'Mother.' –s, *má-báp.* –al, *wálidána ; pidari.*

Parish, *sukúnat ; mahallah ; mauza.*

Park, *ramna ; maidán.*

Parlour, *baiṭhne ka kamra ; khás,* or, *khalwat-khánah.*

Parrot, *tota* (m.); *toti,* (f.).

Parsley, *pársli,* (E.)

Part, (n.), *juz ; ṭukṛa ; hissah.* (concern in,) *alákah.* (side,) *taraf,* (f.). (v.). *bánṭna ; hissah-kar-d,* to take one's –, *tarafdár hona.* to take in bad –, *bura mánna.* to take in good –, *bhala-jánna ; pasand-k.* –ial, *tarafdár.* N. *tarafdári.* –ly, *kuchh.* –ially, *tarafdári se.* –isan, *tarafdár.* –ition, *taksím,* (f.); *baṭwára.* –icularly, (in detail,) *tafsílan.* (especially,) *khusúsan.*

Partner, *sharík ; hissa-dár.* –ship, *sharákat ; hissa-dári.*

Partridge, *títar.*

Party, ...*ki taraf ke log.* (–ies in a suit,) *faríkain.*

Pass, (v.) *jána ; chalá-jána.* (as time,) (*intr.*) *bít-jána.* –away, *ho-jána ; ho chukna.* –time, (*trans.*) *sarf-k.* –current, *jári-hona.* –across, *pár* or *ubúr-k.* –over, (overlook,) *mu,áf-k. ; chhoṛ-d.* come to –. *See* 'Occur.'

to – one's word for, *paimán-k.*; *izhár-k.* the past, *jo guzashtah hai.*

Passage. *See* 'Outlet.' 'Extract.'

Passion. *See* 'Anger.' to be *or* get in a–, *jhaljhaldna.*

Paste, (batter,) *le,i.* (on a pie,) *karast,* (E. crust.). –board, *ṭuṭ.* pastry, *samosah*; *maṭhri*; *pesṭari.* (E.)

Pasture land, *chará-gáh.* to pasture, *charána.*

Pat, (n.) *ṭhak*; *tamáchah.* V. *–d.*; (as a thing flapping,) *ṭhak-ṭhakána.*

Patience, *sabr.* (f.). V. *–k.* Adj. *sábir.* Adv. *–se.*

Patient, a, *bímár ádmi*; *maríz.*

Patron, *murabbi*; *parwar,* as last word in compos.: e.g. *gharíb-parwar.* – of the poor. –age, *ḥimáyat.* –ize, *murabbi hona*; *parwasti-k.*

Pattern, *namúnah.*

Paw, (n.) *panjah*; *changul.* (v.) *ṭápna.*

Pay, (n.) *talab*; *musháharah*; (daily,) *roz-ínah.* (monthly,) *dar-máhah*; *mahína.* (yearly,) *sál-ána.* V. *–d.* (an account, &c.,) *adá-k.* –able, *jo dena hai.* –ment, *ada.*

Pea, peas, *maṭar.*

Peace, *sulḥ,* (f.); *salámat.* (of mind,) *khátir-jama*; *taskín,* (f.). (rest,) *árám* to hold one's –, *chup-rahna.* to break the –, *balwa–k.* –ful, *be-fasád.* –fully, *be-fasád se*; *chup-ke.*

Peach, *shaft-álu.*

Peacock, *mor,* or *mhor.*

Pearl, *moti,* (m.).

Peasant, *kisán*; *grihist*; *ra,íyat.* the –try, *ra,áya.*

Peck, *ṭhongna.*

Peculiar, *kháss*; *mukhtass.* –ity, *khusúsiyat*; *khássiyat.* –ly, *khusúsan.*

Peg, *mekh,* (f.).

Pellet, *goli.* a – bow, *gulel.*

Pen,[1] *ḳalam.* –knife, *–tarásh.* –box, – *dán.* – and ink, *dawát ḳalam.* V. *–band-k.*; *likhna.* *See* 'Restrain.'

Penal, *wájib-us-saza.* the Indian – Code, *majmú,ah táźírát-i-Hind.*

---

[1] As natives always used a reed for writing, there are no words for a 'nib,' or a 'pen-holder.' But '*lohe ka ḳalam*' is in use for the former, and '*ḳalam ki lakṛi,*' for the latter. Natives now use 'nibs.'

Pencil, *pensil*, (E.).

Penury, *tangi; tang-dasti.* -ious, *tang-dil; bak͟hil.*

People, *log; ádmi; k͟halá,ik.* (v.) *basána; ábád-k.*

Pepper, *mirch.* (black,) *gol-.* (red,) *lál-.* V. *-d.* -box, *-dán.*

Perceive. *See* 'See.'

Perfect, (a.) *kámil; púra; sák͟htah; puk͟htah; tamám.* V. *-k.* -ion, *kamál; ikmál; tamámi.* -ly, *bahut ṭhík; tamám-o kamál.*

Perform. *See* 'Do.' -ance (doing,) *fel; kám, &c.* (completion,) *tamámi.*

Perfume. *See* 'Odour.'

Perhaps, *ho sakta hai; sháyad.*[1]

Period, *arsah; muddat; wakt; zamánah;* (long,) *yug.*

Perish. *See* 'Die.'

Perjury, *jhúṭhi-kasam.* to commit -, *-khána; jhúṭhi gawáhi-d.*

Permanent. *See* 'Firm.'

Permission, *ijázat.* V. *-d.; dena* with the inflected infinitive of anything permitted, as in the common phrase, '*jáne do*,' permit him to go.

Perquisite, *dastúri.*

Person. *See* 'Being.' -ate, *bhes-k.; nakl-k.; súrat bandna.* -ation, *by the v. n.*

Persuasion, *targhib*, (f.). V. *-d.*

Perturb. *See* 'Confound.'

Perverse, *muk͟hálif; ziddi.* V. *-hona.* -ness, *zidd; muk͟hálafat.*

Pestle, *soṇṭa.*

Pet, (n. a.) *pyára*, (m.). *-i*, (f.). V. *pyár-k.*

Petition, *darkhwást; guzárish; arz*, (f.); *suwál; nibedon; bayán; bát.* V. *-k.* -er, *sá,il.*

Petticoat, *piṭṭikoṭ.*[2]

Phial, *shíshi.*

Pick, (v.) *chunna; chun-lena.* (flowers,) *toṛna.* - a quarrel, *laṛá,i uṭhána.* -axe, *phauṛa; kudra.*

Pickles, *píkal*, (E.).

Picture, *taswír.* (f.); *nakshah.* -frame, *ḍháṇcha.* *See* 'Draw.'

Piece. *See* 'Part.' -meal, *ṭukṛe-ṭukṛe.*

---

[1] Persian 'it may be,' from '*shudan*,' 'to be.'

[2] Indian ladies don't wear petticoats.

Pierce, *chhedna ; chhed-k.* instrument for –ing, *chhe,-oni.*

Pig, *sú,ar.*

Pigeon, *kabútar.* – house, *-khánah.*

Pile, (heap,) *ḍheṛ,* (f.); *ambár.* (of cloth,) *ro,eṇ.* (post), *khambha.*

Pilgrim, (to Mecca,) *ḥáji.* (generally,) *tírathi.* –age, (to Mecca,) *ḥajj.* (generally,) *tírath.*

Pill, *goli ; ḥabb,* (f.).

Pillage, (n.) *lúṭ.* V. *–k. ; lúṭna.* to be –ed, *luṭna.* one who –s, *lúṭiya.*

Pillar, *situn ; khambha.*

Pillow, *takyah.* –case, *–ye ka ghiláf.*

Pin, (n.) (for clothes, &c.) *pín,* (E.). (small bolt,) *kíl,* (f.) V. *–lagá-d.*

Pincers, *sangsi ; chimṭa.*

Pinch, (n.) *noch.* V. *nochna ; chuṭki-lena.*

Pine-apple, *anannás.*

Pious, *dín-dár ; khudá-tars ;*[1] *sáliḥ ; nek.* piety, *taḳwa; khudá-tarsi.*

Pipe, (smoking,) (native,) *ḥuḳḳah.* (English,) *paip,* (E.). (for e.g. water,) *nal ; nai,* (f.). (cask,) *pípa.* (musical,) *baṇsi.* V. *baṇsi bajána.*

Pistachio, *pistah.*

Pit, *gaṛha ; cháh.* V. *–k.*

Pitch, (n.) *ḳír.* (v.) (e g. a tent,) *khaṛa-k. ; taiyár-k.* *See* 'Throw.'

Pith, *gúda.*

Pity, (n.) *raḥm ; mihrbáni.* V. *–k.* –iful, *raḥím; mihrbán.* –iless, *be-raḥm.*

Place, (n.) *jagah,* (f.); *ja; makán ; gáh,* as last part in compos: *See* 'Rank.' 'Take.' in this place, *is jagah meṇ ; yaháṇ* (v.) *rakhna ;* or by special description, e.g. *khaṛa-k.* to erect; *gáṛna,* place in the ground, *bándh-d.,* to tie up, *and so on.*

Plain, (n.) *See* 'Park.' (a.) (unadorned,) *sáda.* (level,) *bar-á-bar ; samán.* –dealing, *sáda-dili.* –ly, *sáf ; záhiran.* –ness, *sádagi.*

---

[1] From the Persian, '*tarsídan,*' 'to ear.'

Plaint, *nálah.* (in Court). *See* 'Petition.' –iff, *mudda,i; faryádi.* –ive, –ly, *nálán.*

Plan, *tadbír,* (f.); *hikmat; upá,e.* V. *–k.; –banána; –nikálna. See* 'Drawing.'

Plane, (tool,) *randah.* V. *–chalána; randese samán-k.*

Plank, *takhtah.* V. *–lagána.*

Plant, (n.) *paudha; per.* V. *–lagána.*

Plantain, *kela.*

Plaster, *lep.* V. *lepna.*

Plate, *bartan.* –ed, *mulamma.*

Platform, *chabútrah; takhtah; machán.*

Play, (n.) *khel,* (m.); as last word in compos: *bázi.* V. *khelna,* (on an instrument,) *bajána.* –day, *chhutti ka din; tatíl,* (f.). –fellow, *yár; ham-báz.* –fulness, *alol,* (f.). –ful, *alola.* –house, *nách ka ghar.* –thing, *khilauna.*

Pleader, (in Court,) *vakíl; mukhtár.* –ing, *bahs,* (f.). V. *bahs-k.*

Pleasant, *achchha; khúb; khush; dil-pazír.* –ness, *pasanaídagi; khush-taba,i; raghbat.* to please, *khush-k.; rijhána.* –ed, *khush; rázi.* –ing, *khush; makbúl.* pleasure, *khushi.* (will,) *marzi; khushi; ikhtiyár.* please God, *insha alláh.*

Pledge, (n.) *giro; rihn,* (m.). V. *–rakhna.* –d, *marhún.*

Plenty, *bahut; ghanímat; ifrát.* –iful, *bahut; bahutera.* –ifully, *ifrát se.*

Pliers, *chimta.*

Plot, (of ground,) *takhtah; kitah; chaman.* (of evil,) *sázish; bandish.* V. *–k.*

Plough, (n.) *hal* or *hál.* V. *hal-ba,il-k.; jotna; chás-k.* –man, *halwáha; chása.*

Pluck, *torna. See* 'Courage.'

Plug, *datta; thent.*

Plum, *bair,* (f.). –tree, *–gáchh.*

Plunder. *See* 'Pillage.'

Ply, (in cloth, &c.) *tah.* (v.) e.g. a trade, *karna.*

Pocket, *jaib,* (f.). V. *–men rakhna.* –book, *bayáz,* (f.). –handkerchief, *rúmál.*

Point, (of stick, &c.) *nok,* (f.) (dot,), *nuktah,* on the–of, *par; karíb tha kih, &c. thora báki tha kih, &c.*

-ed, *nokila*. to–, (sharpen,) *tez-k*. to –out, *batlá-d*.

Poison, *zahr*,(f.) ; *bis*, (m.). -ed, *-alúdah*. V. *–d*.

Pole, *báns ; chob ; lakṛi ; khambha*.

Police, *polís*, (E.). -office, *thánah*. –officer, *thánadár ; dároghah ; jama-dár ; kánsṭabil*, (E.). (for villages,) *chaukí-dár*. Up-country, they say *kotwál*, for a head police-officer ; and *kotwáli*, for his office.

Polish, (n.) *raughan ; mom-raughan ; pálish*, (E.). V. *–lagá d.* ; *sáf-k*.

Polite, *adabi ; khalíḳ*. –ness, *adab*, (m.) ; *khulḳ*, (f.). –ly, *khulḳ se*.

Pomegranate, *anár*.

Pond, *táláb*, (m.).

Pony, *ṭaṭṭu*.

Pool, (water,) *ḍábar*, (m.).

Poor, *gharíb; kangál; muflis*. (in spirit,) *gharíb; miskín ; nícha*. the poor, *gharíb-log*. *See* 'Poverty.'

Poppy, *post*. one who uses opium, *posti*.

Populous, *ábád ; gul-zár*. –ness, *ábádi ; maamúri*. popular, *ámm-pasand*.

Porcelain, *chín*[1] *ke bartan*.

Porch, *osára ; ḍe,oṛhi*.

Pork, *sú,ar ka gosht*.[2]

Porridge, (oat-meal,[3]) *párich*, (E.). (of rough native flour,) *súji*. (of crushed wheat,) *daliya*.

Porter, (at gate,) *darbán*. (carrier, *ḳuli ; moṭiya ; bardár*. (drink,) *porṭar sharáb*, (f.).

Portion. *See* 'Part.'

Portmanteau, *peṭi ; bakas*, (E.).

Position, *jagah*, (f.). to place in –, *jagah meṇ rakhna*.

Possess. *See page* 75. *Sec.* 13; *dakhl-k*. –ion, *ḳabzah*. –ions, *mál ; daulat ; chíz sab*, and by their special names, as 'milkíyat,' *landed possessions*, *&c*. –or, *dakhl-kár ; ḳábiz ; málik ; sáḥib-i....* (e.g. *khánah*.)

---

[1] *Chín* is China.

[2] You may have English ham and bacon on your table ; but *never* the native animal.

[3] Oat-meal itself is also called '*párich*.'

Possible, *mumkin ; ho sakta hai.* –bility, with *jo.* –ibly, *shâyad ; ho sakta hai.* to be –, *mumkin hona ; ho-sakna.*

Post (for letters, &c.). *See page* 98. *See* 'Appointment;' 'Office;' 'Pillar.'

Posteriors, *chútaṛ ; pichhâṛi.*

Posterity, *pasíni.* to all –, *naslan baad nasl.*

Postpone, (make delay,) *der,* or *deri-k.* (adjourn,) *mau-ḳúf-k.*

Pot, *deg; degcha; degchi; hâṇṛı.*

Potato, *álu.*

Potter, *kumhár.* –y, *maṭṭi ke bartan.*

Poultice, *lo,i.* V. *–lagána.*

Poultry, *murghá-murghi.*

Pound, (n.) *ádha-ser; ek paun,* (E.). (v.) *písná ;* (beat,) *píṭna.* the village –, *beṛha ; paun,* (E.). to impound, *paun meṇ rakhna.*

Pour, *ḍálna ; ḍál-d.* a – of rain, *jhaṛi.*

Poverty, *iflás, muflisi ; tangi; tang-dasti.*

Powder, (for fire arms,) *bárút.* (small dust of anything,) *chúran.*

Power, *ḳudrat ; ḳúwwat ; ikhtiyár ; ḥukm ; háth.* –ful, *zor-áwar ; zabar-dast.* –fully, *zor-se.* –less, *ná-tawán ; kam-zor ; durbal.* –fulness, *zabar-dasti ; baṛá,i ; zor-áwari ; táḳat.*

Practice, *mashḳ.* (v. *–k.*) (habit,) *ádat.* (custom,) *dastúr; riwáj.* V. *hona.*

Praise, *taaríf,* (f.). V. *–k. ; –d.* –worthy, *ḳábil-i-taaríf.*

Prawn, *chiṇgṛi.*

Prayer, *namáz,* (f.). V. *–paṛh-na. See* 'Request.'

Preach, *waaz-k.* –er, *wá,iz.* –ment, (sermon,) *waaz,* (m.).

Precaution, *khabar-dári.* V. *–k. ; khabar-dár hona.*

Precede, *áge-jána,* or *chalna.* –dence in rank, *taḳdím,* (f.). to give ditto, *–dena.* to enjoy ditto, *–lena.*

Precious, (affection,) *azíz ; pyára.* (V. *–rakhna*). (price,) *besh-ḳímat.* V. *–hona.*

Precise. *See* 'Exact.' –ly *ṭhík ; bi,ainihi.*

Preface, *tamhíd,* (f.).

Preference, *pasand,* (f.). ; *cháh; khwáhish.* V. *cháhna;*

pasand-k.; *bihtar samajhna*; *us-se is-ko pasand-k.* to assign a –, *tarjíh-d.* –able, *bihtar*; *dúsron se achchha.*

Preferment, *tarakki*; *barhti*; *barhá,i.*

Preparation, *taiyár-k.* (v. n.); *taiyári.* V. *taiyár-k.*; *intizám-k.* (make,) *banána.*

Prescribe, *kahna*; *hukm-d.* (as a doctor,) *dawa-d.* –ption, *nuskhah.*

Present, (n.). *See* 'Gift.' (a.) *házir*; *sámne*; *pesh*; *ru-ba-ru*; *taiyár*; *maujúd.* –ce, (lit.) *háziri.* (respectfully,) *huzúr.* in the – of many people, *bahut logon ke sámne.* – of mind, *tez-zihn*; *hoshyári.* –ly, *fauran*, &c. *See page* 54.

Preserve. *See* 'Defend.'

Press, (v.) *dabána*; *dabá-d.* (constrain,) *majbúr-k.* (n.) (of people,) *guroh*, (m.); *ghol*,(m.). (for clothes,table things, &c.) *almári*,[1] (oil,) *kolhu.* (printing,) *chhápne ki kal.*[2] –ure, *dabá,o*; *dáb.* –ed labourer, *begár.* –ed labour, *begári.*

Pretence, *bahánah*; *uzr*; *hílah.* V. –*k.*

Pretty, *khúb-súrat*; *suthra*, –iness, –*i.* (somewhat,) *kuchh-kuchh.* *See* Part I. 'Sa.'

Prevalence, *ghalbah.* –ent, *jári*; *phaila hú,a*; *murawwaj.*

Prevent, *mana-kar-d*; *rokna*; *chhenkna*; *atkána*; *báz-rakhna*; *thámna*; N. *rok*; *chhenká,o*; *atká,o*; *muzáhamat.*

Previous, –ly, *áge*; *peshtar.*

Price, *kímat*; *dám.* rate of –, *nirkh*; *bhá,o.*

Prick, (*trans.*) *chubhona.* (*intr.* and *passive*) *chubhna.* (n.) *kánta*; *khár.* –up one's ears, *kán uthána.* –ly, *khár-dár.* –ly heat, *ghamauri.*

Pride, *ghurúr*; *dimágh.* A. *maghrúr*, V. with *hona.*

Prime, (n.) *bahár*, (f.). –minister, *wazír.* (a.) *awwal*; *awwal kism ka.*

---

1 Not Hindústáni; probably Portuguese. *Confer* French, '*almoire*, and Scotch, '*aumrie.*'   2 '*Kal*' is masculine in the western parts.

Prince, *sháh-zádah*, (fem. *-di.*); *kúṇwar; ráj-kumár; jub-ráj.* -ly, *-sa.*

Principal, *awwal; sab se baṛa.*

Principle, *sabab; sabab-i-awwal, jaṛ,* (f.); *bunyád,* (f.).

Print, (v.) *chhápna.* -ed, *chhápa hú,a.* -ing, *by the v.n.* -ing-press, *chhápne ki kal.* -ing-house, *chhápá-khánah.* -er, *chhápne-wála.*

Prison. *See* 'Jail.'

Private, *kháss; khud,* (in compos:) e.g. *khud-kásht,* one's reserved cultivation, or 'home-farm.' -room, *khalwat-khánah; kháss-kamra.* a - soldier, *sipáhi.* in - and in public, *khalwat-o-jalwat meṇ.* -ly, *khalwat meṇ.*

Privy, (n.) *ghusl-khánah; já-e-zarúrat; ṭaṭṭi.*

Probable, *aghlab; mumkin.* -bility, *jo aghlab hai; iḥtimál.* to be -, *iḥtimál hona; 'ho sakta hai.'* -bly, *shakk bahut nahíṇ hai; sháyad; gháliban.*

Proceed. *See* 'Go.' -cedure, *kár-rawá,i;* The Code of Criminal Procedure, *majmú,ah zawábit faujdári.* ditto Civil, *majmú,ah zawábit díwáni.* -ings, *jo sab kám kiya gaya hai; pairavi; kár-rawá,i.*

Proclamation, *ishtihár; manádi.* V. *-k.; -jári-k.; mashhúr-k.; záhir-k.*

Procure, *lána; mangwána; mangwá-lena.*

Prodigal, *fusúl-kharj.*-ity,*-i.*

Produce, (v.) *dena; paidá-k.* (n.) *paidá,ish; paidá-wár; fasl,* (f.). -ductive, *zarkhez.* -ed, *paida.*

Profess, *kahna; waadah-k.* (a trade, &c.) *karna.* -ion, (what one alleges,) *bát; bayán; kahna,* (v.n.); *waadah.* (trade,) *peshah; kám; dhandha.*

Profit, *fá,idah; nafa; maḥásil.* to make -, *-k.; -pána.* -able, *fá,ida-mand.*

Progress. *See* 'Advance.'

Prohibit. *See* 'Forbid.'

Promise, *waadah; iḳrár; paimán.* V. *-k.*

Promissory-note, *ṭip,* (f.); *tamassuk.*

Promote. *See* 'Aid.' (advance,) *baṛhána*; *taraḳḳi-d.* N. *bhaṛti*; *taraḳḳi.*

Pronounce, *kahna*. (sentence,) *ḥukm dena*. -nunciation, *talaffuz.*

Proof, *dalíl*, (f.) (evidence,) *shahádat*; *gawáhi*. V. –d.

Prop, *balli*; *ṭekni*. V. *–rakhna.*

Propagate, *upjána*; *paidá-k.* (by grafting,) *ḳalam lagána.*

Propel, *áge chalána.*

Proper, *durust*; *wájib*; *saḥiḥ*; *ṭhík*, –ly, *ṭhík*; *achchha*; *achchhi taraḥ se.*

Property. *See* 'Possess.'

Prosecute, (any work,) *karna*; *kartá-jána*; *chalána*; *pairavi-k.* N. *ta,aḳḳub*; *pairavi*; *kár-rawá,i.* (in Court,) *muḳaddamah.* –tor. *See* 'Plaintiff.'

Prospect, (view,) *madd-i-nazar.* (e.g. of success,) *ummed.* (f.).

Prosperity, *bhalá,i*; *nek-bakhti*; *daulat*; *baṛhti.* V. *–meṇ hona*; *–meṇ rahna*; *–meṇ guzrán karna.* –ous, the nouns followed by '*meṇ*;' *ba-khair.* His affairs are prosperous, *us ka sab kám ba-khúbi* (or *achchhi taraḥ,*) *chalta hai.*

Protect, *bachána*; *bachá-d.*; *panáh-d.*; *parwarish-k.* (from justice, &c.) *rúposh rakhna.* –tion, *bachá,o*; *ḥifázat*; *muḥáfazat*; *ásra.* (watchfulness,) *nigáh-báni.* self –tion, or defence, *ḥifázat-i-khud.* –or *málik*; *sáḥib*; *ḥáfiz*; *murabbi*; *dast-gír*; *nigáh-bán.*

Provide, *ḥázir-kar-d.*; *taiyár-k.*; *saranjám-k.* –visions, *kháne ki chíz sab.* (for troops, &c., on the march,) *rasad*, (f.). –dent, *khabar-dár*; *dúr-andesh.*

Province, *súbah.* governor of a –, *súba-dár.*

Provoke, *rís–karána.* N. *chiṛh*, (f.).

Prudence, *khabar-dári*; *hosh-yári*; *tadbír*, (f.); *imtiyáz*, (f.). –dent, *khabar-dár*; *hosh-yár.* V. adjs. with *hona.* –tly, *khabar-dári*, *&c.*, *se.*

Prune, (n.) *paṛún*, (E.); *súkhi bair*, (f.). (v.) *chháṇṭna*; *chháṇṭ-k.*

Public, the, *log sab ; ámm-o-khâss ; khalá,ik* a – servant, *sarkár ka naukar.* the – service, *sarkár ki naukari.* (well-known.) *maalúm ; záhir ; mashhúr.* –ly, *záhiran ; sab logon ke sámne.*

Publish. *See* 'Proclaim.' (as a book,) *jári-k.* –er, with '*jo.*'

Pudding, *púding,* (E.).

Puddle, *dabra,* or *ḍabra.*

Pull, *khínch,* (f.). V. *khínchna ; tánna.* (L. B.).

Pulse, (of the body,) *nabz,* (f.) to feel the –, *–dekhna.* –sation, *ṭís.*

Pulse, (grain,) known by its various kinds, e.g. *moṭh ; dál*[1] *; urad ; chana ; múng; kalá,i ; búṭ, &c., &c.*

Pump, (v.) *páni uṭhána.* (n.); *pampah* or *bambah,* being attempts at the English word, natives having no pumps ; and few mechanical contrivances.

Punctual, –ly, *bar-wakt.* –ality, *–hona,* (v.n.).

Punishment, *saza,* (f.). V. *–d.* deserving –, *wájib-us-saza.*

Puppet, *putli.*

Puppy, *pilla.*

Purchase. *See* 'Buy.'

Pure, *sáf; zulál; pákízah.* –ity, –ness, *safá,i ; páki ; neki.*

Purgative, a, *julláb ki dawa,* (f.). V. *jhárna.*

Purgatory, *iráf,* or *aráf.*

Purple, *lál.*

Purport, *mazmún ; matlab ; mani.*

Purpose. *See* 'Intention.'

Purse, *kísah ; kharítah.*

Pursue. *See* 'Chase.'

Push, (n.) *dhakka.* V. *–d. ; ṭhelna.*

Put, *rakhna ; rakh-d. ; baiṭhána ; baiṭhá-d.* –away, *le-jána.*–back, *wápas rakhna.* – crossways, *áṛa rakhna.* – off, (e.g. clothes,) *utárna.* - off, (make delay,) *deri-k. ; maukúf-k.* – on, (clothes,) *oṛhna; kapṛe pahinna.*–out, (e.g.) a person, *nikál-d.* (a light,) *bujhá-d.* (money at interest.) *súd par dena.* –an end to, *khatam-kar-d.*

---

[1] A pleasant dish known as *khichri,* (vulg. *kichary*), is made by mixing '*dál*' and rice, cooked, of course, but served dry.

-to shame, *sharmána; lajwána.* – in mind, *yád dilána.* –to flight, *bhagá-d.; ghálib hona.* – past, *apne pás rakhna.* – up with, *bardásht-k.* – to death, *már-ḍálna; ḳatl-k.*
Putty, *púṭing,* (E.).

Q.

Quack, (as a duck,) *ḳáṇ-ḳáṇ-k.* (oneself.) *láfzani-k.* –ery, *láfzani.*
Quail, *baṭer.*
Quality. *See* 'Kind.' 'Rank.'
Quantity, *miḳdár.*
Quarrel, *jhagṛa; laṛái; ḳaziyah.* V. *–k.; jhagaṛna; laṛna.* –some, *jhagṛálu.* to pick a –, *ḳaziyah uṭhána;* or *bar-pá-k.*
Quarry, (stone,) *sang kì kán.* (lime,) *chúne ki kán.* (game,) *shikár.*
Quarter, (n.) *chauṭhá,i; pá,o; chahárum.* –rúpi, *chau-anni. See* 'Neighbourhood.' –of a town, *maḥallah; ṭola.* –s, *maḳám. See pages* 64 and 91 *note.* (v.) *chár ḥissoṇ meṇ báṇṭna.* –in battle, *amán,* (f.). to give –, *ámán-d.; bachána* –(billet,) *chár-pára-k.* –ly, *si-máhah.*
Queen, (M.), *malikah; ḳai-sar.* (H.) *ráni; mahá-ráni.*
Question, (n.) *sawál,* or *suwál.* (v.) *púchhna; sawál-k.* out of the –, *baḥs ke báhar; behúdah.* –able, *mushtabah.*
Quick, *jald; tez; tund; chust.* N. *jaldi; tezi; chústi; shitábi,* –ly. *See page* 54. V. *dauṛá-d; tez-k.* –(alive,) *zindah.* –lime, *bari.* –sand, *chor-bálu.* silver, *pára.*
Quiet, (a.) *chup; sákin* (as an animal,) *gharíb.* (n.) *árám; ráḥat; khámoshi.* (v.) *ṭhanḍa-k.; sákin-k.* to keep –.(*intr.*)*chup rahna.* –ly, *chup-ke; áhiste.*
Quill, *sháh-par.* (writing,) *par ka ḳalam.*
Quilt, *razá,i.*
Quince, *bihi.*
Quit. *See* 'Abandon.' –tance, *fárigh-khatti.*
Quite, *bil-kull; tamám.*–right, *ṭhík; khúb; bahut achchha.*
Quotation, *iḳtibás.* V. *–k.*

R.

Race, (descent,) *asl*, (f.); *nasl*, (f.); *khándán*. (horse, &c.) *daur*. –course, *ghur-daur*.

Radical, *asli*; *bunyádi*.

Radish, *múli*.

Rafter, *lattha*; *barga*.

Rag, *gúdar*; *gudri*.

Rage. *See* 'Anger.' he has a rage (for, &c.,) *us-ko bara shauk hai, &c.*

Railing, a, *katahra*; *bera*. V. –*lagána*. *See* 'Abuse.'

Railway, *rel-rásta*, (half E.). –train, *rel ki gári,án*. –engine, *injin*, (E.). –ticket, *rel ka tikat*, (E.). –station, *isteshan*, (E.).

Rain, (n.) *páni* (m.); *bárish*; *menh*; *bárán*, (Persian.) V. –*hona*; *barasna*. –y, *páni ka*. a – day, *páni ka din*. the –y weather, *barsát*; *barsát ka mausim*. a storm of –, *jhari*. –coat, *báráni kurti*; if waterproofs, *barsáti kapre*. –pock, (in horses,) *barsáti*. –bow, *dhanak*, (m.).

Raise, *uthána*; *uthá-d*; *khara-k*. –crop, &c. *upjána*.

Raisins, *kishmish*.

Ram, (n.) *bhera*. (v.) *thásna*; *thelna*. –mer, *durmus*. – rod, *bandúk ka gaz*.

Random, at, *ittifákan*; *be-andáz*; *be-tadbír*.

Rank, (position,) *jagah*, (f.); *darjah*; *martabah*. high –, *shán*, (f.); *sar-farázi*; *shaukat*.

Rap, (v.) (at door,) *thonkna*. *See* 'Strike.'

Rapid. *See* 'Quick.'

Rare, *kam*; *jo kam dekhne men* (or *háth men*.) *-áta hai*. N. –*i*.

Rascal, *bad-zát*; *harám-zádah*. –ity, *bad-záti*; *harám-zádagi*. Adv. with *se*.

Rash, *be-liház*; *be-tadbír*. –ness, –*i*. Adv., use the Adjs.

Rate, (n.). *See* 'Price,' 'Market.' (v.) *gáli-d*.

Rather, with *se*. I would rather sleep than eat, *nínd karna mujh-ko pasand hai khána kháne se*. *See* 'Prefer.' (somewhat,) *kuchh-kuchh*.

Raw, *kachcha*. N. *kachá,i*.

Reach. *See* 'Arrive.' 'Power.'

Read, *paṛhna*. –to one, *paṛh-sunána*. –er, *paṛhne-wála*. read, *paṛhá-húʼa*. a –ing, *paṛháʼi*. –ing and writing, (reversed,) *likhni-paṛhni*.

Ready, *taiyár*. –iness, –*i*. V. –*k*.

Real, *asl ; ḥaḳiḳi ; sachcha*. –ity, *ḥaḳiḳat ; asl ḥál*. –ly, *albattah*. (interj.) really now ! *sach bát !* (interrogatively.)

Reap, (lit.) *káṭna ; kaṭni-k*. (fig.) *ḥásil-k*. –er, *kaṭwaiya ; káṭne-wála*. –ing hook, *haswa*, or *hasua*. –time, *kaṭáʼi*.

Reason, (for a thing,) *sabab ; wajh*, (f.). (mind,) *aḳl*, (f.) ; *hosh ; fahm*. –able, *maḳúl ; wájib ; muʼáfiḳ*. –ableness, *sháʼistagi ; maḳúliyat ; durusti ; aḳlmandi*. Adv. with *se*.

Rebel, (n.) *bág̲h̲i*. V. –*hona*. –lion, *bag̲h̲áwat*. –ious, *bág̲h̲i*.

Rebuke, *sar-zanish*.[1] V. –*k*. ; *dokhna ; ilzám-d*.

Receive, *lena ; ḳabúl-k*. ; *milna*. *See page* 50. (a person,) *áne-dena*. (a receipt,) *rasíd ; fárig̲h̲-k̲h̲atti*.

Recent, *nau ; thoṛe dinoṇ ka*, –ly, *thoṛe dinoṇ se ; ab*.

Reckon, *ginti-k*. ; *ginna ; shumár-k*. (fig.) *samajhna ; k̲h̲iyál-k ; ḳiyás-k*. –ing, *ginti ; ḥisáb-k*. (v.n.).

Recollection, *yád*, (f.). V. –*k*. to recollect oneself, *hosh ḳáʼim rakhna ; nahíṇ ghabrána*.

Recommendation, *sifárish*. V. –*k*. a letter of –, –*ka k̲h̲att*.

Recompense. *See* 'Reward'.

Reconcile, *milána ; milá-d*. ; *sulḥ-k*. ; *tasfiyah*, (or *tasfiʼah*)-*k*. N. *mel ; miláʼo ; sulḥ ; tasfiyah*. a deed of –iation, *sulḥ-námah*.

Record, (v.) *likhna*. (put aside in office,) *dák̲h̲il-k*. (n.) (bundle of papers,) *natthi ; misl*. (f.) ; *kág̲h̲azát* –room, *daftar ; daftar-k̲h̲ánah ; muḥáfiz-k̲h̲ánah*. –keeper, *muḥáfiz-i-daftar*, generally called '*muḥáfiz*' only.

[1] From '*sar*,' 'the head,' and Persian, '*zadan*,' 'to strike,' 'to punch.'

Recover, (thing lost,) *pána; milna.* (from illness,) *achchha,* or *bhala ho-jána.* –ery, (of a thing,) *pher-pana,* (v.n.) from illness, *achhá,i; bhalá,i; shifa.*

Recreation, *tafarruj.*

Red, *lál; surkh.* N. *surkhi.*

Redress, *insáf.* V. *–k.,* or *d.*

Reed, *nai; kalam.*

Reference, *zikr;* (v. *–k.*) (for, e. g. another person's opinion,) *ruju.* V. *–k.* 'I refer you to Mr. A.' *A. sáhib se púchhiye.*

Reflection, *soch; fikr,* (f.); *andeshah; ta,ammul.* V. *–k.; sochna; fikrmand hona.*

Refrain, *nahíṇ karna; parhez-k.; báz rahna.*

Refreshment, (by rest.) *árám; ráhat; ásúdagi.* (by food,) *kuchh khána; tífin; jalpán.* V. *árám, &c. lena; kuchh kháne ki chíz lena.* (by amusement,) *bahlána; khush-k.; tamásha dekhna.*

Refuge, *ásra; ot; panáh; ár.* to give –, *d.*

Refusal, *inkár; ná-manzúri;* V. *–k.*

Refuse, (n.) *ákhor; fuzlah.*

Refutation, *radd,* (v. *–k.*); *jawáb.* (v. *–d.*).

Regard. *See* 'Look,' 'Respect.' I regard him as a father, *báp ki tarah, maiṇ uska liház karta húṇ.*

Regiment, *paltan,*(f.); *salári.*

Region, *mulk; jagah,* (f.); *nawáh; taraf,* (f.), or, Pl. *atráf.*

Register, registration; registrar, these words are represented by various corruptions of the English, which must be locally picked up: Vernacular words for similar matters will be found under 'Record.'

Regret, *afsos; hasrat;* (strong,) *soz.* V. *–k.; –khána; pachhtána.*

Regular; (in routine,) *hasb káidah; hasb zábitah; dastúr ke mu,áfik.* –ity, (in work, &c.) *intizám; band-o-bast,* (m.). *tartíb,* (f.); (as to time,) *bar-wakt, pahuṇchna, karna, &c.* a –lation, *á,ín; kánún; hukm.*

Rejection, *ná-manzúri; ná-pasand-k.*(v.n.) *wápas dena*

(v.n.) V. *ná-manzúr-k.*; *wápas-d.*; *ná-pasand-k.*; *pherna.* a rejected (article,) *phirta.*

Reign, *julús*; *saltanat*; *hukúmat*; *amaldári*; *bádsháhi*; *ráj.* V. –*k.* in the reign of A., *bádsháh A. ke aiyám*[1] *men*, or *julús men.*

Reins, *rás*, (f.); *bág*, (f.). V. –*khínchna*; –*khara-k.* to put on the –, –*lagá-d.* (loins,) *kamar*, (f.).

Rejoice, *khush-hona*; *ríjhna*; *shádmán-hona.*

Relate. *See* 'Tell,' 'Connection.'

Release, (n.) *rihá,i*; *khalás*; *khalási*; *chhutti.* V. –*d.*; *chhor-d.*

Relief, *árám.* V. –*d.* (of a guard,) *badli.* V. *badal-k.*

Religion, *dín*; *mazhab.* –gious, *dín-dár.* –giousness, *dín-dári*; *khudá-tarsi.*

Relinquish. *See* 'Abandon.'

Relish, (n.) *zá,ikah*; *mazah*; *niimat ki chíz.* V. *lazíz-k.*; *khush-zá,ikah se khána.*

Remain, (stay,) *rahna*; *thaharna*; *sabr-k.* (be over,) *báki-hona*; *bachna.*

Remains, (of food, &c.) *jo bacha*, or *báki hai*; *ákhor*; *fuzlah.* (mortal,) *murdah*; *lásh*, (f.).

Remark. *See* 'Say,' 'Word,' &c. –able, *ajíb*; *ajúbah.*

Remedy, *iláj*; *upá,e*; *tadbír*, (f.); *chárah.* V.–*k.*;–*batlána.*

Remember, *khátir men rakhna*; *yád men hona.* to call to mind, *yád-k.*; *chetna.* (to cause a person to –,) *yád dilána.* N. *yád*, (f.).

Remind, *yád dilána.*

Remit, (a portion,) *ghatána*; *ghatá-d.*; *kam-k.* (the whole, a penalty, &c.) *mu,áf-k.* –ting, *by v.n.* –tance, *chalán*; *irsál.*

Remove, (*trans.*) *le-jána*; *dúr-k.*; *hatá-d.*; *nikál-d.* (*intr.*) *jána*; *chalá-jána*; *uth-jána*; *hat-jána.* (one from service,) *rukhsat-d.*; *bar-khást-k.*; *maazúl-k.*; (in a coarse way) *nikál-d.*[2] N. *by v.n.*; *dusrí jagah jána.*

---

[1] i.e., *times*, Pl. of '*yaum*,' which is also Hebrew.

[2] Equivalent to our colloquial, '*kick him out.*'

Render. *See* 'Give,' 'Translate.'

Renounce. *See* 'Abandon.'

Renown. *See* 'Fame.'

Rent, (house, shop, &c.) *kiráyah.* (land,) *mál-guzári ; jama ; khazánah ; khiráj.* -free, *lá-khiráj.* rate of –, *nirkh ; sharah.* -roll, *jama-bandi.*

Repairs, -ing, *marammat.* V. *-k.*

Repeat, '*phir.*' or '*pher,*' with appropriate verb. e.g. *phir kahiye,* please say it again. repetition, *by v.n.* -edly, *aksar ; bahut dafe.*

Repent. *See* 'Regret.' -ance, *nadámat.* -ant, *pashemán.*

Reply. *See* 'Answer.'

Report. *See* 'Inform.' -of a gun, *bharáka* -of an occurrence, *khabar ;* (if detailed) *súrat hál.*[1]

Repose, (rest,) *árám ; ráhat ; farághat.* (sleep.) *nínd.* V. *-lena. ; letna ; sona.*

Reprimand. *See* 'Rebuke.'

Reproach, *tan ; tanah.* -ing, *tana-zani.* V. *-k.*

Reproof. *See* 'Rebuke.

Reptile, *kíra ; kirm.*

Reputation, (general,) *nám.* (good,) *nek-námi.* (bad,) *bad-námi.* V. *jánna; ginna.*

Request. *See* 'Petition.'

Require, (desire,) *cháhna.* (a person to do a thing,) *hukm-d.* (to be in need of,) *by hona* and the 3rd Person, e.g., I require a watch, *mujh-ko ghari zarúr,* or *darkár hai.* as may be required, *jaisa zarúr hoga.* -sition, *talab ; iltija,* (f.) ; *hukm.*

Rescue. *See* 'Save,' 'Protect

Resemblance, *musһábih*, *mushábahat.* he resembles his father, *wuh apne báp ka mushábih hai.*

Reservoir, *hauz ; táláb,* (m.) ; *khazánah ; pokhar.*

Resident. *See* 'Inhabitant.'

Resign. *See* 'Abandon.'

Resin, *dhúna.*

Resistance, *rok-tok ; muzáhamat.* V. *-k.*

Resolve. *See* 'Intend.' -lute, *mustakill.*

---

[1] A technical phrase ; properly '*súrat-i-hál,*'='appearance of the event,' a formal report drawn by an investigating officer.

Respect, (v.) *azíz-rakhna; izzat-d.; baṛa jánna*, to pay one's –s, *kisi ki tazím-k; ádáb bajá-lána; salám-k.* (n.) *adab, izzat.* act of showing –, *tazím*, (f.). in all –s, *ba-har-súrat.* in this –, *is amr meṇ kih,* &c.; *is báre meṇ.* –able, *achchha; bhala; mutabar; izzat-dár; wájib-ut-tazím.* –ful, *mu,addab.*

Rest. *See* 'Repose,' 'Remains.' the rest, (people,) *aur sab log.* (things,) *jo báḳi-hai.* –less, *be-árám; be-ḳarár.* –lessness, *be-árámi; be-ḳarári.*

Restrain, *rokna; aṭkána; báz-rakhna; chheṇkna.* –t, *rok; aṭká,o; muzáḥamat.*

Result, *natíjah; ḥásil; phal; nikás; ákhir.* V. these words and *hona:* The enquiry has resulted thus, *taḥḳíḳát ka natíjah yih hai, kih,* &c.

Resurrection, the, *ḳiyámat.*

Retain. *See* 'Keep.' -er, *tábidár.*

Retire, *játa rahna. See* 'Go away, –d, *chhipa.* –ment, *khalwat.*

Retreat, (e.g. of an army,) (n.) *pahlu-tihi.* V. –*k.* (place of private –,) *khalwat-gáh.*

Return, (go, or come back,) *pher-ána; pher-jána; phirna; lauṭna.* (give back,) *wápas-d.* N. *by v. n.* –ed, *phirta; phirta hú,a.*

Revenge, *intiḳám.* V. –*lena.*

Revenue, *khiráj; ámadani; ámad.* (f.). –free, *lá-khiráj.*

Reverence. *See* 'Respect.'

Reward, *inám; bakhshish.* V. *d.; bakhshna.*

Rheumatism, *bá,i.*

Rhinoceros, *gaiṇḍa.* –horn, *khág.*

Rib, *panjari.*

Rice, (in field or husk,) *dhán.* (cleaned, but dry,) *cháwal.* (cooked,) *bhát.*

Riches, *daulat; mál; dhan.* rich, *daulat-mand; dhani.*

Ride, (v.) *sawár-hona; sawári-k.* –ing, *sawári.* a ride, *ghoṛe par hawa khána.* v. n. –er, *sawár.*

Right, (a.) (done well,) *ṭhík; durust; achchha bhala.* (just,) *wájib; nek; ḥaḳḳ ke mu,áfiḳ.* on, *or* to the

–hand, *dáhine*. (n.) *insáf; ḥaḳḳ*. –or wrong, *ḥaḳḳ ná-ḥaḳḳ*. to put –, *durust-k*. –eous, *nek; sádiḳ; musalli*. –ful, *mustaḥaḳḳ*.

Rind, *chhilka*, to take off the –, *chhílna ; chhilka utárna*.

Ring, (v.) (*trans.*) *bajána*. (*intr.*) *bajna*. (n.) *aṇgúṭhi ; angushtari*. (circle,) *dá,irah*.

Riot, *hangámah ; balwa*. V. –*k*. –er, *guhár-log*. –ous, *hangámah kar-ke*.

Ripe, *pakka ; pukhtah*. -en, (*trans.*) *pakána*. (*intr.*) *pakna*. –ness, *taiyári ; pakká,i*.

Rise, *uṭhna; uṭh-jána*. (stand up,) *khaṛa-hona*. (in life,) *baṛhna ; baṛa-hona ; taraḳḳi pána*. (ascend,) *chaṛhna*. (in rebellion,) *balwa-k*. (as plants,) *upajna*. (as bread,) *sújna*. (in price.) *is-ki ḳímat baṛh-ga,i hai*.

Risk, *khatrah*. to run –, –*uṭhána*.

Rival, *ḥaríf; raḳíb*. –ry, *riḳábat*. V. -*k*.

Road, *ráh*, or *rah*, (f.); *rásta*. high–, *saṛak*, (f.). (lane,) *gali*.

Roar, (n.) *ghurrish*. (v.) *ghurrána*.

Roast, (n.) *rost*, (E.); *kabáb*. V. –*k*.

Rob, *lúṭna ; lúṭ-lena*. –ber, *rah-zan*. gang –ber, *ḍakait*. –bery, *rah-zani*. (by a gang,) *ḍáka ; ḍakaiti*. a robbery took place, *ḍáka paṛa*.

Rock, (n.) *patthar ; sang*. (v.) (*trans.*) *hilána ; jhulána*. (*intr.*) *hilna ; jhúlna*.

Roll, (v.) (*trans.*) *lapeṭna*. (*intr.*) *loṭna*. (from side to side,) *loṭ-poṭ-k*. (n.) (e.g. of paper,) *bínḍa*. (rolling about,) *loṭ-poṭ*. dinner–, *rol*, (E.).

Roof, *chhappar*, (f.) ; *chhat*.

Room, a, *kamrah ; koṭhi;* as last part in compos:... *khánah*. (space,) *jagah*, (f.) (stead,) *iwaz*, or *ewaz*. –y, *khula ; kushádah ; baṛa*.

Root, (n.) *jaṛ ;* (fig.) *asl ; jaṛ; bunyád*, (f.). to –up, *ukháṛna*. to take–, *jaṛ pakaṛna*. – and branch, *bil-kull*.

Rope, *rassi ; ḍori*. to–, –*lagá-d. ; –se bándh-d*.

Rosary, *tasbíḥ*, (f.).

Rose, *gul; guláb; gul-áb-*[1] *phúl.* otto of–, *itr-i-guláb.* –bush, *guláb gáchh.* –garden, *gul-istán.* –water, *gul-áb.* –y, *gul-rang.*

Rot, *saṛna.* –ten, *saṛa.* –tenness, *saṛáhind.*

Rough, *kharkhara,* –ness, *kharkaráhaṭ.*

Round, (spherical,) *gol.* to make –, *–k.* (circle,) *dá,irah; ghera.* to put anything – another, *gher-k.* to go a–, *ghum ho-ke jána.* to go –s, (as an officer,) *roungasht-k.* (half E.), all –, *har taraf.* –ness, *gol-shakl,* (f.).

Row, (line,) *ḳatár,* (f.). *See* 'Riot.'

Royal, *sháhi.* –ty, *bádsháhi.* the–family, *kh̲ándán-i-sháhi.*

Rub, (*intr.*) *ragaṛ-k.* (*trans.*) *malna; málish-k.* N. (scraping,) *ragaṛ.* (e.g. with hands,) *málish.* a thing for rubbing body with, *khísah.*

Rubbish, *kurkuṭ; kúṛa; rábish,* (E.)

Ruby, *yáḳút; lál.*

Rude, *gustákh̲; be-adab.* –ness, *–i; –i.* Adv. with *se.*

Rue, (n.) *sudáb.* (v.) *ta,assuf-k.*

Rug, *kammal,* (f.); *kamli.*

Ruin, *kh̲arábi; tabáhi; pareshání.* V. *–k.* a –, *khanḍar.* –ed, *be-marammat; shikastah; ṭúṭa-phúṭa.*

Rule. *See* 'Government.' –er, (for desk,) *mistar.* to –paper, *satar-khaiṇchna.*

Rumour, *afwáh; hawara.*

Run, *dauṛna.* (as time,) *bít-jána.* (as water,) *bahna.* –out, (as water,) *chúna; ṭapakna.* –out, (go done,) *kam hona; ghaṭna.* –away, *bhág-jána.* cause to –, *dauṛána; dauṛa-d*

Rust, *zang; morchah* –y, *zang-álúdah.* This has turned rusty, *is-par zang laga hai.*

S.

Sabre, *shamsher,* (f.)

Sack, (n.) *bora.* (v.) *lúṭna.*

Sacred, *muḳaddas.* a –place, *maḳdis.*

---

[1] See Glossary, Part I. 'A'b.

Sacrifice, *ḳurbán*. V.–*k*. self–, *nisár*. V. –*k*.

Sad, *udás; ghamm-gín; afsurdah*. to –den, –*k*, –ness, *udási; afsurdagi; ghamm*.

Saddle, *zín*, (f.). V. –*bándh-d*. –cloth, –*posh*. –horse, *sawári ká ghoṛa*. saddler, *zíngar; mochi*.

Safe, *mámún; salámat*. N. *salámat; bachá,o; itmínán*. (hanging.) *ḍoli*. –ly, *ba-khair*. *See* 'Save.'

Saffron, *zafarán*.

Sagacity. *See* 'Intelligence.'

Sago, *ságu*.

Sail, (n.) *pál*. (v.) *jaház meṇ chalna*.

Saint, *wali; pír*. the –s, *auliya*.

Salad, *salád*, (E.); *sabzi*.

Salary. See 'Pay.'

Saliva, *thúk*.

Salt, *namak*. –dish, –*dán*. –spoon, –*ka chammach*, or *chamcha*. –petre, *shorah*.

Salutation. *See page* 75.

Same, *ek; ek-hi; eksán; ek ḳism ka; barábar*. this –, *yihi*, that –, *wuhi*. in compos: *ham*. this is the same as that, *yih aur wuh ek-hi haiṇ*. They both arrived on the same day, *we donoṇ ek roz pahuṇche*.

Sample, *namúnah*.

Sand, *ret; reg; bálu*. –bank, *char*. –y, *balu,a*.

Sandal, *sandal*.

Sapphire, *níl-mani*.

Satan, *Shaitán; Iblís*.

Satin, *atlas*.

Satisfaction. *dil-tashaffi; khátir-jami; taskín*. to feel- –*rakhna*. –tory *pasand; achha; khúb*. –fied, *rázi; khush*. V. –*k*.

Saturday, *Sanibár; Saníchar*.

Savage, (a.) *jangli*. (n.) – *ádmi*. *See* 'Cruel.'

Sauce, *sás*, (E.). –pan, *sás-pán*. (E.).

Saucer, *pirich*.

Save. *See* 'Rescue.' to – money, &c., *rúpíye, mál, &c., jama-k*.

Sausage, *sassich*, (E.); *ḳulma*.

Saw, (n.) *ára*. (v.) *áre se chírna*, or *káṭna*. –dust, *búra*. –yer, *árá-kash*.

Say, (speak,) *bolna*, (tell,) *kahna*. people –, *khabar hai; hawara hai*. a –ing *bát; kaha; bayán*. it is commonly said, *aksar sunne meṇ áta hai.*

Scaffold, *machán.*

Scale, (balance,) *tarázu.* (degrees,) *silsilah.*

Scanty, *kam.* N. *-í.*

Scare. *See* 'Frighten.' -crow, *bijh-gáh.*

Scarf, *oṛhni.*

Scatter, *chhitrána;chhiṭkána.*

Scene, (view,) *madd-i-nazar.* (arena,) *akháṛa; khet; maidán.* (show), *tamásha.*

Scent. *See* 'Perfume.'

Scheme, *ḥikmat; tadbír*, (f.); *khayál; mansúbah.*

Scholar, (pupil,) *shágird;* (learned person,) *álim-o-fázil ádmi; maulavi*, (M.); *panḍit*, (H.). -ship, *ilm.* (m.).

School, *ishkúl*, (E.); *maktab-khánah; páṭ-sála.* -master, *ishkúl-másṭar*, (E.). *ustád; guru; mu,allim.*

Scissors, *ḳaiṇchi; miḳráz.*

Scold, (n.) *ranḍi.* -ing, a, *jhiṛki; gáli.* V. *-d.; jhiṛakna.*

Scorpion, *bichchhu.*

Scoundrel. *See* 'Rascal.'

Scrape, (rasp,) *ragaṛna.* (e.g. off rind,) *chhílna; chhíl-d.*

Scratch, (n.) *kharásh.* (v.) *khujlána.*

Scream, (n.) *chilláhaṭ.* V. *chillána; chíkhna.*

Screen, *pardah; ṭaṭṭi; jhámp.*[1] V. *-lagá-d.;* (fig.) *bachána; panáh-d. rúposh rakhna.*

Screw, *iskru*, (E.); *pech; marori.* V. *-d.*

Scruple, *pas-o-pesh; waswás; shakk.* V. *-k.* he overcame my scruples, *us-ne mera pas-o-pesh dabáya.*

Scrutinize. *See* 'Examine.'

Scullion, *mashálchi.*

Scum, *kaf.* V. *-le-jána.*

Sea, *samundar; darya; kála páni.* (m).

Seal, *muhr; chháp.* V. *-lagá-d.* -ed, *makhtúm.* -ing-wax, *lákh.* a stick of -ing-wax, *lákh ki batti.*

Seam, *dokht; joṛ.*

Search, *talásh; khoj; ḍhúnḍh; just-o-ju*, (f.). V. *-k.; taláshna; khojna; ḍhúnḍhna.* -er, with '*jo.*'

---

[1] This is generally moveable; put on and taken off, like shop-shutters.

Season, *mausam*. *See page* 80. –ing, *masálaḥ*. V. *–d*.

Seat, (of body,) *ásan; chútaṛ*. (for sitting on,) *ásan; baiṭhak*, (f.); *chauki; kursi*. to have a good – on a horse, *ásan márna*. (v.) *biṭhána* or *baiṭhána*.

Second, (number,) *dúsra; sáni; doyum*. (time,) *laḥzah*. (v.) *madad-d.; iánat-d.* –ly, *doyum; dúsra yih hai, &c.*

Secret, (n.) *bhed; ráz*, (m.). –crecy, *ráz-dári*. (a.) *poshídah; chhipa; ghá,ib*. –e, *chhipána*. –ly, *chhip-ke*.

Section, *fasl; dafa; jumlah*.

Secure. *See* 'Safe.'

Sedition. *See* 'Revolt.'

See, *dekhna; nazar-k.; tákna*. to be able to –, *sújhna*. (eye-sight,) *sújh*, (f.). –ing, *nazar-k*. (v.n.) –ing that, *chunánchi; chúṇkih*.

Seed, (n.) *bíya; bíj*. –ling, *chára; bíhan*. *–plot, bíhan ka takhtah*. –time, *bone ke din*. –pearl, *rez-i-moti*.

Seek. *See* 'Search.'

Seem. *See* 'Like.' it seems, *maalúm hota hai*. –ingly, *dekhne meṇ*.

Seize, *pakaṛna; pakaṛ-lejána; girift*, or *giriftár-k*. (confiscate,) *zabt-k*. –ure, *pakaṛ*, (f.); *zabti*. (by illness,) *ámad*, (f.).

Seldom, *kam; thoṛe waḳt*.

Select. *See* 'Choose.' 'Extract.'

Self. *See page* 30. –conceit, *khud-pasandi*. –defence, *ḥifázat-i-khud*. –denial, *nisár*. –evident, *khud-záhir*. –interest, *khud-gharazi*, (f.). –ish, *khud-gharz*. –ishly, *khud-gharzi-se*. –murder, *khud-kushi*. –will, *sar-kashi*.

Sell, *bechna; farokht-k*. to be sold, *bikna*. –er, *bá,i; bechwaiya; bechne-wála*; as last part in compos:... *farosh*. buying and –ing, *kharíd-farokht*.[1]

Semi, *nisf; ním; adh; ádh*.

Send, *bhejna*; (goods, &c.), *chálán*, or *rawánah-k*. –for, *bulána; talab-k*.

Sense. *See* 'Intelligence,' 'Meaning.'

---

[1] From the Persian, '*kharídan*,' 'to buy,' and '*farokhtan*,' 'to sell.'

Sentence. *See* 'Decision.' –of book, &c., *jumlah.*

Sentinel, *pás-bán; pahre-wála.*

Separation, *judá,i; mufára-ḳat.* A. *juda; alag; alá-ḥidah; mutafarraḳ.* V. *karna* with the adjs. –ly, *juda-juda; alag-alag; ek-ek.* (by kinds,) *jinswára.*

Sergeant, *dafa-dár; jama-dár; sárjan sáḥib* (half E.).

Serious, *wazani; bhári.* (as injury,) *shadíd.* (of disposition,) *sanjídah.* –ness, *sanjídagi.*

Sermon, *waz.*

Serpent, *sámp; nág.*

Servant, *naukar; chákar; khidmat-gár; mulázim.* the –s, *naukar log. See page* 35. V. *naukari,* or *khidmat-k.* –viceable, *kám ka; mufíd.*

Set, (v.) *See* 'Place.' one's set, *barádari;*[1] *ham-zát; taraf-dárán; dostán.*

Settle, (in a place,) *basána; búd-o-básh-k.* (a dispute,) *tai-k.; miṭa-d.* (an account,) *adá-k.* (in life,) *sar-khud-k.* –ment, *band-o-bast.* –r, *khud-básh.*

Several, *baaze; chand; ko,i ek.* –ly, *ek-ek; juda-juda.*

Severe, *sakht.* –rity, *sakhti.*

Sew, *sína; silá,i-k.* –ing, *silá,i.*

Shade, *sáyah.* lamp –, *fánús.* V. –*d.* –dy, *sáyadár.*

Shadow, *aks; sáya. See* 'Shelter.'

Shake, (*trans.*) *hilána; hilá-d.* (*intr.*) *hilna.* N. *hilá,o.* (tremble,) *kámpna.*

Shallow, (a) *uthla.* (n.) *uthlá,i.*

Shame, *sharm,* (f.); *sharm-indagi; láj,* (f.); *ḥaya,* (f.). to feel –, *lajána.* to put to –, *lajwána.* –faced, *sharm-ru.* –ed, *sharm-sár.* –ful, *mayúb.* –fully, *sharm-se.* (badly,) *bahut kharáb taur se.* –less, –lessly, *b sharm.*

Shape, (n.) *shakl,* (f.); *ḍaul; súrat.* (v.) *banána.* –less, *be-ḍaul.* –ly, *khúb-súrat; sú-ḍaul.*

Share, (v.) *bánṭna; taḳsím-k.; ḥissah-d.* (n.) *ḥissah ḥaḳḳ; ḳismat.* –r, *ḥissa-dár; sharík; bhági.*

Sharp, *tez.* (v. –*k.*). (in point,) *nokíla.* –ness, *tezi.*

---

[1] From the Persian '*barádar,*' 'a brother.'

Shave, *ḥajámat-k.*; *múṇḍna.* –n, *muṇḍla.* a–ing, *chhílan*; *chhilka.*

Shawl, *shál.*

She, *yih*; *wuh. See page* 30.

Sheep, a, *bheṛi.* sheep, *bheṛi,-án.* a flock of –, *bheṛioṇ ka gallah.* –fold, *bheṛi-sála.* shepherd, *bheṛi-wála.*

Sheet, *chádar*, (f.). –of paper, *kág̲h̲az ka tak̲h̲tah.*

Shell, *chhilka.* V. –, *–utár-d.*

Shelter, (n.) *panáh*, (f.); *áṛ*; *sáyah.* V. *–d.*

Sheriff, *názir*; *sherif sáḥib.* (half E.).

Shield, (n.) *ḍhál*, (f.); *sipar.* V. *See* 'Protect.'

Shine, *chamakna*; *raushan-h.*

Ship, *jaház.* V. *–meṇ chaṛhna*, or *chaṛhána.* –master, *sáḥib-i–.* wreck, *–shikani.*

Shirt, *ḳamís*, (f.).

Shock. *See* 'Blow.' (offend,) *chiṛhána.* –ing, –ingly, *bahut k̲h̲aráb.*

Shoe, *júti.* horse –, *nál.* –maker, *júti-wála*; *mochi.* –ing a horse, *nál-bandi.* V. *-k. See page* 90.

Shoot, *chalána*, with the name of the weapon before it, as, *bandúḳ*, (f.) a gun, *tír*, (m.) an arrow. to – rubbish, *kúṛa pheṇkna*, or *ḍálna.* to– as plants, *upajna.*

Shop, *dúkán*, (f.). –keeper, *–dár*, –keeping, *–dári.*

Shore, *kinárah*; *pár.*

Short, *kotáh*, *chhoṭa.* N. *kotáhi*; *chhoṭá,i.* in –, *al-ḳissah*; *alg̲h̲araz.* –en, *–k.* –ly, (soon,) *thoṛi der ke baad*; *jald.* put –ly, *muk̲h̲tasar.*

Shot, (for gun,) *chharra.* gun–, *choṭ.*

Shoulder, *káṇdha.*

Shout, (n.) *shor*; *baland áwáz.* (v.) *pukárna*; *chil-lána*; *lalkárna.*

Show, (n.) *tamásha.* (v.) *dikhlána*; *dikhlá-d.*; *bat-lána*; *batlá-d.*; *záhir-k.*

Shower, *jhaṛi*; *barkha.*

Shrimps, *chiṇgṛi.*

Shrine, *dargáh.*

Shroud, *kafan.* V. *–lagá-d.*

Shun, *kisi se alag-rahna.*

Shut, (a.) *band*; *lagá hú,a.* V. *band-k.*; *lagá-d.* –ter, (venetian,) *jhilmili*; (of bamboo,) *jhámp*; *ṭaṭṭi*; (of wood,) *kapáṭ.*

Sick, *bímár*; *rogi*; *maríz.*

V. *-hona.* -ness, *bímári; rog.* -ly, *sust; káhil* or *káhilah; kam-zor.*

Sickle, *hasú a,* or *haswa.*

Side, *taraf,* (f.); *baghal,* (f.); *páṇjar; jánib; bázu.* (e.g. of a river,) *kinárah.* this-, *is taraf.* that -, *us taraf; pár.* on all -s, *cháron taraf.* to - with, *taraf-dár hona; taraf-kashi-k.* to - against, *dusri taraf lena; mukhtalif hona.*

Sieve, *ghirbál,* (f.); *chalni.* to pass through a-, (*trans.*) *chhánna.*

Sigh, (n.) *áh,* (f.). V. *-khaiṇch-na.*

Sight, *nazar,* (f.); *basárat; sújh.* (spectacle,) *tamásha.*

Sign, (n.) (indication,) *ishárah.* (signal,) *nishán.* V. *-k.; -d.*

Signature, *saḥiḥ; dast-khatt.* V. *-d.; -k.*

Signify. *See* 'Mean.'

Silence, *khámoshi.* V. *-rakh-na; chup rahna.* A. *chup; chup-cháp; khámosh;* (for want of having any reply,) *lá-jawáb.* Interj. *chup! chup raho!* Adv. *chup-ke.*

Silk, *resham.* -en, *-ka; -i.*

Silly, *sádah; múrakh.* N. *sádagi; múrakh-pan.* a -fellow, *sádah lauḥ.*

Silver, *rúpa; cháṇdi.* A. *-ka.*

Simple, (single,) *kháli.* (easy,) *sahl; salís.* (plain,) *sádah.* (in mind,) *gharíb; rást; nek.* -plicity, '*jo*' with these adjs. -ply, *sirf; kháli; fakat.*

Sin, *páp; gunáh.* A., also a -ner, *gunáh-gár.* V. *-k.*

Since, (time,) *jab-se*[1]...*tab-se;*[2] *se.* (cause,) *chúṇ-kih*[1]...*is-wáste.*[2]

Sincere, *rást; nek; sach.* -cerity. *rásti; neki; sachá,i.* -ly, with *se.*

Sinew, *nas,* (f.).

Single, singular, *ek; akela; tanha.* -ly, *ek-ek.*

Sink, (*trans.*) *ḍubá-d.* (*intr.*) *ḍúbna.*

Sir, *miyáṇ; sáḥib; khudá-wand.*

Sister, *bahin.* -in-law, (a man's wife's sister,) *sáli.*

---

[1] In the first clause. [2] In the second clause. *See page* 104.

(a man's brother's wife,) *bhojá,i.* (a woman's husband's sister,) *nanad ; nanand* (a woman's brother's wife,) *bháwaj.*

Sit, *baiṭhna.*

Size, *ḳadar,* (f.) ; *miḳdár.*

Skill, *shu,úr ; hunar ; ilm ; wuḳúf.* –ful, *hunar-mand ; máhir.* –fully, by *se.*

Skirt, *dáman.*

Skull, *khopri ; kásah-e-sar.*

Sky, *ásmán.* –blue, *–rang.*

Slab, *chaṭán,* (f.) ; *sil.*

Slack, *ḍhíla,* (fig.) *sust; narm.* N. *ḍhíl ; susti ; narmi.*

Slander, *bad-námi; gáli ; tuhmat.* V. *–d.* –ous, *bad-nám, &c. ki bát.* –er, with *jo.* –ously, with *se.*

Slap, (n.) *tamáchah.* V. *–d.*

Slaughter, *ḳatl ; k͟hún-rezi.* (V. *–k.*) of animals, *zabḥ ; ḥalál.* V. *–k.* –er, (butcher,) *ḳassáb.* –house, *ḳassáb-k͟hánah.*

Slave, *chera ; launḍa ; bandah ; g͟hulám.* –ery,[1] *bandagi ; g͟hulámi.*

Sleep, *nínd,* (f.) ; *k͟hwáb.* V. *–k.* sleepy, *nindása.* I am very sleepy, *nínd karne ki k͟hwáhish hai.*

Sleeve, *ástín.*

Slender. *See* 'Thin.'

Slice, *salais,* (E.) ; *phánk ; ḳásh.* V. *táráshna ; káṭna.*

Slip, (v.) *khisakna.* (n.) (cover,) *g͟hiláf.* (mistake,) *bhúl ; chúk.* V. *–k.*

Slipper, *slipaṭ,* or *silpaṭ* (E.) ; *pá-posh.*

Slope, (n.) *ḍhálu.* V. (*trans.*) *–k.* –ing, *ḍhál.* to be –, *–hona.*

Slow, *tez nahín ; áhistah ; dhíma.* –ness, *áhistagi.* –ly, *áhiste ; áhiste-áhiste.*

Sly, *mutafanni ; makkár.* –ness, *ḥirfat.* Adv. with *se.*

Small, *chhoṭa ; k͟hurd.* –ness, *–ṭá,i ; k͟hurdi.* –pox, *sítla; chechak.*

Smell, *bu,* (f.) ; *súngh,* (f.). sweet–, *k͟hush-bu,* a nasty–, *bad-bu.* sense of –, *shámmah.* (v.) (*trans.*) *súnghna.* (*intr.*) *bu-d.* ; *bu ka kona.*

---

[1] All slavery, in India is *domestic* slavery; to which our harsh words '*slave*' and '*slavery*' are hardly applicable.

Smile, (n.) *tabassum* V. *-k.*

Smith, (iron,) *lohár.* (gold, &c.,) *sonár ; zar-gar.*

Smoke, (n.) *dhú,áṇ.* V. (*intr.*) *-nikalna.* to-tobacco, &c., *tambáku, &c. pína.*

Smooth, *chikna; samán; barábar; musattah,* V.*-k.* -ness, *chikná,i; barábari.*

Snaffle, (bridle,) *ḳazai.*

Snake, *sámp ; nág ; már,* (Persian.) there are many kinds ; of which the worst are the *guhmanah,* cobra-di capello, and the '*karait.*' which has no English name known to the Author.-of a '*ḥuḳḳah,*' i.e. native (smoking) pipe, *naichah.*

Snare, *phánda ; dám.* V. *phándna ; phánde meṇ pakaṛna.*

Sneeze, (n.) *chhíṇk.* V. *-na.*

Snipe, *cháha.*

Snoring, (n.), *kharráṭa.* V. *-márna ; nák kharkharána,* or *bajána.*

Snow, *barf.* V. *-girti hai.*

Snuff, *súṇgni.* V. *-khaiṇchna.*

So, (therefore,) *pas.* (manner,) *aisa ; jaisa...taisa.* (page 104) ; *is-taraḥ.* (degree,) *is ḳadar ; itna ; eta.* so-so, *aisa-waisa.* Mr. So-and So, *fulánah ; fulánah ádmi.* it may be -, *wuh ho-sakta hai ; so hoga.*

Soak, (*trans.*) *bhíṇga-k.* (*intr.*) *sokna.* -ing, (very wet,) *khúb bhíṇga.*

Soap, *sábún.* V. *-lagána.*

Sob, *ṭhunuk,* (f.). V. *-na. -k.*

Sober, *parhez-gár.* -briety, *parhez,* (f.).

Sock, *mozah ; sák,* (E.).

Socket, ...*dán,* (page 41.); *khánah ; ghar.*

Sofa, *suffah ; kauch,* (E.).

Soft, *narm ; mulá,im.* N. *-í.* -ly, *dhíme-dhíme ; áhiste.*

Soldier, *sipáhi.* native -s, *sipáhi,án.* European ditto, *gore log.* a regiment of -s, *palṭan,* (f.).

Sole. *See* 'Alone.'

Solemn, *sanjídah.* -ity, *-jídagi.*

Solid, (not liquid,) *munjamid.* (firm,) *sakht ; mazbút ; ḳá,im ; pukhtah.* -ity, *sakhti ; mazbúti; pukhtagi.*

Solitary. *See* 'Alone.' -tude, *tanhá,i ; khalwat.*

Some, (of things,); *kuchh; kuchh-kuchh; thoṛa; zarrah-sa.* (of persons,) *ko,i.* –one or other, *ko,i-nah-ko,i.* –more, *aur kuchh.* –times, *baaze waḳt; kabhi-kabhi.* –where, *kahin̤.*

Son, *beta; laṛka; bachcha; pisar,* (p.). –in-law, *dámád.*

Song, *gít.* V. *gána; gún̤-gán̤-k.*

Soon, *jald; ab; thoṛi der ke baad.* as – as, *jab...tab; te-hi.* (*See page* 14) –er, *paihle; us ke áge.* no sooner ...than... *nahín páya, kih.* e.g. his order no sooner reached me, than I carried it out, *us-ka ḥukm mere pás pahun̤chne nahin̤ páya, kih main̤-ne usko taamíl kiya.*

Soreness, *dard,* (m.). to be sore. *–k.* a–, *ghá,o; zak͟hm; násúr; phaphola.*

Sorrow, *afsos; g͟hamm; ranj.* A. *afsurdah; ázurdah; g͟hamgín; ranjídah.* to be –ful, *afsos, &c. khána;* adjs. and *hona.* sorry, *pashemán.* I am very sorry I am late, *afsos hai kih main̤-ne der ki hai.* (use-less,) *ná-kára; ná-chíz; kamínah.*

Sort. *See* 'Kind.' *ḳism.* V. *ṭhík-k.; tartíb-k.; sudhár-na; sab chízon̤ ko apni jaghon̤ men̤ rakhna.*

Soul, *rúḥ,* (f.); *nafs; ján; ji.* with heart and –, *dil-o-ján-se.*

Sound, (n.) *sabd; áwáz,* (f.); *shor; shor-shár; hab-gab; háon̤-ghdon̤.* (of fire-arms,) *dhán̤-dhún̤.* V. *–k.; pu-kárna; chillána.* (any instrument,) *bajána.* (*intr.*) *sabd, &c. d.; bajna.* –in health, *tan-durust.* to be ditto, *tan-durust hona.* –ness of health, *tan-durusti.* –in quality, *mazbút; puk͟htah; be-aib; mustaḥkam.* –ness of ditto, *mazbúti; puk͟hta-gi.* -as a business, *pakka; ṭhík; sab achchha.* a– e.g. thrashing, *k͟hūb saza (dena, pána,).*

Soup, *shorbah,* corruptly, *shurwah.*

Sour, *khaṭṭa; tursh.* N. *tur-shi.* to turn –, *k͟haṭṭa ho-jána.*

South, *dakhan; janúb*

Sow, (n.) *sú,ári.*
Sow, (v.) *bona ; rompna.* –ing, *bo,á,i.*
Space, (time,) *arsah ; muddat.* (place,) *jagah,* (f.) ; *fásilah.* –cious, *khula ; farákh.*
Spade, *kudáli ; bel ; belchah.*
Span, (of hand,) *bálisht ; wajab.* (arch,) *mihráb.*
Spare. *See* 'Thin' (excess,) *barhtı ; fáltu.* (v.) (e. g. life,) *bachána.* (give,) *de-d.* –time, *fursat.* a –liver, *parhez-gár.* N.–*i.*
Sparrow, *ghauriya.*
Speak, *bolna ; kahna ; bhákhna.* (converse,) *bát-chit,* or *guft-o-gu-k.* (chatter,) *bakna ; bak-bak-k.* (incoherently,) *bukhlána. See* 'Language.'
Spear, *ballam ; barchhi.* V. –*lagá-d.*
Special, *kháss ; makhsús.* –ly, *khusúsan.*
Spectacle, *tamásha.* –tator, *dekhne-wála.*
Spectacles, *chashmah.*
Speech. *See* 'Language.' a –, *takrír,* (f.) ; *bahs,* (f.). –less, *be-zábán ; lá-jawáb.*
Speed, (n.) *jaldi ; shitáb,* or *shitábi ; daur.* V. *daurána ; chalána.* –ily, *jaldi, &c. See page* 54.
Spend, *kharj,* or *kharch-k.* (lavishly), *urá-d. ; bar-bád-k.* –thrift, *fazúl-kharj.* N. (waste), -*i.* –(time,) *sarf-k.*
Spice, *masálah.* hot–, *garm–.*
Spider, *makra ; makri.*
Spill, *girá-d.*
Spin, *kátna ; sút-kátna.* –ning wheel, *charkh.*
Spinage, *isfánáj ; ság.*
Spine, (body,) *rírh,* (f.). (plants,) *kánta.*
Spirit, *rúh,* (f.) –of God, *rúhu-l-láh.*[1] (breath,) *dam.* (ghost,) *bhút.* (temper,) *mizáj.* (manliness,) *mar-dánagi.* (liquor,) *arak.* (juice,) *ras ; dúdh.* –less, *be-dil ; be-jigar.*
Spit, (for cooking,) *síkh,* (f.). V. –*lagána.*
Spit, (v.) *thúkna.* N. *thúk.* –toon, *pík-dán ; ugál-dán.*
Spite, *kínah ; zidd,* (f.). –ful, *kína-wár ; ziddi.* Adv. with *se.*

[1] According to Muhammad, Jesus Christ.

Spleen, *tilli*. (disease of,) *–ka rog*.

Splendour, *shaukat; jila*, (f.); *jilwat; shán*, (f.); *raushani*. –did, *alí-shán; mujalla; umdah; sar-faráz*.

Spoil, *kharáb*, or *be-kár-k.*; *bigáṛ-d*. spoilt, *kharáb*; *kuchh kám ka nahin*. the–s, (e.g. of war.) *lúṭ-páṭ; ghanímat*.

Sponge, *isfanj*. –gy, *phulka*.

Spoon, *chammach; chamchah*.

Sport. *See* 'Play.' (hunting, &c.,) *shikár*. –sman, also adj., 'relating to–,' *shikári*. –ive, *khush-taba; shokh*.

Spot, (stain,) *dágh*. (place,) *jagah*, (f.); *sar-zamín*, (f.). –ted, *dághi*.[1] V. *dághi-k*.

Sprain, (n.) *maroṛ; murak*. V. *maroṛna, murakna*.

Spread, (e.g. a carpet,) *bichhána; bichhá-d*. (e.g. disease,) (*trans.*) *phailána*. (*intr.*) *phailna*.

Spring, (season,) *bahár*, (f.); *basant; rabi*. (of water,) *chashmah-e-áb*. (leap,) *kúd*, (f.); *uchhál*, (f.); *chhaláng*, (f.) V. *kúdna; jast-k.*; *uchhalna; chhalángna*. to –at, *lapakna*.

Sprinkle, *chhiṭna; chhiṭ-k*.

Spur, *káṇṭa*, V. *-d.*, or *márna*.

Spy, (n.) *jásús*, his work, *jásúsi*. –glass, *dúr-bín*, to spy, *dekhna; tákna*. (furtively,) *jhánkna; jhánk lena*.

Square, (n.) *chauk*. (a.) *chau-kona; chau-khúṇṭa; chauras*.

Squeeze, *dabána; dabá-d*.

Squirrel, *gilehri*.

Stable, (n.) *istabal*. *See* 'Firm,' &c.

Stack, *ṭál; ḍheṛ*. V. *–k*.

Staff, *asa; lakṛi*. (of office,) *chob*.

Stag, *bárah-singa*.

Stage, (e.g. of a theatre,) *tamásha-gáh*. (journey,) *manzil*, (f.). (platform,) *machán; takhtah*. –coach, *ḍák-gáṛi*.

Stain. *See* 'Spot.'

Stair, –case, *siṛhi*.

Stall, *thán*. (public,) *aṛgaṛa*.

Stammer, *hakla*. V. *–k.*; *haklána*.

Stamp, *muhar*, (f.); *chháp*. V. *–lagá-d*.

---

[1] Means also a prisoner who has been branded, or otherwise marked; as by his name being entered in the list of ex-convicts.

Stand, (n.) *páyah ; ghora ;... dán.* (*page*,41.)–ing, *khara.* (v.) *khara-hona ; khara rahna.* –up, *uthna; uth-ke khara hona, &c.* –down, *níche jána; utarna.*–in the way, *sámne hona.*–out of the way, *hat-jána.* –good, *ká,im rahna.* of long –ing, *bahut roz ka. See* 'Endure.'

Star, *tára ; sitárah.*

Starch, *kalap ; kánji.*

Stare, *ghúrna; dekhte rahna.* N. *ghúr.*

Start, (n.) (sudden movement,) *chaunk.* V. *chaunkna*, e.g.a carriage, *chaléna.* for a place, *rawánah hona.* to startle, *chaunkána.*startling, *ta,ajjub ka ; ajíb.*

Starve, *bhúkh se marna.*

State. *See* 'Government.' (condition,) *hál; hálát ; asl hál.* (dignity,) *kadar*, (f.).; *martabah; shán*, (f.) ; *sarfarázi.*(v.)*kahna ; bayán-k.; bolna; samjhána ; izhár-k.* –in writing, *kalam-band-karke bayán-k.*–ment, *bát ; bayán ; izhár ; arz*, (f.) ; *guzárish; iltimás*, (f.).– in writing, *súrat-hál ; suwál; darkhwást; ripot*, (E.).

Station, *chauki ; jagah*, (f.). (railway,) *isteshan.* (E.). (v.) *rakhna ; khara-k. muta,aiyan-k.; tainát-k.*

Stay, *rahna; thaharna; sabr-k.*

Steak, *ishtek*, (E.).

Steal, *chori-k. ; chorána ; chorá-lejána.*

Steam, *dhú,án.*–boat, *dhú,án-kash ; ág-bot*, (half E.).

Steel, *faulad ; loha.*

Stem, (family,) *asl ; nasl ; bunyád*, (f.). –of tree, *shákh.*

Step, *kadam; deg.* V.–*rakhna.* (in relationship) *sautela...* e.g. *sauteli-ma.*

Stew, *istew.* (E.). V.–*k.*

Steward, *ná,ib ; gumáshta ; kár-pardáz.*

Stick, *lakri ;* (walking,) *asa.* (v.) (e.g. bone in throat,) *atak-jána.* (together,) *sat-jána.* stuck, *sat-gaya ; sátá-hú,a.*(*trans.*)*jorna; lagá-d.; satá-d.*

Still, (a.) *chup ; chup-cháp ; be-harakat.* (adv.) *tau-bhi ; tá-ham ; par.*

Sting, *dank.* V.–*márna.*

Stir, (*trans.*) *hilá-d.* (*intr.*) *hilna.* (n.) *haṛbaṛi; khalal.*

Stirrup, *rikáb*, (f.). -leather, *rikáb-dawál*, (f.).

Stitch, (v.) *sína; ṭáṇkna; ṭáṇk-d.* (n.) *ṭáṇk*, (f.); *ṭáṇka.*

Stocking, *mozah; pá-e-tábah.*

Stomach, *midah*, or *medah.*

Stone, *patthar; sang.* of stone, with '*ka*,' -ny, *pathríla.* -ny hearted, *sang-dil.*

Stool, (foot,) *pá-o-dán; moṛha; ishṭúl*, (E.) night-, *komod*,[1] (E.).

Stoop, *jhukna; jhuk-jána.*

Stop, (*intr.*) *khaṛa rahna; aṭakna.* (*trans.*) *rokna; thámna; aṭká-d.* -page, *rok; aṭká,o; aṭak.*

Store, *dúkán*, (f.); *jins sab; ambár; ḍher.* - house, *dúkán*, (f.); *gola.* stores, e.g. for a journey, *sar-anjám; sámán; chíz sab; sab chíz.*

Stork, *dhanes; bogla.*[2]

Storm, *túfán; áṇdhi.* -y, *túfáni.*

Story. *See* 'Tale.'

Slove, (moveable,) *aṇgeṭhi.* (fixed,) *chúlha.* (oven,) *tanúr.*

Stout, *moṭa; mazbút.* N.-*i.*

Straight, *sídha; sojha.* N.-*i.*

Strain. *See* 'Pull.' (liquids,) *chhánna.* a-er, *chhánna.*

Strange, (unfamiliar,) *be-gánah; ghair.* (wonderful,) *ajíb; ajúbah.* -ness, *ajnabiyat.* a -ger, *ghair ádmí; be-gánah ádmi; bi-desi ádmi.*

Strap, *tasmah; dawál*, (f.).

Stratagem, *ḥílah; fareb; dagha.*

Straw, *bichálí; po,ál; bhúsa.*

Stream, *darya; sota.* V. *jári-hona.*

Street. *See* 'Road.' *isṭríṭ*, (E.).

Strength, *zor; táḳat.* (of liquors,) *tundi; kaṛwá,i.* V. *mazbút-k.; zor-d.*

Strict. *See* 'Severe.'

Strike, *ṭhokar-d.; zarb-d.; márna.* -e.g. tents, *girá-d; kholna.* - against ...*par lagna.*

---

[1] In India, this word—'commode'—must never be used in any other sense. The accent is on the last syllable.

[2] Names of birds are mostly vague; as identity between many English and many Indian birds is wanting.

String, *sutli; ḍori.* shoe–, *fitah.*
Strive. *See* 'Endeavour.'
Stroke, (blow.) *choṭ; zarb; ṭhokar,* (f.); *ṭhoṇk.* – of pen, &c., *dágh; nishán.*
Strong, *zabar-dast; zor-áwar; zor ka; mazbút.* (as liquor,) *kaṛwa; ḳawi.*
Stubborn, *sar-kash; gardan-kash.* N. *–i.* Adv. *–i se.*
Stud, (shirt,) *isṭaḍ,* (E.).
Study, *paṛhna; taalím lena.* –dent, *shágird.* –dious, *miḥnati.*
Stupid, *kund; kund-zihn; ná-dán; be-wuḳúf; náḳis-ul-aḳl.* –ity, *ḥimáḳat; be-wuḳúfi.* a – fellow, *be-wuḳúf ádmi; aḳl ka putla.*
Subdue, *dabána; kisi par ghálib hona; ḳábu meṇ lána.* –ed. (conquered,) *maghlúb.* (meek,) *gharíb; narm.* –er, *ghálib.*
Subject, (underling,) *tábi; tábidár; farmáṇ-bardár; ḥukm-bardár; asámi; ra,iyat.* A. *tábi.* (v.) *See* 'Subdue,' he is subject to fever, *us-ko bukhár aksar áta hai.* –, e. g. of a lecture, *mabḥas.*
Submit to, *mánna; ḥukm sunna; tábi-hona.* (e.g. for orders,) *pesh-k; sámne rakhna.* –mission, *tábi-dári; ḥukm-bardári; zer-ḥukumi.*
Subscribe. *See* 'Sign.' –ption, (to a charity &c.,) *chandah.*
Subsistence, (means of living,) *roz-gár; khána-pína; khúrák-poshák,* (f.); *par-wasti; peshah; dhanda.* –allowance, *khúráki.* –ing, *zindah; zindagi meṇ; ḥai.*
Substance. *See* 'Thing.' (essence,) *hír.* (abstract,) *khulásah; mukhtasar ḥál; mazmún.* –tial, *mazbút; ḳá,im.*
Substitute, (n.) *ewazi; ḳá,im-maḳám.* V. *–k.; –rakhna; muta,aiyan-k.*
Suburb, *shahar ka dáman.*
Successful, *kám-yáb.* N. *–i.* V. *–hona.* to succeed a person, *píchhe ána; ḳá,im-maḳám hona.* –cession, *ḳá,im-maḳámi.* –fully, *barakat-se; nek-bakhti-se.* –ively, *ek par ek; áge-píchhe; tábaṛ-toṛ.*
Such, *aisa* – a one, *fulánah.*

Suck, *chúsna ; khaiṇchna ; pí-lena.* a –ing babe, *dúdh ka bachchah.*

Sudden, –ly, *achának; nágáh.* N. *nágahání.*

Sue, (in Court,) *muḳaddamah-k.* (ask,) *máṇgna ; iltimás-k.*

Suffer. *See* 'Allow.' (endure,) *bardásht-k,* (pain, or other feeling,)...*uṭhána ; ...khána.* –ing. *See* 'Pain,' &c.

Sufficient, *bas ; káfi.* V.–*hona.* N. *kifáyat.* –ly, *bas ; zarúrat ke mu,áfiḳ.*

Sugar, *chíni ; shakar ; misri.* (brown,) *khánḍ.* –candy, *misri.* –cane, *úkh,* (f.); *katári.*

Suggestion, *saláḥ,* (f.); *ishárah ; tadbír,* (f.). V. *–d. ; –batlána.*

Suicide, *khud-kushi.* V. *–k.*

Suit, (n.) (dress.) *joṛa.* (in Court,) *muḳaddamah.* (v.) (please,) *pasand-hona.* (fit,) *milna ; achchha baiṭhna.* (trans.) *milá-d.* –able, *pasand ; achchha ; mu,áfiḳ.*

Sulphur, *gandhak.*

Sum. *See* 'Total.' –of money *zar ; mablagh.* (v.) *joṛna ; jama-k.*

Summer, *garmi ka mausam.* *See page* 80.

Summon, *bulána ; talab-k.* a –s of court, *talabi-parwánah ; samans,* (E.).

Sun, *súraj ; siráj ; khurshíd ; áftáb.* –heat, *dhúp,* (f.). to bask in the –, *dhúp khána.* –shine, *dhúp,* (f.); *ghám.* –rise, *tulu-i-áftáb.* – set, *ghurúb-i-áftáb.* –ny, *dhúp ka ; ghámi.* –day, *itwár ; rabi-bár ; yak-shambah.*

Superintendent, *sar-ba-ráh-kár ; sardár.* –dence, *sar-ba-ráh-kári ; sardári.* V. *sar-ba-ráh kár, &c., hona ; sar-ba-ráh-kári, &c.-k.*[1]

Superior,[2] *sab se achchha, baṛa,* (or as the matter of 'superiority' may be.)

---

[1] Superintendents are named according to their work: e.g. *thánadár,* - of a police station. *názir,* a – of process-serving, &c. *muḥáfiz,* a – of records, and so on *ad infinitum.*

[2] The English word 'afsa' (officer), is much used to mean one's immediate 'superior.'

Supper, *rát-ka-khána; sapar*(E.)
Supply, *dena; ḥázir-kar-d.; pahuṇchá-d.* N. *jo káfi hoga; ambár; ḍher.*
Support, (n.) *ṭekni; ásra.* V. *-d.* to – a person, *par-wasti-k.; khána-pína-d.*
Supposition, *khayál; aṭkal.* V. *-k.*
Sure, (certain,) *yaḳíni.* to be–, *yaḳín jánna.* N *-í.* 'to be sure!' surely! *be shakk; albattah; cháhiye kih.*
Surface, *ru*, (f.).
Surgeon, *jarráḥ; tabíb-i-jarḥ.*
Surpass. *See* 'Excel.'
Surround, *gher-lena.*
Survey. *See* 'View.' 'Measure.' – or, *jaríb-kash.*
Suspect, *kisi par shakk rakhna.*–ed, *mushtabah; shakk ki bát.* –cion, *shakk; shubhah; wahm.*
Sustain. *See* 'Support.' –e.g. losses, *uṭhána.*
Swallow, (bird,) *abábil.* (v.) *nigalna; ghúṇṭna.*
Swamp, *daldal*, (f.). –y, *-í.*
Swan, *ráj-háṇs.*
Swear, (use bad language,) *gáli-d.* (e.g. in Court,) *ḳasam khána*, or *lena.*
Sweat, *pasína.* he is sweating, *us-se pasína girta hai*, or *nikalta hai.*
Sweep, (man,) *mihtar*,[1] fem. *mihtráni.* (v.) *jháṛna; jháṛ-d.* –away, *jháṛ-ke lejána.* –ings, *kurkuṭ.*
Sweet, *miṭha; shíriṇ; khush; pasandídah.* –heart, *pyára*, fem. *-i.* –meats, *miṭhá,i.* –ness, *shíríni; miṭhá,i.* –ly, *dil-khushi-se.*
Swell, *súјna; phúlna; uṭh-jána.* a –ing, *waram.*
Swift, *tez; jald.* –ness, *tezi; jaldi.* –ly, *jaldi; jaldi-se; tez; tezi-se.*
Swim, *pairna.* –mer, *pairák.*
Swing, (*trans.*) *jhulána.* (*intr.*) *jhúlna.* a –, *jhúla.* –ing, *jhúla-jhúli.*
Swoon, *be-hoshi.* in a –, *behosh.*
Sword, *talwár*, (f.); *shamsher*, (f.). –sman, *talwár-báz.*
Syllable, *lafz ka juz.*
Sympathy, *riḳḳat.* V. *kisi se – rakhna.* A. *ham-dard.*
Symptom, *nishán; alámat.*
Syringe, *pichkári.* V. *-d.*
System, *ḳá,idah; rasm.*

---

[1] '*Mihtar*' is really a native title of distinction.

T.

Table, *mez*, (f.). –cloth, *mez ki chádar*, (f.); *dastar-khwán*. to lay the –, *mez lagá-d.* or *taiydr-k.* to remove things from the –, *chíz sab le-jána.*

Tail, *dum*, (f.).

Tailor, *darzi.*

Take, *lena.* –away, *le-jána.* –place, *hona.* (accept,) *lena.*; *kabúl-k.*, *pasand-k.* –captive, *pakaṛle-jána*; *giriftár-k.* –effect, *lagna*; *chalna.* –on hire, *kiráye-lena.* –flight, *bhág-jána*; *uṛ-jána.* –the hand of, *háth pakaṛna.* –heed, *khabar-dár hona.* –off, (e.g. clothes,) *utárna.* –down, *níche-lána.* (in writing,) *kalam-band-k.* –up, *uṭhá-lena.* –courage, *himmat rakhna.* –the field, *khet pakaṛna.* – in good part, *bhala jánna.* –in bad part, *bura mánna.* –the side of, *taraf-dár hona.* –out, (extract,) *nikálna.*

Talc, *abrak.*

Tale, *kissah*; *hikáyat*; *nakl*, (f.); *kahání*; *bát*; *khabar*, (f.).

Talk, *bát-chít*; *guft-o-gu*, (f.); *bát.* V. *–k.*: *bolna*; *kahna*; *bakna.* to – to one's self, *áp se bolna.*

Tall, *lamba*; *dírgh.* –ness, *lambá,i.* *See* 'High.'

Tame, *gharíb.* N. *–i.* V. *–k.*; *dabána*; *hilána.*

Tank, (cistern,) *hauz.* (pond,[1]) *táláb*, (f.); *talá,o*; *pokhra.*

Tap, *thap-thapána.* a –ping, *thappa*; *thappi*, which mean also a thing for tapping with, e.g. *a mallet, bat, &c.*

Tape, *fítah*; *niwár.*

Tapering, *gá-o-dum.* V. *–hona.*

Tar, *kitrán*; *al-katra.*[2] V. *–lagá–d.*

Target, *ḍhál*, (f.); *sipar.* -practice, *chánd–*[3]*mári.*

---

[1] In India, artificial ponds are called 'tanks;' a natural pond, or lake, is '*tál*,' as at 'Nynee Tal.'

[2] This is the word most generally used; but is not to be found in either the Persian or the Hindústáni dictionaries.

[3] 'The moon;' the 'bull's-eye' being regarded a a full-moon.

Tariff, *nirkh-námah.*

Task, (lesson,) *sabak.* (labour,) *kám.* to take to –, *dáṇṭna; dhamki-d.*

Tassel, *jhabba.*

Taste, (n.) *mazah.* (fig.) *salíkah.* sense of –, *zá,ikah.* (v.) *thoṛa khána; zá,ikah lena:* of a pleasant –, *maze ka; lazíz.* –less. *be-mazah.*

Tax, *mahsúl; ṭikas,* (E.). V. *–lagána.*

Tea, *chá,e,* (f.). –pot, *–pochi.* –caddy, *–dán.* –kettle, *ketli,* (E.). cup, *–ka piyálah.* –spoon, *–ka chammach,* or *chamchah.*

Teach, *sikhána; sikhlána; taalím d.* –ing, *by v.n.* –er, *ustád; mu,allim; guru; iskúl-másṭar,* (E.).

Tear, (of eye,) *áṇsu.* (rent,) *chír; phák.* to shed –s, *rona.* (to rend,) *chírna; toṛna; pháṛna; ṭháṛ-d.*

Tease, *satána; dikk-k.*

Telescope, *dúr-bín.*[1]

Tell, *kahna; bolna; khabar-d.; bát-bolna; bayán-k.* (count,) *ginna; shumár-k.*

Temper, *mizáj; kho,* (f.); *tabíat.*

Tempest, *túfán; áṇdhi.* A. *túfáni.*

Temple, (M.), *ibádat-gáh; masjid,* (f.). (H.) *pújakhánah; ṭhákur-bári; maṭh,* (Christian,) *girja,* or *grija.*

Tenant, (of house,) *kiráyadár.* (of land,) *asámi; ra,iyat; kásht-kár.* the –ry, *ri,áya; asámi-log.*

Tender, *narm; mulá,im.* See 'Offer.'

Tent, *khaimah; tambu; ḍera.* (servant's,) *pál.* –pole, *chob,* –curtains, *kanát.* –peg, *mekh.* –pitcher, *khalási.*

Terrify. *See* 'Frighten.'

Testament, (Old) *taurát.* (New,) *injíl.* (will,) *wasíyatnámah; wíl,* (E.).

Testimony. *See* 'Evidence.'

Than, *se; az,* (Persian.).

Thanks, *shukr.* to thank, *–k.* –ful, *–guzár.* (N. *–i.*) (grateful,) *ihsán-mand.* (N. *–i.*) –less, *ná-shukr.* Adv. with *se.*

---

[1] Persian '*bína,*' 'vision.'

That, (narration,) *kih.* (demonstrative.) *See page* 30. —very, *wohi.* —is to say, *yane.*

Thatch, (the,) *chhappar*, (f.). (grass,) *ghás*, (f.); *khar.* V. *ghás, &c. lagána.*

Theatre, *nách-ghar; tamásha-khánah; nakl-khánah.*

Thee. *See page* 29.

Their, theirs, them, &c. *See pages* 30 *and* 31.

Then, (time following,) *tab; is-ke baad; baad is-ke.* (time previous,) *tab; us-wakt.; us-ke baad.* now and—, *kabhi-kabhi.*

Thence, —forth, (place,) *wahán-se; us-jagah-se.* (time,) *baad is-ke; us wakt-se.*

There, *wahán; us-jagah men.*—abouts, *wahín-kahín.* here and—, *idhar-udhar; yahán-wahán.*

Therefore, *is-wáste; pas.*

Thereon, —upon, *is-par; tab.*

They, *ye; we. See page* 30.

Thick, *mota; gárha.* N. *motá,i.* to go through—and thin, *ág páni men parna.*

Thief, *chor; duzd.* theft, *chori; sarkah; duzdi.*

Thigh, *jángh*, (f.).

Thin, *patla;* (texture,) *bárík;* (e.g. as skin,) *kághazi* V. *patla-k.* and *hona.* —ness, *patlá,i.*—ly, *kam.*

Thing, *chíz.* (f.); *shai.* one's things, *chíz sab; bastah; mál; mál-o-mata.*

Think, *sochna; khayál-k.; bichárna.* methinks, *mujh-ko maalum hota hai.*

Third, *tísra; siyum.*

Thirst, (n.) *pyás*, (f.); *tish-nagi.* —y, *pyása.* V. *mujh-ko pyás lagi hai; pyása hona.*

This, *yih. See page* 30.

Thither, *udhar; wahán; us taraf.*

Thorn, *kánta; khár.* —y, *kantár.*

Thorough, *tamám; púra.* —ly, *sar-á-sar.*—fare, *sarak*, (f.), *guzar-gáh; ámm-rásta.*

Thou, *tu. See page* 29.

Though, *agar-chih; har-chand; az bas kih.* as —, *jaisa-kih...taisa-kih.*

Thought, *soch; fikr*, (f.); *ta,ammul; andeshah;*

dhyán. See 'Thing.' -ful, *fikr-mand.* (N. *-i.*) *muta,-ammil ; andesha-nák.* -less, *be-fikr ; be-khabar ; be-parwáh.* N.add 'i' to these adjs. adv., nouns and *se.*

Thrash, (corn,) *dá,ona ; dhun-na ; jhárna. See* 'Flog.' -ing floor, *khalihán.*[1]

Thread, *sút ; sutli ; tága ;* (strong,) *dori.* needle and–, *sú,i tága.* to a needle, *tágna.*

Threat, *dhamki ; tan.* V. *-d.; dhamkána.*

Throat, *gala,* or *gulu ; halak.*

Throb, *tís,* (f.) V. *-márna ; tísna.*

Through, *kebích ; men.* (means) *se.* (agent,) *se ; ki márfat.*

Throw, *phenkna ; phenk-d. ; dálna ; bígna* -aside, *bar-taraf phenkna.* -away, *phenk-d.* -down, *girá-d.* -open, *khol-d.* - up, (as a ball,) *uchhálna.*

Thrust, (n.) *dhakka.* V. *-d. ; ghuserna.*

Thunder, *garaj,* (f.). V.–*na.*

Thursday, *bíphe ; brihaspat ; juma-rát.*

Thus, *aisa ; is-tarah ; isi-tarah.*

Ticket, *tikat.* (E.).

Tickle, *gudgudána.*

Tide, (ebb,) *bhátha.* (flow,) *jawár.*

Tidings. *See* 'News.'

Tie, *bándhna ; bándh-d.* a –, *band.* neck –, *gulu-band.*

Tiger, *bágh ; sher.* -gress, *sherni.*

Tight, *tang ;* drawn –, *kasa hú,a.* N. *tangi.* V. *-k. ; kasna ; khínchna.*

Tile, (round,) *khapra.* (square,) *pewal.* V.–*lagána.*

Till, (v), *kheti-k ; chás-k. ; hal-bail-k ; jotna.*

Till, (adv.). *See page* 47, iii.

Timber, *lakri.*

Time, *wakt ; zamán,* or *zamá-nah,* (period of.) *arsah ; muddat.* (cycle of,) *yug.* —when one ruled, existed) &c. *wakt ; aiyám.* -of life, *umr,* (f.) ; *sinn,* (m.) ; (leisure,) *fursat ; farághat.* (delay,) *der,* (f.) ; from–to–, *waktan-fa-waktan.* at all– s, *har wakt ; hameshah.* in – or out of –, *wakt-ná, wakt.* at the proper–, *bar-wakt.*

---

[1] Accent on the last syllable.

Tin, *ḳalai.* V. *-d.* ; *-lagá-d.*

Tipsy, *matwála ; mast.*

Tire, *thakána.* -ed, *thaka ; máṇdah.* -edness, *máṇdagi.* -some, *malál-angez.* a -some fellow, *thakáne-wála ; diḳḳ karne-wála.*

Title, *nám ; ḵhitáb ; laḳab ;* (ceremonious heading,) *alḳáb.* (Pl. of *laḳab.*)

To,[1] (generally,) *ko ;* (approach), *ke pás ;* (transfer,) *ke háth ; ko.* -day, *áj ; imroz.* -and fro, *idhar-udhar ;* face - face, *rú-ba-ru ; ke sámne.* with respect -, *is báre meṇ ; is-ke ḥaḳḳ meṇ.*

Toast, (v.) *seṇkna.* N. *tost,* (E.).

Tobacco, *tambáku.* to smoke -, *-pína.*

Together, *ke sáth ; sáth ; sáth-sáth ; ek sáth ; báham ; ham,* as first part in compos : all -, (action,) *sab mil-ke,* (company,) *sab ek sáth.*

Tomb. *See* 'Grave.'

Tongue, *jíbh,* (f.) ; *zabán,* (f.). *See* 'Language.'

Too, (of excess,) *ziyádah.* (also,) *bhi.*

Tool, *hathiyár.*

Tooth, *dáṇt.* -ache, *dáṇt ka dard.* -brush, *dáṇt ka barúsh,* (E.). -pick, *ḵhilál.* -powder, *or* paste, *manjan.* to cast in one's teeth, *muṇh par bolna.*

Top, *sar.* (toy,) *laṭṭu.* -most, *sabhoṇ se úpar.* -heavy, *sir-bhári.* -sy-turvy, *ulaṭ-pulaṭ ; úpar-níche.*

Torch, *mashál.* -bearer, *-chi.*

Torment, (n). *siyásat ; diḳḳ ; dukh ; ján sozi.* V. *-k.* ; *satána.*

Tortoise, *kachhúa.*

Toss. *See* 'Throw.'

Total, *jumlah ; kull ; kulliyat ; moṭ ; sab le-ke ; jama.*

Touch, *chhúna.* N. *chhu'háwaṭ ;* the sense of -, *lams.*

Tow, (n.) *páṭ ; paṭwah* -ing-rope, *gun.* V. *gun k.*

Toward, towards, *ki taraf ; ke pás.*

Towel, *tauliyah. ; dast-mál.*

Tower, *burj.* V. *baland-hona.*

Town, *shahr ;...púr,* and .. *nagar,* as last part in compos : -sman, *shahr-*

---

[1] 'To' or 'for' '*a place,*' is generally omitted, e.g. '*kal rát-ko Banáras rawánah hú,a,*' 'he started last night *for* Banaras.'

ka ádmi. one of the same –, *ham-shahr.*

Toy, (n.) *khilauna.* (v.) *khelna.*

Trace, (n.) (by which to find,) *surágh* ; *alámat* ; *pata* ; *asar.* (harness,) *jot.* (v.) *khojna* ; *khojh-k.* ; *pag-danḍí-lena.* (by pen, &c.) *khínchna.*

Trade, *tijárat* ; *saudá-gari* ; *kár-bár* ; *kharíd-farokht* ; *byopár.*–er, *saudá-gar* ; *bai-pári.* (travelling,) *banjára* ; *bakas-wála,* (half E.).

Traffic, *áná-jána* ; *ámad-o-raft.* *See* 'Trade.'

Trail, (*trans.*) *ghasíṭna* ; *khínchna.* (*intr.*) *ghasiṭna.*

Train, (of dress,) *dáman.* (followers,) *ḥashmat* ; *ham-ráhi,án.* (sequence,) *tar-tíb,* (f.) ; *silsilah.* (railway,) *gáṛi,án.* (v.) *sikhlána.*

Trample, *pá e-mál-k.* N. –*i.*

Transact. *See* 'Do.'

Transfer, *muntaḳal-k.*

Translation; *tarjamah.* –tor, *tarjumán* ; *mutarjim.*

Transparent, *shaffáf.* N. –*i.*

Transpositon, *inḳiláb.* V. –*k.*

Trap, *kal,* (f.) ;... *dán,* as last part in compos.

Travel, *safar-k.* ; *sair-k.* –ler, *musáfir.* –ling, (adj.) *safari.*

Tray, *khwán* ; *kishti.*

Treacle, *gur* ; *tiryáḳ.*

Treason, *daghá-bázi* ; *namak-ḥarámi.*

Treasure, *khazánah.* –ry, –*khánah.* –er, *khazánchi.* (v.) *azíz-rakhna* ; *ḳadar-k.*

Tree, *darakht* ; *peṛ* ; *gáchh.*

Tremble, *kámpna.* –bling, *larzish.*

Trial, *imtiḥán* ; *jánch* ; *áz-má,ish.* V. –*k.* (in Court,) *tajwíz,* (f.).

Tribunal, *adálat* ; *maḥkamah.*

Trick, *ḥílah* ; *bahánah* ; *fareb.*

Trickle, *girna* ; *rasna* ; *ṭapakna.*

Troop, *guroh,* (f.) ; *tá,ifah* ; *jamá,at* ; *ghol.* troops, *lashkar,* (m.) ; *sipáhi,án.*

Trot, (n.) *dulki.* V. –*chalna.*

Trouble, (n.) *tasdi,* (f.) ; *dukh* ; *diḳḳ* ; *taklíf,* (f.) ; *ranjish.* to feel –, –*uṭhána.* to cause –. –*k.* ; *satána* ; *chheṛna* ; *ranjána.* –d, *ázurdah* ; *fikr-mand* ; *gham-gín.* –some, *múzi* ; *ranj-áwar* ; *diḳḳ-karta* ; *diḳḳ-dár.*

Trousers, *paṭlún*, (E.). *izár*,[1] (f.).

True, *sach ; wájib ; sádiḳ ; durust.* truth, *sachá,i ; rásti ; asl bát ; ḥaḳíḳat.* in truth, *wáḳe meṇ ; fil-ḥaḳíḳat.*

Trumpet, *turhi.* V. *–bajána.*

Trust, *itibár ; itimád.* V. *–rakhna.* (deposit,) *amánat.* –tee, *amánat-dár.* one who trusts, *mutamid.* –worthy, *itibári ; wafá-dár ; ímán-dár.* –worthiness, *ímán-dári ; wafá-dári.*

Tub, *ṭab*, (E.). *tag̲h̲ári.*

Tube, *náli ; nai ; nal.*

Tuesday, *mangal; si-shambah.*

Tumble. *See* 'Fall.'

Tumbler, *tambleṭ*, (E.).

Tumult. *See* 'Riot.'

Turban, *pagṛi ; sar-band.*

Turkey, (bird,) *peru*, or *píru.*

Turmeric, *haldi.*

Turn, (*intr.*) *phirna ; phir-jána ; ghúmna.* (*trans.*) *ghumána;ghumá-d.* to make a–, (circuit,) *chakkar márna; ghúm-ke jána ;* to take a–,(exercise,) *hawa-khána.* to –back, *pher-ána*, or *jána ; lauṭna.* to – out, *nikál-d.* to – one's back, *píṭh-dikhlána* a – ing, *chakkar ; pech.* *See* 'Turner.'

Turner, (trade,) *k̲h̲arádi.* –ing lathe, *k̲h̲arád*, (f.). V. *k̲h̲arádna.*

Turnips, *shalg̲h̲am.*

Tweezers, *chimṭa.*

Twilight, *godhaura*; *shafaḳ ; chirág̲h̲ jaláne ka waḳt.*

Twin, (one.) *tau,am ;* (the two,) *tawámán.*

Twine, (n.), *sút.* *See* 'Climb.'

Twist, *aiṇṭhna ; maroṛna.*

Type. *See* 'Kind.' (printing,) *chháp.*

Tyrant, *zálim ; jafá-kár.*–ny, *zulm ; zabar-dasti ; sitam ; jabr ; zor.* –ous, *zulmi, zabar-dast ; sak̲h̲t.* –ously, *jabran ; zulm, &c. se.*

---

[1] Means, rather, 'drawers.' Natives, unless anglified, seldom wear 'trousers.'

U.

Note.—Many of the words beginning with 'un' *negative*, are not given. *You may turn the sentence into one with* 'not' e.g. *this is untrue* = '*this is* not *true*'—yih sach nahíṉ hai; *or secondly, you may prefix* 'ná' *to almost any adjective; and* 'be' *to almost any noun:* e.g. ná-pasand, ná-maalúm, ná-durust;—be-hosh, be-aḳl, be-sharm. 'Lá' 'g͟hair' and 'kam' are also negative prefixes, *but they are appropriated to certain words*, e.g. lá-wáris, *without an heir;* lá-jawáb, *without an excuse*, g͟hair-ḥázir, *absent. Many words of Saṉskrit origin* (*of which only a few have been given*) *take* 'a' *privative*, (as in Greek,) or 'nir,' e.g. a-dharm, *injustice;* nir-buddhi, *senseless, stupid.*

Udder, *than.*

Ugly, *bad-súrat; bad-shakl.* --ness. --*i.*

Ulcer, *násúr.*

Umbrella, *chhátá; chhatri.* --bearer, *chhatar-dár.*

Unanimous, *ek zabán ka.* --ity, *ek zabán ka ittifáḳ.* --ly, *ek zabán se.*

Unawares, *achának; nágahán.*

Uncertain, *be-ṭhikána; g͟hair-muḳarrar.*

Uncivil, *bad-k͟hulḳ; be-adab.* N. --*i.*

Uncommon. *See* 'Rare.'

Under. *See* 'Below.' --trial, *zer tajwíz*, (f.).

Undergo, (e.g. pain labour, &c.) *khána; uṭhána.*

Understand, *samajhna; bújhna; samajh meṉ lena; wáḳif-hona.* N. *samajh*, (f.); *hosh; aḳl*, (f.); *fahm; wuḳúf.*

Undertake, *bíṛa-uṭhána; háth lagána; karna.* --king, *kám*, or by the name of the thing.

Underwood, *jháṛ; jháṛi.*

Undo, *kholna;* (fig.) *akárath-k.; tabáhi-k.* --done, *khula;* (fig.) *tabáh; shikastah.*

Unfix, *kholna; utárna; nikál-d.*

Unfortunate, *kam-bak͟ht.*

Uniform, (a), *eksáṉ; ek ḳism ka* (n.)*úṛai.* --ity, *barábari; eksáni.* adv. with *se.*

Union, *ittifák*; *ek-dili*; *ekíyat*; *bá-hami*. unite, (join,) *jorna*; *milá d.*

Universe, the, *dunya*, (f.); *álam*; *jahán* --sal, *har-já,i*; *kull*; *tamám*.--sality, *kulliyat*; --sally, *bil-kull*. –sity, *madrasah*.

Unlawful, *khiláf kánún*; *khiláf-i-shara*.

Unless, *agar* followed by *nahíņ*, e.g. unless you do this, I shall not pay you, *agar tum yih kám nahíņ karo, to, maiņ ek paisa nahíņ dúņ*.

Unmarried, *kúņára*. an --person, *muflis*.

Unravel, *udherņa*.

Unroll, *kholna*.

Unruly, *sar kash*; *be-lagám*. N. *sar-kashi*.

Unseen, *ghá,ib*; *nazar se ghá,ib*.

Until. *See page* 47, iii.

Unusual, *khiláf dastúr*; *be-riwáj*; *jo kam dekhne meņ áta hai*.

Unwell, *achchha nahíņ*; *mizáj kharáb hai*: *bímár*; *maríz*.

Unyoke, *kholna*.[1]

Up. *See* 'Above.'

Upon, *par*.

Upright, *khaŗa*. V. --*k*. (fig.), *rást*; *sachcha*; *sídha*; *nek*. N. *rásti*; *sachá,i*; *sídhá,i*; *neki*.

Uproar, *ghul*; *danga*; *haul-jaul*; *khalal*. V. --*k*. Adv. with *se*.

Upset, (v.) *ulṭána*; *ulṭá-d.* (a.) *ulṭa*; *ulṭa hú,a*.

Upshot, *natíjah*.

Urge, (e.g. a horse,) *chalána*. (a request,) *iltimás-k*. he urged me to grant his prayer, *is ki darkhást manzúr karne ko, mujhe dabáya*. or *lá-chár kiya*, or *tangkiya*.

Urine, *pesh-áb*.

Us, *ham*, &c. *See page* 29 and *Notes*.

Usage. *See* 'Custom.'

Use. (n.) *istiamál*. V. --*k*.;

---

[1] The reader will have observed how universally this word is used for all senses of '*disjoining*' as well as of merely '*opening*.' He will hear English children who are allowed to talk English (a bad habit for them in India) say, '*opin mai shoos*,' where the happier children in England say, 'untie my shoes'—(or do it for themselves.)

kám meṇ lena. –ful, *kám ka; kámi.* (salutary,) *mufíd.* –fully, *fá,ide ke sáth.* –less, *ná-kárah* ; *kuchh kám ka nahíṇ.* –lessly, *lá-ḥásil ; be-fá,idah.* –lessness, *lá-ḥásili.*

Usual, *ḥasb-dastúr ; jo jári hai.* -ly, *aksar ; beshtar ; ba-dastúr.*

Usurer, *byáj-k͟hor ; súd-k͟hor.* –ury, *–i.*

Utensil, *chíz,* (f.). (but *name* the – you want.)

V.

Vacant. *See* 'Empty.' –cation, *tatíl,* (f.).

Vagabond, *bad-zát ; luchcha.*

Vain, *dimágh̲i,* to be–, *uṛchalna ; láf-zani-k.* –ity, *k͟hud-faroshi,* in–, *be-fá,idah.*

Valid, *durust; pakka; ḳá,im; mazbút.* –ity, *durusti; mazbúti.*

Value. See 'Price.' –able, *ḳímati ; besh-ḳímat ; giráṇbaha.* V. *ḳímat-lagá-d.* (fig.), *azíz-rakhna; ḳadar-k. ; pyár-k.*

Vanish, *gh̲á,ib-hona ; uṛ jána.*

Vanquish, *gh̲álib-hona ; dabá-d. ; toṛna.*

Variety, *taraḥ-taraḥ ; ḳism-ḳism.* –ious, *chand ḳism ka.* –ously, *aur aur taraḥ se.* to vary, (*trans.*)*badalna; chand taraḥ se karna.* (*intr.*) *badal-jána.*

Varnish, (n.) *bárnish,* (E.); *pálish,* (E.) ; *raugh̲an ; chikná,i.* V. *–lagá-d.*

Vase. *See page* 41.

Vegetables, *tarkári ; sabzi.*

Vehicle, *gáṛi ; sawári.*

Veil, *niḳáb.* wearer of a –, *–dár.* (pretence,) *burḳah.*

Vein, *nas,* (f.) ; *rag,* (f.). – of metal, *asar,* or Pl. *ásár.*

Velvet, *mak͟hmal.*

Vengeance, *intiḳám.* V.*–lena.*

Venture, *himmat-k.* at a –, *ḳismat par.*

Verandah, *barámadah.* *See page* 23.

Verbal, –ly, *zabáni.*

Verdure, *sabzi.*

Verification, *tasdíḳ,* (f.). V.*–k.*

Verily, *ḥaḳíḳat meṇ ; fil-wáḳe.*

Vermicelli, *baramseli,* (E.).

Very, *bahut; nihâyat;* by suffix '*hi.*' e.g. *wu-hi ádmi*, '*that very man.*'

Vessel. *See* 'Dish,' 'Ship.'

Vex, –ation. *See* 'Annoy,' 'Grief,' &c.

Vice, *sharárat; kharábi; badi; zabúni.* (a), *kharáb; bad-kho; zabún.*

Vice... (substitute,) *ká,im-makám.*

Victor, *ghálib.* –ious, *and* to be –ious, *–hona.* –y, *fatḥ; ghalbah; jai.*

View. *See* 'See,' 'Scene.'

Village, *gáṇw; basti; dih; grám,* (L. B.). –together with the lands attached, *dihát; mauza.* –er, *gaṇ-wár; gáoṇ-wála; basti-wála.*

Villain, –ous, *bad-zát; ḥarám-zádah.* –y, *bad-záti.*

Vine, *angúr ka darakht.* –yard, *angúr ka bágh.*

Vinegar, *sirkah.*

Violence, *zor; jabr.* V. *–k.* (adv.) with *se.* (a.) *sakht; zor-áwar; zabar-dast; be-lagám.*

Virgin, *bákirah.* –ity, *bikárat.*

Virtue, *rásti; neki; bhalá,i.* A. *rást; nek; bhala.* by – of his office, *az rú-e-uhde apne; ba-zari,e,* (or *ba-sabab,*) *apne uhde ke.*

Visible, *záhir; nazar meṇ.* –bility *zuhúr.* –bly, *záhi-ran.* vision, (sight,) *nazar,* (f.); *biná,i; basárat.* (in sleep,) *khwáb-khayál.*–ary, *wahmi.*

Visit, *mulákát; bheṇṭ.* V. *–k.* or, by '*jo.*'

Vizier, *wazír.*

Voice, *áwáz,* (f.); *shabd,* vocal, *awáz se; shabdi.* vocal and instrumental music, '*gána-bajána,*'[1] (v.n.).

Volume, *jild,* (f.)

Voluntary, *ikhtiyári.*

Vomit, (n.) *kai; ubká,i; radd.* V. *–k.*

Voyage, *safar-i-darya.* –r, *jahází- musáfir.*

Vulgar, (public,) *ámm.* (mean,) *nícha; kamínah; páji. See* 'Common.'

Vulture, *gidh.*

---

[1] Lit. 'to sing (and) to play.' Page 11, *Note.*

W.

Wade, *helna.*
Wafer, *ṭikli.*
Wager, *shart; hoṛa; háṛi.* V. *-k.; bándh-lena.*
Wages. *See* 'Pay.'
Wagon, *chhakṛa; gáṛi.* (car used in religious processions, &c.) *rath.*
Waist, *kamar,* (f.). -band, *or* belt, *-band.* -coat, *wáskiṭ,* (E.).
Wait, *rahna; sabr-karna; rah-jána.* -ing, *intizár.* (on one), *khidmat; mulázamat.* V. *-k.* -er, (general,) with '*jo.*'; *ummedwár.*(servant), *khidmat-gár.*
Wake, (*trans.*) *jagána; jagá-d.* (*intr.*) *jágna.* awake, *jágna; bedár.* -ful, *bedár; be-khwáb.* -fulness, *bedári.*
Walk, (n.) *sair; hawa-khána,* (v.n.).(v.)*chalna; ḳadam-k.* (take a -,) *sair-k.; hawa-khána.*
Wall, *díwár,* (f.). -of a tent, *ḳanát.*
Wallow, *loṭna.*
Walnut, *akhroṭ.*
Want, (need,) *ḥájat; iḥtiyáj.* (deficiency,) *kuchh kami; aib.* (poverty,) *tangi.* (v.) (desire,)*cháhna; ḥájat hona.* (be deficient,) *kam hona.*
War, *laṛa,i; jang,* (f.). V. *-k.* -like, *jangi.* -equipments, *sámán-i-jang.*
Warm, *garm.* V. *-k.*N.*garmi; tapish.* a -bath. *garm-ábah.* to -oneself, *tápna.*
Warn, *chitána; khabar-d.; ágáh-k.* a -ing, *khabar,* (f.); *ittila,* (f.).
Was, *tha, &c. See page* 11.
Wash, *dhona; dho-d.; sáf-k.* -ing, *dholá,i.*-er, (person,) ...*sho,* as last part in compos: -erman, *dhobi.* -erwoman, *dhobin.*
Wasp, *birni; zambúr.*
Waste, (what is over after manufacture, &c.,) *síṭhi; síṭh,* (f.). (squandering,) *isráf.* (a desert,) *wírána.* (v.) *ghaṭána; uṛá-d.; barbád-d.; kharáb-kar-d.* ful, *fuzúl-kharj.*-fulness.*fuzúl-kharji.*
Watch, (n.) (pocket,) *ghaṛi.* -man. *See* 'Sentinel.' -post, *chauki* (protection,) *ḥifázat; nigáh-báni; kha-*

barddári. –ful, *be-dár ; kha-bar-dár.* Adv. with *se.* (v.) *ḥifázat, &c. k.*

Water, *páni,* (m.) *áb,* (Persian,) ; *jal.* –fall, *áb-shár.* –fowl, *murgh-ábi.* –ing, *áb-páshi.* –ing-pot, *loṭa.* –pot, *ghaṛa ; ka.si.* –man, *bihishti; páni-wála.*–melon, *tarbúz.* –servant, *áb-dár.* –y, *tar ; ábi.* (v.) *páni-d. ;* (irrigate), *paṭána ; áb-páshi-k.* to sprinkle–, *páni chhíṭ-karke-d.*

Wave, (n.) *mauj,* (f.). (v.) *hilána ; hilá–d.*

Wax, *mom.* -en, *mom ka.* –cloth, *mom-jámah.* sealing –, *lákh.*

Way. *See* 'Road.' by the –, i.e. on the road, *darmiyán ráh ke.* by the –, e. g. by the way, I ought to mention, &c., *kahte hú,e ; játe hú,e.* by way of...(e.g. kindness,) *az ráh-i-mihr-báni.* costs of the –, *ráh ka kharch.*

We, *ham.* *See* 29. ; *ham log.*

Weak, *kam-zor ; ná,tawán ; za,íf.* –ness, *kam-zori ; ná-ṭáḳati ; zof.*

Wealth. *See* 'Riches.'

Weapon, *ḥarbah ; hathiyár.*

Wear, (out, as clothes), *pur-ána ho-jána.* (clothes, &c.), *pahinna ; oṛhna ; bándhna ; lagá-d. ; rakhna.*

Weather. *See page* 80.

Weave, *binna.* –ing, *bináwaṭ.* –er, *júláhah ; táṇti.*

Web, *thán.*

Wednesday, *budh ; chár-shambah.*

Weed, *ghás,* (f.) ; *jangli ghás.* when plucked up, *ghás-pát ; ákhor.* V. *–ukháṛna.*

Week, *haftah.*

Weep, *rona ; áṇsu-girá-d.*

Weigh, (*trans*) *taulna ; wazn-k.* (*intr.*) *itne wazn ka hona.* (ponder,) *wazn-k. ; jáṇchna ; sochna.* –ty, *bhári ; wazni ; sangín ; giráṇ.* all lit. and fig.

Welcome, *mubárik,* (also by way of address). V.–*bád-k.* *See* 'Agreeable.'

Well, (a.) *achchha ; bhala ; khúb,* (which are also interjs.) to be–, *–hona.* (in good style,) *achchhi taraḥ.* –enough, *kam-besh.* as – as possible, *maḳdúr bhar.* this, as – as that, *yih, aur wuh bhi.*–fare, *khairiyat.*–done! *shábásh! bahut achchha!* –known, *khúb-maalúm; mashhúr.* –wisher, *khair-khwáh.*

West, *pachchham; maghrib.*

Wet, *bhínga; tar; gíla.* –ness, *tari.* V. *bhingána.*

What, –ever. *See pages* 33 *and* 39.

Wheat, *gehúṇ.*

Wheedle, *phuslána; chum-kárna.*

Wheel, (n.) *charkh; pahiya; chakkar.* (v.) e.g. a barrow, *chalána.*

When. *See page* 104. –ever, *jab kabhi...tab.*

Where, –ever. *See pages* 104 and 62. –abouts? *kaháṇ; kis taraf?*

Whether, *khwáh...khwáh; kya...kya* (e.g. whether rich or poor,) *khwáh daulat-mand, khwáh gharíb.*

Which. *See page* 33. which of these two do you prefer, *in donoṇ meṇ se kaun pasand karte ho?* which is which, I can't say, *kaun yih hai aur kaun wuh hai, maiṇ nahíṇ kah-sakta húṇ.*

While. *See page* 47. iii. also, 'Space.' a long *or* good –, *bahut der tak; muddat-i-daráz.* a little –, *thoṛi der tak; chhan-ek.*

Whip, *chábuk; koṛa.* V. –*márna*, or –*se márna.*

Whirl, *ghúmna; phirna.* –pool, *gird-áb.*–wind, *gird-bád.*

Whiskers, *múchh*, (f.).

Whisper, *phasphasáhaṭ.* V. *phasphasána.*

Whistling, *síṭi; safír*, (f.). V. –*bajána.*

White, *safed.* N.-*i.* V.-*k.* a –man, *gora.* a –ant, *díwak.* –wash, *puchára.*

Who, –ever. *See pages* 33 *and* 39.

Whole, (a) *kull; tamám; sab.* (n.) *kulliyat.* –some, *mu,áfik; sajíwan; zulál.* –ly, *bil-kull; maḥz.*

Why? *kyúṇ? káhe? kis wáste?*

Wick, *batti.*

Wicked. *See* 'Bad.'

Wicker, –work, *jafari.*

Wide. *See* 'Broad.'

Widow, *ráṇḍ; bewa; be-shauhar.* –er, *raṇḍú,a; be-zan.*

Wife, *joru ; zaujah ; ḳabílah.*

Wilful, *khud-pasand ; sar-kash.* –ly. *See* 'Intention.'

Will. *See* 'Pleasure.' 'Power.' (testament,) *wasíyat-námah.* –ing, *taiyár; rázi; rizá-mand ; khush.* –ingness, *taiyári ; rizá-mandi ; khushi.* –ingly, *khushi-se.*

Win, *jítna ; ghálib-hona.*

Wind, *hawa,* (f.) ; *bád,* (Persian.).

Window, *khirki ; ghurfah.*

Wine, *sharáb,* (f.) *mai; mad; dáru,* (f.). *bádah,* (Persian.).[1]

Wing, *par; pankh,*(fig.)*baghal,* (f.). V. *pankh márna.*

Wink, (n.) *chashmak.* V. *–k.*

Winter, *járe ka mausam.*

Wipe, *poṇchhna ; poṇchh-d.*

Wire, *tár. See page* 98.

Wisdom, *aḳl,* (f.) ; *hosh ; dánist.* A. *aḳl-mand ; hosh-yár ; dánish-mand.* to have–, to be wise, the adjs. and *hona.* wisely, *aḳl se.*

Wish. *See* 'Desire.'

Wit. *See* 'Wisdom,' 'Jest.'

Witch, *ḍáyan.*

With, (accompanied by,) *ke sáth; le-kar; ma,i.*[2] (instrument, manner,) *se; ke sáth,* (cause,) *ke máre; ke bá,is ; ke sabab; se* –draw, *le-jána.* –hold, *nahíṇ-d ; báz-rakhna.*–stand. *mukhálif-hona.* –in, *bhítar ; andar.* –out, *báhar;* (destitute of,) *be ; bila.*

Witness, *gawáh ; sháhid; sháki,* (L. B.). eye–, *chashm-díd gawáh.*

Wizard, *ojha.*

Wolf, *bheṛiya.*

Woman, *aurat ; zan,* (p.) *stri ; ranḍi.*–'s property, *strí-dhan.* appertaining to

---

[1] This word will remind you (later on) of the beautiful song, '*tázah ba tázah, naụ ba nau,*' where occur the line and refrain.

> '*Bádah-i-dil-kusha bijo—*
>
> *Tázah ba tázah, nau ba nau—*'
>
> 'Bring forth the heart-expanding wine—fresh and afresh.'

[2] This word is nearly equivalent to '*and.*' It is used of what is closely connected with a thing already named ; as 'a case *wit* (or *and*) its evidence.' *See page* 118, for two illustrations of this.

women, *zanáni.* –'s apartments, *zanánah.* –ly, *aurat-sa.*

Wonder, *ta,ajjub; ḥairat; taḥaiyur.* V. *–k.* –ful, *ajíb; ajúbah.* -fully, *ajíb taraḥ se.*

Woo, natives never 'woo;' in L.B. they employ a broker, called '*ghaṭak.*'

Wood, *lakṛi; hezim.* of –, *lakṛi ka.*

Wool, *ún; pashm.* of –, *–ka.*

Word, *bát; bayán; lafz; sukhun; shabd.* – by –, *lafzan.* (news,) *khabar,* (f.); *bát; ittila,* (f.).

Work, *kám; kár; kár-bár; kár-o-bár.* *See* 'Trade,' 'Labour,' –man, *kárigar.*[1] –shop, –place, *kár-khánah; dúkán,* (f.). V. *kám, &c. k.; miḥnat-k.*

World. *See* 'Universe.' –ly affairs, *úmúr dunyávi.*

Worm, *kirm; kíṛa.* glow –, *shab-táb.* –eaten, *kirm-khurdah.*

Worn, –out, *purána; ho-gaya.* *See* 'Tired.'

Worse, *us-se kharáb;* (in health,) *áj wuh aur bímár hai,* or *áj bímári aur sakht hai.* worst, *sab-se kharáb.*

Worship, (M.) *ibádat;* (H.) *púja.* V. *–k.* your–! *ḥuzúr' janáb; janáb-áli; gharíb-parwar; jahán-panáh; dharm-avatár, &c.*

Worsted, *ún ka sút.*

Worth. *See* 'Price,' 'Value.' a rupi's –of cloth, *ek rúpíye ka kapṛa.* it's not – while, *kuchh parwáh nahín; taklíf mat uṭhá,íye.*

Wrestling, *kushti.* V. *–k.* –tler, *kushti-gír; pahlwán.*

Wretch, *kam-bakht; be-chárah.* –ed, *be-nasíb; kangál.* (contemptible,) *ná-kára.* –edness *kam-bakhti; be-nasíbi; shikasta-ḥáli.* –edly, *tangi-se; kharáb ḥál men.*

Wring, *machoṛna.* (out water,) *páni nikál-d.*

Write, *likhna; likh-d; kalam-band-k.* a –ing, *lekha.* –er, *kátib; nawísandah;* as last part in compos:... *nawís*

[1] Accent on first syllable.

or...*navís.* e.g. *naḳl-navís,* a copyist. –ten, *likha hú,a; nawishtah; ḳalam-band; taiyár.* –ting materials, *dawát-ḳalam; ḳalam-siyáhi.* the art, or act, of –ting, *ḳalam-bandi; ibárat; tasníf,* (f.).

Wrong, (a.) *ná-durust; ṭhík. nahíṇ; is meṇ bhúl hai; achchha nahíṇ,* (unjust), *be-insáf; ná-ḥaḳḳ; ghair-wájib.* right or –, *haḳḳ-ná-ḥaḳḳ.* N. *be-insáfi ki bát; zulm.* –doer, with '*jo.*' –fully, *be-insáfi se.*

X.

[Nil.]

Y.

Yard, (court,) *saḥn.* (measure,) *gaz.*

Yawn, *jamhá,i* V. *–k.; jamhána.*

Year, *baras; sál,* (p.); (in dating), *san.* during this–, *im-sál.* during last –, *guzashte sál.* for years, *barasoṇ se; sálha sál se.* –ly, *sályánah,* or *sáliyánah.* every –, *har sál; sál-basál.* advanced in—s, *buḍḍha; sinn-dár.* of tender –s. *See* 'Young.' the new –, *nau roz.*

Yellow, *zard.* N. *i.*

Yes, *háṇ; ji háṇ.* *See page* 56, *Note* 2.

Yesterday. *See page* 69.

Yet, (e.g. *yet* he did not obey me,) *lekin; magar; tau-bhi; tá-ham.* (for all that,) *par.*[1] there is *yet* this to be said, *yih bhi kahna hoga.* he has not come *yet, ab-tak.*

Yield, (n.) *paidáwár; fasl,* (f.). (v.) *dena.*

Yoke, (n.) *jú,a,* or *jú,áth.* (v.) *jotna.*

You, your; yourselves. *See pages* 28, 29, *and* 30, 7.

---

[1] See page 115, line 9. '*magar haḍḍi na' nikli*'; *par na' nikli.*

Young, *jawán; júba.* under age, *kam-sinn; khurd sál.* grown-up, but –, *siyána.*

Youth, a, *jawán; nau jawán.* time of youth, *jawáni.* –fully, *jawán-sa.*

Z.

Zeal, *josh; tezi; garmi.* –ous, *tund; tez; garm.* a –ot, with '*jo*' (devotee,) *záhid.* –ously, *josh, &c. se.*

Zephyr, *bád-i-saba.*

Zest, *hasrat.*

Zig-zag, *kaj-o-pech.*

Zone, *iklím; mintaka.*

GENERAL INDEX.

NOTE.

A single figure, (as '23,') indicates *the page*. When that figure is followed by a comma and another figure, then the first figure indicates the page, and the second, the section on that page. A second or third figure *not referring to a Section*, is separated from the preceding figure by a semi-colon

A.

B.

C.

D.

E.

F.

G.

H.

I.

N.

O.

P.

R.

S.

T.

FINIS.